D0934997

Pre-Colonial African Trade

Pre-Colonial African Trade

Essays on Trade in Central and Eastern Africa before 1900

Edited by
RICHARD GRAY
and
DAVID BIRMINGHAM

London
OXFORD UNIVERSITY PRESS
NEW YORK NAIROBI
1970

Oxford University Press, Ely House, London W.1

GLASGOW NEW YORK TORONTO MELBOURNE WELLINGTON
CAPE TOWN SALISBURY IBADAN NAIROBI DAR ES SALAAM LUSAKA ADDIS ABABA
BOMBAY CALCUTTA MADRAS KARACHI LAHORE DACCA
KUALA LUMPUR SINGAPORE HONG KONG TOKYO

Printed in Great Britain by Ebenezer Baylis and Son Ltd.
The Trinity Press, Worcester, and London

Preface

Nine of the chapters of this book were originally presented to seminars which we have recently conducted at the School of Oriental and African Studies, University of London, and at the University of California at Los Angeles. Many of them represent progress reports from young scholars at an early stage of their research in this comparatively unexplored sector of pre-colonial African history. To this kernel we are pleased to be able to add contributions from Professor Brian Fagan, Dr. M. Abir, Dr. Andrew Roberts, and Mr. Joseph Miller, and we express our gratitude to the Reverend Dr. Aylward Shorter, W.F., for his help and comment on Chapter 10, and to the *Journal of African History* and the Cambridge University Press for permission to reprint Professor Fagan's article. We should like to thank all the members of the seminars for their discussion of earlier drafts, and also our research students and colleagues at the School for their comments and criticisms of our opening chapter. We should also like to thank Mr. Richard Brain of the Oxford University Press for his extensive and skilled editorial assistance.

London, October 1968

J.R.G.
D.B.B.

I

Some Economic and Political Consequences of Trade in Central and Eastern Africa in the Pre-Colonial Period

RICHARD GRAY and DAVID BIRMINGHAM

Modern economic development in Africa has often been seen as an encounter between two extremes: self-sufficient homesteads, the inward-looking units of a subsistence economy, have been confronted by a vigorous, world-wide, alien industrial economy. This abrupt dichotomy, so arresting in twentieth-century Africa, nevertheless obscures and distorts our understanding of the earlier, pre-colonial period. Here the significant economic categories are by no means so sharply contrasted; the pace of change was often more gradual, and its impetus depended to a greater extent on local, indigenous initiative. Here one can begin to discern a series of innovations which together constitute a mode of economic organization midway between subsistence and a fully-fledged market economy.

Foremost among these earlier initiatives were those connected with the growth of trade. The beginnings were slender yet pervasive. Among the basic needs of a subsistence economy, two items—iron and salt—were of relatively rare occurrence in Bantu Africa.[1] Good, easily-worked deposits of iron ore, together with the knowledge of smelting, were by no means so common as has sometimes been assumed, while, although most communities produced a substitute for mineral or coastal salt, the demand for quality salt was persistent and widespread. From the early iron age onwards, the tools, weapons, and a basic condiment of many homesteads were often obtained only by the indirect filtration of commodities coming from an area far beyond the social and political horizons of the people concerned. In addition to these essentials, strong arrow-poison was sometimes sought over great distances,[2] and occasional luxury items were often added fairly

[1] See below, Ch. 2, pp. 26, 28. [2] e.g. by the Kamba, see below, Ch. 4.

rapidly, consisting of shell-beads, red ochre, and even the rare import from the coast or overseas.

Faced with this long history and with the great range of exchange transactions, our first task is to identify and define the categories and phases through which trade in Eastern and Central Africa has passed. Even at a very simple and early stage it is difficult to distinguish the different phases of trade primarily on the basis of geographical scale or the distances and commodities involved. The distinction between village and regional trade, suggested by Vansina,[1] becomes blurred right at the start. There is remarkably little evidence to suggest that 'local trade from village to village within a given population' was restricted to local products. Even in early iron age communities of the first millennium A.D., homesteads or villages already benefited from transactions which extended over several hundred miles and involved several commodities not produced by the local community. Nor is it clear how this local activity is distinguished from regional trade, defined by Vansina as that 'conducted over greater distances either between culturally different peoples within a single state, or between neighbouring peoples'. This trade, he suggests, had 'connexions with the political structure'; in particular, markets were organized by the state, and it involved the exchange of 'foodstuffs, specialized products from local industry, and products which come from markets specialized in the long-distance trade, such as European goods, salt, or copper'.[2] But the exchange of foodstuffs must surely have taken place at both levels; stateless societies were by no means excluded from the exchange of salt, copper, or exotic luxury imports; and while the organization of markets by a political authority may sometimes indicate a greater commercial dynamism than local village trade, state markets do not by themselves constitute a decisive innovation sufficient to demarcate distinct categories of trade. Clearly the items of trade are an unreliable index; nor, in the final analysis, does the significance of this pre-colonial trade depend on the area, distance, or communities involved, even, as will be seen, when they include Vansina's third category of long-distance caravan trade. Instead of a geographical criterion one must employ an economic analysis. If the operation and impact of exchange transactions, the role of trade and the level of economic activities associated with it, are examined more closely, two principal

[1] J. Vansina, 'Long-Distance Trade-Routes in Central Africa', *Journal of African History*, III, 3, 1962, 375–90.

[2] ibid., 375–6.

Contents

List of Maps

Map 1. Central and Eastern Africa, showing the peoples, places, and political areas principally discussed in this book

phases of trade in the pre-colonial period can be discerned, the vital distinction resting not on spatial categories but on the contrast between the economic activities directly related to trade.

The first phase is subsistence-oriented trade, in which trade remains closely associated with subsistence agricultural production, and is subservient to the local kinship system. In this phase the exchange of goods makes virtually no impact on the subsistence economy nor does it generate a wide range of activities divorced from supplying the basic needs of subsistence agriculture. The impulse towards innovation and economic specialization is continually suppressed and shackled. Meillassoux has shown how, in a subsistence economy, defences are erected against the economic and social changes which would otherwise follow from external trade. Restrictions and prohibitions are imposed on the production and exchange of iron tools. The few exotic, luxury items are carefully assimilated into the category of bride-wealth, and circulate only among the elders, in contrast to the subsistence foodstuffs which are redistributed to the younger producers. The objects associated with bride-wealth, including the imported items, are given a conventional, social value, which cannot be measured against that of other objects. In such a system there is, therefore, nothing approaching a universal, monetary value, and the significance of the exchange transaction remains intimately dependent on the social status of the parties concerned.[1]

The significant contrast to subsistence-oriented trade is then the phase in which trade freed itself from these subsistence and kinship shackles, and a market-oriented trade began to create a number of far-reaching economic innovations directly dependent on commercial opportunities. For market-oriented trade, as compared to subsistence-oriented trade, by itself generated new forms of wealth: a whole range of goods (e.g. ivory, slaves, cattle, or wax) acquired new economic values which they did not possess in the subsistence economy. Organized markets handling a multiple exchange of goods were often developed, although, at least in theory, trade could of course become market-oriented (i.e., responsive to the market principle of supply and demand) without the existence of actual, physical markets. Almost always this second phase seems to have involved the invention, or introduction, and the increasing acceptance of an indigenous or imported currency, for this enabled traders to bring an increasing

[1] C. Meillassoux, 'Essai d'interprétation du phénomène économique dans les sociétés traditionelles d'auto-subsistance', *Cahiers d'Études Africaines*, 4, 1960, 38–67.

number of commodities within a common frame of values.[1] New means of capital accumulation were formed, a new field of consumer demand for imports was created, and, above all, new forms of economic specialization were stimulated. The production of export goods, whether by miners, hunters, or craftsmen, assumed an unprecedented importance, while individuals, and in some cases whole communities, began to adopt the role of professional merchants.

Market-oriented, professional trade did not, however, produce in the pre-colonial period an economy integrated by the market principle. Most Africans continued to depend for their livelihood primarily on subsistence agriculture, and the production of vital foodstuffs was only very marginally affected by market demands. Even in societies most affected by market-oriented trade, the changes were generally confined to a relatively restricted sector of an economy which remained predominantly one of subsistence agriculture, until rail and motor transport solved the problem of bulk exports from tropical Africa. Yet within their restricted sector the changes promoted by market-oriented trade were historically of a fundamental significance which has not, perhaps, been fully appreciated. The fact that in such a situation the market principle operated only peripherally, and that market price did not affect future production by allocating resources among alternatives, is thought, by an anthropologist and an economist, to confine these peripheral markets to the sphere of subsistence economies as opposed to a 'Western economy'.[2] An historical analysis, however, demands an intermediate category in which sectors of the economy were tentatively beginning to respond to market opportunities.

Confronted with the civet cat farms of Enarea and Kaffa,[3] or the more common example of the development of a corps of professional ivory-hunters,[4] an historian must conclude that here were cases in which production was already intimately dependent on a market-oriented trade. And this dependence was only one aspect of a fundamental economic change, which, however limited and restricted were its sphere and impact, carried with it a momentum of its own. Here perhaps one should distinguish between the innovations associated with market-oriented trade and other forms of economic specialization

[1] Our appreciation of this factor has been sharpened by discussions with Mr. Peter Greenhalgh and Dr. Andrew Roberts.

[2] P. Bohannan and G. Dalton, *Markets in Africa*, Anchor Books, Doubleday, New York, 1965, 10–12.

[3] See below, Ch. 6, p.125.

[4] e.g. amongst the Cokwe, Baganda, and Nyamwezi; see below, Chs. 9, 5, and 3.

in pre-colonial Africa. The fairly common practice of a pastoral group living in symbiosis with agriculturalists within the same community, as for example the BaHima and BaIru in Ankole, or the close relationship which often developed between hunter-gatherers and agriculturalists, are instances of specialization which often did not involve far-reaching commercial innovations. In those cases where symbiosis did not give rise to a market-oriented trade, the exchange of products remained an isolated, relatively static response, and, although it supported an extensive specialization, the trade itself remained a simple operation intrinsically linked to subsistence patterns and unproductive of a commercial momentum.

So far we have been concerned with two abstract models, both of which lie between the extreme categories of a self-sufficient subsistence economy and a fully-fledged market economy. Between these two extremes, we would suggest that two contrasted phases of trade-related economic activity can be discerned, one restricted to supplementing subsistence needs and the other oriented to market conditions. These abstract categories are difficult, if not impossible, to divide with a hard and fast line. In practice the populations of Central and Eastern Africa lived in varying degrees of dependence on subsistence production and market exchange, and subsistence-oriented trade often continued to co-exist with an incipient, developing commerce. A consideration of some concrete examples may help to make clear the distinction that we have in mind. Let us begin with a most effective description of trade at a subsistence level. Miracle's account[1] of Tonga trade reveals the startling extent and importance of a people's trade which other specialists assumed to have been 'largely non-existent'. He describes a network in which thirty different goods were exchanged with ten other neighbouring peoples; in which distances of up to three hundred miles were covered; and in which the Tonga successfully acted as middlemen in the exchange of several items (hoes, fish, ochre, bamboo shafts, *impande* shells, and a range of overseas goods such as beads, cloth, and guns). Important deposits of salt occur at Mazabuka in Tonga territory and this may well have provided the original advantage around which this trading pattern developed. It must have been stimulated also by the fact that the Tonga had no local iron-ore deposits and were therefore always dependent on the import of a vital commodity. Miracle goes on to argue that this trade served purposes

[1] M. P. Miracle, 'Plateau Tonga Entrepreneurs in Historical Inter-Regional Trade', *Rhodes-Livingstone Journal*, XXVI, Dec. 1959, 34–50.

other than merely supplying the needs of a subsistence economy: trading helped to raise the standard of living, and by increasing the range and volume of goods it increased the wealth that could accumulate. Yet if we analyse the economic impact and social function of Tonga trade it would seem to fall largely in the category of a subsistence-oriented trade. The wealth produced by trade had not become anything like a necessity for any of the people involved, the profits were rapidly redistributed through the kinship system, and they did not become an essential mechanism for obtaining or organizing the services and allegiance of others. E. Colson has emphasized the ephemeral nature of the *mwami* or rich man in Tonga society, and she considers that 'the ideal of self-sufficiency' helped to determine their conduct of trade.[1] The most important economic function served by trading profits seems to have been an additional insurance against times of scarcity, though even here recourse to hunting and the collection of wild flora was probably of much greater significance than the import of grain in exchange for trade goods.[2] Trade remained seasonal (largely confined to the post-harvest period of the dry season) and it involved no specialist organization: there were no market-places and no established currency, for, although hoes seem to have been usually acceptable for further exchange, there is uncertainty about this, and there was no fixed rate of exchange. Pre-colonial Tonga trade, despite the distances and items involved, seems therefore to have stayed essentially geared to the subsistence economy: it did little or nothing to support an administrative élite; it does not seem to have produced either professional traders or specialist industrial skills intimately linked with the export market, although if more were known about their activity as middlemen, Tonga traders might emerge as far more significant. With the data available at present, however, it seems that the Tonga had not evolved the basic institutions of a market-oriented commerce, capable of inducing radical economic change.

At a fairly early stage Lozi trade seems to have fulfilled somewhat similar purposes. Gluckman[3] describes how the Lozi economy was organized around the ownership of different types of land which produced varied goods and foodstuffs. This involved large-scale co-

[1] In Bohannan and Dalton, 1962 edition (Northwestern University Press, Evanston, Ill.), 604, 609.

[2] Miracle (1959).

[3] M. Gluckman, *Economy of the Central Barotse Plain*, Rhodes-Livingstone Papers 7, Livingstone, 1941.

operation and exchange, which was in turn facilitated by easy river transport. The production and distribution of surplus foods in turn stimulated other local specializations, in particular the work of the Totela, Kwangwa, and Old Mbunda blacksmiths. But the manner in which this flourishing exchange was effected reveals the relatively limited economic purposes that it served. For it was carried on, we are told, by gifts between kinsmen, by barter between strangers, and by tribute. The last of these was probably the most important economically and was certainly by far the most significant socially. The courts of the king and of his councillors acted as clearing-houses or redistributive centres: within the central plain, the Lozi gave of their surplus to the king, royals, and councillors, and freely begged for items which they needed; outside the plain, the subject tribes brought their specialities and were given in exchange the things they lacked. This complex exchange operation enabled the region's economy to support a large administrative élite, it raised the standard of living of many of its participants, and promoted a few, isolated cases of industrial specialization. It remained, however, relatively static, was intimately linked with the subsistence economy, and completely lacked the dynamism generated by market opportunities.

In the case of the Lozi, the decisive break-through seems to have occurred when this relatively closed barter system was transformed by the arrival of large supplies of overseas products. This change operated in two principal ways. In the first instance, the king at the centre of the traditional exchange system, with special stores and access to goods now required for export, was well placed to benefit by the new opportunities for making substantial commercial profits, while the new range of imports increased the possibilities for storing wealth and accumulating capital. Trade and production for export (including hunting) began, therefore, to assume an immensely enhanced significance, which was strengthened by a second set of factors, linked with the introduction of exchange media. Cloth became the principal medium, assisted by beads, bullets, gunpowder, and conus shells; as their use increased not only was economic specialization greatly stimulated but also the whole pattern of exchange began to be expanded beyond recognition. It began to overflow its former static channels, and assumed the force of a creative mobility. In passing it should be noticed, as Gluckman points out, that while the new opportunities for trade could at first strengthen the central political authority, the increased use of exchange media could in time produce radically different consequences by obviating the necessity for the royal clearing-house and by weakening the importance of kinship barter links. But the essential fact for our analysis is that within a few years trade had begun to transform the Lozi economy. The exchange of goods was no longer subsistence-oriented; it had begun to be part of a developing market-oriented commerce. The Lozi were still far from entering, however tenuously, an industrialized market economy, but in pre-industrial categories they had effected the crucial transition.

In the case of the Lozi this transition occurred rapidly under the stimulus of a direct, long-distance connection with overseas trade. But has this always been an essential element in the emergence of a powerful innovatory trade? Should long-distance caravans indeed be recognized as the most notable, distinguishing feature of our second phase of pre-colonial trade? Do they really merit, as Vansina has suggested, a separate category of their own? Over a large area the evidence, though at present by no means conclusive, suggests that this contact has played a significant, perhaps decisive, role. For the centuries of medieval Arab trade, it is only in the regions of direct contact, in the hinterlands of Sofala and the Zambezi, that archaeologists have so far discovered the hall-marks of a developed commerce in the Eastern African interior. The bundle of unused hoes, the specialized metallurgy, and the accumulation of wealth in trade goods at Ingombe Ilede stand in this respect in sharp contrast even to the situation at the Ivuna salt-pans, which would seem to have more in common with, say, the Tonga exploitation of the salt resources at Mazabuka. Again the commercial renown and significance of the great, later entrepreneurs of this area—the Yao, Bisa, Kamba, and Nyamwezi—are intimately linked with their exploitation of the opportunities offered by the overseas market. For interlacustrine trade the decisive watershed, like that of the Lozi, seems also to have been the introduction of overseas trade goods and the need to meet the demands of overseas markets. Similarly, in parts of West Central Africa, such as the Lunda territories, the second phase began with the opening of the overseas market from the fifteenth century.

Yet this is by no means the whole story, for the evidence from the Kongo kingdom and the excavations at Lake Kisale in Katanga seems to lead to a very different conclusion. When the Portuguese arrived at the mouth of the Congo they stumbled upon a developed commercial system, centred on the royal capital, but, unlike that of the Lozi, already operating a complex, well-established currency system with standardized units based on the *nzimbu* shells (*Olivancillaria nana*) collected at Luanda, or on standard lengths of palm cloth imported from Loango and elsewhere. Here also salt and iron were still among the principal items exchanged, but trade had already produced, and was in turn sustained by, a wide range of specializations—copperwork, pottery, baskets, nets, and superb textiles made from the raffia palm—while the market was already an established institution.[1] Here, then, was a commerce already far advanced from mere subsistence production, and here the opening of the overseas market does not seem to have altered in any radical way the role which commerce played in the economy of the area. The demands and opportunities of the Atlantic trade increased the distances involved, weakened the royal control of commercial profits, and of course ended by subverting the whole commercial structure with its attendant local industries; but it would surely be difficult to argue that the long-distance caravans of the *pombeiros* performed an economic function significantly different from those of the regional governors which had previously carried the *nzimbu* from Luanda, the copper from Bembe, or the raffia cloth from Soyo and elsewhere, while it is highly significant that as late as the mid-seventeenth century the newly opened routes to Stanley Pool and into the Kasai basin were dominated not by overseas goods but by the interchange of purely African products. There would seem to be strong grounds for suggesting that for the first two centuries the expansion of scale had for the most part merely acted as an additional stimulant to a pre-existing pattern of exchange and economic specialization.

The evidence available from the excavations at Sanga, Lake Kisale, is far less definite, but it also strongly suggests that, when this area was still completely isolated from any direct contact with overseas markets, it had already developed a high degree of economic specialization linked with and dependent upon commerce. Apart from the excellence of the metallurgy found with all three pottery types at the Sanga burials, which in itself is evidence of a highly developed specialization generally found elsewhere only in association with flourishing trading systems, the crucial evidence so far which suggests commercial sophistication at Sanga is, of course, the celebrated copper crosses. Here, unfortunately, the chronological position is by no means clear as yet: with the Kisalian ware (with an eighth or ninth century carbon dating) crosses were found in only two of the twenty-nine burial

[1] See, for example, the account in G. Balandier, *Daily Life in the Kingdom of the Kongo*, London, 1968, Ch. 4. See also P. Martin's description of Loango, below, Ch. 7, pp. 141–3.

groups; with the Mulongo ware (undated) crosses were found with every burial; but it was only with the Red Slip ware (undated, though probably a good deal later than the Kisalian) that literally hundreds of copper crosses were found.[1] If the evidence of the beads found with the Red Slip ware is to be trusted, this latter abundance may well date from the eighteenth century onwards when the Katanga area was already in relatively close contact with overseas markets, but the occurrence of crosses in association with the Kisalian and Mulongo wares at least suggests an increasing acceptance of an indigenous currency and standard of value long before the overseas markets were exerting any effect in the area. And currency, of course, in turn suggests a commerce already decisively more significant than subsistence-oriented trade.

Taken together the evidence of these two examples demonstrates that the essential distinguishing features of our second phase are not inevitably dependent on the stimulus of overseas trade or long-distance caravans. In these two cases the riches of the environment—mineral wealth, or in the case of the Kongo its strategic position athwart the contrasted areas of forest, coast, and savannah—were apparently sufficient to stimulate a market-oriented trade. In both cases agriculture together with hunting and fishing may well have supported a considerable density of population, and the emergence of a market-oriented trade may often have owed much to those agricultural systems which enabled some populations, or significant sections of them, to spend some, or all, of their time away from their fields in the pursuit of durable wealth. It would appear therefore that, by themselves, the changes brought by long-distance, direct caravan trade, linked with overseas markets, are insufficient to merit a separate category. Caravans carrying goods to and from overseas markets may in some cases have provided the occasion for the transition from subsistence-oriented trade, but they were not an indispensable prerequisite. The use of a currency system may well have been a more critical and essential step. In the study of pre-colonial trade the crucial questions relate to the nature and results of this transition, and in so far as overseas markets are concerned the most rewarding research may investigate the caravans' encounter and interaction with indigenous trading systems. Indeed, in the case of the successful entrepreneurs studied in this volume—the Kamba, Nyamwezi, Cokwe, and Thonga[2]

[1] J. Nenquin, *Excavations at Sanga, 1957*, Tervuren, 1963.

[2] The Thonga traders of Delagoa Bay discussed in Chapter 13 should not be confused with the Tonga (or Ila-Tonga) on the middle Zambezi, who are also discussed in this chapter.

—the growth of long-distance caravan trade involved an intimate dependence on the energies and initiatives generated by the exploitation of a wide range of local, indigenous commercial opportunities, and it was their vitality which produced the most significant consequences of trade in the pre-colonial period.

So far, we have been primarily concerned with identifying the categories or phases of trade, but for an understanding of the economic changes brought by it we should consider some of its specific, individual characteristics. Indeed, what is probably the most important single consequence of trade—the creation, maintenance, and expansion of lines of communication—cuts across both phases, being of similar, vital significance in both. As has been seen, the supplementation of subsistence production sometimes involved journeys of several hundred miles, and Fagan[1] has argued convincingly that early technological advance may well have diffused along these tracks and not merely in the wake of migration or political conquest. One wonders whether more advanced techniques such as wire-drawing and the production of cotton cloth, specialities often linked with a developed commerce, might not have spread along trade-routes. The diffusion of American food-crops provides another obvious example of far-reaching innovation, while Vansina has suggested[2] that the great cultural similarities between peoples south of the equatorial forest may in part result from commercial contacts.

The other major economic consequences of trade are linked more closely to the second phase. Indeed, the most obvious and far-reaching change associated with a market-oriented trade was the creation of a remarkably broad-based consumer demand for clothing, bracelets, beads, and other imported objects. In itself this demand was a potent tool for the transformation of subsistence economies, and was perhaps the most substantial legacy of this early, pre-colonial trade. Other innovations tended to be more restricted in their impact. By imparting a high price to a whole range of goods which were not highly valued in the subsistence economy, and by importing an assortment of luxury items some of which were relatively durable, commerce made possible the storage of wealth on an unprecedented scale. In tropical Africa land was seldom a marketable commodity, hence its ownership did not represent a form of realizable capital accumulation; wives, trade goods, and livestock were alone available to perform this function, and as a result of trade the possibilities of investment widened and the ruling

[1] See below, Ch. 2. [2] Vansina (1962), 388.

groups often increased their economic power and influence. Although one should not accept the social strictures of a seventeenth-century Capuchin too uncritically, there is probably some truth in Francesco da Roma's account of how the nobility in the Kongo had assumed a luxurious, care-ridden arrogance: sumptuously dressed, travelling in hammocks borne by relays of their servants, they monopolized the ownership of cattle, and, burdened with the preoccupations of property-owners—'how to cultivate their lands, how to sell their harvests, how to recapture fugitive slaves'—they had somewhat lost the carefree, easy laughter of the commoners.[1] Because of the paucity of opportunities for productive investment in pre-colonial tropical Africa, an increase of wealth normally resulted merely in an increase in immediate consumption, often redistributed to kinsmen or subjects, or occasionally used in the construction of more elaborate buildings. While it is undeniable that this fact seriously limited the economic impact of commercial profits, one productive outlet has, nevertheless, too often been disregarded. For by far the most important economic consequence of the new wealth generated by market-oriented commerce was its unprecedented mobilization and concentration of economic skills. The archaeological record of commercial centres and great mining complexes, together with the contemporary and traditional accounts, bears witness to the technical ability and potential of their skilled artisans. Here was a reserve of skilled labour and a human investment of immense significance. Indeed, the pre-colonial economic tragedy of East and Central Africa principally consists of the dissipation and disruption of these industrial and specialized skills under the impact of violence and the slave trade, so that eventually they were judged by colonial governments to be irrelevant and incapable of exploiting the opportunities which improved communications were to bring to twentieth-century Africa.

One class of skills, those of the trader himself, was even more intimately linked with sophisticated trade and managed in a few rare cases to adapt itself and survive into the colonial era. We know extraordinarily little as yet about the role and organization of the professional traders of pre-colonial Africa. We know most about the *pombeiros* or *mussambazes* of the Portuguese. But one of the most exciting results of recent research on this subject has been to turn

[1] (ed.) F. Bontinck, *La Fondation de la mission des Capucins au Royaume du Congo* (1648) par Jean-François de Rome, Louvain, 1964, 98, 99, 105, 108, 115–17. See also W. Rodney, *A History of the Upper Guinea Coast 1545–1800*, Oxford, 1069.

attention to the entrepreneurial initiatives of whole sections of distinct ethnic groups—peoples who made their name as traders, pioneers on the frontiers of economic opportunity, whose power and influence hinged on an acute awareness of commercial forces allied to a tough capacity to operate over enormous distances on foot. Their achievements, more perhaps than any other set of facts, should effectively destroy the stereotype of a pre-colonial Africa prostrate and passive before the forces of the outside world.

At this stage of our knowledge it is still rash to attempt to generalize about the secrets of success in group enterprises. Yet as one considers some of the major examples of our area—the Kamba, Nyamwezi, Yao, Bisa, Cokwe, and Thonga—one is struck by the negligible role played by political leadership, especially in the early stages of commercial expansion. It has often been assumed that the development of market-oriented trade over long distances required a large-scale political system to organize ancillary services. In West African kingdoms, such as Mali and Ashanti for instance, the state appears to have sometimes provided security and defence for traders; it helped to supply the means of transport; it ensured the upkeep of roads and ferries; it established safe market-places and organized a judiciary to settle disputes; it may even have fostered labour specialization to ensure that a marketable surplus be produced. These state-supplied facilities were paid for by a system of taxation based on road tolls, on a turnover tax, or on tribute to the sovereign. In Eastern and Central Africa, however, similar close links between states and organized trade have not, on the whole, been established. It has been found that forms of security other than political authority could be afforded to traders who travelled beyond their homeland; at times, this protection was based on religion or magic; or it could be secured by employing traders who obviously presented no threat to the country through which they travelled, as with the Kamba use of women traders;[1] in some cases caravans passing through foreign territories may have had a sufficient supply of superior weapons to afford protection against numerically superior local forces: the Arab traders in East Africa were a notable case of such traders relying on fire-power for their safety. Much more important than external protection, however, was the skill with which traders made themselves indispensable to the host communities which they visited. Just as early European traders on the

[1] See below, Ch. 4.

African coasts created a local taste for foreign brandy and textiles in order to ensure for themselves a ready welcome—even as slave traders—so the African trading entrepreneurs of Central and Eastern Africa created a local demand for the material goods, or the specialist skills, which they had to offer.

It seems that many of these early entrepreneurial groups may have been people who originally had much in common with the seasonal Tonga traders. Participants in a barter system designed to supplement a subsistence economy began to exploit their own special sets of opportunities. Most seem to have started with the possession of a special skill over and above the practice of agriculture: they began with a reputation as hunters, smiths, fishers, or weavers. At a later stage they began to seek benefit from a geographical advantage, such as their position athwart a potential line of communication or between regions of wealth and prosperity, or from their ability to meet a peculiar set of ecological needs; they then went on to gain acceptance among their neighbours, and those with whom they soon came into contact, as people who alone could satisfy an ever-widening range of economic needs. As they operated further and further from their base, resilient, elastic lineage links became far more important to them than any formal political hierarchy, and in some cases they were able to take advantage of more remote affinities in language or a dimly-remembered common origin.[1] In this expanding zone of influence, military prowess often counted for far less than diplomatic skill. The Cokwe, for instance, were able to penetrate the Lunda territories as hunter-traders with little or no resistance because they paid fifty per cent of their ivory takings to the local chief, thus providing him with a new, unforeseen, but extremely welcome source of revenue and making it unlikely that he would allow any hostility from his people towards the visitors. Not only protection but other facilities required by traders could also be obtained without the need for a political umbrella. Transport methods could be devised which did not depend on a ruler conscripting his subjects as carriers in lieu of tribute dues. Family businesses could co-opt free men and women of their own clan into co-operative caravanning ventures of the Cokwe or Bisa type, which

[1] Far to the north of the interlacustrine area, for instance, it was the Pari, a minute Lwo-speaking group situated near Gondokoro in the southern Sudan, who as early as the 1840s were exploiting their affinities with the Acholi, to become the first importers of overseas goods from the Indian Ocean: R. Gray, *A History of the Southern Sudan 1839–1889*, Oxford, 1961, 38.

spread rapidly and successfully with no overall political authority.[1] Responsibility for the upkeep of roads is a subject that has not been investigated, but the task may not have been as difficult in the southern and eastern savannahs as it was in parts of the West African forest. A study of ferries would certainly prove interesting, as it was one of the functions of the Mwata Yamvo's Lunda government to ensure that ferries were supplied and manned on the routes of the empire.[2] The Maravi were apparently skilled at building makeshift bamboo bridges which they could throw across swollen streams.[3] Perhaps other traders, such as the Nyamwezi or the Cokwe, were able to buy the services of local watermen, or were able to route their lines of communication to avoid the necessity of crossing unfordable rivers.

Accepting that the supporting services for large-scale specialized trading are not necessarily provided by political authority, one none the less has to recognize that the growth of states is often associated with the growth of market-oriented trade. One of the earliest documented examples of a kingdom which owed its strength, if not its very origins, to trade was the Mbundu kingdom of Ndongo.[4] Ndongo was apparently built to dominate the trading system of the Kwanza valley. The crucial commodity which it controlled was high-quality rock-salt mined in Kisama and carried in natural slabs far into the interior. A larger and more important state which derived its strength from its commercial position was the empire of Lunda, which grew in the eighteenth century to be one of Africa's largest suppliers of slaves to the outside world. The empires of Mutapa and the Rozwi Mambo also seem to have owed much of their power to trade, in this case the control of the gold trade south of the Zambezi. Yet another trading power may have existed on the north bank of the lower Zambezi where, before the Portuguese conquest, the Malawi channelled ivory to the Arabized traders along the river.[5] These spectacular examples of areas of intensive trade which evolved sophisticated political systems contrast sharply with equally important commercial systems of Central Africa which threw up no such 'empires'. The Nyamwezi succeeded in spreading their influence from the Indian Ocean to the Copper Belt without any initial allegiance to a central political system.

[1] See below, Ch. 9.

[2] A. Verbeken and M. Walraet, *La Première Traversée du Katanga*, Brussels, 1953.

[3] A. C. P. Gamitto, *King Kazembe*, Lisbon, 1960, I, 50.

[4] See below, Ch. 8.

[5] E. A. Alpers, 'The Mutapa and Malawi political systems' in T. O. Ranger (ed.), *Aspects of Central African History*, London, 1968.

It was only once the trade network was established that leaders such as Mirambo began to form a wider political hegemony.[1] The Yao, the Bisa, and the Kamba, all eminently successful trading peoples, never created any centralized state; although in the case of the Kamba the absence of political authority was apparently a factor leading to their decline.[2] More spectacular still is the case of the Cokwe who destroyed the Lunda empire and took over much of its trade without replacing it with any political structure.

Future research may clarify and explain some of these differences in the relationship between politics and trade. Here we can only offer a few tentative suggestions as to why some traders operated within a political framework and some without. The first, and possibly the most significant, factor was the nature of the commodities traded. In particular, the trade in rare or semi-rare minerals probably required organization and controls of a different order from that of other forms of trade. Mining is a precisely located activity, as well as being a potentially lucrative one, and the trade to gold, copper, or salt mines could become the focal centre of rapidly growing economic and political power. Furthermore, since precise territorial possession either of the mines or of the main routes to them is essential to a mine-based economy, the trader or entrepreneur must be able to defend his position from external—or indeed internal—aggression. The normal means of defence was an armed force which, once available, could also be used to extend the limits of the state. Additional forms of protection were also adopted, for instance by the Teke, who successfully spread the disconcerting—and probably false—rumour that they were cannibals who ate hostile foreigners in order to protect their position as middlemen in the copper trade from Mindouli. One of the earliest and most notable armed forces to be assembled in West Central Africa was the one used by the kings of Ndongo to protect their salt trade from the Portuguese. For decades the Portuguese were unable to gain a footing on the south bank of the Kwanza, where a series of armies protected the salt supply routes. In a similar manner the early Luba states may have evolved their military skill because of the necessity to protect the highly valued Katanga copper trade. In addition to providing a focus for concentrated economic development and a need for effective territorial defences, centres of mineral production probably also required more complex marketing facilities and security procedures

[1] See below, Ch. 3.	[2] See below, Ch. 4.

than other trade centres. The provision of such facilities in the West African gold-mining areas led to the growth of extremely centralized trading empires. One problem of such centralized production, however, was the mobilization of sufficient labour. Early Akan states met this problem by purchasing slaves, both from their Sudanese and from their Portuguese customers. In Central Africa the pattern seems sometimes to have been to allow the foreign trader to come in and do his own mining under licence from the ruling power. Thus the trader was responsible for supplying the labour. This seems to have been the system both at the Ivuna salt-pans and at the Bembe copper mines.[1] It is not yet clear on what basis the gold mining in the Mutapa domains was conducted. The mines were fairly widely scattered, which may have made control difficult, but the political authority seemed, to the Portuguese at least, to be fairly centralized, and external access to the major gold-producing areas on the plateau to the south was effectively prevented by the Rozwi Mambo.

If mineral extraction was likely to be associated with state formation, the ivory trade presented a rather different situation. Ivory hunting did not require the possession of a particular site to the same degree as did mining. Not only was there no need to build a long-term defence system such as a mining community would require, but since ivory hunting, like wax collecting and rubber tapping, rapidly exhausted an area if intensively carried out, the consolidation of a political organization in one place would have been quite unrewarding. A flexible, semi-nomadic association was required, not a territorially determined fief. Thus the collectors of animal and vegetable produce tended to spread their influence over wide areas in which they were sometimes destructive of existing peoples and institutions, but in which they had not the incentive, the time, nor the skill to evolve state structures of their own. Time and again, however, one is reminded in the following essays that the skills and specialisms associated with the rise of market-oriented trade in these hunted and collected commodities were as great, if not greater, than those associated with the development of specialist trade in the more familiar state trading structures.

When studying political organization, the differing effects of such commodity-types as iron and ivory, salt and wax, copper and rubber, gold and goats, can be assessed. One vital factor has been left out of account, however, and that is slaves. At various times and in various

[1] See below, Ch. 2 and Ch. 8.

parts of Eastern and Central Africa slaves came to be one of the most important of all items of trade. The slave trade seems to have been one eminently conducive to the growth of states. In some cases the process of acquiring slaves was by direct military action; this was probably the manner in which Kasanje obtained slaves in its early years. The building of an army for slave-raiding purposes can naturally lead to territorial expansion which in turn can lead to the control of new market and supply centres. Raiding, however, is often only an early phase of development in the life of a slave-trading state. It is followed by a much more important phase in which tribute becomes the key to the supply of slaves. The ability of African rulers to obtain slaves by taxation may emphasize a key difference between African and Western European states. In Europe, but not in Africa, the key to power and wealth was mastery of the land. In Africa the real key to production and prosperity was men and women; land was rarely in short supply and therefore no especial value was attached to its ownership. The manner in which a chief commanded the productive services of his subjects was complex, but an understanding of it is probably the key to understanding the Central African tribute system and the methods used to accumulate slaves for export. The relationship between chief and subject went through various shades, father and son, householder and retainer, landlord and villein, master and slave, warlord and captive. Within this range the chief might on occasion be persuaded to exchange the services of subjects for material returns; if he thought that the guns, cloth, drink, and tobacco which traders offered him for a subject whom they would take away into slavery, more than outweighed that subject's life work as a producer at home, he might indulge in slave trading. The alternative would usually be to forgo any prospect of acquiring exotic goods, thus clearly making the temptation to indulge in such traffic very great. The opportunities for gaining durable material  wealth from the slave trade obviously encouraged rulers to expand their possessions and increase the number of people over whom they ruled. Such expansion often took place by warfare which initially provided prisoners of war, a ready source of slaves, and subsequently provided new subjects on whom taxes could be levied in the form of men. One further advantage which a ruler gained from expanding his fief derived from his position as the final arbiter in judicial matters; it was he who could condemn recalcitrants, or alleged recalcitrants, to be sold into foreign bondage. This use of judicial processes to obtain export slaves may have been a major factor in the trade, and inevitably put pressures on the administration of justice which tended to warp pre-existing values.

If the gains to be derived from the slave trade provided one of the sharpest incentives to imperial expansion in Central Africa, it also provided the means by which kings consolidated their authority over vassal chiefs. The system of patronage involved handing out material possessions, as well as offices, and the rich imports received at royal courts filtered down through the ranks and into the provinces to provide repayment for loyalty, tribute, and service. The paying and receiving of tribute was a two-way process in African states, and did not result in the same massive concentration of wealth at the top as occurred in mediaeval Europe or pre-Columbian America. The benefit which a vassal derived from paying his tribute was not feudal protection—unless against reprisals for non-payment—but returns in kind. At the lowest level the returns might consist of a feast accompanied by music and dancing at the chief's village. At a higher level the reward for generous tributary payments would consist of rich fabrics and foreign intoxicants.

We have argued, in effect, that Africa's most important wealth, both to itself and to others, was man-power. We have further argued that through the tribute and tax systems of a political hierarchy it was possible to convert this wealth into a tradeable form which could be exchanged for material possessions, sometimes of exotic origin. It can now be asked whether the tribute structure could be used—and was used—to assemble production surpluses of other tradeable commodities for export. The answer appears to be that it sometimes was so used although often not until foreign trade items had been introduced to stimulate the exchange economy. Although a state might have the means of concentrating goods for trade, it often did not have the specialist skills to handle production and redistribution. Thus the Lunda empire did not have hunters capable of exploiting the ivory potential in its territory and had to rely on foreign Cokwe hunters. Once these hunters arrived, however, they did channel half their production through the tribute system since the ground tusk of every elephant killed had to be paid to the ruler on whose land it fell. So, too, with the rubber trade; chiefs among the Bashilange could collect rubber readily enough, but could not arrange head transport over the 800 miles to the coast and so had to rely on Imbangala and Bihe traders to export it to the coast through their existing trade networks.[1]

[1] Pogge's account of the Bashilange in *Mittheilungen der Afrikanischen Gesellschaft in Deutschland*, IV.

It would seem, therefore, that although slaves, the richest and most prized of all possessions, were the item of trade most frequently and immediately channelled through the tribute system and the one which contributed most strongly to the growth of states, the system could be adapted to cater for other varieties of trade.

In trying to understand why some of the trading systems of Africa developed within the framework of a state and some did not, another factor, in addition to commodities, has to be taken into account. This is time. One of the difficulties in studying the chronology of the Lunda empire is to decide at what stage in its growth it became a recognizable centralized state. Although the initial political impulses from Luba probably reached the Lunda country in the first half of the sixteenth century, and although some external trading may have begun at a similar period, it seems likely that it was at least a hundred years before a recognizable state structure emerged, with the Mwata Yamvo at its head and royally appointed commissioners governing the satellite territories. For a considerable period the early trade of the Lunda probably resembled much more closely that of the nineteenth-century Cokwe than that of nineteenth-century Kazembe. The centralization of the Mwata Yamvo's authority and the political expansion of Lunda influence mainly took place in the eighteenth century, as shown by the history of Lunda domination among the Pende, the Yaka, the Luapula, and other peoples. It may well be that time was the most crucial of all the factors governing state growth, and if the Nyamwezi had had another 150 years before the colonial conquest they might have built an empire in East Central Africa comparable to the Lunda empire in West Central Africa.

Some consideration should also be given to the harmful effects which trade could sometimes have on previously flourishing kingdoms. It is particularly notable that one of the most flourishing empires of fifteenth-century Central Africa, Kongo, is usually held to have disintegrated under the impact of overseas trade. We argued above that Kongo showed signs of an advanced form of trade before the arrival of the Portuguese; soon after the opening of Portuguese trade, however, the kingdom developed signs of severe political strain. It can be argued that Kongo was unaccustomed to the effects of foreign trade and unable to resist the pressures of traders from overseas. The kingdom lay in a backwater of Africa, untouched by the world trading community which had established such effective links with both Western and Eastern Africa. The West African communities in particular had evolved means of holding at bay traders from the Sudan and were able to use these, in a way that Kongo was not, to confine Europeans to the coast. In addition to lacking the mechanisms for effective resistance to foreign economic intrusion, Kongo may also have lacked the positive commercial institutions with which to meet the intensive demands of overseas trade. Benin, as a contrasting instance, had developed to a far greater extent the necessary means of accumulating surplus goods, the necessary markets, guilds, taxation, and transport to meet the demands of foreign export. Kongo did not, and foreign traders therefore had a greater incentive to establish for themselves a system of state trading which met types of demands quite different from those of the old Kongo commercial structure. The Portuguese moved in and rapidly undermined the authority of the king by assuming extra-territorial rights and establishing, with the help of missionaries, parallel judicial and administrative authorities. The dual system worked moderately well until about 1540, but then rapidly broke down until twenty years later Kongo was overrun by the Jaga, who expelled the Portuguese and ended their experiment. This apparent decline of Kongo when faced with the demands of European traders leaves a large unanswered question about the destructive effects of early European contact. Perhaps one of the weaknesses of the more sophisticated and structured empires was insufficient flexibility; they were not always able to adapt rapidly to new commercial circumstances. If given time, as in the case of the Angolan slave trade, African entrepreneurs were capable of establishing effective institutions to meet new trading demands, but this could not be done quickly. Another apparent example of inflexibility when faced with rapid economic change was the Lunda empire, which was unable to survive the abolition of the Atlantic slave trade and allowed the Cokwe to capture the initiative in the new ivory trade.

If some states failed to benefit politically from the new sources of commercial wealth and power, economically the failure of market-oriented trade to produce sustained economic growth in the pre-colonial period was even more marked. We have already suggested that transport difficulties were largely responsible for the lack of any large-scale modification of the subsistence economies. Local skill and ingenuity could create small yet significant commercial advances towards a market economy, but so long as it remained impossible to exploit on any considerable scale the agricultural and mineral riches of tropical Africa for the outside world, the profits of African traders and exporters depended to an alarming extent on wasting assets: ivory, wild rubber, surface minerals, and slaves. The tensions inherent in this situation, together with the increasing import of cheap firearms during the nineteenth century, at least in part explain why the early commercial initiatives of, for example, the Yao, Kamba, and Nyamwezi, were increasingly marred and distorted by raiding and outrage, while in West Central Africa the Cokwe adoption of firearms and their purchase of slaves was but the last stage in the violence long associated with the Atlantic slave trade. Another nineteenth-century development, the Ngoni migrations, disrupted large areas including the Thonga and Rozwi trading systems dealt with in this book, and although with time the military regimes established in their wake might have developed and re-established earlier trading links, their immediate impact was commercially disastrous.

Yet in the long run indigenous entrepreneurs were threatened less perhaps by the spread of violence than by alien competition. One of the most notable features of some areas was the success of local initiatives in containing or defeating foreign traders by exploiting native advantages and by rapidly responding to frontier opportunities. The Afkala of Southern Ethiopia, who beat the long-established, well-organized Jabarti merchants by operating with smaller profit-margins; the Nyamwezi, whose profits from local trade supplied the 'capital' for their caravans, which for long competed successfully with those from the coast; and the interlacustrine kingdoms, whose combination of political and, it is now argued, commercial strength enabled them to confine the Zanzibaris to a purely external role, are all cases in point.[1] But over Eastern and Central Africa as a whole this encounter with alien competition was by no means uniformly so successful, at least in economic results. In one area, the gold-producing plateau of the Rozwi, where the threat of foreign traders had been faced for centuries, the problem of competition was solved under the Changamire Mambos by the total exclusion of the Portuguese. The economic price, however, exacted by this solution was a royal monopoly, which exhibited many of the characteristics of administered trade as defined by Polanyi,[2] and effectively inhibited the growth and impact of market-oriented commerce.[3] As in the case of the relationship between states and trading

[1] See below, Chs. 6, 3, and 5.

[2] K. Polanyi, C. M. Arensberg, and H. W. Pearson, *Trade and Market in the Early Empires*, New York, 1957, 262–3. Compare also his account of the rather similar case of Dahomey, *Dahomey and the Slave Trade*, Seattle, 1966.

[3] See below, Ch. 12.

systems, time was also of possibly crucial importance in determining the success or failure of the local response to the challenges of market opportunities. The corridor between Lakes Malawi and Tanganyika provides a striking illustration of this factor. Despite considerable potential in the shape of local specializations and exchange, no entrepreneurs emerged in this area, for here the expansion of opportunities practically coincided with the arrival *en masse* of the Nyamwezi and coastal traders.[1] On a far greater scale, the coming of colonial rule exposed African traders throughout Eastern and Central Africa to a well-nigh overwhelming competition. Lacking the long-established foundations available in West Africa, and hampered by some, if not all, of the difficulties previously described, African entrepreneurs were suddenly exposed to the full-scale demands of an industrialized market economy in a situation where not only the terms of trade but also the structure of political control were decisively employed against them. The alien impetus to development in twentieth-century Africa virtually disregarded and overrode these earlier economic initiatives, considering them but a feeble and unproductive cul-de-sac, yet despite these severe handicaps, it may well be that subsequent research will reveal, as in West Africa, significant continuities between the modern African entrepreneurs—the lorry-owners, shop-keepers, and cash-crop farmers—and the earlier, pre-colonial traders.

[1] See below, Ch. 10.

2

Early Trade and Raw Materials in South Central Africa[1]

BRIAN M. FAGAN

Some years ago J. Vansina[2] published a lucid analysis of long-distance trade in Africa in which he argued that the regional trading networks already in existence in the far interior played a critical part in the later development of the ivory and slave trades. Ultimately, however, the expansion of trade in later centuries has its roots in the early development of inter-village traffic in raw materials during the first millennium A.D. The archaeological evidence for early trade in Central and South Central Africa is both limited and unsatisfactory; this essay is an attempt to place the evidence into a theoretical context.[3]

The fundamental economic changes which took place at the beginning of the African Iron Age led to major alterations in population distribution, settlement patterns, trading practices, and social organization over much of the subcontinent. Nowhere were these more dramatic than in South Central Africa, where the transition from food gathering to food production coincided with the introduction of metallurgy into the region.

Later Stone Age hunter/gatherers lived in small camps of several families, exploiting the natural environment within a comparatively small distance of their home bases.[4] The critical factor in hunter/

[1] Reprinted from *J. Afr. Hist.*, X (1969), 1, 1–13.

[2] J. Vansina, 'Long-distance trade-routes in Central Africa', *J. Afr. Hist.*, III (1962), 375–90.

[3] This essay has benefited from presentations and discussions at the 'East Africa and the Orient' conference held in Nairobi in March 1967, and at a seminar on Iron Age Africa held at the State University of New York, Binghamton, in April 1968. I am grateful to the Ford Foundation, the University of Illinois, Urbana, and the State University of New York, Binghamton, for financial support to attend these meetings. Dr. Bernard Riley kindly prepared the original sketch for Map 2.

[4] R. B. Lee, 'The subsistence ecology of the !Kung Bushmen', unpublished Ph.D. thesis, University of California, Berkeley (1965). I am grateful to Dr. Lee for much unpublished information on !Kung economic practices.

gatherer subsistence is the distribution of water relative to game and vegetable resources, so that the amount of territory covered by one camp varies from area to area. The degree of contact, and hence presumably of trading and social intercourse, varies with the density of population relative to natural resources, as well as with the range of each camp's food-gathering activities. Among some !Kung bands today, the amount of visiting and trading contact between camps varies with the availability of food.

Most hunter/gatherer groups in Southern Africa before the period of Bantu and European contact were largely self-sufficient in raw materials. Although cases are known of trade in such commodities as ochre and some other raw materials, most of life's requirements were obtained from local sources, and the amount of regional trade was much smaller than it is under similar conditions today.[1] Rock paintings depict a wide range of economic activities, while abundant evidence from archaeological sites indicates that the camp of Later Stone Age times was very self-contained.[2] Wood and bone were combined with stone to furnish the essentials of material culture, while water could be carried in antelope-stomach bags and other such containers, made from materials readily available to the hunter.

With the new food-producing economies, however, trade became far more important, for many requirements of a more complex economy and material culture had to be met from other sources than those available locally. While such items as skins, grain, hut poles, and other commodities were frequently a significant part of inter-village trade,[3] three basic raw materials were of vital importance to the Iron Age farmer. Iron, copper, and salt were responsible above all for the development of complex inter-regional bartering networks which were based on a comparatively steady, but informally structured, demand for raw materials.

IRON

Iron ore and iron implements were essential to the functioning of an Iron Age agricultural economy. Cultivation on any scale required hoes and axes; these were made from iron ore obtained from ferricrete

[1] J. Desmond Clark, *The Prehistory of Southern Africa*, London, 1959, 219; R. B. Lee, personal communication.

[2] Creighton Gabel, *Stone Age Hunters of the Kafue*, Boston, 1965; B. M. Fagan and F. van Noten, *The Hunters of Gwisho*, Tervuren, forthcoming.

[3] M. P. Miracle, 'Plateau Tonga entrepreneurs in historical inter-regional trade', *Rhod.-Liv. J.*, XXVI (1959), 34–50.

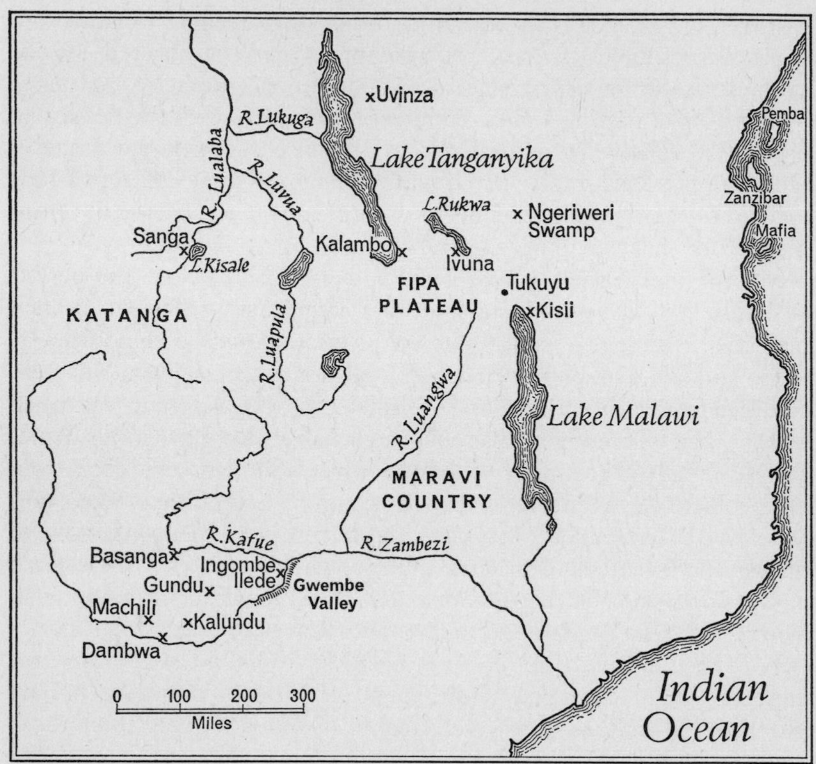

Map 2. Iron Age Sites in South Central Africa

layers, bog iron deposits, and sometimes mines.[1] Supplies of iron ore are comparatively plentiful in many areas, but not in others, where there is limited archaeological evidence for the importation of the raw material. The Machili site, in Southern Zambia, dated to A.D. 96±212 (C-829), yielded a few lumps of a foreign substance identified tentatively as ferricrete.[2] The site lies in a sandy area, and the ferricrete was imported by man, presumably for iron smelting. In later centuries there are numerous historical records for the trading of iron tools from areas where the people were skilful metallurgists.[3]

During the Early Iron Age, iron tools were confined to small,

[1] C. M. Schwellnous, 'Short notes on the Palabora smelting ovens', *S. Afr. J. Sci.*, XXXIII (1937), 904–12.

[2] J. Desmond Clark and B. M. Fagan, 'Charcoals, sands, and channel-decorated pottery from Northern Rhodesia', *Amer. Anthrop.*, LXVII (1965), 354–71.

[3] David Livingstone records trade between the Toka and Kololo in iron hoes, which were also given as tribute.

functional artifacts such as arrow-heads, spear-heads, razors, and occasional axes and hoes.[1] Such artifacts are fairly common in the deposits of the Kalomo mounds, as are iron rings and strip bangles.[2] Unfortunately, preservation conditions at early sites preclude the discovery of many iron artifacts, but a few iron tools of similar types to those found with Kalomo-type occupation are known from the Dambwa site, dating to the eighth century, and also from the lower levels of the Gundu mound near Batoka, dating to the fifth century, as well as from sites in Central Zambia.[3]

The simple iron artifacts made during the Early Iron Age did not require extensive metallurgical activity, resulting in a small demand for ore compared with that in later centuries, when ironworking was both widespread and an important attribute of political and commercial power. But the existence of trade in iron ore and finished artifacts was probably a factor in the development of a standardized but simple metallurgy over much of South Central Africa during the earlier Iron Age, although the limited range of technological skills available to the metalworkers also affected their products.

By the fourteenth or fifteenth century, the inhabitants of Ingombe Ilede in the Zambezi valley were in possession of iron tools of ceremonial type which were far more elaborate than the artifacts of the Early Iron Age farmer. Single bells, long-bladed hoes, and wire-drawing tools were deposited in graves at the site.[4] The hoes were unworn, whereas those found in the deposits of the village itself had been heavily utilized. Iron slag is rare at Ingombe Ilede; even in recent times, metallurgy was rarely practised in this area. One has the impression that the inhabitants of this site were manufacturing their own domestic artifacts, most of which were of similar design to Early Iron Age tools. Their ceremonial implements are more elaborate, and were almost certainly obtained by trade. It is as if the iron trade received a new dimension in later centuries with additional traffic in more elaborate artifacts which were passed to groups with lesser metallurgical skills, while domestic tools were made in most areas for local

[1] B. M. Fagan, 'Pre-European ironworking in Central Africa, with special reference to Northern Rhodesia', *J. Afr. Hist.*, II (1961), 199–210.

[2] B. M. Fagan, *Iron Age Cultures in Zambia*, I, London, 1967, 88–91.

[3] B. M. Fagan and T. N. Huffman, 'Excavations at Gundu and Ndonde, near Batoka', *Archaeologia Zambiana*, III (1967), 34; D. W. Phillipson, 'The Early Iron Age in Zambia: regional variants and some tentative conclusions', *J. Afr. Hist.*, IX (1968), 2, 191–212.

[4] B. M. Fagan, D. W. Phillipson, and S. G. H. Daniels, *Iron Age Cultures in Zambia*, II, London, forthcoming.

consumption. But many more discoveries will have to be made before this tentative hypothesis can be supported by firm evidence.

SALT

Salt was an important commodity for Iron Age peoples, and was widely traded during the first and second millennia. Deposits from which cake salt of comparatively good quality can be extracted are rare, and were the object of considerable trading activity in Iron Age times. Although salty water was sometimes obtained by boiling certain river grasses or reeds,[1] much of the salt came from such localities as Uvinza[2] and Ivuna in Tanzania,[3] the Kiburi and Mwashya pans in Katanga,[4] and the extensive Basanga salt workings in Central Zambia.[5] The archaeological record so far includes little information on salt trading, for few of the known localities have been investigated.

The Ivuna salt-pans, nine miles south-east of Lake Rukwa, were studied in a campaign of excavations in 1966.[6] A long sequence of Iron Age pottery associated with salt-making activity was recovered from dumps round the pans, and has been radiocarbon-dated to the period A.D. 1215±110 to 1410±110.[7] Some of the salt-workers lived in villages built on dumps overlooking the salt lake; they cultivated sorghum, kept cattle and small stock, and buried their dead near the huts which were uncovered in the occupation levels in the dumps.

Broken pots, and much salt-flecked earth associated with them, are grounds for assuming that salt-working and, presumably, trade in cake salt were important activities. The pottery from the later levels of the dumps comes from several different cultural traditions, which may tentatively be assigned to one or other of the various tribal groups living in the area today.[8] Such a mingling of pottery types may imply

[1] Ernest Gray, 'Notes on the salt-making industry of the Nyanja people near Lake Shirwa', *S. Afr. J. Sci.*, XLI (1945), 459; Mrs. Beverley Brock, personal communication.

[2] V. L. Cameron, *Across Africa*, New York, 1877, 228.

[3] B. M. Fagan and J. E. Yellen, 'Ivuna: ancient salt-working in Southern Tanzania', *Azania*, III (1968), 1–43.

[4] J. Vansina (1962), 386.

[5] The Basanga salt-workings were described by the Rev. Arthur Baldwin in his diaries, and were examined briefly by the writer, Mr. T. N. Huffman, and Mr. Robin Fielder in 1967.

[6] B. M. Fagan and J. E. Yellen (1968).

[7] B. M. Fagan, 'Radiocarbon dates for sub-Saharan Africa, V', *J. Afr. Hist.*, VIII (1967), 520.

[8] A number of different groups live in the area, including the Namwanga, Siceela, Wanda, and others, whose pottery styles are distinctive enough for us to be able to distinguish them the one from another (B. M. Fagan and J. E. Yellen, 'The potmakers of Ivuna', in preparation).

that different peoples have collected salt from the pans at various times, or that the control of the trade changed hands from time to time. Alternatively, the archaeological record may reflect both cultural diversity in the Ivuna region and also regular visits by peoples from outside the immediate area who sought salt. Pots were an essential part of the salt-making process used at Ivuna until recent times, and may be taken as an accurate yardstick of the salt trade. When more is known of the archaeology of Southern Tanzania it may prove possible to plot the distribution of Ivuna pot types over a wide area, for Ivuna salt is traded as far east as Tukuyu at the present time, and the nearest alternative source of cake salt is about 150 miles away.[1] Sophisticated methods of trace element analysis are now being applied to pot clay and other materials;[2] they are to be applied to the Kisii pot trade in Northern Malawi,[3] where pottery is traded over large areas from a single manufacturing source on the eastern shore of the lake. Once the association of salt-making and a particular type of pot is established,[4] such analyses might prove informative when applied to wares found at or near localities such as Ivuna.

Cake salt is produced by a process of boiling and evaporation, and is readily handled in containers of standard size, thereby providing a stable commodity of exchange (as does the copper ingot). Such a standardized unit of exchange would have been a basis for regional trade centred on Ivuna, the salt being handled from village to village by barter of other materials, such as iron tools from the Fipa plateau and also grain. While much of the trade may have proceeded on the basis of inter-village barter, others may have travelled to the pans to collect salt themselves, a process that was certainly in progress at Ivuna in the nineteenth century[5] and also elsewhere—for example, Katanga and Malawi.[6] The result of the Ivuna trade in an essential commodity was a degree of direct and indirect contact between peoples living up to 150 miles away or more from each other, and also the creation of a network of regional trade.

Although the earlier levels at Ivuna contain a different type of

[1] Ngeriweri Swamp, Saja (Mr. H. Sassoon, personal communication).

[2] L. Perlman and F. Asaro, 'Deduction of provenience of pottery from trace element analysis',University of California Reprint, no. UCRL-17937 (1967).

[3] Professor J. Desmond Clark, personal communication.

[4] Illustrations published by Ernest Gray (1945) show pots in use for salt-making in Malawi of a very similar form to those commonly found at Ivuna (our classes I and II).

[5] Mrs. Beverley Brock, personal communication.

[6] Ernest Gray (1945).

pottery,[1] there is no reason to believe that the methods of salt-working changed in later centuries. We may expect to uncover evidence of Early Iron Age salt-working from other localities where the stratigraphy is more complete. But Ivuna is an indication of the type of evidence which the archaeologist may expect to find in future investigations of earlier sites.

COPPER

Copper is another raw material which was highly prized during the Iron Age, especially for ornamentation and also as a trade commodity. The evidence for copper trade as opposed to that in salt is easier to reconstruct from the archaeological record as the results are more tangible, in the form of artifacts or by-products of metallurgical activity.

Early Iron Age sites in South Central Africa contain few copper fragments. An occasional ring or fragment of strip bangle is found in the deposits of early settlement, such as Dambwa, where the few copper ornaments can only have been imported from outcrops at least 200 miles away.[2] By the seventh century the inhabitants of the Kalomo mounds possessed copper-strip bangles, such ornaments occurring slightly earlier than the wire type with a fibre core, which was established by the eleventh century.[3] The quantity of copper is small enough at all the sites to indicate that the material had an ornamental significance, but that, as far as can be established from present evidence, copper had not acquired the great commercial significance which is associated with it in the later centuries of the Iron Age.

The early history of the African copper trade is still almost unknown, although important series of copper artifacts have been excavated at Sanga in Katanga, and at Ingombe Ilede in Southern Zambia. Sanga has been radiocarbon-dated to the late seventh to ninth centuries,[4] while the graves at Ingombe Ilede have been provisionally assigned to the fourteenth or fifteenth century.[5]

Our knowledge of the owners of the Sanga cemetery near Lake Kisale is confined to a description of the contents of fifty-six graves,

[1] The earlier Ivuna wares have no connexion with either modern vessels or the Early Iron Age channel-decorated pottery tradition found at Kalambo Falls.

[2] B. M. Fagan, D. W. Phillipson, and S. G. H. Daniels (forthcoming).

[3] B. M. Fagan (1967), 123.

[4] J. Nenquin, 'Two radiocarbon dates for the Kisalian', *Antiquity*, XXV (1960), 140, 132.

[5] D. W. Phillipson and B. M. Fagan, 'The date of the Ingombe Ilede Burials', *J. Afr. Hist.*, X (1969), 2, 199–204.

most of them containing more or less complete pots, together with a range of iron tools and copper ornaments and ingots, including some remarkable necklaces, and a very small number of glass beads and East Coast sea-shells.[1] Jacques Nenquin has divided the burials into three distinct groups, whose stratigraphical relationships are somewhat problematical. The major group, the Kisalian, is represented by twenty-seven graves, and is dated to the seventh to ninth centuries. Copper ingots were found in only two graves of these people, although they are characteristic of the site as a whole; certain composite copper chains also belong to this culture.

Nenquin's second group, the Mulongo, is known from six graves, whose stratigraphical relationship to the Kisalian graves is not exactly established, although the distinctive Mulongo pottery shares some features both with the first group and with the Red Slip ware graves, which are demonstrably later than the Kisalian. Copper croisettes were found in all the Mulongo graves, but they were even more common in the Red Slip graves, over 360 ingots being found in the four graves of the group which have been excavated.

Although the stratigraphical and chronological relationships of the three Sanga pottery groups are still imperfectly known, the increase in copper ingots within the three groups of graves is striking, and may perhaps indicate an increasing importance at the end of the first millennium for copper as a trade metal as opposed to an ornamental one.

Most of the copper objects from the Sanga necropolis are ornamental in concept, consisting of bangles, elaborate wire chains of sophisticated design, and also a number of minor artifacts such as needles. Copper croisettes are found in two forms—the so-called Handa type,[2] and also a diminutive form, most of which were found in the later graves. Nenquin records that one group of Handas was tied together with string;[3] they are of a type widely known from South Central Africa.

Sanga lies in the middle of an area where copper outcrops are abundant, as well as salt deposits. The archaeology of this mineral-rich region is almost unknown, but is vital to our understanding of the Iron Age of South Central Africa. The site provides abundant evidence for sophisticated methods of copperworking in the Katanga area by the

[1] J. Nenquin, *Excavations at Sanga, 1957*, Tervuren, 1963.

[2] James Walton, 'Some features of the Monomotapa culture', *Proc. Third Pan-African Congress on Prehistory (1955)*, Livingstone, 1957, 336–56.

[3] J. Nenquin (1963), 194.

eighth century, reflected both in the ornaments of the inhabitants and in the large number of ingots found in later graves at Sanga.

A dual attitude to copper as a metal seems to be characteristic of the peoples of Sanga. On the one hand it has an important ornamental role, as evidenced by elaborate chains and bangles. On the other, standardized ingots are common possessions. Such objects have no ornamental significance, but may be interpreted as symbols of wealth and possibly as a form of rudimentary standardized currency, or units of exchange. The implications of this dual attitude are far-reaching; the scope of the copper trade is widened, and formalized by the use of standard units of exchange, whereas in earlier centuries, and away from the main centres of commerce, the traditional and informal methods of barter in essential commodities still continue, for the volume of trade in raw materials is insufficient to require any more regular form of exchange unit.

According to Vansina,[1] Sanga may have been involved in direct long-distance trade, but the archaeological evidence does not yet support this tempting hypothesis, for imports from coastal regions are rare, confined to a few East Coast sea-shells and glass beads, and may merely reflect the final processes of long-distance hand-to-hand trade as opposed to formal caravans. But the greater use of copper ingots may well indicate an increasing concern with larger-scale trade and the development of long-distance trade-routes.

Evidence of copper trade comes from Ingombe Ilede in the Middle Zambezi valley, far away from mineral outcrops. Several of the central burials, from fourteenth or fifteenth century horizons, were deposited with copper cruciform ingots of a type found from Rhodesia in the south to as far north as Katanga.[2] Three skeletons were buried with complete sets of wire-drawing equipment, closely similar in form to Venda specimens described by Stayt many years ago.[3] A typical outfit consists of a series of hammerheads, tongs, spikes, and the wire-drawing plates themselves. Lengths of rectangular cross-section trade wire were found at the heads of three burials, and had been bent around sticks to form standardized lengths of wire, presumably for trade purposes. One burial also contained a bundle of finer wire which had obviously been drawn from the trade lengths on the site, and was presumably made for eventual conversion into ornaments. The gauge of the finer wire is similar to that used to make the bangles which were fabricated by

[1] J. Vansina, *Kingdoms of the Savanna*, Madison, 1966, 35.

[2] James Walton (1957).

[3] H. Stayt, *The BaVenda*, Oxford, 1931.

winding copper wire round a fibre core from the *Raphia* palm.[1] Numerous copper bangles, beads, needles, a razor, and fragments of wire complete the inventory of artifacts in this metal.

Ingombe Ilede lies in a flood-plain area where outcrops of copper are unknown; all supplies of the metal had to be imported. The artifacts suggest that the ornamental role of copper was very important, to the extent that the principal inhabitants were importing both ingots and trade wire, and then converting the latter into bangles for their own use. Whether or not they were re-exporting the finished bangles it is impossible to establish; but, with an important salt-trade outlet in the area,[2] conditions would have been favourable for the handling of finished ornaments for local markets, as well as the standardized ingots favoured in the Zambezi trade.

The strictly commercial importance of copper is clearly seen at Ingombe Ilede. The cruciform ingots have remarkably similar weights; the trade wire is bent in standardized lengths, which obviously had an established value in long-distance trade circles. This is in contrast to the strictly ornamental functions of the metal, which were of regional and local concern to Iron Age traders. Perhaps we may glimpse in the Ingombe Ilede site the overlapping of two distinct trading patterns, the one based on local demands for salt, copper ornaments, and other prosaic commodities; the other on an increasing volume of long-distance traffic in ivory, copper, and other raw materials, a trade which may have depended on its standardization of commercial units, and perhaps even on a form of rudimentary 'currency' in the form of copper bars, etc., to function effectively.

Such distinctions are hard to draw from the archaeological record, but the archaeologist will be able to learn much by carefully controlled studies of the distribution of ingots and other artifacts commonly handled in the more important centres of commercial activity such as Sanga and Ingombe Ilede. We may hope one day to learn more of the extent of the more sophisticated trade systems which flourished with the aid of a series of 'monetary units' which may have served as a means of storing wealth and also as a medium of exchange.

LONG-DISTANCE TRADE

Although South Central Africa was basically self-sufficient in minerals and other essential raw materials during the first millennium, the

[1] Identification by Kew Botanical Gardens, London.
[2] B. M. Fagan, D. W. Phillipson, and S. G. H. Daniels (forthcoming).

tenuous trading patterns of the far interior absorbed a certain number of exotic commodities, such as glass beads and sea-shells, which may reflect a different type of trade.

The evidence for contact between the East Coast of Africa and the South Central African interior during the Early Iron Age is confined to a few finds of exotic imports in the deposits of early farming villages in Southern Zambia[1] and some isolated specimens from Malawi.[2] The earliest dated imports yet recorded from Zambia are East Coast species of cowrie shell (*Cypraea annulus* L.) found in the lowest levels of two Early Iron Age mounds on the Batoka plateau in an area with no mineral outcrops or special economic importance. A shell found at the base of the Kalundu mound is dated to A.D. 455±95 (SR-123), while two others from Gundu mound near Batoka itself date to A.D. 440±85 (GX-1114).[3] The associated occupation levels belong to the earliest Iron Age cultural tradition in Zambia.

Our limited archaeological finds of glass beads and sea-shells do not indicate a formalized trade in such commodities during the Early Iron Age. The copper and iron objects which survive in the archaeological record from this earliest period are functional or decorative in nature, and do not reflect any overriding concern with standard-sized ingots or exotic objects as a primary motive for trade. Copper ornaments are rare, and may indicate that Early Iron Age trade was essentially informal and concerned almost wholly with local raw materials. This is in contrast to the picture in later centuries, when copper at least appears to have had a comparatively formal role in long-distance trade.

Unquestionably imports were reaching the far interior via the Zambezi valley from the early centuries of the Iron Age, for it is most likely that the imports on the remote Batoka plateau arrived there from the Middle Zambezi area. The discoveries at Ingombe Ilede have, however, filled in many gaps in our knowledge of long-distance and local trade at an early stage in its development. The site lies some 32 miles downstream of the Kariba Dam, on the flood plain of the Zambezi, in an area formerly rich in ivory and salt but not in minerals. Ingombe Ilede[4] was inhabited by Iron Age peoples who practised a mixed farming economy based on the cultivation of cereals (including

[1] B. M. Fagan, *Southern Africa during the Iron Age*, London, 1966, 93.

[2] K. R. Robinson, 'A preliminary report on the recent archaeology of Ngonde, Northern Malawi', *J. Afr. Hist.*, VII (1965), 169–88.

[3] B. M. Fagan, 'Radiocarbon dates for sub-Saharan Africa, VI', *J. Afr. Hist.*, X (1969).

[4] B. M. Fagan, D. W. Phillipson, and S. G. H. Daniels (forthcoming).

sorghum), kept cattle, goats, chickens, and dogs, and also depended to a considerable extent on hunting and food-gathering to supplement their diet. The so-called gold burials from the centre of the site, already mentioned, were associated with large numbers of imported objects.

The foreign imports from the central burials include sea-shells and glass beads—commodities known to have been widely handled during the Iron Age.[1] Three species of sea-shell were found with the skeletons and give an idea of the range handled in the trade. Two burials were associated with *conus* shells; all of them were cut off at the base, leaving only the basal disk for trading, the common form in which this species was handled. There is abundant evidence that *conus* shells were widely traded in the Iron Age.[2] Cowrie shells were also common finds at Ingombe Ilede, being associated with several of the less important burials. All the cowries had been split down the back, before being worn in the hair or on clothing. A third sea-shell species (*Polynices mammilla*) was represented by a single group of shells deposited with a burial at the southern borders of the settlement. This East Coast species is known to have been traded during the Iron Age, although it was not as popular as the cowrie or *conus*.

Glass beads are the most commonly found import at Ingombe Ilede, as well as in many sites in the interior. An extensive literature, principally concerned with their use as dating evidence, has grown up in recent years,[3] from which it seems that their principal value is as indicators of the extent of trading networks rather than for dating purposes. The Ingombe Ilede beads were found in long strings around the necks or waists of the central burials. Most of the cane beads were Indian reds, opaque dark blues, turquoise, and yellow forms. Less frequently found are wound green beads, a string of 'melon' specimens, three carnelians, and a series of flat green and white beads, which are similar in form to the freshwater shell types also found at the site. The trade in glass beads at this time seems to have been based on a comparatively limited number of shapes and colours, which had a very wide chronological range during the Iron Age. Only rarely does one

[1] A few fragments of imported cotton cloth were found with one of the burials; the remaining fabric is thought to be of local manufacture: B. M. Fagan, D. W. Phillipson, and S. G. H. Daniels (forthcoming).

[2] Joan R. Harding, 'Conus shell ornaments (*Vibangwa*) in Africa', *J. R. Anthrop. Inst.*, XCI (1961), 52–66.

[3] J. F. Schofield, 'Southern African beads and their relation to the beads of Inyanga', in R. Summers, *Inyanga*, Cambridge, 1958, 180–229.

find a large collection of glass beads outside important commercial settlements such as Zimbabwe and Mapungubwe. Beads were traded into the interior in large strings. Once imported, they were used for the adornment of important individuals, and disseminated in small numbers into regional trading networks.

The primary preoccupation of the coastal trade was with the export of raw materials, including gold, ivory, copper, and iron. Gold was mined even in the early centuries of the Iron Age,[1] but the range of objects made from this metal was limited, being confined to beads of various shapes, metal sheet, and wire bangles. A gold sheet backing-plate, a considerable number of beads, and some bracelets were found at Ingombe Ilede. There were no signs of gold slag or of other by-products of goldworking such as were found at Mapungubwe, for example.[2] Frey[3] has demonstrated that the Ingombe Ilede beads were made with the same techniques as those used to manufacture Rhodesian gold ornaments. Since there are no gold outcrops near Ingombe Ilede, all the metal must have been traded, perhaps either in the form of dust in porcupine quills or as finished objects.[4] We cannot, of course, estimate how much gold passed through the hands of the chieftains of Ingombe Ilede, but they seem to have retained a proportion of the metal for their own adornment. Gold was apparently never an important metal for domestic use, for it is normally only found in contexts where long-distance trade was important, and may, like copper, have been a monetary unit of fixed value.

We have argued elsewhere that ivory was the staple of the East Coast trade,[5] but its importance in the archaeological record has been underrated because it is rarely found or described by excavators. At Ingombe Ilede, ivory fragments are scattered throughout the deposits and elephants are abundant in the region; it appears likely that the inhabitants of the settlement recognized the economic value of elephant tusks. Fragments of ivory are sometimes found in Batoka plateau villages, but whether these were collected for local ornamentation or for trade we cannot tell.

[1] Roger Summers, 'Iron Age industries of Southern Africa, with notes on their chronology, terminology, and economic status', in W. W. Bishop and J. D. Clark (eds.), *Background to African Evolution*, Chicago, 1967, 687–700.

[2] L. Fouché, *Mapungubwe*, Cambridge, 1937.

[3] E. Frey, 'Goldworking at Ingombe Ilede', in B. M. Fagan, D. W. Phillipson, and S. G. H. Daniels (forthcoming).

[4] G. M. Theal, *Records of South Eastern Africa*, London, 1898, IV, 43.

[5] B. M. Fagan (1966), 91.

Three out of the four raw materials found at Ingombe Ilede were imported by the inhabitants from outside the Gwembe valley. Gold, copper, and ivory were attractive commodities to those who wished to exploit the trading networks of the Zambezi and receive exotic objects from downstream. Minerals were obtained from the plateau country on either side of the river, a commercial process in which the Lusitu salt deposits probably had a role. Livingstone[1] speaks of widespread salt trade in this area in the mid-nineteenth century, the flourishing regional trading networks of the last century resulting in constant interaction between the plateaux and the Gwembe. At the time when Ingombe Ilede was occupied, similar trade, also based on local demands for raw materials, carried minerals to the Zambezi trade-routes and resulted in the dissemination of exotic objects far into the interior.

The staples of the coastal trade are well defined in both archaeological and documentary records. Undoubtedly, a great deal of the commerce was conducted initially by bartering, a process of trade which led to more formalized trade-routes in later centuries, reflected in the ready Portuguese annexation of well-trodden roads to the goldfields and ivory grounds of the interior,[2] and the increasing number of ingots and other artifacts of possible monetary significance in the archaeological record.

Ingombe Ilede demonstrates the critical importance of regional trade-routes in the development of Iron Age trade. The inevitable demands of metallurgist and farmer led to continued if irregular contact between communities living up to several hundred miles apart, which developed into complicated barter networks extending over enormous areas. Political and social considerations, as well as economic factors, prompted the evolution of many complex commercial relationships. The successive masters of the East Coast trade used local trading networks as a starting-point for their trade, stimulating demands for raw materials. The result was economic and political change, and the development of sophisticated centres of metallurgical and commercial activity in the far interior, reflected in such finds as Sanga and Ingombe Ilede.

In Early Iron Age sites and in settlements far away from the outcrops of copper and gold, we find scattered foreign imports in early middens, which are the earliest signs of one of the dominant historical processes of the last two thousand years. The diffusion of more

[1] C. and D. Livingstone, *Narrative of an Expedition to the Zambezi and Its Tributaries*, London, 1865, 225.

[2] Eric Axelson, *Portuguese in South-East Africa, 1600–1700*, Johannesburg, 1960.

advanced metallurgical techniques and artifacts, more sophisticated agricultural methods, and the establishment of important chieftainships, could not have taken place without the greater mobility of products and people caused by the informal trading networks between countless Iron Age villages through South Central Africa. But the character of this type of trade in local materials is quite different to that of the long-distance commerce in raw materials and exotic luxuries which developed around such centres as Sanga or Ingombe Ilede. One of the big questions for future research is to plot and assess the influence and impact of the sophisticated commercial centres, whose locations were determined by many different factors, such as proximity to outcrops or to well-established trade-routes. How much interaction did they achieve with their less fortunate and humble neighbours with their less advanced technologies and agricultural methods? How much of a distinction can be drawn between the two types of commerce? Trading activities are as important an agent of social and political change as population movements and the sword, a point which the archaeologist and the historian sometimes tend to forget.

3

Nyamwezi Trade

ANDREW ROBERTS

Throughout the nineteenth century, the Nyamwezi were the most important traders among the peoples of what is now the interior of Tanzania.[1] This essay, however, is by no means exclusively concerned with the Nyamwezi, who are far from constituting a discrete and homogeneous tribal group, let alone a political entity.[2] In the present context the appropriate unit for consideration would seem to be either a chiefdom or group of historically related chiefdoms, or else the whole area within which the Nyamwezi peoples conducted trade. As yet, too little research has been done to make possible the first kind of study, indispensable though such small-scale analysis would be for a proper understanding of Nyamwezi trade. But for this very reason it may at present be useful to attempt a rather general sketch of the scope and nature of trade in western Tanzania. Such an approach may at any rate go some way towards explaining how the Nyamwezi achieved their

[1] In 1967 I spent six months in historical research among the western Nyamwezi (Galagansa), Galla, Sumbwa, and Vinza, while Research Fellow in Oral History at the University College, Dar es Salaam. I have drawn where possible on my fieldnotes, and I should like to acknowledge here the co-operation I received from my informants and the assistance of my interpreter, Mr. Leonard Msholwa. None the less, this essay remains very largely based on literary sources, and such evidence needs to be checked against the results of more extensive fieldwork. We may therefore expect further light on the present topic from the researches of Mr. Alfred Unomah (University of Ibadan) in Unyanyembe; Mr. John Collinson (Oxford University) in southern Nyamweziland; and Mr. C. F. Holmes (Boston University) in the Kwimba chiefdoms of Usukuma.

I am grateful to the Editors and to Dr. Cyril Ehrlich for their comments on a draft of this essay.

[2] See R. G. Abrahams, *The Peoples of Greater Unyamwezi, Tanzania*, London, 1967; *The Political Organisation of Unyamwezi*, Cambridge, 1967; and the literature cited therein. 'Nyamwezi' simply means 'of the moon' and hence 'of the west', since the new moon is first seen in the west. For a short account of Nyamwezi history see my 'The Nyamwezi' in Andrew Roberts (ed.), *Tanzania before 1900*, Nairobi, 1968.

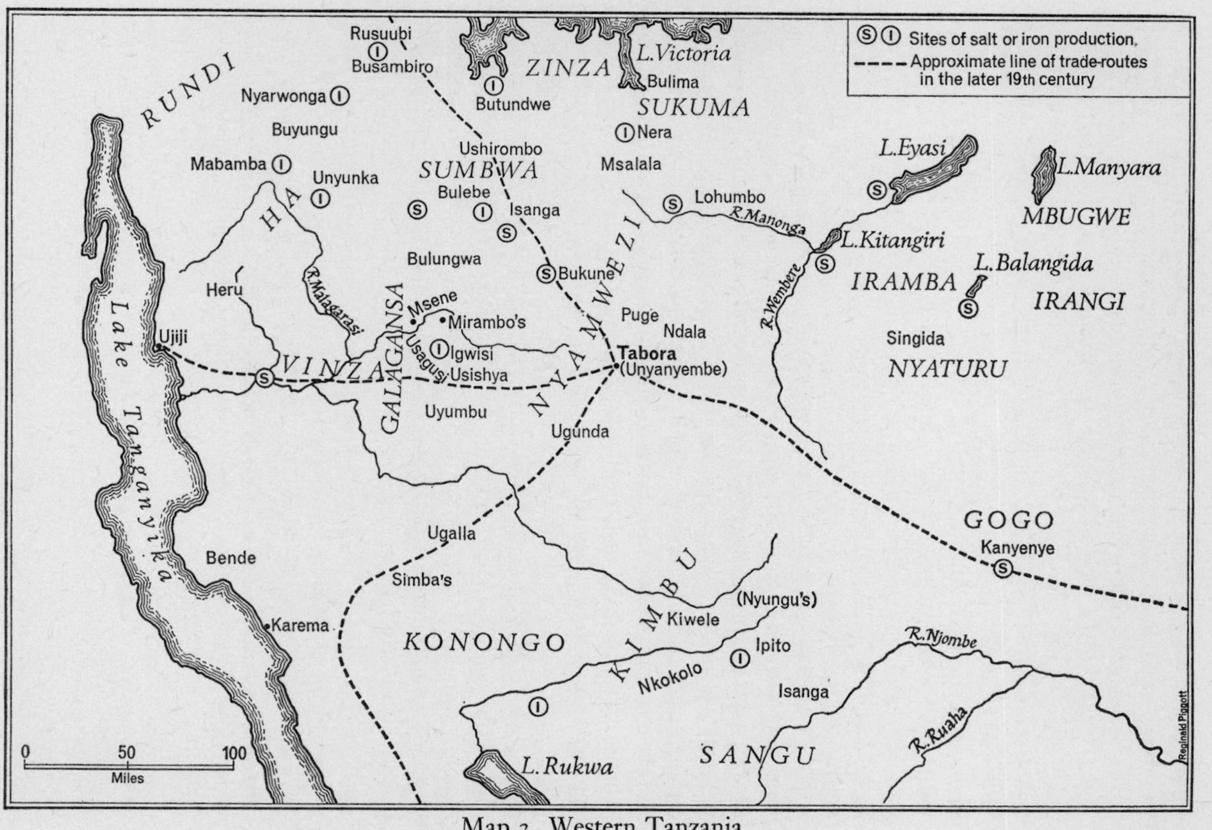

Map 3. Western Tanzania

commercial pre-eminence. It will indicate how, in this part of Africa, networks of regional trade could have been extended to form the basis of long-distance trade-routes, and how the two types of trade interacted: regional trade providing the capital, as it were, for long-distance enterprise, while long-distance trade provided new incentives for more intensive regional production and exchange.[1] In conclusion, the essay will survey the evidence—as yet very fragmentary—for other forms of economic change resulting from the increased scale of Nyamwezi trade during the nineteenth century.

The Nyamwezi peoples, who number some 300,000, occupy a large part of the tableland bounded by Lake Victoria, the Wembere valley, the Southern Highlands, the Lake Rukwa depression, the escarpment east of Lake Tanganyika, and the highlands of Burundi and Rwanda. This tableland may to some extent be regarded as an historical unit, for in some respects the ecology is broadly similar and there has been extensive movement over the area for at least the past two centuries, promoting a measure of uniformity in social customs and institutions. The terrain is for the most part fairly flat and presents few obstacles to human movement. There are few perennial rivers, but water can usually be found close to the surface. The main ecological contrast is between the plains in the north, which have largely been cleared of tree-cover, and the *miombo* woodland in the south.[2] Cattle are herded in the north, especially by Tusi and Taturu; in the south, however, cattle-keeping is restricted by the widespread incidence of tsetse, due to the tree-cover and the survival of a variety of game. (The incidence of tsetse has of course been partly determined by human factors; some areas in the west are known to have supported cattle before they were depopulated during the upheavals of the later nineteenth century.) In the woodland areas, hunting and honey-collecting have long been important features of the economic cycle, and the Kimbu in particular may be described as semi-nomadic.[3] But throughout the whole region agriculture has been practised on a shifting rather than an intensive basis, for the soil is generally poor. The main subsistence crops, sorghum, bulrush millet, and maize (which was introduced during the last century) can often only be grown on the same plot for three or four

[1] This point is adumbrated in the useful account of trade in W. Blohm, *Die Nyamwezi*, 1, Hamburg, 1931, 166–72.

[2] This is of course an over-simplification: see Abrahams, *Greater Unyamwezi* (1967), and sources cited therein for further details.

[3] Cf. A. E. M. Shorter, 'Ukimbu and the Kimbu chiefdoms of southern Unyamwezi', D. Phil. thesis, Oxford University, 1968.

consecutive seasons, and for this and other reasons homesteads change sites every ten to fifteen years. Except in special circumstances settlement tends to be dispersed rather than concentrated.

These factors may largely account for the small scale of political organization throughout the region.[1] Territorial chieftainship, of a type common elsewhere in eastern and central Africa, has been present in the region since at least the seventeenth century. But until the later nineteenth century there was little pressure for chiefs to exercise authority over large numbers of people. There was no serious competition over land-use such as might call for regulation by superior authority, nor were there areas sharply defined by geography as natural economic or strategic units. Chiefs had no special weapons, and few resources, with which to exercise physical power, and disaffected subjects could easily move elsewhere. Until about a century ago, most chiefs were respected primarily as rain-makers, magicians, and arbitrators. In their role as mystical guardians of the land, they regulated the cycle of economic activities, but they normally had little political or military power. Many chiefdoms can never have comprised more than a thousand people, while many were much less than a thousand square miles in area. And most of these small chiefdoms were essentially autonomous. Apart from those of the Ha and Zinza (who were subject to greater influence from the interlacustrine kingdoms), there is no indication that they were united under paramountcies before the rise of the nineteenth-century warlords.

All the same, there were important links between chiefdoms. Those formed through secession might continue to recognize the original chiefdom as senior; some were linked for specific historical reasons by joking relationships; while certain dynastic genealogies strongly suggest the temporary or permanent subordination of one chiefdom to another. Such political ties extended the lines of economic exchange, whether on the basis of reciprocity between equals or on that of tributary relations. Moreover, social horizons were further enlarged through the agency of semi-secret societies, such as those of the snake-experts (*wayeye*), the porcupine-hunters (*wanunguli*), or the spirit-cult of the *baswezi*. There is no good evidence that such societies exercised political functions, nor that they had any centralized organization, but they maintained their own hierarchies, corresponding to progressive

[1] Cf. Abrahams, *Political Organisation* (1967); Hans Cory, *The Indigenous Political System of the Sukuma*, Kampala, 1954; Shorter (1968, D. Phil. thesis); also A. E. M. Shorter, 'The Kimbu', in Roberts (ed.) (1968).

stages of initiation into their medical and magical secrets, and to some extent they overrode the ties of family and chiefdom. From what little is known of the history of these societies, it would seem that they spread rapidly as a result of the expansion of trade in the last century; yet it would also seem reasonable to suppose that they had long since provided networks of communication through which people might learn about new ideas, new goods, new opportunities.[1]

It is difficult to provide any very reliable picture of the growth and development of trade in western Tanzania, since so much of the evidence comes from the later nineteenth century, when all kinds of economic exchange had been more or less affected by the expansion of long-distance trade in ivory and slaves. It is, however, possible to make some reasonably informed guesses as to the character of trade in the whole region around the early nineteenth century, even if quantification is impossible. Inferences can be drawn from the location of different economic resources, on the assumption that trade in commodities of immediate usefulness in the subsistence economy is likely to be relatively long-established. Traditions from western Nyamweziland and Uvinza speak of immigrant groups from the north exchanging grain crops for pots with earlier inhabitants, fishermen who lived along river banks and only cultivated root crops.[2] Pottery was probably an important item of early trade elsewhere in the region, but I have no special information on this.[3] Dried fish, in which there is a considerable trade today, is likely to have been in some demand, for there are few rivers which can supply fish throughout the year.[4] Forest products—bark-cloth, bark boxes, axe- and spearshafts, honey, and beeswax—were traded between villages and no doubt were in special demand in the sparsely wooded northern plains. Conversely, livestock, especially cattle, is and was exported from the north, while within tsetse-free areas cattle have long been the chief medium for paying bride-wealth and fines.[5]

[1] Cf. Andrew Roberts, 'Enlargement of Scale among the Nyamwezi' (paper presented to the Social Science Conference, University of East Africa, 1968); T. O. Ranger, 'The Movement of Ideas: 1850–1939', in I. N. Kimambo and A. J. Temu (eds.), *A History of Tanzania*, Nairobi, forthcoming. Travelling groups of dancers, such as those used to publicize the *baswezi,* would have been important in this connection.

[2] Fieldnotes; Andrew Roberts, 'Uvinza in the Nineteenth Century', *Azania,* III, 1968.

[3] Blohm indicates that pottery was especially made in Ugunda: (1931) I, 155.

[4] The sociological restrictions on such exchanges should not be overlooked: for example, the Sumbwa have a taboo on the eating of fish (cf. D. Livingstone (ed. H. Waller), *The Last Journals of David Livingstone*, London, 1874, I, 308).

[5] See Abrahams, *Greater Unyamwezi* (1967), 34, and p. 58 below.

The two most important items in early trade were probably iron and salt.[1] Surface outcrops of ironstone are fairly common in western Tanzania,[2] but there seem to be few places where ores near the surface are rich enough to repay the effort of extracting them. Such places can be fairly well pinpointed from the evidence of African informants today and that of early European travellers, though we must bear in mind that sites of iron-extraction were sometimes worked only for a relatively short time before being abandoned. The main area of iron-extraction and iron-working was in the north, among the northern Ha and Zinza; the latter were specially famous as smiths. We know of iron-workings in Bulima (north-western Sukumaland), Nera, Butundwe, Rusuubi, and Busambiro.[3] In the Ha chiefdom of Buyungu, there were iron-workings at Nyarwonga, Mabamba, and Unyunka.[4] Only two workings in Nyamwezi country are known to me: Isanga, in Mhunze chiefdom, and Igwisi, in Busangi.[5] According to Broyon, there were iron-workings somewhere 'south and west' of Mirambo's capital; iron was also worked in Ukonongo.[6] Finally, there was an important iron-working in the Kimbu chiefdom of Ipito.[7]

The available evidence thus suggests that in western Tanzania, as in other parts of Africa, iron was a relatively scarce commodity. Its

[1] See above, Ch. 2.

[2] Cf. R. F. Burton, *The Lake Regions of Central Africa*, London, 1860, II, 6; H. M. Stanley, *How I Found Livingstone*, London, 1872, 353, 376; White Fathers, *À l'Assaut des Pays Nègres*, Paris/Lille/Algiers, 1884, 283.

[3] R. F. Burton, 'The Lake Regions of Central Equatorial Africa', *Journal of the Royal Geographical Society* (*JRGS*), XXIX, 261, 269; J. H. Speke, *What Led to the Discovery of the Source of the Nile*, London, 1864, 298; A. Schynse, *À Travers l'Afrique avec Stanley et Emin Pacha*, Paris, 1890, 83; A. Sigl, 'Bericht über den Handelsverkehr von Tabora', *Deutsches Kolonialblatt (DKB)*, III, 1892, 165 (by 'Msalala' he probably means Nera); *Chroniques Trimestrielles . . . des Pères Blancs*, 66, 1895, 339; O. Baumann, *Durch Massailand zur Nilquelle*, Berlin, 1894, 211; White Fathers, *Près des Grands Lacs*, Lyons/Paris, 1885, 16.

[4] R. C. Greig, in Kasulu District Book, National Archives of Tanzania (NAT); Dantz, 'Die Reisen des Bergassessors Dr. Dantz', *Mitteilungen . . . aus den deutschen Schutzgebieten*, XV, 1902, 147; cf. C. H. B. Grant, 'Uha in Tanganyika Territory', *Geographical Journal*, LXVI, 1925, 418.

[5] Fieldnotes; J. A. Grant, *A Walk across Africa*, London, 1864, 87–8 (he refers to a place near Bukune, which might well be Isanga); J. Macqueen, 'The Visit of Lief ben Saeid to the Great African Lake', *JRGS*, XV, 1845, 372. Burton ('Lake Regions', 261) reported 'raw iron worked at Msene's', but his testimony on this is not at all certain, and he may have been referring to Isanga or Igwisi.

[6] P. Broyon, 'Description of Unyamwesi', *Proceedings of the Royal Geographical Society (PRGS)*, XXII, 1877–8, 36; Stanley (1872), 533; E. Diesing, 'Eine Reise in Ukonongo', *Globus*, XCV, 1909, 327.

[7] Shorter (1968, D. Phil. thesis), 372, 434.

scarcity was aggravated by the fact that the craft of iron-smelting was practised only by certain families who transmitted the necessary technical and magical skills.[1] It is remarkable that at Igwisi, for example, the ore was extracted and smelted, not by the local people, but by Ha craftsmen from Buyungu, while at Isanga the workers came from Rusuubi.[2] Burton reported that the 'working of iron at Nera is confined to certain villages; the others occupy themselves exclusively with cultivation and cattle.'[3] In Uzinza and Buha, these families of smiths are called *walongo*; they appear to have formed a caste-like endogamous group, though this has yet to be confirmed by modern ethnography.[4] Such smiths monopolized the production of iron and the forging of new implements; although there were smiths in many villages, their skills were usually confined to reworking worn implements.

This scarcity of iron was naturally a major stimulant to trade. Throughout the region, iron was needed in a variety of forms: as hoe-blades for cultivation; as knife-blades and axe-heads for building and other crafts; as spear-blades and arrow-heads for hunting, fishing, and fighting. In 1883 it was reported that many people would make a fifteen-day journey to obtain iron in Busambiro.[5] As late as 1937 the smiths of Buyungu exchanged locally-made hoes for cattle from the Rundi.[6] The northern Nyamwezi introduced iron hoes (presumably from Uzinza) to the Nyaturu.[7] Iron hoes from the north-west were reworked to make spears, not only among the Sukuma and the Wakiko

[1] For some descriptions of these, see J. A. Grant (1864), 130–1; F. Stuhlmann, *Mit Emin Pascha ins Herz von Afrika*, Berlin, 1894, 117; R. Stern, 'Die Gewinnung des Eisens . . .' in F. Stuhlmann, *Handwerk und Industrie in Ostafrika*, Berlin, 1910, 152–63; Blohm (1931), I, 164–8; C. C. de Rosemond, 'Iron Smelting in the Kahama District', *Tanzania Notes and Records (TNR)*, 16, 1943, 79–84; Greig in Kasulu District Book (NAT). For the spread of iron-working and iron-using in East Africa, see J. E. G. Sutton, 'The Iron Age in East Africa' in P. L. Shinnie (ed.), *The Iron Age in Africa* (forthcoming).

[2] Fieldnotes. Among the Bemba in north-eastern Zambia, iron-working was mainly carried out by immigrant Lungu: A. D. Roberts, 'A Political History of the Bemba' (Ph.D. thesis, University of Wisconsin, 1966), 231, 246.

[3] Burton, 'Lake Regions', 269.

[4] Cf. Baumann (1894), 207, 211. The *walongo* are sometimes listed as a separate tribe: Abrahams, *Greater Unyamwezi* (1967), 17; but the name is presumably derived from a common Bantu root for 'kiln'; the same etymology may apply to the Lungu of the Tanzania-Zambia border. See also *Tanzania Zamani*, 4, 1969, 14–22.

[5] White Fathers (1885), 16.

[6] Greig, in Kasulu District Book (NAT); but it is not clear whether the hoes were made from local ores or the scrap of imported ironwork.

[7] Baumann (1894), 190. The Iramba obtained their hoes from *walongo* who are said to have once lived on the Iramba plateau. (Personal communication from Mr. P. Pender-Cudlip, who has been recording Iramba traditions.)

fishermen of the lower Malagarasi, but also among the western Masai and 'Wahumba' (Baraguyu).[1] Iron was also drawn to make a fine wire used in anklets, bracelets, and necklaces.[2] In view of the abundant evidence, to which I shall return, for an extensive trade in iron hoes and wire in the later nineteenth century, we may assume that such trade, if on a smaller scale, has a much longer history.

Sources of salt, as of iron, are common enough in western Tanzania, but they too are mostly of poor quality. Most, if not all, villages were acquainted with techniques for extracting salt from saline grass and from lake and river beds. But such processes were usually laborious and such salt as they yielded was often very impure or unpalatable. Only in a few places was it possible to produce enough salt to meet more than immediately local demands. In the later nineteenth century, the only places in or near the region where salt was both produced and traded in any quantity were the salt-pans of Ivuna, south of Lake Rukwa;[3] Kanyenye, in Ugogo;[4] Lake Balangida, north of Mount Hanang; Singida; Lake Eyasi; Lake Kitangiri;[5] on the river Manonga, in the northern Nyamwezi chiefdom of Lohumbo; at Bukune and Bulungwa, south of Kahama; a few sites in northern Buha;[6] and the brine springs in Uvinza, on the lower Malagarasi.[7] Of all these sources, the last-named was much the most important, for the numerous springs yielded a plentiful supply of brine, which had only to be evaporated to produce an exceptionally pure salt. Unlike iron-working, salt-working could be undertaken by anyone, but there were some restrictions on production. The brine springs in Uvinza and the salt-pans in Bulungwa, for example, could only be exploited for a few months each year during the dry season, since they were flooded by

[1] Fieldnotes; P. Kollmann, *The Victoria Nyanza*, London, 1899, 158; Stanley (1872), 545; Sigl (1892), 165. The Masai and 'Wahumba' may also have obtained iron from Irangi, but this seems to have been a minor source: Baumann (1894), 186, 247; cf. P. Fuchs, *Wirtschaftliche Eisenbahn-Erkundungen . . .*, Berlin, 1907, 102–3.

[2] Cf. J. A. Grant (1864), 87–8; Stern (1910), 157–8; P. Reichard, *Deutsch-Ostafrika*, Leipzig, 1892, 355.

[3] See above, Ch. 2.

[4] Burton, *Lake Regions* (1860), I, 308; J. Becker, *La Vie en Afrique*, Paris, 1887, I, 448.

[5] Baumann (1894), 133, 189, 247; H. S. Senior, 'Sukuma salt caravans to Lake Eyasi', *TNR*, 6, 1938, 87–90; Kollmann (1899), 147; Schynse (1890), 182.

[6] L. Decle, *Three Years in Savage Africa,* London, 1898, 365; Sigl (1892), 165; J. A. Grant (1864), 88; D. Herrmann, 'Uber Salzgewinnung in Unyamwesi', *DKB*, XIX, 1908, 21; R. Kandt, *Caput Nili,* Berlin, 1905, 223; Fuchs (1907), 115, 176; Broyon (1877–8), 36; Dantz (1902), 143–7.

[7] Burton, *Lake Regions* (1860), II, 37; V. L. Cameron, *Across Africa*, London, 1877, I, 232; H. M. Stanley, *Through the Dark Continent,* London, 1880, 325.

rivers during the rains. In Uvinza, work at each spring could only begin after a priest had made an offering to its resident tutelary spirit, while Lakes Eyasi and Balangida were only visited by Iramba under the leadership of experts in salt-magic.[1]

From the distribution of these various sources of salt, which mostly lie along a line running east and west across western Tanzania, one might infer that well before the nineteenth century salt was traded widely, especially to the north and to the south. It is certainly likely that the Uvinza springs have been exploited ever since the early iron age (perhaps since the fifth century A.D.). We cannot be sure how long they have been important in the trade of western Tanzania, but it is very probable that the Vinza salt industry was further stimulated by the foundation of the original Vinza chiefdom in about 1800, which would have extended the range of social contacts and created a social group that would profit directly, through taxation, from increased salt production.[2]

From the foregoing survey, we may conjecture that the trade of western Tanzania may well, by 1800 or so, have involved exchanges over considerable distances. It is, however, clear that it was only about this time that the region began to participate in long-distance trade and thus to be linked to economies outside Africa. It was, of course, elephant ivory which was the cause of such contact and which brought into being the long-distance trade routes of this part of Africa. Until then, ivory had no commercial value for the Nyamwezi and their neighbours. It was used only as a symbol of chieftainship: chiefs wore ivory bracelets and were sometimes buried between elephant tusks.[3] The Nyamwezi began to hunt elephant in earnest, and to exchange their tusks and the teeth of hippo, only when they became exposed to the demand for ivory in India, Europe, and America. The process by which this happened is not yet clear. The kingdom of Buganda obtained goods from the coast during the eighteenth century,[4] and it is

[1] P. Pender-Cudlip, personal communication.

[2] Excavations in 1967 revealed, at two sites, three levels of occupation. In the top layers were found clay-lined pits and a mass of burnt potsherds—clear evidence of the salt industry as it was described by Burton and later travellers. Charcoal in the lowest levels yielded radio-carbon dates of A.D. 420 ±160 and A.D. 590 ±200: J. E. G. Sutton, 'The Archaeology of Uvinza and its Salt Industry', *Azania*, III, 1968. Vinza traditions of origin are briefly discussed in Roberts, 'Uvinza in the Nineteenth Century' (1968), 64-6.

[3] Fieldnotes. The Kimbu are said to have hunted elephant long ago for their meat, and there was a considerable mystique attached to elephant hunting long before the ivory trade reached Ukimbu: Shorter (1968, D.Phil. thesis), 122, 249.

[4] See below, Ch. 5.

possible that Nyamwezi traders played some part in conveying them thence; but there is no evidence for this. But it is worth noting the westward migration into Ukimbu during the eighteenth century of Sagara lineages who brought with them conus shells derived ultimately from the coast. The founders of the Igulwibi dynasties in Ukimbu are said to have moved south-west from Iramba in search of ivory, and the genealogical evidence would place this event in the later eighteenth century.[1] It certainly seems likely that by this time traders in western Tanzania were beginning to make contact with traders further east who were in direct contact with the coast.

According to traditions still related in the western Nyamwezi chiefdoms of Usagusi, the first Nyamwezi to reach the coast included Mpalangombe and Ngogomi, who set out from Usagusi for the coast after failing to obtain chieftainships. They pushed on through Gogo country, where

> they met people tilling the soil with wooden tools. So they sold their iron hoes for domestic animals. . . . When they were in Uzaramo they were told that further to the east there was a big lake. They asked to see it and went on as far as Bagamoyo. . . . Here they went to Bushiri and found beads and cloth. This Bushiri was a light-skinned man. . . . They came back again and began looking for ivory. They carried this to Bagamoyo where the long-bearded men lived. These were the first Arabs. When the Arabs saw this, they wanted to go to the countries where the ivory was obtained.[2]

This story should not, of course, be taken wholly at face value. As an explanation of how the Nyamwezi rose to fame as ivory traders, it has something of the character of a 'mythical charter'. It may well conflate the experience of a whole century of trade. The name Bushiri may well be an anachronism, while the reference to selling hoes to the Gogo may simply be an ascription to the pioneers of later trading practices. And several versions of the story, as told in the villages of chiefs today, give more weight to the political than to the economic results of this adventure: their primary purpose is to explain how Usagusi first obtained conus shells from the coast as new emblems of chieftainship; it has not been considered so important to remember exactly how contact with the Arabs was first established, or what changes this meant in trading practices. On the other hand, the story may do no more than telescope into a single dramatic event a sequence of journeys and exchanges

[1] Shorter (1968, D.Phil. thesis); also 'The Kimbu' in Roberts (ed.) (1968).
[2] Interview with Msongela Hangai, near Kaliua, 5 July, 1967.

which could have elapsed quite rapidly. And it is certainly very plausible that the pioneers of trade between Nyamweziland and the coast should have included men from Usagusi. Not only is this one of the oldest groups of Nyamwezi chiefdoms; its inhabitants would already have been accustomed to travelling as traders, to obtain salt from Uvinza or Bulungwa and hoes from Igwisi, Isanga, or Buyungu. Such trade, moreover, would have been facilitated by the ready access of Usagusi to the products both of the southern woodland and the grazing-grounds of the north; indeed, until the later nineteenth century, cattle were herded and sold in Usagusi itself.[1]

If the stages by which direct contacts were established between the coast and the western interior remain somewhat obscure, it is at least fairly clear that this development took place around 1800. This may be inferred from the place of the pioneer traders in the dynastic genealogies of Usagusi; furthermore, Baumann heard the story about Mpalangombe and Ngogomi in 1892 and dated their adventure to the reign of Swetu, a chief of Unyanyembe in the early nineteenth century.[2] The Sumbwa of Ushirombo remember that Kafuku, son of chief Imaliza, was the first man from their country to reach the coast, and we know from Burton that Kafuku was killed by the Gogo in about 1830.[3] By 1811, Nyamwezi country was well known for its ivory at Zanzibar: in that year, Captain Smee wrote there of 'the Meeahmaizees, whose country is said to be three months journey from the East Coast of Africa; elephants abound in it. . . .'[4]

As yet, we cannot be sure whether in fact it was the arrival at the coast of traders from the west which first stimulated the coastal traders to press far inland. But as trade increased in Zanzibar in the early nineteenth century, more journeys to the interior would have been made from the Mrima coast opposite the island. Thus coastal traders would have been brought into contact with the country lying north of the well-established routes from Kilwa to Lake Malawi.[5] By about

[1] Fieldnotes; Burton, *Lake Regions* (1860), I, 405; and see p. 58 below.

[2] Baumann (1894), 234; but he hazards the date of 1830, which is certainly too late; see below.

[3] Mwami Kizozo, 'Habari za Usumbwa' (serialized in *Mhola Ziswe*, Tabora, June-Dec. 1959, and *Wangaluka,* Tabora, Jan. 1960–Dec. 1961), Sept. 1959; Burton, *Lake Regions* (1860), I, 263, 307.

[4] Smee to Hamilton, 25 Sept. 1811, Marine Records Misc. 586, India Office Archives, London. (This passage is reproduced in R. F. Burton, *Zanzibar—City, Island and Coast,* London, 1872, II, 510.)

[5] For these, see E. A. Alpers. 'The Role of the Yao in the trade of East Central Africa' (Ph.D. thesis, London, 1966).

1820, one Arab expedition had crossed Lake Tanganyika and visited the main Luba kingdom, west of the river Lualaba.[1] Such early expeditions usually travelled west by way of the upper reaches of the Ruaha and Njombe rivers. By the 1820s, they were trading in a market in Sangu country. Here they met Nyamwezi caravans bringing slaves and ivory, and in about 1830 the coast men induced the Nyamwezi to carry their own goods north to Unyanyembe.[2] By this time, traders from the east coast had reached the neighbourhood of Ujiji, on Lake Tanganyika, by way of Ugunda, Usishya, and Usagusi; and soon afterwards the paternal grandfather of Tippu Tip visited Uyowa.[3] In 1839 the Imam of Zanzibar, Sayyid Said, negotiated with Nyamwezi envoys for the security of Arab caravans up country.[4]

Until the 1840s, it seems that the traders from the coast preferred to take the southern route to the far west, through Sangu country, rather than the more direct route through Ugogo which had been pioneered by the Nyamwezi. But in the 1840s, as Burton learned, coastal traders began to use the Gogo route, since the southern route was disturbed by wars among the Sangu and also, perhaps, by the northward advance of the Ngoni.[5] As a result, caravans from the coast began to frequent Unyanyembe, which hitherto had been bypassed by the main route to Lake Tanganyika.[6] It was probably during the 1840s that Tippu Tip's father married into the chiefly family in Unyanyembe, while Arab settlements were founded at this period in Msene, west of Uyowa; at Ujiji; and in Puge, north of Unyanyembe.[7] In 1852, a group of Arabs fled from a war in Puge and sought better protection from Fundikira, chief of Unyanyembe. They were allowed to settle near the capital, at a place called Kazeh, which later became

[1] Tippu Tip, tr. W. H. Whiteley, *Maisha ya Hamed bin Muhammed*, Nairobi, 1966, 65, 69. Stuhlmann considered that the Arabs first reached Lake Tanganyika in about 1825: F. Stuhlmann, *Beiträge zur Kulturgeschichte von Ostafrika*, Berlin, 1909, 208.

[2] Burton, 'Lake Regions', 300; *Lake Regions* (1860), II, 57, 224.

[3] Macqueen (1845), 372; cf. W. D. Cooley, 'The Geography of N'yassi', *JRGS*, XV, 1845, 207; Tippu Tip (1966), 95.

[4] E. Burgess, 'Letters from Mr. Burgess, dated Sept. 11th, 1839', *Missionary Herald*, LXXXVII, 1840, 119.

[5] Burton, *Lake Regions* (1860), I, 302, II, 272.

[6] Unyanyembe probably expanded southwards in the 1840s, no doubt to increase its share in long-distance trade. Shorter, 'The Kimbu', in Roberts (ed.) (1968), 105.

[7] Tippu Tip (1966), 9; Baumann (1894), 234, 242; Burton, *Lake Regions* (1860), I, 327. In about 1847 Guillain heard at the coast that several Arabs and Swahili from Zanzibar stayed two or three years among the Nyamwezi: C. Guillain, *Documents sur l'histoire, la géographie et le commerce de l'Afrique Orientale*, Paris, 1856, II, 380.

known as Tabora.[1] By 1860, this settlement had become the major entrepôt up country; it was the meeting-point of trade-routes to Ujiji, the interlacustrine kingdoms, and Katanga.[2] And Nyamweziland became still more important with the exploitation of the eastern Congo by Tippu Tip in the 1870s and the consequent increase of trade between Ujiji and the east coast.

A careful examination of the East African ivory trade would obviously be of great importance for understanding the history of trade in western Tanzania. As yet, there is no adequate study of the subject, but this is not the place to attempt one.[3] My concern here is rather to indicate the relationship between the ivory trade and older forms of trade in the region, and to trace some of its more general economic effects. In some parts of Africa, the ivory trade was undoubtedly mainly wasteful and destructive. In western Tanzania, however, it is clear that despite its grave drawbacks it did have the effect of increasing very considerably the volume and flow of trade in general. The ivory trade not only introduced new items of commerce; it also greatly extended the range of older forms of trade, and hence the production of goods which had long been in demand. Fundamentally, of course, long-distance trade consisted of the export from the interior of a commodity, ivory, which was of no practical use there, in exchange for imports produced only overseas—beads, mass-produced cloth, guns. In practice, however, the conduct of such trade involved extensive trade in commodities which were both produced and consumed in the interior. This was true of all caravans, but especially those of Nyamwezi and other up-country traders—which at least in Burton's day greatly outnumbered those led from the coast.[4] It was by trading in the resources of their own homelands that the Nyamwezi obtained the means to make long-distance ventures, just as it was the credit of

[1] Burton, *Lake Regions* (1860), I, 327; J. H. Speke, *Journal of the Discovery of the Source of the Nile*, London, 1863, 82. Baumann (1894), 234, says that Tabora was founded in 1846 and that the date was well-known to Arabs living there (i.e. in 1892). Becker and Reichard, however, asserted that Arabs first settled in Unyanyembe between 1810 and 1830: Becker (1887), II, 29; Reichard (1892), 345.

[2] Becker (1887), I, 211, thus describes the excitement of caravans approaching Tabora: 'La joie éclate partout, et bien loin est le souvenir des jours de morne tristesse et de rudes privations. C'est que Tabora, comme Bagamoyo, Oudjidji et Nyangoué, est une des capitales de l'Afrique, un séjour de délices et d'éxubérante licence.'

[3] R. W. Beachey, 'The East African ivory trade in the nineteenth century', *Journal of African History (JAH)*, VIII, 1967, 269–90, is based on a very incomplete survey of even the published source material.

[4] Burton, *Lake Regions* (1860), I, 341.

money-lenders in Zanzibar which financed Arab-led expeditions from the coast. It is not too much to say that in order to sustain long-distance trade, older patterns of production and exchange were transformed.

A large ivory caravan—and for self-defence it might number several hundred (some ran into thousands)[1]—could not carry food for a long journey such as that between Tabora and the coast (which usually took ten weeks). Instead, it carried goods with which to buy food. Furthermore, all caravans had to pay tolls at various points along a trade-route and had to be supplied with an acceptable medium of payment. To these ends, as well as to buy ivory itself, a caravan leaving the coast stocked up with imports, especially cloth, beads, and metal wire. Parties going to the coast, however, stocked up with local products, especially hoes. Iron hoes were in great demand along the central caravan route between Tabora and the coast, for throughout Ugogo, Usagara, and Uluguru the known sources of iron were evidently much scarcer even than in western Tanzania. Iron was smelted in the Itumba and Ngulu hills,[2] but the supply seems to have fallen well short of local demand. At all events, the Nyamwezi provided the Gogo with iron hoes, partly to obtain grain and partly to pay the heavy tolls imposed by the Gogo.[3] Among the Sagara, spears and 'assegais' were made from hoes brought by Nyamwezi caravans.[4] The Luguru also depended on iron brought from Unyanyembe; at this distance, indeed, it was too precious to use in the form of hoes, and instead the Luguru used it to make axes and adzes for carving their wooden hoes and digging-sticks.[5]

More generally, the extended scale of trading operations resulting from the ivory trade set a special premium on commodities of universal utility, such as hoes, for these could serve as a form of currency. The demand for hoes on the caravan routes meant new opportunities for trading in hoes within the older trading networks. Musonga, chief of

[1] In 1850, Krapf heard of Nyamwezi caravans numbering three or four thousand: J. L. Krapf, *Travels, Researches and Missionary Labours in East Africa*, London, 1860, 421.

[2] J. T. Last, 'A Visit to the Wa-Itumba Iron-workers', *PRGS*, n.s.,V, 1883, 586–9; T. O. Beidelman, 'Iron-working in Ukaguru', *TNR*, 58/59, 1962, 288–9.

[3] Burton, *Lake Regions* (1860), I, 311. Schloifer noted in 1906 that Gogo would make a five-week journey to buy hoes in Uzinza (O. Schloifer, *Bana Uleia: ein Lebenswerk in Afrika*, Berlin, 1941, 223). This was presumably because they could no longer charge tolls and in any case were visited by few caravans, following the shift of Tabora's trade northwards to Lake Victoria and the Uganda Railway (cf. Decle (1898), 352; Fuchs (1907), 119).

[4] Burton, *Lake Regions* (1860), I, 237.

[5] R. Young and H. A. Fosbrooke, *Land and Politics among the Luguru*, London, 1960, 31.

Ipito in Ukimbu in the 1850s, was specially well placed, for he controlled iron-workings there and was thus able to supply both his own traders and foreigners with hoes for paying tribute to the Gogo.[1] By 1880, Sukuma brought hoes (presumably from Uzinza) for sale to caravans at Tabora.[2] We may reasonably conjecture that iron production increased considerably during the latter part at least of the nineteenth century, though unfortunately we have no reliable estimates for any particular centre.[3] It is no surprise to learn from the songs of the iron-workers that they regarded themselves as the true producers of the wealth to be had from the coast: 'Only the charcoal of the *mubanga* tree brings you the fine clothes and sights of the coast.'[4]

The salt trade may also be presumed to have benefited from the growth of the ivory trade, since salt, like iron, was a scarce necessity in general demand and could serve traders as a form of currency. Burton reported that salt from Ugogo (presumably from Kanyenye) was supplied to western Usagara and eastern Unyamwezi: 'no caravan ever passes through the country without investing in the salt-bitter substance.'[5] The Sumbwa sold hoes in Iramba in exchange for salt from Lake Eyasi, which was also taken by the Sukuma to the western shores of Lake Victoria and as far as Uganda.[6] Grant noted that Nyamwezi brought salt to Karagwe with which to buy ivory from Bunyoro, Ankole, and Butumbi. The coastal traders' settlement at Tabora became a market for salt as well as hoes: Taturu brought salt thither from Iramba (presumably Lake Kitangiri), to be exchanged for grain and beads.[7] Still more salt was brought to Tabora from Bulungwa and from Usukuma—some, no doubt, from Lohumbo and some from Lake Eyasi.[8]

The salt trade of Uvinza gained most of all from the general expan-

[1] Shorter (1968, D.Phil. thesis), 437; Lyndon Harries, *Swahili Prose Texts,* London/Nairobi, 1966, 257.

[2] Reichard (1892), 349; cf. ibid., 438.

[3] Sigl, the first German commander at Tabora, estimated that in 1890–91 150,000 hoes were sold in Tabora, most of which came from Msalala (? i.e. Nera) and Busambiro: Sigl (1892), 165. But Stern (1910), 51, cites an estimate by Pére Brard in 1897 that 30,000 hoes were produced each year in Uzinza. In 1889 many smelters in Busambiro were deserted and many *walongo* had moved westwards—perhaps to escape Ngoni raids: Schynse (1890), 73–4.

[4] Stern (1910), 155, 157.

[5] Burton, *Lake Regions* (1860), I, 308; he also asserts that the Sukuma partly depended on Gogo salt, which seems doubtful ('Lake Regions', 261).

[6] Mwami Kizozo (June, 1960); Baumann (1894), 247.

[7] J. A. Grant (1864), 159; Burton, *Lake Regions* (1860), II, 221.

[8] Herrmann (1908), 21; Sigl (1892), 165.

sion of trading networks, since Vinza salt was far better than any other produced in the interior and could be produced in greater quantities than was usually possible. Furthermore, Uvinza lay athwart the caravan route from Tabora to Ujiji, which by the 1840s, if not before, had become the main point of departure for traders visiting the countries around Lake Tanganyika. In the second half of the nineteenth century, Vinza salt was sold as far north as Lake Victoria and Burundi; as far east as Ugogo; as far south as the Ruaha valley; all round Lake Tanganyika; and over much of the eastern Congo.[1] Traders from western Unyamwezi came to Uvinza to obtain salt with which to buy hoes in Buyungu for equipping expeditions to the coast.[2] This widespread demand for Vinza salt stimulated production on an exceptional scale. For a few months each year, the brine springs around the lower Ruchugi became the scene of intense and sometimes acrimonious activity. Estimates made by European travellers between 1879 and 1900 suggest that during this period it was common for 20,000 people to work at the springs each year. Some of them were Vinza, but the majority were foreigners, from Ujiji, Burundi, Unyamwezi, and as far away as Lake Victoria. Since local supplies of food were unreliable, most visitors only stayed as long as was necessary to produce as much salt as one man could carry away. This quantity—about 25 kg.—could be produced in about ten days. Some visitors, however, obtained salt through barter (whether with other visitors, Vinza workers, or the Vinza chiefs, who accumulated salt by taxing the producers); while a few obtained salt in payment for cutting and carrying wood for the salt-workers.[3]

The role of copper as a 'lubricant' of long-distance trade in East Africa has already been noted by Alison Smith.[4] On present evidence, the copper trade seems in western Tanzania to have been essentially ancillary to the ivory trade. Copper was chiefly in demand for making wire with which to fashion anklets, bracelets, and necklaces; the wire also served as a form of currency.[5] A 'white' variety, imported from

[1] Burton, 'Lake Regions', 261; Cameron (1877), I, 232; Reichard (1892), 397; Baumann (1894), 247; Becker (1887), II, 312; H. Ramsay, 'Bericht über seine Bereisung des Nordostufers des Tanganyika', *DKB*, VII, 1896, 771; *et al.*

[2] Fieldnotes.

[3] Roberts, 'Uvinza in the Nineteenth Century' (1968), 68–70.

[4] Alison Smith, 'The Southern Section of the Interior, 1840–1884' in R. Oliver and G. Mathew (eds.), *History of East Africa*, Oxford, 1963, I, 264–5.

[5] Burton, *Lake Regions* (1860), I, 149, 396; Cameron (1877), I, 194, 210, 227; Broyon (1877–8), 31; Becker (1887), II, 187–8; Decle (1898), 318, 369.

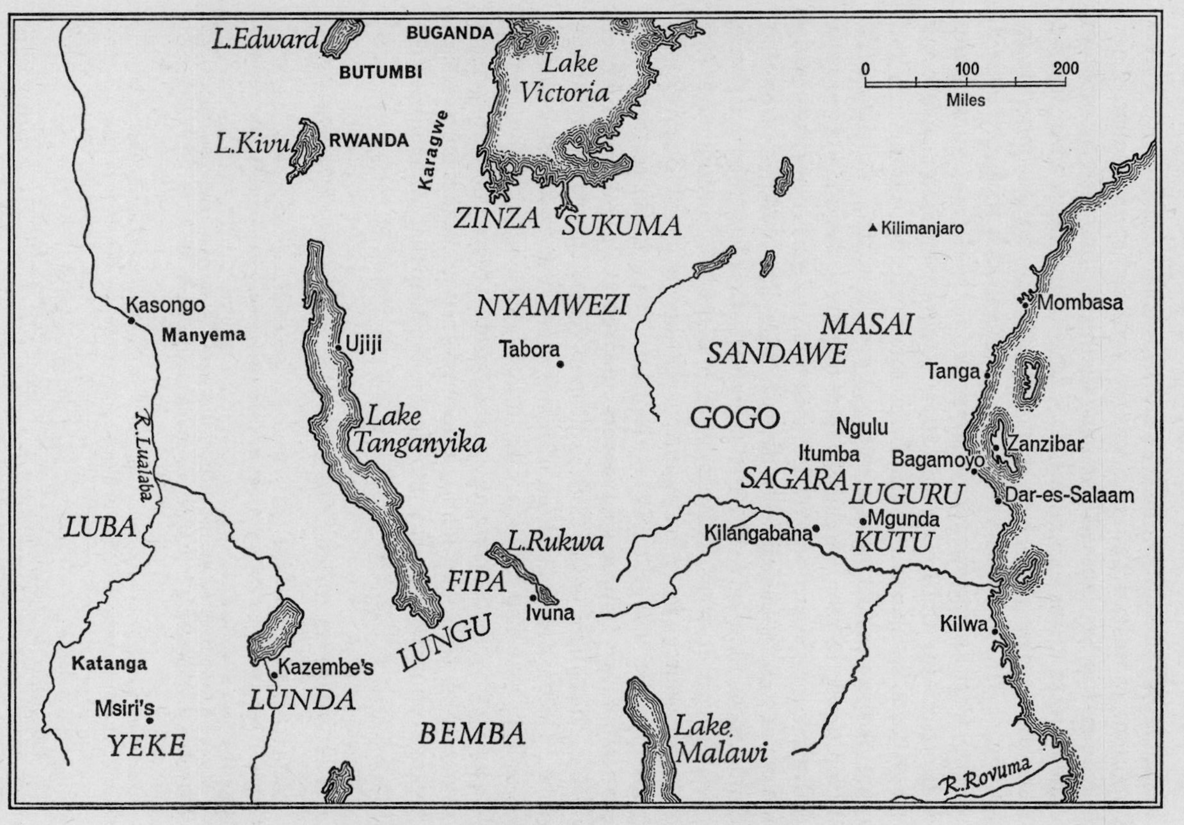

Map 4. Tanzania and the Eastern Congo

India, came inland from Zanzibar, in exchange for ivory.[1] Also important, in western Tanzania, was the 'red' copper of Katanga. This, of course, has been mined for many centuries, but there is no clear evidence that it was exported east of Lake Tanganyika much before 1800. It appears, however, that Buganda obtained copper from Karagwe in the later eighteenth century,[2] and this probably filtered through from Katanga by way of connected networks of regional trade. A direct caravan trade between Katanga and western Tanzania seems not to have developed until well into the nineteenth century. At the court of the Lunda king Kazembe, east of Katanga, 'Tungalagazas' were reported in 1806,[3] and these have tentatively been identified with Galagansa, or western Nyamwezi.[4] But today at least the Galagansa do not claim to have pioneered trade with Katanga. Traditions from the Sumbwa chiefdom of Ushirombo indicate that traders from there were bringing copper from Katanga by the 1830s.[5] According to a less authentic source, there are traditions of the people of Bugoi (Ujiji) going on a year's safari to the south of Lake Tanganyika for copper in pre-Arab days.[6] Copper spears were adopted as insignia by chiefs of the Ha, but there is no clear indication when copper first reached Buha.[7] Livingstone met an old man at Tabora in 1872 who said that as a small boy he had accompanied his father to Katanga by way of Ufipa.[8] By the 1830s, certainly, the Nyamwezi were known to obtain copper from Katanga and to be accustomed to using brass wire.[9] Katanga copper was thought more prestigious than that from the coast;[10]

[1] Burton, *Lake Regions* (1860), I, 150–51; Burton (1872), II, 413, 415.

[2] See below, Ch. 5.

[3] A. Verbeken and M. Walraet, *La première traversée de Katanga en 1806*, Brussels, 1953, 75.

[4] Smith (1963), 265. Verbeken and Walraet (1953) hazard a connexion with the Serra Canganza in Angola; more likely is Ngalanganja, west of the Zambezi sources. See also below, p. 215.

[5] Mwami Kizozo (Oct. 1959); this account first mentions such an expedition in the reign of Makaka, who succeeded in Ushirombo soon after the death of the trader Kafuku. See p. 49.

[6] Kibondo District Book (excerpted copy on file in the National Museum, Dar es Salaam, the original appears to be lost). Swann heard a story explaining the origin of Lake Tanganyika which involved a stranger carrying copper to Ujiji from the south: A. J. Swann; *Fighting the Slave-Hunters in Central Africa*, London, 1910, 78–9.

[7] Kasulu District Book (NAT).

[8] Livingstone (1874), II, 180.

[9] Cooley (1845), 212–13. Burton, *Lake Regions* (1860), II, 65, heard that people at Ujiji learned from the Arabs how to make brass from zinc brought from the coast and copper from Kazembe's (i.e. from Katanga).

[10] As late as 1880, Becker (1887), II, 187–8, gathered that among the Bende, Nyamwezi, and Gogo, only chiefs could wear ornaments of red copper, but I found no confirmation of this.

though it is not clear how far this was due simply to its colour and how far to relative scarcity compared with Indian copper. It is at least likely that in the first half of the century there were few Nyamwezi expeditions to Katanga; Burton gives the impression that in the 1850s Arab traders predominated on the routes thither.[1]

About this time, however, Katanga was visited by a headman from the Sumbwa chiefdom of Bulebe. He returned home, but his son Ngelengwa ('Msiri') settled in Katanga, took over a chiefdom, and by exploiting his access to trade from both east and west coasts built up an extensive brigand empire.[2] By the late 1860s, several Nyamwezi had formed settlements to the east of Katanga, south and south-west of the south end of Lake Tanganyika.[3] By 1880, Nyamwezi controlled most of the copper trade going north-east from Katanga.[4] The copper was bought in and around Katanga with imports from the coast—cloth and firearms; it was commonly sold in Nyamweziland for cattle or ivory.[5]

Crops and livestock also played an important part in the caravan trade of western Tanzania. People living along caravan routes found it profitable to produce crops for sale, and as commercial contacts increased it became easier to make up local deficiencies through trade. Ugogo, for example, was normally a source of food for caravans, but the region has long been subject to severe famines, and in 1884 a group of missionaries on their way to Tabora encountered a party of Nyamwezi 'with loads of corn which they were carrying to sell at high price in the famine-stricken Ugogo'.[6] A similar trade, clearly

[1] Burton (*Lake Regions* (1860), II, 148) says that caravans to Luba country (which was traversed by one of the routes to the copper mines of Katanga) were wholly composed of slaves: the Nyamwezi, 'unmaritime savages', refused to advance beyond Ujiji. It must of course be remembered that Burton obtained his information from Arab rather than Nyamwezi traders.

[2] A. Verbeken, *Msiri Roi de Garenganze*, Brussels, 1956. Informants in Bulebe added little to this. It is said that Msiri went to Katanga for copper to buy ivory from the Gogo: E. Verdick, in A. Verbeken, *Contribution à la géographie du Katanga*, Brussels, 1956, 72.

[3] Livingstone (1874), I, 291, 308–12; II, 282. These were also known as Garaganza, but some may have been natives not of Nyamweziland but of the territory ruled by Msiri which became known as Garenganze—evidently in allusion to Ugalagansa (western Nyamweziland).

[4] J. Thomson, *To the Central African Lakes and Back*, London, 1881, II, 46–7; cf. ibid., II, 215.

[5] Stern (1910), 158.

[6] E. C. Hore, *Tanganyika*, London, 1892, 249. Hore's party in fact had to buy the corn for themselves. In 1876, Wilson met 'a caravan of grain going to the south' from southern Sukumaland: C. T. Wilson and R. W. Felkin, *Uganda and the Egyptian Sudan*, London, 1882, I, 78.

ancillary to the caravan trade, was that in the tobacco of Ukutu: Thomson reported that this 'has already a wide-spread reputation in the interior and at the coast; and small trading caravans of Wanyanwesi not unfrequently come all the way from Unyanyenbe for the "soothing weed", which they barter to the Wagogo and other tribes'.[1] As for livestock, Burton says that goats and sheep were not exported to the coast from west of Usagara, but goats, from whatever source, were certainly brought to the coast by Nyamwezi in the 1880s.[2] Cattle were also taken to the coast by Nyamwezi;[3] most were driven all the way from Nyamwezi and Sukuma country, for the Gogo were disinclined to sell cattle.[4] In the 1850s cattle were sold for beads in the Kimbu chiefdoms of Kiwele and Nkokolo, and in the later nineteenth century cattle were kept specially for trading purposes in the western Nyamwezi chiefdom of Uyumbu.[5] The caravan trade also gave a special value to the donkeys bred in Nyamweziland. These were reported as plentiful in 1831, and they soon came to be used as pack-animals in Nyamwezi caravans bound for the coast.[6] They do not seem to have been used for carrying ivory, for tusks could not easily be slung on such small animals. Instead, they were loaded with other trade goods and caravan paraphernalia, in saddle-bags of giraffe or buffalo hide.[7] Later in the century, Nyamwezi donkeys seem to have been less commonly used; Stanley spoke of then as 'strong and large, but vicious and wild', and they were thought less useful than those from Masailand or from Muscat stock.[8] Both Masai and Nyamwezi donkeys, however, were sold at the coast in the 1890s.[9]

As elsewhere in Africa, the ivory trade prompted a notable expan-

[1] Thomson (1881), I, 163–4; cf. Schynse (1890), 191.

[2] Burton, *Lake Regions* (1860), II, 413; Harries (1966), 180; A. Burdo, *Les Belges dans l'Afrique Centrale,* I, Brussels, 1886, 203 (describing a caravan of Mirambo's in 1880). A Nyamwezi ivory caravan is shown driving sheep and goats into Bagamoyo in a drawing reproduced in R. Schmidt, *Deutschlands Kolonien,* Berlin, 1898(?), I, 180.

[3] Harries (1966), 180; Swann (1910), 162; Baumann (1894), 251.

[4] Becker (1887), II, 472. Towards the end of the century, one Sukuma trader took a large caravan with cattle to the coast every two years: Schynse (1890), 174–5; H. von Schweinitz, 'Das Trägerpersonal der Karawanen', *Deutsche Kolonialzeitung,* 1894, 20.

[5] Burton, 'Lake Regions', 300, 305; fieldnotes. But just to the north of Uyumbu, in Usoke and around Mirambo's capital, there were no cattle by 1878, due to warfare, raiding, concentration of settlements, and the spread of tsetse: White Fathers (1884), 282; Thomson to Mullens, 4.8.78 (Urambo), London Missionary Society Archives (LMS), CA/I/3D.

[6] Macqueen (1845), 373; Cooley (1845), 213; Guillain (1856), II, 355.

[7] Burton, *Lake Regions* (1860), I, 348; II, 30.

[8] Stanley (1872), 529; cf. ibid., 540; Baumann (1894), 251; Deniaud, 5.9.80, in *Chroniques Trimestrielles,* 8, 1880, 287; but they were highly praised by Burdo (1886), 396.

[9] Baumann (1894), 251.

sion of trade in slaves. Slaves from Nyamweziland were on sale in Zanzibar in 1811.[1] Until 1830 or so, Nyamwezi sold slaves as well as ivory to Arabs at Isanga, in south-eastern Ukimbu.[2] Slaves from Nyamweziland were taken to Zanzibar in the 1840s and to Kilwa in 1850.[3] Burton noted that the Nyamwezi were used to selling criminals and captives, though they sold each other only in extremities.[4] Mirambo exported slaves to the coast and towards the Nile valley:[5] these presumably consisted largely of captives taken in his campaigns between Lake Victoria and Lake Rukwa. But western Tanzania was never regarded as a mere hunting-ground for slaves.[6] This was due partly to the valuable links which had been developed between local trade and caravan trade and partly to the opening up, in the 1870s and 1880s, of new areas of exploitation. During this period, both traders from the coast and Nyamwezi brought great numbers of slaves to Ujiji and Tabora from all round Lake Tanganyika, especially from Burundi, Manyema, and around the south end of the lake.[7]

However, this extensive traffic was not primarily directed to the coast. To the end, most slaves exported from the mainland passed through Kilwa, which drew mainly on its southern hinterland, north and south of the Rovuma river.[8] In western Tanzania, by contrast, the slave trade chiefly served demands for slave labour within the interior. The Gogo sold ivory in order to obtain slaves, as did the Kimbu of Nkokolo.[9] Nyamwezi and other long-distance traders bought slaves both to obtain ivory on the route to the coast[10] and to work on their farms. As early as 1839, it was reported at the coast that some Nyamwezi owned four or five hundred slaves.[11] This may well be an

[1] See reference p. 49, n.4. It is not certain whether these 'Meeahmaizees' were what would be called Nyamwezi today: the term was used very loosely in the early nineteenth century to include, for example, the Ha. Cf. Cooley (1845), 207; Macqueen (1845), 372; Burgess (1840), 119.

[2] Burton, 'Lake Regions', 300.

[3] Guillain (1856), II, 309; Krapf (1860), 423.

[4] Burton, *Lake Regions* (1860), II, 31, 33.

[5] A. Burdo, *Les Arabes dans l'Afrique Centrale*, Paris, 1885, 40–41.

[6] Cf. Reichard (1892), 479.

[7] For Nyamwezi participation, see Cameron (1877), I, 255, 277.

[8] Cf. Baumann (1894), 243–4; also E. A. Alpers, *The East African Slave Trade*, Nairobi, 1967, 17; J. Christie, in E. Steere (ed.), *The East African Slave Trade*, London, 1871, 63.

[9] Burton, *Lake Regions* (1860), II, 409; Thomson (1881), II, 274; Burton, 'Lake Regions', 305. Gogo hunted ivory while their slaves grew crops: *Bull. Soc. Géog. Lille*, IV (1895), 324.

[10] 'The best [ivory] in the [Zanzibar] market was held to be the fine heavy material brought down from Ugogo by the Wanyamwezi porters who on their long journey collect ivories of many different kinds': Burton (1872), II, 410.

[11] Burgess (1840), 119. In 1881 Becker passed through the Nyamwezi chiefdom of Ugunda and wrote of 'un petit bourg, fort de 500 habitants, dont 40 hommes libres et le reste

exaggeration, and in any case many such slaves were doubtless held for future sale rather than for actual employment. All the same, Burton gathered that the Nyamwezi employed slaves from the region of Ujiji, the kingdoms west of Lake Victoria, from Ugalla, and from Ufipa.[1] As late as 1890, when slaves could no longer be openly sold on the east coast, Nyamwezi were buying slaves in Buddu, southern Buganda.[2] Slaves, indeed, were almost as much a form of currency as hoes or salt. They were relatively cheap: in Burton's day, five or six were needed to buy a tusk in Ugogo,[3] and at Karema in 1882 a slave was worth less than a donkey, a cow, or a sack of salt. To buy a slave was in fact the first ambition of anyone who managed to get his hands on a piece of cloth.[4]

The principal customers for slaves in western Tanzania were the Arabs themselves. Hore noted in 1879 that the slaves brought from Manyema to Ujiji were mostly sold there to work as servants, boatmen, carriers, bodyguards, or cultivators for Arab traders settled there (who usually owned between twenty and a hundred). Wissmann, in 1887, observed that less than a quarter of the slaves exported from Kasongo, in Manyema, reached the coast; they were absorbed by the Arabs in Tabora and especially Ujiji, where it was said that a working slave could not survive the climate more than a year. And besides being used in general domestic employment, slaves were directly employed in the ivory trade. Burton considered that the indiscriminate use by ivory dealers of slaves as commercial agents had contributed to the rapid rise in ivory prices in the interior.[5] With the spread of firearms in the 1870s and 1880s,[6] ivory traders became less dependent on the skills of local hunters armed with heavy spears; instead, they tended

esclaves!'—though this was probably an exaggeration since he also implies that the freemen were all councillors (*wagabe*): (1887), II, 98, 100.

[1] Burton, *Lake Regions* (1860), II, 33.

[2] Stuhlmann (1894), 186. Isike, chief of Unyanyembe, resorted at times to low cunning to enslave his subjects: Reichard (1892), 468.

[3] Burton, *Lake Regions* (1860), II, 406; but he does not say whether these were male, female, or children.

[4] Becker (1887), II, 320, 244. Reichard (1892), 466, was struck by the readiness of the Nyamwezi to gamble away their freedom.

[5] Hore to Thompson, 16.4.79, LMS/CA/2/IB; H. von Wissmann, *My Second Journey through Equatorial Africa*, London, 1891, 246; Burton, *Lake Regions* (1860), II, 370.

[6] Cameron (1877), I, 201; Stanley (1880), 313, 322; H. von Wissmann, *Unter Deutsche Flagge*, Berlin, 1889, 251; Becker (1887), II, 509; Baumann (1894), 211. The gun trade in the western interior was under way by 1858: Burton, *Lake Regions* (1860), I, 233; II, 308. See also R. W. Beachey, 'The Arms Trade in East Africa in the late nineteenth century', *JAH*, III, 1962, 451–67.

(especially in Manyema) to employ bands of their own slaves, armed with guns. In 1873 the Sultan of Zanzibar formally abolished the slave trade in his dominions, and despite extensive evasions this eventually induced some slave traders to seek a living in the interior. It also inevitably lowered slave prices there, so that slaves were even more commonly used in ivory trading and raiding, and in agriculture.[1]

On the other hand, slaves played only a minor role in the actual porterage of ivory to the coast. This was a skilled and arduous task best performed by fit and experienced young men: undisciplined and demoralized captives would have been of very little use. Some Europeans believed that the slaves sold at the coast had been used to carry down ivory, but as Reichard pointed out an Arab caravan had to reckon on taking into the interior trade goods weighing between a half and two-thirds of the ivory it could expect to return with. It thus made better sense to engage porters at cheap rates for the round trip.[2] In the early part of the century, coastal traders employed 'servile gangs hired on the coast' for safaris up country, but by about 1850 most caravans on the routes through Tabora used free men, especially Nyamwezi.[3] Some of the richer chiefs and Arab colonists employed their more trusted men as regular porters, and this practice increased when slaves became both cheaper in the interior and less negotiable at the coast, but even in Tabora in 1890 there were said to be few slave porters.[4]

In view of such indications that long-distance trade stimulated an increase in various forms of production and exchange, we must enquire how far food production was affected. Most of the activities contributing to the trade of western Tanzania were concentrated in the dry season, between May and November, when there are few or no agricultural tasks demanding attention. Making iron and salt; hunting elephant and other game; collecting tree-bark and honey; carrying ivory to the coast: all these could be pursued without disrupting the annual agricultural cycle. All the same, it would surely have been difficult for the traditional small-scale agriculture of the region to accommodate the pressures created by the expansion of trade. The region came to be settled by groups with no place in the traditional

[1] Reichard (1892), 478–9; Stuhlmann (1894), 62.

[2] S. T. Pruen, *The Arab and the African*, London, 1891, 214; Reichard (1892), 485.

[3] Burton, *Lake Regions* (1860), I, 337.

[4] Cf. Capt. Colomb, *Slave-Catching in the Indian Ocean*, London, 1873, 387; Livingstone (1874), II, 202; Becker (1887), II, 403; Alpers (1967), 24; Pruen (1891), 130; Stuhlmann (1894), 64.

subsistence economies: Arab and Swahili traders, and large numbers of imported slaves. Ordinary people also became increasingly mobile, and were obliged in the course of trade and travel to obtain their food in exchange for goods or labour. Thus foodstuffs had to be produced for consumption outside the family compound or even the local chiefdom. Finally, the growth of the ivory trade, together with the invasions and depredations of the Ngoni from the 1850s, brought about great changes in military organization. Chiefs such as Mirambo, Nyungu ya Mawe, or Isike had large followings of warriors who spent little or no time in cultivation and whose most productive activity was cattle-raiding.[1] And not only did such leaders withdraw able-bodied young men from the subsistence economy: the progress of an army might ruin the fields of many villages and the threat of war compel villagers to abandon the most crucial tasks of cultivation.

It is, in fact, fairly clear that the expansion of trade in the nineteenth century, for all its destructive effects, did bring about some notable changes in the scope and scale of agricultural production. Crucial to this was the introduction of new crops. Traders from the east coast brought rice to be planted in their own settlements up country. Around 1860, rice was still very much a foreigners' crop,[2] but over the next twenty years it was adopted in Nyamwezi villages, especially those along the line of caravan routes.[3] The special advantage of rice was that it could be grown in areas hitherto unavailable for cultivation—the grassy corridors (*mbuga*) along the line of streams and rivers which are flooded in the wet season. Reichard, who visited Nyamweziland in the early 1880s, noted that before the onset of the rains channels were dug to hold and distribute the water.[4]

Maize and cassava also appear to have been introduced to western Tanzania during the nineteenth century, presumably as a result of travel between Nyamweziland, the coast, and the Congo.[5] Burton

[1] See, e.g., Storms, in Becker (1887), II, 507–8; Aylward Shorter, 'Nyungu-ya-Mawe and the "Empire of the Ruga-rugas"', *JAH*, IX, 1968, 241.

[2] Burton, *Lake Regions* (1860), I, 331, 397; Speke (1863), 102, 651; Speke (1864), 201.

[3] Cameron (1877), II, 297, 299; R. Böhm, *Von Sansibar zum Tanganjika*, Leipzig, 1888, 54 (Ngulu, Ugunda); Becker (1887), I, 417 (Mirambo's); I, 430 (Simba's); Wissmann (1889), 251, 255; Baumann (1894), 101; Kandt (1905), 189 (southern Buha and western Nyamwezi). In 1880 Mirambo gave a field of rice (as well as forty acres of millet) to the missionary Southon: Southon to Thompson, 1.6.80, LMS/CA/3/2A.

[4] Reichard (1892), 378.

[5] Cf. Stuhlmann (1909), 208–9. American crops probably reached the countries east of Lake Tanganyika some time after they reached the countries immediately west of it, where their abundance was noted by Livingstone (1874), II, 153, and Thomson (1881), II, 52, 59, 152.

heard that maize, cassava, and sweet potatoes were abundant in Nkokolo, an important trading centre in Ukimbu,[1] and he found 'the finest manioc' in Uvinza, while at Msene maize and cassava were 'plentiful enough to be exported'.[2] By 1880, both crops were grown in southern Buha and at Mirambo's and were also on sale at Tabora.[3] Reichard guessed that maize accounted for 18% of Nyamwezi food crops and noted that it had become the staple crop in Bende country; by 1890, cassava was common in Uzinza.[4]

These innovations helped to increase overall food production, both by extending the area under cultivation and, by diversifying, reducing dependence on any one crop; resistance to famine was thus increased, especially of course by the adoption of cassava. And the effect of new crops was naturally reinforced by the more widespread trade in, and use of, iron hoes, which can be assumed to have increased agricultural productivity. Furthermore, as we have seen, slaves were used as agricultural labourers both by Nyamwezi and by traders from the coast. Only indeed through changes in agricultural habits could it have become possible to supply food to the large stockaded villages which were formed in many places for security against marauders and invaders. The capitals of some chiefs, such as Mirambo, had several thousand inhabitants.[5] Many, as dependants of the chief, subsisted on war-booty and tribute, but if each householder had depended on cultivating millet alone, many would only have found room to do so at a distance of two days or more—and thus could not have inhabited the village at all continuously.

So far, I have tried to sketch the impact of long-distance trade on various forms of economic activity in western Tanzania. I shall now briefly consider how far this involved changes in economic organization. In general, the region was far from becoming a 'market economy'. Markets themselves were not, on the whole, characteristic of the region. They appear to have been long established in the southern Ha chief-

[1] Burton, 'Lake Regions', 305. In general, however, maize and cassava were little cultivated in Ukimbu before this century: Shorter (1968, D.Phil. thesis), 103–4.

[2] Burton, *Lake Regions* (1860), I, 397, 408; cf. White Fathers (1884), 289.

[3] Wissmann (1889), 238; Becker (1887), I, 222, 417. In 1877, south of the river Manonga, Wilson noted that maize was 'much more largely grown here than it is further north': C. T. Wilson, 'Journey from Kagei to Tabora and back', *PRGS*, II, 1880, 618.

[4] Reichard (1892), 384; Schynse (1890), 73; Baumann (1894), 71.

[5] Southon's description of Mirambo's capital in 1879 is quoted by Alison Smith (1963), 281; he guessed, however implausibly, that there were about 15,000 inhabitants, who were supplied with food by cultivators living at a distance from the capital. Hore, however, had noted in 1878 that there were 'tiny plots' of maize throughout the town (1892), 54.

dom of Heru,[1] and in other areas around Lake Tanganyika, including Ujiji.[2] Markets were also held in some Sumbwa chiefdoms,[3] but even in the later nineteenth century they were not usual among the Nyamwezi. Near the Arab settlement in Msene, Burton reported 'an African attempt at a soko or bazaar'[4] but in 1882 the only significant markets in Nyamwezi country seem to have been those at Tabora and at Mirambo's capital. And whereas at Tabora—essentially an enclave of coastal culture—prices were based on supply and demand, at Mirambo's the prices were fixed by Mirambo himself.[5] Apart from Tabora, the great ivory entrepôt, such markets were mainly concerned with exchange of food crops, cattle, meat, vegetables, salt, iron hoes, cotton, and bark-cloth. In general, the trade of the region was conducted not through regular markets but in *ad hoc* gatherings at a caravan halt, or by visiting a particular place of commercial interest, such as a centre of salt or iron production.

Partly for this reason, no single currency of exchange gained general acceptance. Burton reported that cowries were used as currency in Karagwe—they were brought there from the coast by Nyamwezi caravans;[6] but there is no indication that the Nyamwezi themselves, or their neighbours, used cowries for this purpose. Several varieties of beads were used as currency along the main trade-routes, and there were recognized names, indicating standards of value, for different quantities. In Ujiji, the pipe beads called *masaro* appear to have remained in circulation for several decades, even though in 1893 they were said not to be used as ornaments.[7] But Ujiji, like Tabora, was essentially an offshoot of the commercial culture of the coast. In most villages, beads or imported cloth were accepted not as currency in the strictest sense, but because a particular variety was in local and temporary demand for actual wear. Burton and later travellers complained of the fluctuations in the taste for beads; they also noted that once the novelty of imported cloth had worn off, it was often rejected in favour of more durable skins and bark-cloth for actual wear, and beads

[1] C. H. B. Grant (1925), 518; J. H. Scherer, 'The Ha of Tanganyika', *Anthropos*, LIV, 1959, 862; A. Leve, 'Wha (Deutsch-Ostafrika)', *Globus*, LXXIX, 1901, 76.

[2] Hore (1892), 70, 152; cf. Livingstone (1874), II, 182–3; Decle (1898), 317.

[3] Mwami Kizozo, interview at Ushirombo, 3.11.67.

[4] Burton, *Lake Regions* (1860), I, 397.

[5] Becker (1887), II, 157. Stuhlmann, in 1890, noted a market-place in Ndala, north-east of Tabora: (1894), 100.

[6] Burton, *Lake Regions* (1860), II, 185.

[7] ibid., I, 398; II, 392–3; White Fathers (1884), 301; Decle (1898), 314.

and wire for trade.[1] Even where cloth was in use as a currency, its negotiability was liable to be limited by political conditions: Becker found that the *satini* cloth used as currency in Tabora was useless at Mirambo's,[2] probably because of the hostility and lack of trade between the two centres. Thus caravans had to stock up with a variety of beads and cloth, and also with commodities which were bulkier but less subject to the whims of fashion and politics: copper and iron wire, hoes, and salt.[3] And sometimes certain commodities were bartered only against certain others: the Gogo, for instance, sold food for hoes and ivory for slaves; in both cases, they obtained equipment needed to secure further supplies. As for credit, this was, as Burton reported, unknown in Nyamweziland except among Arab traders.[4] Mirambo, whose operations were certainly on a large enough scale to make him interested in the idea,[5] was denied such opportunities by political circumstances: he could not, for example, accept payment for cloth from Wissmann in a note for dollars in Tabora, since he had no credit there or elsewhere.[6] However, Rumanika of Karagwe, who was on much better terms with Arab traders, sold ivory to Speke for promissory notes redeemable in Zanzibar, and in Buganda Nyamwezi porters accepted part-payment in notes on Rumanika.[7]

If patterns of exchange continued to be more responsive to local and particular than to large-scale, universal economic pressures, so too economic specialization did not develop very far. The carriage of ivory to the coast became a most important feature of Nyamwezi life, but it was not essentially a specialist activity. As we have seen, it was possible to accommodate six-month safaris within the annual agricultural cycle without undue strain. Caravans under Nyamwezi leadership usually left for the coast in April or May and set out on the return journey in

[1] Burton, *Lake Regions* (1860), I, 149; cf. ibid., II, 73, 388; *Chroniques Trimestrielles*, 66, 1895, 340; Wilson and Felkin (1882), 48. Travellers' impressions of local clothing are often contradictory, but it is probable that imported cloth only became popular when durable stuffs were introduced near the end of the century: cf. Baumann (1894), 229, 252. Some cloth was locally woven from locally grown cotton: Cooley (1845), 213; Burton, *Lake Regions* (1860), II, 30; Cameron (1877), I, 275–8; Hore (1892), 85–6; J. T. Moloney, *With Captain Stairs to Katanga*, London, 1893, 104; but this does not seem to have been an important item of commerce.

[2] Becker (1887), II, 157.

[3] Cf. Decle (1898), 354.

[4] Burton, *Lake Regions* (1860), II, 30.

[5] In June 1882 caravans arrived at Mirambo's from the coast and were despatched by him to Uganda, Karagwe, Usukuma, Katanga, and Manyema: Griffith to Thompson, 1.7.82., LMS/CA/4/4C.

[6] Wissmann (1889), 260. Mirambo simply gave the cloth to Wissmann.

[7] Speke (1863), 237, 449.

September.[1] Thus during much of the year there were a large number of men both able and willing to join a caravan. Burton reported that 'porterage, on the long and toilsome journey, is now considered by the Wanyamwezi a test of manliness'; Swann observed that 'not one of them was allowed to marry before he had carried a load of ivory to the coast, and brought back one of calico or brass-wire'.[2] Stuhlmann estimated that about a third of the male population of Nyamweziland went to the coast each year as traders or porters.[3] In this way, of course, many Nyamwezi became accustomed to living for a large part of the year away from home. As Raum has observed, the Nyamwezi porter 'learned to live in two economies'—the subsistence economy at home and the wage economy of the caravan. 'Among the porters a shallow kind of specialization developed: there were cooks, tent boys, carriers, personal servants; selected men were trained as askaris. The caravan personnel formed a community of its own with its own interests and "culture", expressed, for instance, in songs and stories.'[4] Once arrived at the coast, the Nyamwezi usually stayed there for a time, enjoying 'the dear delights of comparative civilization'; porters made a living for themselves either as labourers—cutting grass or carrying stones—or cultivating a plot of vegetables and cassava.[5] Burton found that many Nyamwezi traders took their ivory over to Zanzibar, where the Nyamwezi had their own quarter.[6] Traders were obliged to spend some time in bargaining at the coast: 'a lot of two hundred tusks is rarely sold under four months.'[7] But Indian merchants were quite prepared for protracted bargaining, knowing that a Nyamwezi caravan

[1] Guillain (1856), II, 380. Krapf found groups of Kimbu and Nyamwezi living at the coast in February 1850 and says that the latter stayed from December to March: (1860), 420–21. Burton met a Nyamwezi caravan on its way to the coast in January 1859: *Lake Regions* (1860), II, 268; he also says that the Nyamwezi 'came twice a year, in our mid-summer and midwinter': (1872), I, 343; but the dry season seems to have been the more favoured period for service in caravans organized by traders from the coast: *Lake Regions* (1860), I, 339.

[2] Burton, *Lake Regions* (1860), I, 337; Swann (1910), 58.

[3] Stuhlmann (1894), 89.

[4] O. F. Raum, 'Changes in African Tribal Life', in V. Harlow *et al.* (eds.), *History of East Africa*, II, Oxford, 1965, 169. This description seems to refer primarily to the German period, but it agrees well enough with Burton's observations: *Lake Regions* (1860), I, 143–6, 337–62. For other impressions of Nyamwezi caravan life see Wilson and Felkin (1882), 42–7; E. Baur and A. Le Roy, *À Travers le Zanguebar*, Tours, 1886, 193; White Fathers (1884), 282; Reichard (1892), 437; Harries (1966), 180–83; Blohm (1931), I, 170–72; Schweinitz (1894), 19.

[5] Burton, *Lake Regions* (1860), II, 30.

[6] ibid., I, 38–9. Burton's later recollections of Nyamwezi in Zanzibar are in his least sympathetic vein: (1872), I, 343.

[7] Burton, *Lake Regions* (1860), I, 39.

would eventually become anxious to get home in time for the sowing season in November.[1] The demands of the Nyamwezi subsistence economy largely regulated the availability of porters at Tabora and the coast. One reason, indeed, why west-bound caravans found it difficult to retain Nyamwezi porters beyond Tabora was probably that by the time they arrived there late in the year they were needed at home.[2]

If porterage became a seasonal rather than a full-time occupation for the Nyamwezi, the same would seem to be true of actual trading—and in Nyamwezi caravans the two activities were not sharply distinguished. A young man often used the wages earned on safari (which were usually paid in cloth) to begin trading on his own account. On his second or third expedition he might carry two small tusks of his own; with experience, he might become a caravan guide (*kiongozi*) and thus earn much more cloth for investment, and eventually he might become rich enough to fit out a caravan of his own.[3] But many traders continued to be farmers; even the most successful seem seldom to have become wholly engaged in commerce. And as long as there was an expanding 'trader's frontier' the enterprising trader was likely to find more scope there than at home, where wealth could still only be realized in terms of political advancement. Some traders, being sons of chiefs, might themselves become chiefs and so turn their own profits to political account, while continuing to organize caravans. Others used a trading fortune to carve out a chiefdom of their own, often far from Nyamweziland. One such was Kilangabana, who with Mpalangombe and Ngogomi had been a pioneer of trade from Usagusi to the coast. By 1830, he was established in Kisanga in Sagara country, athwart the route from Tabora to the coast.[4] Mgunda, in Ukutu, was another,[5] and the most famous of such adventurers was Msiri of Katanga. It is, of course, difficult to say of such figures whether their ambitions were primarily commercial or political. Msiri's conquests might well be considered incidental to his achievement in expanding the trade of Katanga; in the local conditions, the new scale of operations

[1] See Reichard (1892), 438–43, for details of the process.

[2] Burton, *Lake Regions* (1860), I, 340. A further deterrent, in the 1870s and early 1880s, to porterage west of Tabora was the hostilities between Mirambo and Arabs in Tabora.

[3] Fieldnotes; cf. Blohm (1930), I, 167–70.

[4] Fieldnotes; Macqueen (1845), 372; Burton, *Lake Regions* (1860), II, 258; D. O. Kilosa to P. C., Eastern Province, 7.8.34 and 11.8.38 in NAT/61: 1C/II, 310, 358.

[5] Thomson (1881), I, 167–8; V. Giraud, *Les Lacs de l'Afrique Équatoriale*, Paris, 1890, 89–90. Cf. Reichard's account of the rise and fall of a Makua ivory hunter and trader; (1892), 434.

called for a new political order. It is clear that several other Nyamwezi achieved a special status as foreign experts in more or less distant countries. Some settled as traders and craftsmen in what is now north-eastern Zambia,[1] as well as in Katanga and Manyema. Others became advisers to Gogo chiefs, and prompted Stanley to remark that the Nyamwezi 'are like Scotchmen, they may be found almost everywhere throughout central Africa, and have a knack of pushing themselves into prominence'.[2] Baumann encountered Nyamwezi colonies in Usandawe and Irangi, and himself established one in Mbugwe; he was much impressed by their 'civilizing' influence in such remote areas.[3]

Probably the most specialized economic pursuit in Nyamweziland was ivory-hunting. Recruitment to this craft was more open than to iron-working, but more selective than to porterage. Hunters were organized in societies, which like others in the region were based on experience and achievement rather than birth. Like iron-working, hunting called for both practical and magical skills, and a hunting expedition had to be led by a *fundi* who knew the special medicine and songs for attracting elephants.[4] (This knowledge was part of general hunting lore: a man was a hunter rather than an elephant hunter, even if he concentrated on elephant.) Each hunter worked with a group of four or five apprentices (*bahemba*), who might or might not be his relatives. After an apprentice had killed several elephant, his *fundi* would give him insignia and hunting-charms of his own. The dry season was best for hunting, but since ivory was always in demand, many hunters worked through much of the year. They travelled widely, wherever game was most abundant; they were not tied to any particular territory, so long as they shared their crop with the local chief.[5] As ivory became scarcer in their homelands, Nyamwezi hunters went further afield: from Tabora to Manyema and as far north as Butumbi, near Lake Edward.[6] In the last two decades or so of the

[1] Livingstone (1874), I, 321–2, 331; II, 254, 256, 331 (and references in p. 57, n.3 above); Giraud (1890), 238–42, 260; Moloney (1893), 250.

[2] Cotterill, in J. F. Elton, *Travels and Researches among the Lakes and Mountains of Eastern and Central Africa*, London, 1879, 398; E. Gleerup, in P. Hassing and N. Bennett, 'A journey across Tanganyika in 1886', *TNR*, 58/9, 1962, 143; Stanley (1872), 253.

[3] Baumann (1894), 235, 253, 257. Nyamwezi colonization increased considerably under German rule, especially in Tanga district, due to labour migration.

[4] Cf. Baumann (1894), 243; Blohm (1931), 97–101.

[5] Interview with Lutumbika, the son and grandson of ivory-hunters, at Kaliua, 2.9.67; cf. Stuhlmann (1894), 86–7.

[6] Baumann (1894), 243; Stuhlmann (1894), 86, 262. Nyamwezi today say that those who settled in Katanga in the last century became known as Yeke since this is the word for

nineteenth century, western Tanzania and the eastern Congo were increasingly frequented by other groups of hunters: indeed, 'Makua' became a generic name for hunters in the interior as in the countries near the coast.[1]

The production of iron and salt, however, appears to have been much less specialized. Iron-smelting, indeed, was an exclusive occupation, but it was seasonal and smiths usually grew their own food.[2] Salt, as we have seen, was produced on a relatively large scale in Uvinza, but this industry was open to all comers and was strictly seasonal. In 1880 there was a brisk trade in food for salt, and in 1902, shortly after the German occupation, it was reported that many Vinza obtained food through making salt for exchange rather than through cultivation. But it is unlikely that even the Vinza in the neighbourhood of the brine springs became dependent on trade for a livelihood: only a few years before, food had been unobtainable, probably due to a recent agreement between the three chiefs that salt-workers should provide their own.[3] Nor was food-production highly specialized. One Arab at Tabora, Salim bin Sef, had abandoned trade for agriculture: he employed a great many slaves in cultivating extensive plantations of cassava and grain,[4] but he seems to have had no African counterparts.

Any discussion of changes in African economic organization raises the question of the relationship between trade and politics. This subject is of course crucial to the history of western Tanzania and has already received some attention.[5] Here I want only to remark on the role of political authorities in the expanded trade of the later nineteenth century. As we have seen, most of the region was governed during the last century by a multitude of small chiefs with limited political authority and economic resources. Many chiefs participated in long-distance trade, but even the great warlords, such as Mirambo, had

---

hunter (*muyege*). Baumann found that the ivory trade in the country west of Lake Victoria was almost entirely in the hands of 'Warambo'—traders from the former dominions of Mirambo.

[1] Baumann (1894), 62, 232, 243; Stuhlmann (1894), 804; cf. Reichard (1892), 427; Livingstone (1874), II, 185.

[2] But in 1882 Last found that the Itumba iron-workers 'almost completely neglect cattle-keeping and agriculture .... all the produce of their labour has to go for food:' (1883), 586.

[3] Roberts, 'Uvinza in the Nineteenth Century' (1968), 70.

[4] Becker (1887), II, 30; cf. Moloney (1893), 68.

[5] Andrew Roberts, 'Political Change in the Nineteenth Century', in Kimambo and Temu (eds.) (forthcoming); Abrahams, *Political Organisation* (1967); Shorter, 'Nyungu-ya-Mawe' (1968).

difficulty in mobilizing and monopolizing the economic resources of their dominions: such empires were highly dependent on *raubwirtschaft*.

There were certain basic advantages enjoyed by all chiefs. Chiefs obtained a special share of their subjects' labour and produce; and not only the harvests but animal and mineral wealth. The three Vinza chiefs shared a tax of one-tenth of the salt output of the brine springs, and a levy on salt production at Lake Kitangiri formed the basis of the Iramba chief's power.[1] From hunters, chiefs usually exacted one elephant tusk from every pair, though in return the hunters received cloths and livestock.[2] In this way, a chief might accumulate a large stock of ivory and either send his own men with it to the coast or else sell it to coastal traders, who bought most of their ivory in the villages of chiefs.[3] Many chiefs also derived a substantial revenue from road tolls (*hongo*). The western Gogo were specially well placed for this, since water was very scarce in their country and large caravans were wholly dependent for survival on Gogo co-operation.[4] The exactions of the Vinza chiefs were also notorious,[5] since it was scarcely possible to avoid their countries when travelling between Tabora and Ujiji, and they controlled the ferries across the Malagarasi. As yet, it is difficult, except in the most general terms, to assess the economic and political effects of such taxation: we lack the necessary quantitative information. It would appear that there were some broad guide-lines as to the proper rates for road tolls: complaints of 'blackmail' by European travellers ill-acquainted with local custom should not be taken at face value.[6] But in the late nineteenth century, such guide-lines would have been greatly complicated both by political considerations and by changes in values and prices resulting from the rapid growth of trade.[7]

[1] Roberts, 'Uvinza in the Nineteenth Century' (1968), 70; P. Pender-Cudlip, personal communication.

[2] Fieldnotes (Lutumbika). [3] Cf. Reichard (1892), 444.

[4] L. Heudebert, *Vers les Grands Lacs de l'Afrique Orientale*, Paris, 1900, 240–41; cf. Pruen (1891), 184; Schweinitz (1894), 20.

[5] Cf. Becker (1887), I, 428, and many travellers' reports.

[6] Southon, in 1880, spoke of 'the customary mhongo' in Uvinza (journal entry, 27.9.80, LMS/CA/J3/31). Several travellers reported how much they had to pay in tolls, but without indicating what percentage of their total loads these charges represented. Wilson asserted that 'the various chiefs are supposed to levy the tax at so much for every bale of barter goods, but there is no check', and in practice a few days' journey through Ugogo might cost 20–25% of the total property of a caravan: Wilson and Felkin (1882), 58. A missionary caravan in 1889 was charged rates ranging from 1% to 7% in seven chiefdoms between Tabora and Lake Victoria: Schynse (1890), 93.

[7] Cf. Burton, *Lake Regions* (1860), II, 229, 409–10; Speke (1864), 240; Reichard (1892), 436; Thomson (1881), I, 294–5; H. M. Stanley, *In Darkest Africa*, London, 1890, II, 403.

Mirambo himself deplored the somewhat haphazard methods of levying tolls, for he realized that they seriously discouraged foreign traders.[1]

It was, however, impossible for chiefs to monopolize long-distance trade as long as hunters retained half their ivory crop and could sell it direct to traders. And towards the end of the century, at least in areas where chiefs were of little consequence, hunters divided their proceeds not with local chiefs but with traders who supplied them with guns and powder.[2] Indeed, it would seem that few if any chiefs were able for long to retain control over trade in and possession of guns. Cameron noted that whereas in Burton's day 'a musket was an heirloom for a chief . . . when I passed through Ugunda nearly every village could turn out at least half its men armed with muskets'.[3] Isike of Unyanyembe was thought to have thousands of guns at his disposal, but many of these must have been in private hands: from the 1870s Nyamwezi porters were commonly paid in firearms as well as cloth.[4] This circumstance, of course, seriously undermined the ability of Nyamwezi chiefs, even within their own chiefdoms, to present a united front against European invasion.

It will have become all too clear in the course of this essay that although there is a good deal of evidence about Nyamwezi trade before 1900, much of it is fragmentary and uneven in quality. None the less it does indicate clearly that important changes took place in the economic life of the Nyamwezi and their neighbours during the nineteenth century. Under the stimulus of trade with the world outside Africa, there was a real break away from the limited scope of earlier trade. We must not, of course, overlook the measure of economic growth—notably through the exchange of iron and salt—before the establishment of long-distance trade. But the links with the coast brought about a qualitative change in the nature of Nyamwezi trade. Instead of being directed simply to the maintenance of subsistence economies, production began to be directed towards sustaining complex and extensive trading networks which met certain needs of industrial and plantation economies far from Nyamweziland. This transformation involved a real measure of commercial enterprise and risk-taking. Nyamwezi traders—like the Bisa in north-eastern Zambia—increasingly made fine

[1] Becker (1887), II, 167; Southon, journal entry, 27.9.80, LMS/CA/J3/31.
[2] Baumann (1894), 243.
[3] Cameron (1877), I, 201; Burton, *Lake Regions* (1860), II, 308.
[4] Wilson and Felkin (1882), 43; Becker (1887), II, 509.

calculations of the material profit to be derived from satisfying the wants of people far beyond the orbit of their own subsistence economies.[1] No less important, many of the Nyamwezi and their neighbours were bold enough to supplement their familiar staple crop, or even replace it; and recent experience has belatedly taught us the considerable hazards of such fundamental experiment in poor tropical soils. (No doubt cultivators with slaves—who might be sold if food ran short—were readier to take such risks than those without.) It need hardly be stressed that changes in the production and distribution of food are essential to any sound process of development away from the subsistence economy, and judged by this basic criterion there was a real element of significant economic growth in western Tanzania during the nineteenth century.

Yet if we recognize this measure of achievement, we must also ask why in fact it was not more considerable: why markets did not become more common, why currencies remained so particular, why there is so little sign of the emergence of true entrepreneurs. The answers, surely, are not far to seek. On the economic side, the unfavourable environment must never be forgotten. Unyanyembe might strike weary travellers as a land of milk and honey after the tribulations of arid Ugogo,[2] but the abundance was only relative. In general, the margin between sufficiency and real want in western Tanzania is a narrow one, and a livelihood is not nearly so easily won as in, for example, the plantain belts around Lake Victoria or Kilimanjaro. And if so basic a factor as food-production remained uncertain, so too was the *primum mobile* of the whole system of long-distance trade—the supply of ivory. No trade system could long survive which was so heavily geared to the uncontrolled exploitation of a natural asset. From this point of view, the economies of western Tanzania had all the stability of towns spawned by a gold rush. In such a fevered atmosphere, a more or less balanced response—in terms of the allocation of labour or the development of commercial confidence through currency, credit, prices—was scarcely feasible.

The political and military hazards facing the Nyamwezi trader were hardly less formidable. So rapid an expansion of economic opportunities was bound to be a disturbing influence among so many small polities. An enlarged economic frame was essential if any large-scale

[1] Cf. Livingstone (1874), I, 311; R. F. Burton, *The Lands of Cazembe*, London, 1873, 33–4n.

[2] Cf. Burton, *Lake Regions* (1860), II, 7; also Becker as cited in p. 51, n.2.

political organization was to emerge, but at this place and time—as is shown by the careers of empire-builders like Mirambo or Nyungu ya Mawe—the process of political transformation involved intense and prolonged competition and disruption. This was aggravated by the fact that the ivory trade opened up the region for the first time to the trade in firearms; as so often, this helped to shift the locus of physical power away from the old dynastic leaders towards adventurer-traders. Thus it was that instead of concentrating exclusively on 'business', like those Arabs with a secure base in Zanzibar, Nyamwezi such as Msiri had to expend much energy and wealth on providing security for themselves by creating private armies and setting up as chiefs at strategic points on a trade-route. Moreover, the very fact that Arabs and Swahili were also engaged in trade up country was a source of friction. The most obvious example of this is Mirambo's running war, hot and cold, with certain Arabs in Tabora; another was the expulsion of Mnwa Sele, chief of Unyanyembe, who had sought to impose duties on Arab as on other caravans entering Tabora.[1] But the very passage of relatively wealthy foreigners along the trade-routes provoked unrest. In contrast to up-country traders, linked by joking relationships and blood-brotherhood to the various peoples along the way, coastal traders seldom 'belonged', and were thus more prone to be regarded simply as milch-cows, to be squeezed for what they could yield. This attitude was too purely rapacious to make for good business. Finally, we must remember that western Tanzania, in the second half of the nineteenth century, was the scene of Ngoni migration, settlement, and raiding, and their 'snowball' technique of growth ensured that Ngoni marauding, and their search for new pastures, continued to be a threat to settled agriculture and the movement of caravans until the German conquest.

It would seem, then, that we are obliged yet again to conclude that only rule by representatives of a superior technology could provide the preconditions for sustained advance from the subsistence economy. This was, indeed, partly due to the very manner in which the region had become already linked to, and in a sense dependent on, the economies of the industrialized world. Yet if, on a long view, this essay may be said to report on progress towards an inevitable dead end, this progress, however illusory, may help to suggest that the local economies were less inflexible and more inventive than is commonly supposed.

[1] Cf. Speke (1863), 77–8.

And as we look more closely into the role of African initiative in the economic history of the colonial period, it will surely be necessary to discover how far there has been continuity from earlier processes of economic change.

4
The Kamba and the Northern Mrima Coast

JOHN LAMPHEAR

In the nineteenth century there was a Swahili saying which went: 'When the flute is heard in Zanzibar, all Africa east of the Lakes must dance.' From the early part of the century traders from Zanzibar had been establishing themselves in a number of commercial towns on the mainland opposite the island and had pushed their caravans (and concurrently their commercial influence) far inland. Indeed, the very name 'Swahili' became synonymous with a vigorous, if not aggressive, trading people, who by their own ingenuity and initiative opened a new commercial network which efficiently drew off ivory, slaves, and other trade items from areas even beyond the Great Lakes.

It is paradoxical, then, that a careful examination of the commerce of the northern Mrima coast, from Pangani northward to the settlements above Mombasa, clearly indicates that the initiative for and the exploitation of the interior trade during the first half of the century lay not with the coastal Swahili, but with indigenous peoples of the interior. Mombasa, chief of the northern Mrima commercial towns, depended in turn upon the commercial systems of the Nyika and the Kamba peoples of its hinterland for the vast majority of its trade items throughout the earlier decades of the century. When direct Swahili caravan penetration of the interior eventually did begin to develop along this section of the coast, it was not so much a spontaneous explosion of Swahili commercial activity as a more gradual response to the decline of the indigenous commercial systems, and it was facilitated largely because of the political activities of two other peoples of that hinterland, the Shambala and the Masai.

It is difficult to say exactly when and to what extent trading connexions between the northern Mrima coast and the interior had been established. There are some hints in early missionary journals that the

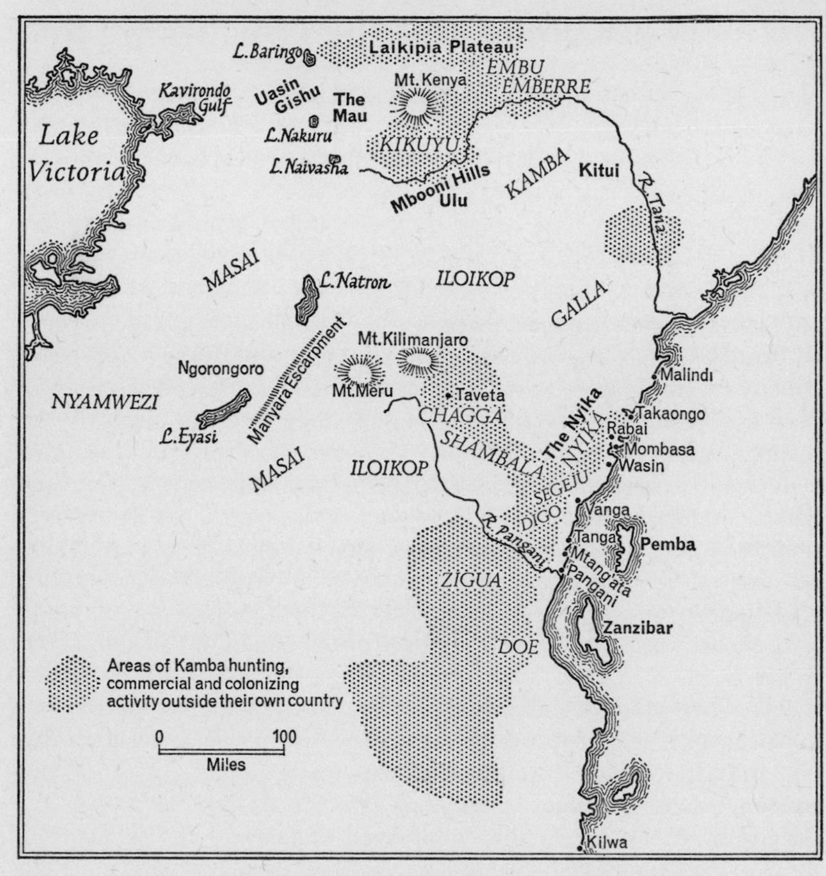

Map 5. The Hinterland of Mombasa and the Northern Mrima Coast, *c.* 1850

Mazrui, or even perhaps their predecessors, themselves ventured into the interior to trade, but that political unrest on the coast and incursions of warlike people in the interior obliged them to abandon such activity.[1] By at least the middle of the eighteenth century the Mazrui-dominated coast had made alliances with peoples living immediately behind the towns and a certain amount of trade was being conducted between the coast and the interior. In 1845 the missionary J. L. Krapf was told that in former times the Mazrui 'had established friendly connexions with the Interior and they enriched themselves. . . .'[2]

The northern Mrima interior trade began to develop to an appreciable extent, however, only at the turn of the eighteenth century, and it was then conducted largely through the efforts and initiative of the peoples collectively called 'Nyika' by the Arab and Swahili residents of the coastal towns. Many of the Nyika were the staunch allies and friends of the Mazrui and they had probably been subjected to a certain amount of Arab influence for at least a couple of centuries before the Mazrui rose to power.[3]

Nyika traders kept many of the Swahili coastal towns supplied with a variety of items including ivory, gum copal, honey, beeswax, grain, foodstuffs, and timber for building dhows. In exchange they obtained salt, beads, cloth, iron hoes, and other coastal trade goods, and it would appear that Swahili trade into the interior was, at least by the latter part of the eighteenth century, being carried on for them by the Nyika.[4]

The Nyika sent most of their caravans to the north and north-west. In the former direction were the Borana Galla, warlike herdsmen who

[1] J. L. Krapf, *CMS–172*, June, 1847–Dec., 1848, 61, 65; J. Rebmann, *CMS–53*, 1849, 13. For abbreviations, please see Note on p. 101.

[2] Krapf, *CMS–167*, 1845, 20–21; H. C. Baxter, 'Pangani: The Trade Centre of Ancient History', *TNR*, June, 1949, argues that commercial activity between the coast and the far interior may have been going on from as early as the fifth century, B.C. In the sixteenth century, A.D., the Portuguese seem to have been at least vaguely aware of the Kilimanjaro area. See R. F. Burton, *Zanzibar*, I, London, 1872, 49; H. H. Johnston, *The Kilimanjaro Expedition*, London, 1885, 6; G. S. P. Freeman-Grenville, 'The Coast, 1489–1840', in R. Oliver and G. Mathew (eds.), *History of East Africa*, I, Oxford, 1963. Oral tradition of the Chagga people may well indicate some kind of Arab or Swahili activity from the beginning of the eighteenth century. See K. Stahl, *History of the Chagga*, The Hague, 1964, 307; Rebmann, *CMS–53*, 18.

[3] A. H. J. Prins, *The Coastal Tribes of the N.E. Bantu*, London, 1952, 37, suggests that it was mostly Nyika blood which was mixed with that of the Arabs to produce the hybrid Swahili. See also Krapf, *CMS–172*, 127.

[4] T. H. R. Cashmore, 'Notes on the Chronology of the Wanika', *TNR*, 1961, 155; Prins (1952), 38; Krapf, *CMS–171*, 1847, 18; id., *CMS–174*, 1849, 68; id., *CMS–176*, 1851, 130.

had been pushing their way southward for many years. There were Galla to the north-west, too, but not as many, and after crossing their country and the semi-arid expanse of waste-land called the 'nyika' which runs just inland parallel to much of the Kenya coast, the Nyika encountered the Kamba, a people with whom trade could be easily and profitably conducted. The Galla and the 'nyika' must have severely restricted the amount of commercial activity which the Nyika were able to carry on with the Kamba. By the dawn of the nineteenth century the Giriyama Nyika were trying to make a treaty with the Galla so that their caravans could push more directly across into Ukamba. The Galla rejected the Nyika overtures and pillaged caravans whenever possible, but still the Nyika commerce was able to prosper to such a point that just before the middle of the century Krapf could write that 'the inland trade was formerly in their hands almost exclusively'.[1]

Ironically, however, the same trading contacts with the Kamba people to the west and north-west, to whom the Nyika probably owed much of their earlier commercial pre-eminence, were soon to become a major factor in its eventual limitation and decline.

Oral traditions of the Kamba themselves as well as the traditions of many other peoples scattered throughout East Africa remember that originally they were a wandering, widely dispersed people.[2] It is probable that from about the seventeenth century small groups of people who were all to call themselves Kamba were gradually moving up into the Mbooni hills of the Ulu area of Kenya. The Kamba claim

[1] Krapf, *CMS–173*, 1848, 15. Also id., *CMS–172*, 66; Rebmann, *CMS–53*, 10.

[2] The oral traditions of the Kwere and other tribes just inland from Dar es Salaam recall that at a date probably early in the seventeenth century they and the Shirazi coastal settlers were forced to seek help from one Mwene, leader of the warlike Doe people, in repelling the Kamba who were causing trouble in the area. Defeated, the Kamba fell back to the north until they eventually reached their present country in Kenya, which tradition claims had been recently vacated by an early wave of Galla invaders. See *TDB*, II, 82–4; IV, 39; Krapf, *Travels in East Africa*, London, 1860, 392–3; id., *CMS–177*, 1852, 64; G. Lindblom, *The Akamba*, Uppsala/Appelberg, 1920, 570–71. In the middle of that same century the Nyamwezi of western Tanzania also claim to have had contacts with the Kamba, a group of Kamba hunters arriving at that time during the earliest stages of Nyamwezi political formation, and establishing one of their first ruling dynasties. See R. G. Abrahams, *The Political Organisation of Unyamwezi*, Cambridge, 1967, 31–2. It seems certain that there were some definite early contacts between these two peoples who were to become the foremost traders in East Africa: H. E. Lambert ('Land Tenure among the Akamba', *African Studies*, 1947) claims that it is only with the Nyamwezi that the Kamba even now maintain a 'joking relationship' (*utani*) although their territories are at present separated by more than 300 miles. See also Lindblom (1920), 14. The Chagga and the Teita peoples of the Kilimanjaro area and the Duruma Nyika of the Kenya north coast also remember early instances of Kamba strangers establishing clans or dynasties. See Stahl (1964), 51; Prins (1952), 39, 102.

that before their settlement in Ulu they were primarily a hunting people, but the Mbooni hills were probably fertile enough to reward intensified agricultural activity, and hunting may have been largely eclipsed for a time.[1]

In the Mbooni hills the Kamba at first appear to have formed a compact settlement, and traditions indicate that the plains below the hills were occupied by fierce pastoral people. Perhaps it was because of them that the Kamba clustered themselves on their easily defended hilltops; perhaps they clung to the hills because the rainfall was heavier, more adequate for crops, than down on the plains. Whatever the reason, the original Kamba settlements did not long remain clustered in Ulu, however, and probably by a date early in the eighteenth century whole groups of them were hiving off and spreading out in all directions from the Mbooni range to establish themselves on other hilltops. The major settlements at this time seem to have been eastwards into Kitui, an area considerably drier than the original ones in Ulu, and seem to have been necessitated largely because of an expanding Kamba population and resulting economic pressures in the Mbooni highlands. Kamba hunting activities, if somewhat neglected during the period of Ulu settlement, soon regained a good deal of their former importance as Kamba settlers pushed into increasingly less fertile areas further away. Hunting bands pushing even further eastwards from the eighteenth-century Kitui settlements were probably the first Kamba to make contact with traders from the coast. There are indications that before their settlement in Ulu the Kamba may have owned cattle, but with the proximity of hostile pastoralists (and perhaps the favourable agricultural conditions of the Mbooni hills) the Kamba gave up herding almost entirely. The settlers moving into Kitui and beyond found that conditions there were more fitted to pastoralism, as well as hunting, than to intensive agriculture, and the first tusks of ivory bartered by Kamba hunters to coastal traders were probably in exchange for Nyika cattle.[2]

Once having learned that ivory was considered valuable by the peoples living nearer the coast, the mobile and independent hunting bands of the Kamba began to intensify their elephant-hunting activities.

[1] See the traditions recorded in Lindblom (1920), 353–4, 476; see also C. Dundas, 'History of Kitui', *JRAI*, 1913, 481; J. Middleton and G. Kershaw, *The Kikuyu and Kamba of Kenya*, London, 1965, 68.

[2] Lambert (1947), 133–4; Krapf, *CMS–174*, 1849, 57, 63; Middleton and Kershaw (1965), 68; Lindblom (1920), 353–4, 476. Lambert is of the opinion that these earliest Kamba migrations out of Ulu were at the very beginning of the eighteenth century. Supporting evidence is found in *KLC*, I, 594; II, 1285–6.

By the earlier part of the nineteenth century Krapf's colleague, Rebmann, could observe that Unyika had been largely hunted out, the elephants and other larger game retreating back into the at least temporary sanctuary of the more inland forests, and by 1849 Krapf noted that 'many Wakamba are engaged in hunting elephants . . . [and] these animals have been much destroyed in Ukambani.'[1]

It appears that the Kamba, traditionally a more mobile and more skilled hunting people than the Nyika, increasingly began to monopolize ivory-hunting activities as the retreating herds put the Nyika further and further away from profitable hunting grounds. Gradually the mobile Kamba hunting parties began to take over a good share of the transportation phase of the trade, the hunting parties easily assuming the role of commercial caravans by marching directly from the hunting grounds to the coast with their spoils. The Kamba were able to realize a greater profit by conveying their tusks down to the coast than by selling them to Nyika caravans in the interior; while the Nyika, allowing the Kamba to take over the greater part of the collecting and carrying phases of the trade, jealously prevented them from entering Mombasa and other coastal towns, and became powerful middlemen, channelling Kamba caravans into market centres such as Kwa Jomvu and Shongi.[2]

By the early part of the nineteenth century Kamba commercial activity was growing very rapidly indeed. A fresh series of Kamba expansions occurred at this time, apparently to find fresh hunting grounds and to expand their indigenous trading network. Krapf was informed that 'they felt themselves induced to extend their hunting and mercantile expeditions northward as far as they could and so likewise to the westward'.[3] To the north, Kamba expansion was halted at the Tana River by Galla who occupied the plains beyond, while to the west the Kamba crossed the headwaters of the Tana and entered the forests of the Kikuyu and other peoples of the Mt. Kenya area. Relations between the Kamba and Kikuyu seem to have been rather temperamental. At many times the two peoples were embroiled in feuds, and war-parties ranged back and forth across the Tana. On many other occasions, however, the climate was more amicable and commerce could flow smoothly between them. Much of their trade

[1] Krapf, *Travels* (1860), 140; (from Rebmann's journal), 235; id., *CMS–174*, 67.

[2] id., *CMS–174*, 10, 44, 57–8.

[3] ibid., 58; *KLC*, II, 1286–7, records in detail the nineteenth-century occupation of the various outlying areas of what is now Ukamba.

seemed to depend on which people had the more successful cultivation season, and grain and livestock were bartered accordingly. The Kikuyu living near the Ithanga hills obtained iron ore from neighbouring Kamba. The Kamba were also able to market handicrafts including chains, snuff-boxes, weapons, and medicines to the Kikuyu, and as their contacts with the coast became more developed the Kamba (not unlike the Nyika down on the coast) became middlemen in the interior trade, exchanging coastal trade items for ivory and livestock. At other times, the Kikuyu themselves travelled to Kamba villages to trade tobacco and other items for the coastal goods kept in ready stock by Kamba merchants.[1]

Other peoples of the Mt. Kenya area such as the Emberre, Tharaka, Mwimbe, and Embu were similarly touched by the expanding Kamba commercial system. Kamba hunting parties penetrated deep into their forests, and if any Mt. Kenya peoples discovered an elephant which had been killed by Kamba arrows the ivory was divided between themselves and the hunters. As with the Kikuyu, the Kamba were able to carry on a trade in handicrafts with the Mt. Kenya peoples, supplying them with arrow-heads, arrow-poisons, and decorated collars, clubs, and gourds. The Embu and the Emberre were so influenced by Kamba trade that they, at least for a time, became 'junior partners' in the Kamba interior trade. Caravans of Embu and Emberre, stocked with coastal trade items obtained from the villages of Kamba middlemen, set out for the regions beyond Mt. Kenya and traded with peoples living as far away as Lake Baringo. After obtaining a good supply of ivory and tobacco, the caravans would return to the Kamba villages where their goods could be sold to the Kamba who, in turn, would convey them to the coast. The Embu also seem to have been traders in their own right, carrying on a traffic in the special kind of wood used in the manufacture of Kamba arrow-poisons throughout Ukamba.[2]

The Kamba also sent caravans of their own into the areas beyond Mt. Kenya where they traded with the 'Wabilikimo pygmies', who can probably be identified as Dorobo or possibly some other Dorobo-like hunting people. The Kamba hunted elephants in their country and

[1] *KLC*, II, 1333; I, 111, 113; C. Dundas, 'Organization of Some Bantu Tribes', *JRAI*, 1915, 236; Lindblom (1920), 17; Krapf, *CMS–171*, 29; J. Kenyatta, *Facing Mount Kenya*, London, 1938, 69; W. S. Routledge, *With a Prehistoric People*, London, 1910, 16.

[2] Lambert (1949), 2; Middleton and Kershaw (1965), 19; G. Orde-Brown, *The Vanishing Tribes of Kenya*, London, 1925, 153, 156, 164, 166, 229; Krapf, *CMS–174*, 49, 67; id., *CMS–176*, 49, 58, 67; id., *Travels* (1860), 314, 316–17.

also bartered coastal goods, arrows, and arrow-poisons with them in exchange for honey and ivory.[1]

Another important area into which Kamba commercial activity spread was southwards into what is today Tanzania. During the closing years of the eighteenth century and on into the early decades of the nineteenth century, bands of Kamba hunters and traders left Ukamba and settled throughout a vast area of north-eastern Tanzania which included Unguu, Usagara, Uzaramo, Usambara, Uzigua, Upare, and Ukwere. In many cases these bands of Kamba were all-male vanguards which hunted and traded their way to the south. Only after establishing themselves as a colony in a suitable hunting area did they send back for additional colonists, including women. The Kamba, although always an alien minority, were respected as fighters and in general stubbornly clung to their own cultural traits, spoke their own language, and often refused intermarriage with the local people. Often they would switch allegiance from one local headman to another, launching a devastating series of raids against their former patron (an easy way of collecting additional trade items) before moving off to their new locality, and are remembered to have tried to subject the Kaguru people to their rule. The Kamba seem to have used their Tanganyika settlements as a means of expanding their commerce in indigenous crafts and marketed arrow-poisons, weapons, meat, skins, and beer to the Kaguru, Nguru, and other peoples. The reason for the establishment of these colonies was undoubtedly commercial. As the missionary J. T. Last reported:

> Their chief object in leaving Ukambani was hunting. . . . [They] settle down . . . and cultivate the ground for food until they have remained long enough to get a good stock of ivory and teeth by hunting, then they return home. It seems that they are continually going and coming.[2]

A final area of Kamba commercial expansion was eastwards, towards the coast. In many places throughout Unyika and Uteita the Kamba established themselves in colonies not unlike those to the south.

[1] ibid., 302; id., *CMS–176*, 9.

[2] J. T. Last, *CMS–16;* J. J. Erhardt, 'A visit to the Masai', *PRGS*, 1883, 149–50; *CMS–7A*, 1853, 18; Krapf, *CMS–173*, 55–6; id., *CMS–177*, 88; *TDB*, II, 92–3, 119; T. O. Beidelman, 'Some Notes on the Kamba of Kilosa District', *TNR*, 1961, 182, 185, 187–8, 192; Lindblom (1920), 11, 569. It is interesting to note that many of these Kamba colonies were located precisely in the areas where the seventeenth-century wars with the Doe were supposed to have occurred.

A cursory examination of these eastern settlements might lead one to conclude that these settlements, unlike those of other areas, were originally founded for reasons unconnected with commerce. In his published account, Krapf mentioned that the Kamba colony at Rabai (near Mombasa) was founded in 1836 by Kamba famine refugees, and this was borne out by the up-country Kamba who looked down on them as *mabikilambua*, 'those who have followed the rain'.[1]

In his unpublished journals, however, Krapf indicated that there were Kamba settlements in Unyika by at least the 1820s, and he clearly stated that the early Kamba settlements in Unyika had been undertaken because of expanding Kamba commercial interests to serve as 'an outlet [for their trade items] to the coast of Mombas, where a considerable part of them fixed their abodes on the territories of the Wanika tribe [which] together with the Suahili on the coast soon perceived the great advantage they derived from their intercourse with the Wakamba. . . '.[2]

It seems, then, that Kamba commercial settlements had been established for some years before the 1836 influx of famine refugees into Rabai. Indeed, if it is remembered that the arid expanses of the 'nyika' lie between Ukamba and Rabai it would seem absurd for bands of starving Kamba to push into that wilderness where conditions were as bad, if not considerably worse than any area of Ukamba, unless they knew that there were previously-settled colonies of their own tribesmen waiting to receive them in the alien land beyond.[3]

Largely because of Krapf's description of the 1836 Rabai refugees, subsequent writers[4] have assigned rather too much importance to the role of famines in the development of Kamba commercial activity. That famines were one important aspect in the development of Kamba trade cannot be disputed. Indeed, the Kamba themselves are able to recall events in the past by associating them with a list of named famines. It would seem, however, that most of these famines occurred during the middle or latter part of the nineteenth century, well after Kamba commercial activity was in full swing, and when the Kamba were expanding into more arid and inhospitable areas further from the Mbooni range. Many of the later famines were rather more disruptive

[1] Krapf, *Travels* (1860), 142; Lindblom (1920), 11.

[2] Krapf, *CMS–167*, 24; id., *CMS–171*, 4; id., *CMS–174*, 57.

[3] H. R. Johnstone ('Notes on the Tribes Occupying the Mombasa Sub-District', *JRAI*, 1902, 263), is also of the opinion that the Rabai settlement was originally undertaken at the end of the eighteenth century for definitely commercial purposes.

[4] e.g., D. A. Low, 'The Northern Interior', in Oliver and Mathew (eds.) (1963), 314.

than conducive to commerce. In general, the role played by famines in the development of Kamba trade is a rather negative one. A group of Kamba, whether trading or hunting, far from their *utui* would at least be able to support themselves, whether or not they killed any elephants or did much profitable bartering, without depleting their home-village grain supply. In this way the possibility of famine may have played an important part in the development of Kamba trade, but the famines themselves surely were something less than the 'crucial point' in such development.

Rather, it seems clear that Kamba society had some distinctive traits which enabled them to become the pre-eminent trading people of this part of East Africa.

The period of confinement in the Mbooni hills, whether it was voluntary or imposed, gave birth to the Kamba *utui* political system. The *utui* was the territorially compact group of homesteads, usually clustered on one or perhaps two or three adjacent hilltops. The Kamba had no chiefs as such, but it was usual for *asili*, 'outstanding individuals', to rise to positions of leadership through their own exceptional personalities, abilities, or wealth. Several *motui* might temporarily ally themselves into a larger *kibalo* grouping in times of war, but for all daily requirements the *utui* was a 'tribe in miniature, self-supporting, socially and economically complete'.[1]

The *motui* probably formed the basis for Kamba migration out of Ulu, and they certainly organized Kamba hunting activities and, later, Kamba commercial caravans. Except perhaps during the period of Mbooni confinement, hunting played an extremely important role in Kamba economy and the Kamba were renowned for their skill in tracking and hunting. Many of the Kamba's rituals and observances were concerned with it: before setting out on a hunt diviners would seek omens, beer would be consumed, dances held, sacrifices offered, and talismans blessed and received to ensure good fortune. Once into the bush observances relating to the conduct of hunters, taboos pertaining to novices, and rules governing the division of spoils were prescribed. The leaders of the hunting parties were the same 'outstanding individuals' who led the men of their *utui* in other activities, especially raids, for in the words of a Kamba elder: 'Was it not war to hunt such animals as the elephant . . .?' Skilful hunters were regarded with awe and even ascribed an aura of the supernatural. Hunting was

[1] Lambert (1947), 134; Krapf, *CMS–174*, 63; Lindblom (1920), 149; also Dundas (1913), 487.

done primarily with bows and poisoned arrows, and the Kamba seem to have been expert archers, although pits, snares, and other traps were also less frequently used.[1]

The Kamba were also able to produce and market a whole variety of indigenous trade items to many different peoples of the interior. Kamba arrow-poisons, for example, brewed from the bark of a tree and fortified with the poison glands of scorpions and snakes, seem to have been in great demand over a large portion of central East Africa. Even other hunting peoples who manufactured their own poisons preferred the Kamba variety (the recipe of which was kept as a closely guarded secret) wherever they could obtain it.[2] The Kamba were also skilled in the production of various handicrafts. Iron ore, washed from streams in the manner of gold prospectors, was smelted by Kamba smiths and fashioned by craftsmen into ornamental chains and other decorations without equal in East Africa. Von Höhnel, who had very little else good to say about the Kamba, was forced to admit that their handicrafts betrayed 'an artistic skill and taste far exceeding anything we had noticed elsewhere in Africa', and by the 1840s Krapf could write that even the coastal Swahili realized that 'the iron of Ukambani is of excellent quality . . . [and they] consider it superior to the iron which they get from India'.[3] Trade in a special kind of beer, game-meat, saliferous sand, foodstuffs, tobacco, beeswax, and bark bags also went on. Intra-tribal markets seem to have occurred spontaneously and rather infrequently, but were traditionally one of the few times for *ibalo* rather than *motui* relations. It seems that women (often the older ones, past the age of child-bearing) very often served as the actual traders in such indigenous commerce, being afforded a certain immunity even during times of feuds and warfare.[4] Of course, it is quite possible that intensive specialization in the production of crafts

[1] Lindblom (1920), 465–8; C. W. Hobley, *Ethnology of the Akambe*, Cambridge, 1910, 44–5; Dundas (1915), 238; W. A. Chanler, *Through Jungle and Desert*, London, 1896, 66; C. Guillain, *Documents sur l'histoire . . . de l'Afrique Orientale*, Paris, 1856, 111, 212; A. Neumann, *Elephant Hunting in East Africa*, London, 1898, 22.

[2] Hobley (1910), 44; Lindblom (1920), 455; J. Boyes, *John Boyes, King of the Wakikuyu*, London, 1911, 119; R. A. J. Maquire, 'Il Torobo', *TNR*, 1948, 17; M. Merker, *Die Masai*, 1905, 159; W. D. Raymond, 'Tanganyika Arrow Poisons', *TNR*, 1947, 57.

[3] L. von Höhnel, *Discovery of Lakes Rudolf and Stephanie*, London, 1894, II, 308; Krapf, *CMS–14*, 68; also Hobley (1910), 29; Lindblom (1920), 369, who indicates that trade in Kamba chains formed the basis for the eventual establishment of Kamba colonies as far afield as the Kavirondo gulf.

[4] Hobley (1910), 31, 33–4, 156; Beidelman (1961), 192; von Höhnel (1894), II, 318; Krapf, *Travels* (1860), 315; id., *CMS–174*, 68; Lindblom (1920), 353, 526, 580; Lambert (1947), 137.

developed only with the 'golden age' of Kamba commerce. Some activity undoubtedly pre-dated it, but the response to the increasing commercial demands of the nineteenth century probably intensified these and gave rise to new activity as well. Unquestionably the part played by famines cannot be assessed unless viewed against the whole framework of Kamba society in which hunting, colonization, indigenous crafts, political organization, and a certain amount of what can only be called natural commercial ability were at least all equally important parts.[1]

By the 1840s the Kamba settlements at Rabai and elsewhere in Unyika were unquestionably centres of commerce. As in the Tanganyika colonies, the Kamba remained aloof from the local people who both feared and respected them. Krapf found them

> the principal traders between the Interior and this coast. . . . They travel in caravans of 200–500 men, and carry from the Interior slaves, ivory and the horn of the Rhinoceros and a few other articles. . . . They are always out on hunting excursions and kill with their arrows every animal which they can obtain.[2]

Other Kamba settlements grew up along the trade-routes through Unyika and Uteita and a notable one at Maungu mountain seems to have existed to supply passing caravans with provisions and water. The Kamba caravans, whether originating from the coastal colonies or from up-country *motui*, hunted and traded their way between the coast and the interior with regularity, often trying to establish a string of blood-brother relationships in the *motui* passed along the way, thus affording themselves with places of safety and rest, and possibly the chance of securing provisions and additional trade items as well.[3]

Increasingly outfitting their own caravans to collect trade items in Ukamba and acting as entrepôts for Kamba, Nyika, and Swahili goods, the Kamba settlements in Unyika appear (for at least a time) to have

[1] Lindblom (1920), 339, gives a complete list of the famines; also see 351; H. R. Tate, 'Notes on the Kikuyu and Kamba Tribes', *JRAI*, 1904, 135; Dundas (1913), 485; Chanler (1896), 406–7.

[2] Krapf, *CMS–166*, 1845, 9, 21; id., *CMS–172*, 74; id., *Travels* (1860), 143–4; Lindblom (1920), 11; Prins (1952), 39.

[3] Krapf, *CMS–174*, 13; Rebmann, *CMS–52*, 1848, 9; Middleton and Kershaw (1965), 72; Guillain (1856), 111. A good picture of a typical Kamba caravan can be gleaned from Krapf, *Travels* (1860), 286, 300–310, 315, 347; Guillain (1856), 212; Lindblom (1920), 345–6. The Kamba, unlike most East African tribes, did not carry loads on their heads, but rather by means of a strap around the forehead, thereby enabling them to manage heavier and bulkier loads, such as tusks. See Neumann (1898), 144.

seriously threatened the firm Nyika control of middleman activities between the coast and the interior. It can be supposed that the end of Mazrui power at Mombasa in 1837 affected their staunch allies and friends, the Nyika. No sooner had Omani power supplanted the Mazrui than a series of slave-raids was conducted by the new rulers against the Nyika, recently weakened by severe famines. The Kamba seem to have grasped the opportunity and joined the Omani raids, attacking Nyika villages near Ndara. A great deal of ill-feeling was thus caused, and it was probably during this time that the Kamba may have briefly usurped the Nyika role of middlemen.[1]

If the Kamba did wrest control of middleman activity from the Nyika that control seems to have been rather short-lived, and although Rabai and other Kamba settlements were to continue as rivals to Nyika entrepots, the local middlemen seem to have regained much of the Ukamba traffic from the early 1840s. By that time, relations between the Nyika and the Arabs seem to have been largely repaired, and although they were nominally governed by four Swahili sheiks from Mombasa and Swahili traders took up permanent residences at some of their markets, the Nyika apparently were allowed a great deal of independence and freedom in handling their own affairs.

Mombasa could well afford to allow the peoples of her interior to conduct their own commercial affairs, for it is clear that by the middle of the nineteenth century the city was prospering and was unquestionably the most important centre along the coast of East Africa despite the troubles between Mazrui and Omani factions during the '20s and '30s. Krapf indicated that the city's population grew by several thousands to about 12,000 between 1844 and 1853. Between 2,300 and 2,600 frazilas (about 45 tons) of ivory per year were being supplied to the town at mid-century, mostly through the efforts of indigenous peoples of the interior, especially the Kamba and Nyika.[2]

By at least as early as 1844 the Swahili residents of Mombasa were beginning to form their own trading caravans to go up-country to Uchagga. Originally they went with camels to bring back loads of ivory from various of the more than one hundred fragmentary Chagga chiefdoms (Machame and Kilema seem to have been the most frequently visited), but by the late 1840s increasingly they purchased

[1] Cashmore (1961), 156; Prins (1952), 57; Freeman-Grenville (1963), 158–60; *TDB*, II, 15; Krapf, *CMS–167*, 14; id., *CMS–172*, 127; id., *CMS–174*, 12; id., *CMS–177*, 24.

[2] Guillain (1856), 211, 217, 235–9, 265–6, 331; Krapf, *CMS–179*, 49; see also Burton (1872), II, 75.

7

slaves, secured by Chagga chiefs in internecine feuds with their neighbours. It is notable that the Chagga, unlike the Kamba, were not very skilled hunters and seem to have lacked the inclination to leave their own area. Perhaps the feuding Chagga chiefs were reluctant to deplete their fighting forces by sending their own caravans off to the coast, and in any event preferred to let the Swahili come to them, although Swahili caravan traffic was probably never very heavy until late in the century.[1] Just to the north of Mombasa, Takaongo and other largely independent Swahili villages had succeeded in opening somewhat limited trading relations with otherwise hostile neighbouring Galla people. In what would appear to have been an additional active attempt to expand their commercial range, the Mombasa Swahili took steps to secure this trade for themselves during the 1840s.[2]

Despite these isolated attempts at commercial expansion, however, it is clear that at mid-century Swahili caravan traffic to Uchagga or direct trading contacts to the north were far less important to the commerce of Mombasa than was the trade conducted by the efficient trading systems of the Kamba and Nyika. Fresh incursions of hostile peoples along the route from Mombasa to Uchagga had made a crossing of the 'nyika' even more dangerous than ever. The Mombasa Swahili can, therefore, hardly be blamed for taking the role of rather passive recipients when placed at the end of an indigenous commercial network which was prepared to assume the dangers and difficulties of collection and transportation and then deposit annually 45 tons of ivory on Mombasa's doorstep. The infrequency of Mombasa caravans to Uchagga, or for that matter to anywhere else in the interior, can be seen from Krapf's statement of 1848 that the caravan leader Bana Kheri was 'the only Suahili of Mombas . . . acquainted with the inland tribes'.[3]

[1] Krapf, *CMS-165*, 1844, 12; id., *CMS-172*, 79, 147; id., *CMS-179*, 1853, 24; Rebmann, *CMS-52*, 29, 35, 42; id., *CMS-51*, 1848, 51; id., *CMS-53*, 6, 11, 13–15; id., *CMS-54*, 1849, 9; Guillain (1856), 208; Johnston (1885), 541; Stahl (1964), 45, suggests that the Chagga may have had trading contacts with Kamba, Nyamwezi, and Nyika caravans (although Rebmann, *CMS-53*, 10, shows that this was clearly not the case with the latter) as early as 1825. The Kilema Chagga have traditions that may indicate an early eighteenth-century contact with the coast. See Rebmann, *CMS-53*, 18.

[2] Krapf, *CMS-168*, 1845, 20; id., *CMS-169*, 1846, 7, 11–12; Rebmann, *CMS-51*, 31–2; id., *CMS-52A*, 1848; C. Pfefferle, *CMS-0-21*, 1851, 11.

[3] Krapf, *CMS-173*, 11; id., *CMS-172*, 144; id., *Travels* (1860), 222, 231; Guillain (1856), 266, 280, 331. In 1849 Guillain (1856), 211, 266, noted the arrival of a single Kamba caravan with 300–400 frazilas of ivory, while a Swahili one from Uchagga in the same year returned with only 40.

At mid-century, while the Mombasans were passively receiving the bulk of their trade goods, the Kamba and the Nyika were even further expanding their commercial activities. The Nyika, for their part, were busy extending their middleman activities to the north where they, like the Swahili traders of Takaongo, established at least some trading contacts with the Borana Galla (ironically, the same people who were simultaneously the most notorious and feared raiders of Kamba, Nyika, and Swahili commerce). The Galla sent some ivory caravans of their own to a number of Nyika market-villages near their borders and even allowed a few specially designated Nyika traders to enter Galla country to buy ivory, copal, and rhino horn in exchange for coastal trade items and slaves.[1]

The Kamba, with their far-flung trading empire, seem to have reached perhaps the apogee of their commercial power at this time as bands of hunters, traders, and colonists moved further afield. This peak of Kamba power was exemplified in the career of Kivoi, the most successful and enterprising of the Kamba caravan leaders. Although frequently referred to as a 'chief', there is little doubt that Kivoi was in fact only an *asili*, an 'outstanding individual', who through his own efforts became the leader of a Kamba section in Kitui. By the late 1840s Kivoi's trading and collecting activities carried him frequently to such far-off places as the Mt. Kenya forests, Ukikuyu (where he seems to have maintained a permanent depot for the storage of ivory), Mt. Kilimanjaro, and beyond, and to Unyika and the coast around Mombasa. He was the only Kamba caravan leader allowed by the Nyika to enter Mombasa, where he was personally known to the Arab governor and where he would affect Swahili garb to please the coastmen. Often he personally led his caravans, which usually seem to have numbered several hundred men and women and even a few musketeers, to their various destinations. At other times he remained at home, surrounded by slaves and retainers, overseeing a brisk middleman's trade with Kikuyu and Mt. Kenya peoples who regularly visited his village, while he delegated temporary command of his caravans to lieutenants. He seems to have been powerful enough to levy taxes on neighbouring Masai, and his own people feared and respected him as a

[1] Guillain (1856), 111, 217, 235–9, 265–6, 331; Krapf, *CMS–168*, 8, 28; id., *CMS–166*, 14–15; id., *CMS–167*, 2, 25, 28; id., *CMS–174*, 10; id., *CMS–179*, 28; id., *Travels* (1860), 120; Rebmann, *CMS–51*, 39, 45; E. S. Wakefield, *Thomas Wakefield*, London, 1904, 46, 49; C. New, *Life in East Africa*, London, 1873, 128; Burton (1872), II, 67; W. H. Jones, *CMS–0–14*, 1878, 9.

great magician and rainmaker. He was formulating a plan to send his ivory down to the coast via the Tana river by boat just before his death. At the end of Krapf's first visit to him in Ukamba, Kivoi presented the missionary with a quantity of beads and a piece of American cloth so that he could buy food on his return trip to the coast in a curious reversal of what was to become later the normal interchange between Europeans and inland African leaders.[1]

In 1849 Krapf considered that the Kamba's profit from the ivory trade had 'placed them among the wealthiest tribes of Eastern Africa'. By that year the Kamba traders had obtained such vast quantities of coastal trade items that they refused to sell their ivory for anything other than livestock, a Swahili trader being

> obliged first to buy a quantity of those animals (cattle, sheep and goats) before he is able to obtain the amount of ivory which he requires, as no Mkamba will sell this article for the commodities which are brought from the coast and which consist chiefly in cotton cloth . . . beads, brass wire, red ochre, black pepper, salt . . . [and] blue zink [*sic*].[2]

The Mombasa Swahili, however, devised an ingenious way of securing a good profit from the Kamba ivory trade:

> A Mombassian takes for instance a slave girl who he bought at Kiloa . . . for 7 or 8 dollars or German crowns and carries her to the Wanika-country, selling her for 2 large and 2 small cows which are worth 18 dollars on the spot—with these he proceeds to the neighbouring Wakamba, who bring ivory from the Interior, and buys there a piece of ivory which sells at Mombas [for] 40 or 50 dollars, which sum he then takes and goes or sends to Kiloa at the proper season where he buys another supply of slaves. . . .[3]

Traditionally, neither the Nyika nor the Kamba had been slave-owners. Although the latter frequently went on raiding expeditions, prisoners were seldom taken, even pregnant women and adolescent girls being dispatched with clubs (they were unworthy of an arrow), and only little girls or infant baby boys were taken, the former growing up to be Kamba wives and the latter adopted by Kamba families. Indeed, it was common for Kamba men to refer jokingly to their foster-sons as 'my children which I produced with my bow'. Adult prisoners occasionally were taken under special circumstances and a

[1] Krapf, *Travels* (1860), 295, 298, 314; id., *CMS–172*, 150, 152; id., *CMS–174*, 43–5, 50; id., *CMS–176*, 45, 59, 66, 119; Guillain (1856), 212; Dundas (1915), 237–8.

[2] Krapf, *CMS–174*, 58.

[3] Krapf, *CMS–179*, 30.

few were taken back to Ukamba to become herdsmen, but more often they would be held for ransom or maimed and sent back to their people as a warning of Kamba power.[1]

As late as 1845 Krapf noted that 'the Wanika in general have no slaves . . . except they be very rich', but only a few years later the picture was beginning to change and even 'those Wanika who have got a little wealth by trading do very soon imitate the Suahili in employing slaves for their domestic and agricultural business'. By 1853 he observed that the Kamba, too, were buying slaves at the coast, 'not only females but also males for cultivating their ground and feeding their herds'. The Coastal Swahili, no longer legally able to export slaves to Arabia, were beginning to look inland for a new market, and the Nyika and the Kamba, as yet another indication of their booming prosperity, had rapidly become their best customers.[2]

Much misunderstanding has been engendered by a statement of Krapf's to the effect that the Kamba did not allow Swahili caravans to trade with 'Ukambani, Kikuyu, Mberre, Uembu, Udaka, and other inland countries'.[3] This led Lindblom to write that Ukamba 'lay like a wall between the coast and the interior' prohibiting virtually all Swahili caravan traffic from penetrating that country, and D. A. Low has more recently referred to the 'battle' for control of the Ukamba route between the Kamba and the coastmen.[4]

In the same narrative, however, Krapf rather cryptically indicates that some coastal caravans *were*, in fact, allowed to enter Ukamba, albeit with Kamba guides, and in several other places in his unpublished journals he refers to Swahili and Nyika caravan activity within Ukamba.[5] In none of the early accounts is there any mention of active Kamba resistance to Swahili caravans entering their country, although there are indications that they discouraged such activity by spreading fantastic stories of fierce pygmies and cannibals inhabiting the interior. Certainly Burton's account of a caravan dispersing throughout Ukamba in small groups to barter for trade items does not suggest any kind of overt Kamba resistance, and it is probable that in the middle of

[1] Hobley (1910), 45–8, 193, 196; Lindblom (1920), 202–3; Krapf, *CMS–179*, 24.

[2] Krapf, *CMS–167*, 15; id., *CMS–173*, 34; id., *CMS–179*, 27; also id., *Travels* (1860), 357; Guillain (1856), 266, 268.

[3] Krapf, *Travels* (1860), 552.

[4] Lindblom (1920), 12; Low (1963), 316.

[5] See for example Krapf, *CMS–176*, 117: 'A merchant who proceeds from the coast to Ukambani in quest of ivory must first exchange his goods for cattle in Ukambani before he is able to get ivory.' Also id., *CMS–166*, 23; id., *CMS–174*, 64, 69, 75; Rebmann, *CMS–53*, 10.

the nineteenth century the Kamba were more worried about keeping the caravans of Mt. Kenya peoples from going directly to the coast than they were about the very limited Mombasa caravan penetration of the interior.[1]

Before the middle of the nineteenth century Swahili caravans were, in fact, beginning to make determined efforts to penetrate the far interior, but the major centre for this activity was not Mombasa, but rather the heretofore less important towns of the southern section of this northern Mrima coast. No people with a commercial skill approaching that of the Kamba inhabited the hinterland of this portion of the coast. The Digo and Segeju peoples who lived along the southern section of the northern Mrima were apparently engaged in some commercial activity during the first part of the century, sending ivory caravans of their own as far as Unyamwezi and trading with the Swahili at market-villages near Tanga and other coastal towns; but unlike the coastal areas around Mombasa, elephants could still be found along this part of the coast and the local people were hunting them and selling ivory to these Mrima towns as late as the 1850s, albeit at very high prices. There is nothing to suggest that this indigenous commerce of the south was anything as far-flung or sophisticated as the system developed by the Kamba and Nyika inland from Mombasa, and indeed Digoland, at least, was one of the areas frequented by Kamba ivory-collecting parties, while by the 1840s the Digo and the Segeju had become embroiled in an internecine feud which virtually ended their commercial activity.[2]

Although lacking an indigenous trading people equal to the Kamba, other factors invited development of the interior trade by this southern section of the northern Mrima. In the first place, this portion of the coast was much better watered than areas to the north, the arid stretches of the 'nyika' of Mombasa's hinterland giving way to rolling green hills where permanent water could always be found. Also, if this area lacked a dynamic trading people, it also lacked the fierce nomadic Galla and other hostile tribes that preyed constantly on Mombasa's caravan traffic.

During the first four decades of the nineteenth century the Sham-

[1] Krapf, *CMS–171*, 42; id., *CMS–176*, 58, 60.

[2] Burton, *The Lake Regions of Central Africa*, London, 1860, II, 409; id. (1872), II, 111, 119; Erhardt, *CMS–16*, 1854, 13; id., *CMS–7A*, 6, 8; Krapf, *CMS–165*, 13; id., *CMS–173*, 4–5, 8, 16, 20; id., *CMS–177*, 6, 36; id., *CMS–175*, 1850, 6; id., *Travels* (1860), 415; *TDB*, II, 2, 8; *KLC*, III, 2510; E. C. Baker, 'Notes on the Wasegeju', *TNR*, 1949, 34–5.

bala kingdom of Usambara had grown up under the able leadership of Shebuge and later his son, Kimweri za Nyumba. There are indications that the political expansion of Shebuge may well have been due to underlying commercial interests. By a date very early in the nineteenth century Shebuge was making visits to a hill near the coast where he met with merchants of Pangani, Tanga, and other Mrima coastal towns and obtained 'goods, beads and bars of iron' from them. The Swahili inhabitants of these towns 'recognized the rule of Vuga (the capital of Usambara) and year after year they sent tribute'.[1]

After Shebuge was killed in battle against the Zigua in about 1820, Kimweri spent the early years of his reign in strengthening and more efficiently organizing his kingdom, which has been estimated at 16,000 square miles containing perhaps half a million people. His cabinet members included the *Mdoe*, a sort of 'minister of finance', whose duties included collecting tribute from the governors of the twenty-five or more Shambala districts and conveying and selling trade items to the Swahili traders at the coast. The king employed 'Ala' (probably Dorobo) and Kamba hunters to supply him with ivory and there was a royal monopoly in the trade of slaves. Of even more importance to the commerce of this part of the East African coast, Kimweri established a 'pax Shambala' over much of the hinterland of the southern section of the northern Mrima coast where Krapf reported there was 'more civil order and security than in any other country of this coast'. The Shambala were never to become the same dynamic trading people as the Kamba. Unlike the Kamba, they relied on outside sources (alien hunters for ivory and military campaigns against their neighbours for slaves) for most of their trade items. By as early as the 1850s Kimweri's kingdom was in decline, with many of the formerly subject peoples in revolt, and the Zigua, recently armed with muskets by the Zanzibaris, making serious incursions along the Pangani. By the 1870s the kingdom was rent by civil war and the Swahili were able to dominate the

[1] Abdallah bin Hemedi 'l Ajjemy, *The Kilindi*, Dar es Salaam, 1963, 78, 79; J.E.F. Mhina, *The Shambala*, 1966, 4–5, 7. See also *TDB*, II, 6, which indicates that Shebuge exercised a very real political control over the coastal towns. It has recently been suggested by Fr. A. Shorter, 'Ukimbu and the Kimbu Chiefdoms of Southern Unyamwezi', Oxford D.Phil. thesis, 1968, 427, that Sumbwa caravans were beginning to journey to the northern coast of Tanzania at approximately the same time as Shebuge's expansion, and it can be reasonably assumed that their route passed through at least some parts of the Usambara kingdom. Perhaps early contacts with them provided Shebuge with at least part of the incentive to expand his kingdom so as to include the easiest avenues to the interior and the coastal towns. (See also Ch. 3, above, and Ch. 10, below.)

kingdom both commercially and politically. Still, the 'pax Shambala' established by Shebuge and Kimweri was never seriously threatened, and although the frontiers of the kingdom were often turbulent, the Swahili traders of the southern section of the northern Mrima were consistently able to route their caravans through the untroubled heartland and northern areas of the kingdom.[1] Yet as important as the 'pax Shambala' of Kimweri's empire were the activities of the Masai peoples further inland.

At a date which corresponds almost exactly to Kimweri's consolidation of his ordered and commercially orientated kingdom behind this part of the Mrima coast, a people known as the 'Enganglima', who appear to have been a 'Kwavi' (or more accurately 'Iloikop') people inhabiting a considerable part of the East African hinterland roughly between Mounts Kenya and Kilimanjaro, were heavily defeated by the Masai. There has been considerable confusion in understanding who these 'Kwavi' people were. Briefly, a whole collection of peoples, who have been termed the 'Maa-speakers', seem to have moved gradually down the Rift Valley from an as yet undetermined location in the north-west, probably arriving in the Lake Nakuru area of Kenya about the seventeenth century. At some point during their southward migration, the people of Maa became divided into two groups and lost contact for a fairly long period of time. When the two groups again came into contact they did so as two distinct peoples, one group calling themselves 'Masai' and the other being known by the general name 'Iloikop'. The Maa-speakers had encountered previous groups of invaders as they moved down the Rift including the Kalenjin peoples, the Tatoga, and the Dorobo, and the Iloikop seem to have assimilated more of these non-Maa elements than did the Masai, who remained a purely pastoral people. The Masai seem to have been contemptuous of their 'lost' cousins and gave them a whole series of rather degrading nicknames. They may have referred to some of the Iloikop groups as 'Kwavi', but the Swahili seem to have applied the term to all Iloikop generally and even to some Masai and 'Masai-like' Bantu-speaking peoples.[2]

[1] Krapf, *CMS–173*, 43, 48, 79; id., *CMS–177*, 21, 73, 88; id., *Travels* (1860), 268, 275, 385; Erhardt, *CMS–7A*, 3–4; id., *CMS–16*, 34; Abdallah (1963), 82, 110; Mhina (1966), 5, 8, 10, 20; E. V. Winans, *Shambala*, London, 1962, 20, 140; Burton (1872), II, 229, 418.

[2] The first chapter of A. H. Jacobs's Oxford D.Phil. thesis, 'The Traditional Political Organization of the Pastoral Masai', 1965, gives the best existing account of early Masai history: see especially 29–36. Also C. Hollis, *The Masai*, Oxford, 1905, iii; H. A. Fosbrooke, 'An Administrative Survey of the Masai', *TNR*, 26, 1948, 3–5; J. E. G. Sutton, 'The Archaeology of Kenya and Northern Tanzania', *Azania*, I, 49, 52.

In the 1830s a severe drought (probably the same one which drove Kamba settlers to Rabai) seems to have set the Enganglima and Masai herders moving in search of adequate pasture for their stock. Clashes between the two peoples seem to have become more severe until finally they became embroiled in a major war which ended in complete defeat for the Iloikop. Early accounts and Masai tradition remember the Iloikop as an extremely fierce and aggressive people who had constantly harassed their neighbours and done much to disrupt interior commercial activity. Probably they were the people who had kept the early Kamba settlers in Mbooni from moving down onto the plains, and their *murran* had launched frequent raids even to the environs of the towns in the southern section of the northern Mrima coast. Krapf went so far as to remark that had they not been defeated by the Masai 'the intercourse of . . . weaker tribes (Chagga, Kamba, Teita, Shambala) with the Interior would in all probability have been cut off by these Wakuafi who infested the countries adjacent to the sea-coast'.[1]

Their defeat undoubtedly brought more settled conditions to much of the hinterland of the southern area. By the 1840s their raids against Tanga and the other Mrima towns were only a memory, and they were so weakened that the Vanga Swahili could launch slave-raids against their camps near Taveta. By 1853 they had 'long disappeared' from the eastern frontiers of Usambara, and at mid-century the Swahili were in agreement that approaches to the interior were much safer in the south than inland from Mombasa.[2]

The pioneer of the Swahili inland caravan traffic which had its origins in the towns of the southern section of the northern Mrima was reputed to be one Kasimu of Vanga, under whom the redoubtable Bana Kheri had his tutelage. It seems that these first Mrima traders tried to push all the way across Masailand to the shores of Lake Victoria and possibly on even to Uganda. During the late 1830s and early 1840s their caravans seem to have been in rivalry with those coming up to the Lake from Unyanyembe, but, by a date which Erhardt set at before 1847, the Mrima caravans were penetrating only to the Mt. Meru area and the Manyara escarpment, before cutting north to the forests of the Mau, where they traded for 'Masai' ivory with Dorobo hunters. The northward shift may have been caused by an unfavourable resolution of their commercial rivalry with the Unyanyembe traders, or perhaps by

[1] Krapf, *Engutuk Eloikob*, Tübingen, 1854, 3; also Jacobs (1965), 62; Fosbrooke (1948), 5; *KLC*, III, 2542; *TDB*, I, 191.

[2] Krapf, *CMS–173*, 27–8; id., *CMS–172*, 144; Erhardt, *CMS–72*, 7.

hostility and internecine warfare in the Lake Eyasi and Ngorongoro area.[1]

Again, it seems that the Masai may have been responsible, however indirectly, for opening possible avenues of approach and pacifying large areas of the East African hinterland. Swahili caravans working their way up from Mounts Meru and Kilimanjaro towards Mt. Kenya found the Kikuyu people hostile, and they failed to penetrate their country until virtually the end of the century. To the west of Mt. Kenya, however, a nomadic people from the north, who can probably be identified as Borana Galla, were driven back out of the Laikipia plateau by the Masai probably in 1842.[2] Shortly thereafter, it seems, Swahili caravans began using the Laikipia as a means of circling to the north-east of Mt. Kenya to open commercial relations with the Meru, Embu, and other Mt. Kenya peoples. There was probably some disruption of trade in the area when the Laikipia Iloikop peoples advanced down the plateau in the 1860s, but by the 1870s the Purko and allied Masai dealt them a heavy defeat in the areas around Lake Nakuru and once again pacified (if not depopulated) the Laikipia plateau. To the west the Losegelai and other Uasin Gishu (Iloikop) groups were handed a series of defeats by the Masai culminating in the early 1850s, and once again the Swahili caravan traffic seems to have followed closely on the wake of these wars. It is indeed ironic that the Masai people who have often been vilified as an aggressive, warlike people who prevented coastal commercial expansion into the northern part of East Africa seem almost unquestionably the ones who opened the way. The first European observers actually to penetrate Umasai found that tales of Masai attacks on caravans had been greatly exaggerated, for, if the Swahili took care not to provoke unduly the Masai, not only could their country be passed without incident but trade could be carried on with them along the way.[3]

[1] Krapf, *Travels* (1860), 277; id., *CMS-173*, 9, 15; id., *CMS-173*, 61; id., *Engutuk Eloikob* (1854), 28; id., *CMS-177*, 25; J. Christie, *Cholera Epidemics*, London, 1876, 2, 12, 238 (from a letter to Christie from Charles New); Erhardt, *CMS-7A*, 80. For indications of hostilities along this route see Erhardt, ibid.; Fosbrooke (1948), 11; Jacobs (1965), 65; *TDB*, I, 45, 206–7.

[2] Krapf, *CMS-177*, 73; J. Thomson, *Through Masailand*, London, 1885, 306, 309–10, 312, 572; von Höhnel (1894), II, 276, 284, 287, 290; K. R. Dundas, 'Notes on the Origin of the Kikuyu', *Man*, 1908, 137–8; Hollis (1905), 1; Jacobs (1965), 66–7; the date was arrived at by comparing Routledge (1910), 15, and C. Cagnolo, *The Akikuyu*, Nyeri, 1933, 202.

[3] Jacobs (1965), 66, 68–9, 81; Thomson (1885), 353, 381, 389; Johnston (1885), 408, 555; von Höhnel (1894), I, 232; Christie (1876), 206, 209; Jacobs (1965), 93, goes so far as to state that 'at no time did the pastoral Masai attempt to . . . prevent caravans from entering their territory. . . .' This is certainly an exaggeration but no more so than the frequently expressed picture of Masai savagely resisting all forms of commerce.

During the second half of the century the Swahili caravans were penetrating to Lake Baringo, to the Kavirondo gulf, and finally to Karamojong and other areas beyond Mt. Elgon. The earlier accounts make it clear that most of the caravans which pioneered these routes were from the southern towns of the northern Mrima, but by the 1860s there are more frequent mentions of Mombasa caravans plying these routes as well.[1] This development of direct Mombasan caravan activity, so atypical of the town's commerce during the first half of the century, resulted from a number of factors. To begin with, the Masai victories over the Iloikop did not seem to benefit Mombasa's hinterland quite as much as they had the southern area. The Iloikop of Mombasa's interior had been stunned but not totally defeated in the wars of the 1830s. For a time, the Kamba were able to adopt a more direct route to the coast as beaten Iloikop bands pulled back out of the 'nyika' area; but the Borana Galla soon came pouring into the void left by the Iloikop and thus extended their caravan-raiding activities, which they carried on with a ferocity equalling if not surpassing that of the Iloikop. The Iloikop withdrew to the borders of Ukamba where they recouped their losses and soon were threatening a full-scale invasion of Mombasa's coast once again. The Kamba were forced to adopt a more circumambulatory (but none the less dangerous) route to the coast, and may well have been experiencing renewed pressures below their hilltops. There followed a confused series of wars and raids in the 'nyika' area, at a given point the Galla controlling the region for a year or two, and the Iloikop gaining sufficient strength to push them out at another. It is indeed a credit to Kamba caravan organization and fighting skill that they were ever able to conduct as voluminous a trade as they did, but the more unsettled conditions of the 'nyika' area fiom the 1840s onward probably began to hamper ever more seriously the flow of that commerce. By 1869, even after the Kamba had launched successful military campaigns against the Galla, Rebmann could pessimistically observe that 'such is the unsettled condition of these countries [the 'nyika' areas] at present that there is far less prospect of an extension of our mission inland than there was 20 years ago'.[2]

From the 1850s until virtually the end of the century, Mombasa's

[1] Burton's works trace the routes during the 1850s, New, Wakefield, and Christie examine them during the 1860s and 1870s, and the Thomson and von Höhnel accounts deal with the final expansion beyond Elgon in the 1880s.

[2] Rebmann, *CMS-55*, 1869, 4; id., *CMS-50*, 1847, 3; id., *CMS-52*, 2, 7, 44-5; id., *CMS-52A*; id., *CMS-53*, 14; Guillain (1856), 280; Krapf, *CMS-167*, 19; id., *Travels* (1860), 362; id., *CMS-173*, 1, 17, 27; id., *CMS-174*, 11-12, 35, 38, 72; id., *CMS-176*, 12.

hinterland was in a state of extreme chaos, the Iloikop becoming bold enough to raid even the suburbs of the city itself. The Mombasan caravans which were able to penetrate the interior did so only by slipping southward down the coast to head inland from one of the more peaceful southern towns, following one of the routes pioneered by the southerly Swahili.[1]

Simultaneously with the more vigorous incursions of hostile peoples in the 'nyika', the Kamba were beginning to encounter a variety of difficulties with commercial activity in the interior. The same mobile and independent *utui* system which had facilitated the development of Kamba commerce in the first place lacked the overriding unity and authority necessary for the development of an ordered country such as Kimweri's Shambala kingdom. As the century progressed there were indications that feuds and quarrels between the various areas of Ukamba were becoming more frequent. It seems that many of these feuds may have been engendered by commercial conflicts, for as early as 1849 Krapf could note that certain areas of Ukamba forbade other Kamba to trade in their countries and even sent their caravans down to the coast at different seasons so as not to clash *en route*. There are also indications that increasingly some Kamba began to abandon any pretence of legitimate trade, employing their *utui* organizations as highly efficient bands of robbers which would waylay bona fide caravans, killing their members, stealing their goods, conveying them the remaining distance to the coast, and selling them to the middleman villages.[2] It is possible that whole areas of Ukamba may have given up trading for the easier, but just as lucrative, occupation of bandits. The Kilungu Kamba, who were 'fierce robbers who waged war against the rest of the Kamba', and the Aendi of Kilima Kibombu near the 'nyika', who found it 'more profitable to take ivory ready for sale (from legitimate caravans), than to hunt elephants in the wilderness', seem to have been just such people.[3]

As mentioned above, the early commercial rivalry between the

[1] Burton (1872), II, 58, 61, 71, 73; New (1873), 297; Thomson (1885), 64, 66, 122; Christie (1876), 211; Jones, *CMS–0–14*, 1, 4, 5; W. J. Russell, *CMS–0–25*, 1876. In many of the accounts the 'Masai' are referred to as raiders of Mombasa's coast, but this was apparently another case of referring to Iloikop by the wrong name: Wakefield (1904), 179, noted that the Masai and Iloikop 'are not always distinguished by the natives about here, "Wakwavi" being almost the synonym for "Masai" and *vice versa*'.

[2] Krapf, *CMS–174*, 50; id., *CMS–176*, 45, 59, 131; id., *Travels* (1860), 311–12; Dundas (1915), 237; id. (1913), 484–5; Neumann (1898), 431; *KLC*, I, 400, 406.

[3] *KLC*, II, 1286; Krapf, *CMS–176*, 20–21; see also Krapf, ibid., 16, 18, 23; Lindblom (1920), 17.

Kamba and Nyika, although largely resolved so as to satisfy both parties, did create a certain ill-feeling which, even in the first half of the century, was expressed by each of the tribes extracting exorbitant *hongo* from caravans of the other passing through their respective countries. By the 1870s the ill-feeling was being expressed in outright conflict. The Kamba and the Giriyama Nyika had a brief war in 1874, and a few years later the Kamba were fighting against Mbaruku, a last remnant of the Mazrui family, who with his renegade Swahilis and Nyika allies was raiding Kamba and Mombasa commerce in the 'nyika'.[1]

To the west things were even worse. It will be recalled that the Kamba had hunted out much of their own territory during the early part of the nineteenth century and that their subsequent expansions were dictated to a considerable extent by a desire to find fresh hunting grounds. The Emberre, Embu, and other Mt. Kenya peoples seem eventually to have become tired of Kamba hunting-parties encroaching on their lands. Even at mid-century there were hints of growing dissatisfaction among the Mt. Kenya peoples. During his stay in Ukamba in 1851 Krapf was told by Rumu wa Kikandi, an Embu caravan leader who was employed by up-country Kamba middlemen as an extension of their interior commercial network, that he and his people were getting little profit because of the Kamba and that they would like to establish their own relations with the coast. Indeed, the redoubtable Kivoi met his death at the hands of a party of Mt. Kenya people and there seem to have been rather frequent quarrels and wars over commercial matters for at least some years before he was killed.[2] By the early 1870s the Emberre sought the help of Swahili traders, who by that time were sending caravans into the areas north-east of the mountain via the pacified Laikipia plateau. Together with these traders, the Emberre were able to drive the Kamba from their territory, and even before this time an Emberre woman called Churume had rallied her people's warriors in an earlier attempt to rid themselves of the intruders.[3]

Kamba-Mt. Kenya relations were undoubtedly further soured by the later-nineteenth-century development of Kamba slave-raiding activity, which was itself a significant indication of the sharp decrease of Kamba prosperity. For by the second half of the nineteenth century

[1] Krapf, *Travels* (1860), 294, 342, 249; T. H. Sparshott, *CMS–0–26*, 1874, 42; Jones, *CMS–0–14*, 3, 9; Praeger, *CMS–0–22*, 1877, 3; Wakefield (1904), 172–3.

[2] Krapf, *CMS–176*, 49, 58, 60, 103–4.

[3] *KLC*, I, 942; Orde-Brown (1925), 54.

the Kamba were no longer purchasing slaves from the Swahili so much as supplying that commodity as a trade item to the coast. Kamba raids went out against the Kikuyu and the other Mt. Kenya peoples, the Pokomo, the Masai, and even areas as far removed as Marsabit. By the latter part of the century ivory was becoming increasingly difficult to obtain in the same large quantities that it once had been. Kamba hunting-parties were forced to go as far afield as Samburu and Turkana (more than 300 miles north-west of Ulu) and even to the southern end of Lake Tanganyika and Songea (more than 600 miles to the south-west).[1]

The Kamba were able to carry on a greatly diminished commerce with the coast until the early part of the twentieth century, but Swahili caravans increasingly used Ukamba as an avenue to the more distant interior and the golden age of Kamba commercial activity was long past. Taking into consideration their lack of overriding authority and co-ordination, together with the virtually insurmountable difficulties and dangers that such activity entailed, the Kamba achievement can still be seen as a truly remarkable one. That they should eventually decline from that golden age because of over-extension, the depletion of the once great herds of elephant, and various internecine conflicts is not nearly so astounding as the fact that it was mainly through their efforts that Mombasa could rank at the forefront of the East African coastal towns by the middle of the century.

The Swahili caravans which by the late 1880s had penetrated to the last frontier of the inland ivory supply, not so much as a result of any conscious 'outflanking' of the Kamba as by the fortuitous pacification of various areas of the interior and the resulting commercial expansion of the southern section of the northern Mrima, were to enjoy only a brief period of booming commerce before the coming of a new era made the whole system of caravan trade, however courageous and enterprising, a relic of an outdated past. The vanguard of the Europeans who established themselves in Ukamba at the end of the nineteenth century were met with armed resistance, but soon resistance was forced to give way to superior firepower, administration, and technology. Kivoi was to become a legendary figure to some of the Kamba, while others smeared rocks with fat along the old trade-routes as

[1] Hobley (1910), 343, 351–2; von Höhnel (1894), I, 331; L. Decle, *Three Years in Savage Africa*, London, 1898, 489; *KLC*, I, 193, 603; Dundas (1913), 484; Lindblom (1920), 13, 20, 343; Chanler (1896), 407; Neumann (1898), 92; Beidelman (1961), 181; *TDB*, IV, 39.

offerings to other departed caravan leaders. Kamba pride in their commercial ability lived on in the answer of a Kamba elder to a European's offer to establish Asian shopkeepers in Ukamba: 'We don't want any Indians . . . we know how to keep shops ourselves.' Many Kamba hid away their few remaining bits of ivory, hoping that these new intruders would soon go away and that the old commerce might revive, but by 1896 the ringing of workmen's hammers knocking in the first spikes of the Uganda Railway sounded the knell of the once great Kamba trade.[1]

A Note on Sources

The majority of my unpublished sources are from the archives of the Church Missionary Society, Waterloo Road, London. In citing references to this material in the footnotes I have used the CMS classification number and have given the page number in each case; for example, 'Krapf, *CMS-172*, 5', refers to page 5 of document 172 in the CMS file for J. L. Krapf. The *Kenya Land Commission, Evidence and Memoranda* has been abbreviated as *KLC* with the relevant volume number shown by a Roman numeral. The *Tanganyika District Books* have been abbreviated as *TDB*, and *Tanganyika Notes and Records* as *TNR*.

[1] *KLC*, II, 1342; Lindblom (1920), 21–9, 349, 353, 469, 550; Decle (1898), 485.

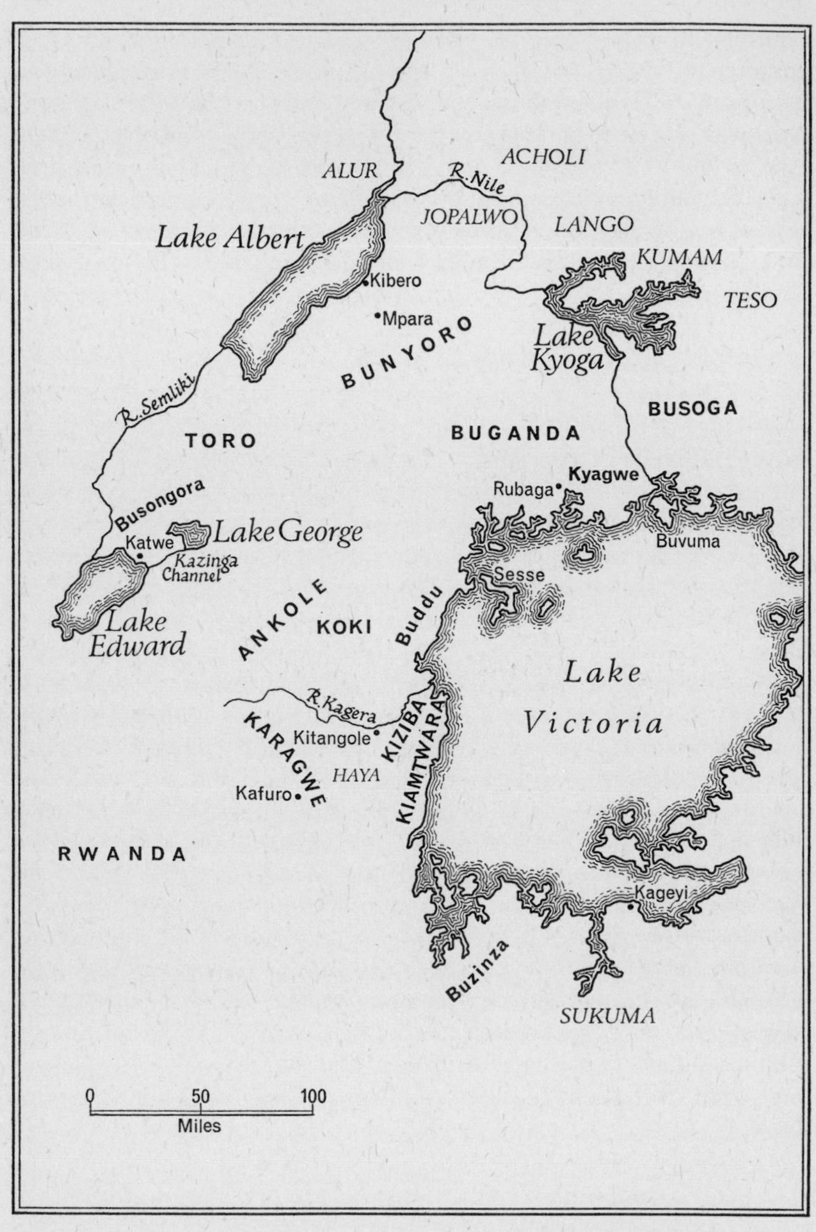

Map 6. The Northern Interlacustrine Region in the Nineteenth Century

5

The Northern Interlacustrine Region

JOHN TOSH

The northern interlacustrine region of East Africa[1] is well known for its political achievements before the beginning of the colonial period, but historians have been reluctant to credit the region with commensurate importance in the commercial field. Christopher Wrigley has pointed out that, for all its ecological advantages, pre-colonial Uganda had no significant trade. The foundation of the economy was of course agriculture, and 'apart from very minor exceptions . . . the products of the soil did not enter into trade'; salt, fish, and iron goods occasioned a little inter-tribal traffic, but supply and demand were reasonably uniform over the whole region, and trade brought no significant changes to the subsistence economy. Even the Zanzibari traders in Wrigley's opinion caused no appreciable change in the traditional economic system.[2] Seen in the context of modern development, this view is fair enough; with the partial exception of Buganda, the interlacustrine region retained its essentially subsistence economy throughout the nineteenth century, and since then industry and commerce have been developed along entirely fresh lines. There are, however, sources available which give a more detailed picture and convey an impression of greater vigour and potential in pre-colonial trade than is generally admitted.

From the 1860s onwards, the lake region was exposed to a constant stream of European visitors; few of them wrote anything approaching a general economic assessment of the area—the notable exception was

[1] The area dealt with in this chapter includes Buganda, Busoga, Bunyoro, Ankole, and Toro. Where appropriate, some mention is also made of Rwanda and the Haya states (notably Karagwe) in the south. I am indebted to Peter Greenhalgh for drawing my attention to a number of references, and to Professor Roland Oliver and Dr. Michael Twaddle for their helpful comments on earlier drafts.

[2] C. C. Wrigley, *Crops and Wealth in Uganda*, Kampala, 1959, 11–12.

Emin Pasha, Governor of Egypt's Equatoria Province from 1878 to 1889[1]—but the scattered references in their accounts are nevertheless our most valuable source. Many of their observations concern exclusively African transactions. A distinction must, however, be made here between indigenous trade, which was restricted to the region and a traditional feature of its economy, and those other aspects of trade which were a response to the quickening commercial tempo caused by the Arab and Swahili traders from the coast. Emin Pasha was well aware of this issue, though he found it hard to say whether the progress he saw was mainly due to the 'active commercial spirit' of the inhabitants or to the trading expeditions and permanent settlements of the coastmen.[2] The problem is perhaps best approached by looking at the commodities of pre-colonial trade.

It has been said that, apart from a rough distinction between a gardening economy based on the plantain in the east and a pastoral economy in the drier lands of the west, everyone in the interlacustrine region 'was producing much the same things by similar techniques and in similar conditions'.[3] But there were items of specialized production which loomed large in the daily life of the inhabitants. Chief of these were salt and iron.

Poor quality salt could be procured from the ashes of certain plants and even from cow's urine, but natural salt was considered an essential. Buganda used to import it by canoe from the east side of Lake Victoria, and in the 1880s she was also obtaining expensive supplies from as far south as Buzinza.[4] In the interlacustrine region itself, however, there were only two salt-producing centres of any significance. One of these was the settlement of Kibero on the eastern shore of Lake Albert in Bunyoro. Here, the villagers owed their livelihood to the salt deposits, and Kibero was reputed to be the main centre of population on the lake in the 1880s. European observers varied in their estimates of the quality of salt produced there, but James Grant in 1862 found that it 'was perfectly pure in colour and taste'. Salt has been traded at Kibero for as long as Nyoro traditions recall, and the area supplied was a large one; by the late nineteenth century it covered 'almost the whole of [B]Unyoro, [B]Uganda and the surrounding countries', including

[1] See especially (ed.) G. Schweinfurth and others, *Emin Pasha in Central Africa*, London, 1888, 111–23, for his survey of trade among the Banyoro and Baganda.

[2] Schweinfurth (1888), 111–12.

[3] Wrigley (1959), 11.

[4] T. H. Parke, *My Personal Experiences in Equatorial Africa*, London, 1891, 440; Schweinfurth (1888), 121, 122; J. Roscoe, *The Baganda*, London, 1911, 438.

Acholiland and Alurland to the north.[1] The scale of the trade is illustrated by Emin's statement in 1885 that 'the salt deposits of Kibiro ... constitute one of the most valuable portions of Kabarega [of Bunyoro]'s dominions', and by that time Buganda had designs on the place.[2]

Further south in Busongora, the salt-lakes of Katwe flourished as another commercial centre. The crystallized slabs of salt from the bottom of the lakes were inferior in quality to the Kibero product, but the business supported an estimated population of 2,000 in 1889. H. M. Stanley's description in that year is of a bustling centre of regional trade frequented by Banyankore, Banyaruanda, and Batoro, who came with a variety of trade goods including grain, bark-cloth, vegetables, and iron tools.[3] And, like Kibero, Katwe became a political factor of some importance. The chief of Busongora never seems to have been a free agent; in the 1870s Stanley heard that he was paying a tribute of salt to the Kabaka of Buganda. At one stage Ankole controlled the place from across the Kazinga channel, and by the 1880s Kabarega was in possession; Stanley's arrival with the Emin Pasha Relief Expedition in 1889 caused the Banyoro soldiers to abandon Katwe, but by 1891 they had apparently returned.[4] It is possible that Kabarega's efforts to recover Toro were intended not only to keep open communication with the Zanzibari traders from the south but also to secure a monopoly of salt supplies in the interlacustrine region. If in the long run this policy had been successful, it would have caused considerable embarrassment to Buganda, which was wholly dependent on imports for her heavy consumption of salt.[5]

Natural salt, then, was clearly a much sought after article in short supply, and its trade had repercussions on the pattern of rivalry between the states. There is nothing in the European accounts to indicate that the salt trade was a recent development; rather, the scarcity of this essential commodity suggests that it was an article of

[1] W. Junker, *Travels in Africa During the Years 1882–1886*, London, 1892, 524; J. W. Grant, *A Walk Across Africa*, London, 1864, 296; M. Posnansky, 'Pottery Types from Archaeological Sites in East Africa', *J. African Hist.*, 2 (1961), 192; A. T. Mounteney-Jephson, *Emin Pasha and the Rebellion at the Equator*, London, 1890, 36; Schweinfurth (1888), 176.

[2] Schweinfurth (1888), 176; Junker (1892), 524.

[3] H. M. Stanley, *In Darkest Africa*, 2 vols., London, 1890, II, 311–16.

[4] Stanley, *Through the Dark Continent*, 2 vols., London, 1878, II, 473; Stanley (1890), II, 316; G. Schweitzer, *Emin Pasha: His Life and Work*, 2 vols., London, 1898, II, 195.

[5] Schweinfurth (1888), 122.

inter-tribal trade long before either the coastmen or the Europeans reached the region.

Much the same factors made ironware commercially important. Hoes and spear-heads were no more dispensable than salt in a predominantly agricultural region, which was constantly putting dynastic disputes to the test of war. Deposits of good iron-ore near the earth's surface were much less common than might be supposed. Buganda was almost totally deficient in this respect, and, until the conquest of eastern Kyagwe and Buddu in the eighteenth century, relied on imported iron; even then, she continued to get pig-iron from Koki and spear-blades from Bunyoro.[1] In the 1850s the spears made in Karagwe were held in high esteem at Tabora; but it was in Bunyoro that the richest deposits of iron-ore were to be found, and the Banyoro seem to have been the most important purveyors of iron goods in the region, trading them both to the Baganda and to the segmentary peoples across the Nile.[2] The smelting and the working of iron on this scale were important additions to the subsistence economy and must have maintained a significant number of specialists. We know much less about the iron trade than the salt trade. There is, for instance, no evidence that it caused concentrations of trade comparable to Katwe, but its economic importance can hardly be denied.

Salt and iron were thus two articles of trade which were essential to everyday life. But there were other indigenous products which were traded over considerable distances for their luxury value. The first of these was bark-cloth. From at least the reign of Semakokiro onwards, the making of bark-cloths was a vigorous domestic industry in Buganda, and they had become standard clothing for the common people by the late nineteenth century. Plain and dyed bark-cloths were exported to Karagwe, Rwanda, Busoga, and Bunyoro, for none of these countries produced cloth of comparable quality. Outside Buganda, bark-cloth was generally worn only by the wealthy, but the Baganda were assured a steady demand since bark-cloths were apparently worn out in a month.[3]

Another well-established article of exchange was coffee. The cultivated plant was unknown, but wild coffee produced small beans

[1] M. S. Kiwanuka, 'The Traditional History of the Buganda Kingdom', London Ph.D. thesis (1965), 332; Roscoe (1911), 379; Grant (1864), 271.

[2] R. F. Burton, *The Lake Regions of Central Africa,* 2 vols., London, 1860, II, 184; Schweinfurth (1888), 122, 113; Junker (1892), 471.

[3] Roscoe (1911), 403, 434; Schweinfurth (1888), 119–20; S. W. Baker, *Ismailia,* 2 vols., London, 1874, II, 251.

which were chewed as a stimulant. The traditions of the Haya states show that in the eighteenth century traders from Kiziba were taking coffee to the neighbouring states of Kiamtwara and Karagwe. In the nineteenth century the coffee plant flourished in Bunyoro and Buganda, and it was these countries which supplied Karagwe, where it was customary for guests to be presented with a handful of beans. European travellers found that the toasted beans made an excellent beverage, and Emin remarked with considerable foresight on the commercial potential of interlacustrine coffee.[1] But its place in the African economy was small, as was the case with tobacco. Like coffee, tobacco was a luxury with a long history; pottery tobacco pipes from the seventeenth century have been found at the Ankole capital site of Bweyorere. It was in Ankole that much of the best tobacco grew in Emin's day, and a surplus was exported to Karagwe and Bunyoro.[2]

Clearly, in a handful of commodities at least, quite a brisk trade affecting widely separated quarters of the interlacustrine region must have been carried on before the arrival of the coastal traders. But it is easier to record the existence of this trade than to describe the nature of the commercial process involved, for it was precisely at this level that the coastal traders made their greatest impact, especially as regards media of exchange. The subsequent European accounts may therefore be a most unreliable guide in this matter. They give very little evidence that the northern interlacustrine region was equipped with an indigenous form of currency. Roscoe claims that ivory discs were used as currency before either beads or cowrie-shells arrived from the coast, but this statement can hardly be accepted at face value without any indication of the economic context. Cows and probably also iron hoes served as units of account; the latter may conceivably have been a medium of exchange, though we have no direct evidence for thinking so. What is quite clear is that there was little or no means of hoarding currency as wealth and thus securing the economic services of others.[3]

For the most part, it would therefore seem, trade was carried on by barter, and the lack of currency was partly offset by the existence of recognized markets where traders could rely on finding the fullest range of goods and customers. Later on, Arabs frequented these markets, but the European descriptions are of essentially African

[1] H. Cory, *History of Bukoba District*, Mwanza, n.d., 75, 77; Junker (1892), 482; Burton (1860), II, 181, 187; Parke (1891), 459–60; Schweinfurth (1888), 118.

[2] Posnansky (1961), 193; Schweinfurth (1888), 78, 112; Grant (1864), 158–9.

[3] Roscoe (1911), 412–13, 456, 457; Roscoe, *The Banyankole*, London, 1923, 78.

markets to which the coastmen came as outsiders. As Emin wrote when stressing the commercial bent of the Africans: 'whoever visits the markets of Werahanje [i.e. Bweranyange] in Karagwa [*sic*], Rubaga in Uganda, and Mpara Nyamoga in Unyoro will find convincing proofs of this fact', and he supported this assertion by giving a vivid detailed description of Mpara. Kibero was another such centre where in Emin's time ox-hides, skins, iron-ore, spear-heads, brass bars, and glass beads were brought in exchange for salt; on the other side of Bunyoro there were frontier markets to which the Baganda came with bark-cloths and plantains, and the Banyoro with hoes and salt, while further east in Lake Kyoga the islands of Namulumuka and Kaweri were established places for trade between the Banyoro and the Kumam.[1] It is hard to tell whether these markets were seasonal or in session regularly throughout the year. Probably those which dealt mainly in salt and iron goods fell into the second category, since these commodities were worked by specialists who had no other livelihood and could practise their skills all the year round. As for the traders themselves, there is no evidence that they were professional entrepreneurs; rather, they were engaged in subsistence farming or one of the few specialized activities and took time off to barter their surpluses.

Yet if there were no professional traders and no one trading people before the arrival of the Arabs, some parts of the region seem to have been commercially more prominent than others. The available evidence strongly suggests that Bunyoro was the most important. Casati in the 1880s noted how the Banyoro 'exhibit their gifts in industries and commerce', and Samuel Baker had been equally impressed. It may be objected that these glowing reports merely reflect the tendency for Europeans to travel through Bunyoro, but the vital concentrations of salt and iron there lend substance to their accounts. Furthermore, Bunyoro derived substantial advantages from her strategic position as the northernmost interlacustrine kingdom: on two sides—the north and the east—her territory was contiguous with the non-Bantu areas inhabited by the Lango and the Acholi, with whom Bunyoro had ancient dynastic links. The initiative in trading with the Lango was apparently taken by the Jopalwo, a group of Lwo-speaking clans in north-east Bunyoro. In return for goats, cattle, butter, and later ivory, they traded metal hoes which the Lango needed both for agricultural use and for turning into spear-heads. Neither the Lango nor their

[1] Schweinfurth (1888), 112–13, 180; Roscoe (1911), 456; Paulo Kagwa, 'Kakungulu Omuzira wa Uganda', 10 (MS. in Makerere College Library).

eastern neighbours, the Kumam and Iteso, knew the art of smelting, and in time the Banyoro established commercial links with these latter tribes as well. This traffic in ironware is the basis for D. A. Low's statement that the Banyoro dominated the trade round Lake Kyoga in the nineteenth century.[1]

In two other areas—Buganda and Karagwe—the European accounts also give an impression of particularly vigorous commercial activity. But here it is more difficult to assess the place of indigenous trade, since these were the kingdoms most frequented by the Zanzibaris. Karagwe's dominance of the other Haya states may indeed have been due to her skilful handling of long-distance trade. The case of Buganda poses different problems; her eminence undoubtedly predated the arrival of the Arabs. Buganda's food supplies were the most plentiful in the region; they depended on a plantain economy which provided food all the year round with minimum human effort, thus freeing manpower for other activities. But this potential for entrepreneurial activity was not realized by the Baganda. Their dealings with the surrounding tribes were on a predatory rather than a commercial level, and this tendency was strongly encouraged by the Kabaka in order to provide, at no cost to himself, rewards in the form of captured women and livestock for his chiefs and those Baganda who were anxious to better themselves. Iron and salt were obtained by plunder and tribute,[2] as well as by trade. According to their own traditions, the Baganda seldom travelled abroad to trade; instead, they waited for foreigners to come to them.[3] Only on Lake Victoria is there any indication that they were involved in an extensive commercial network. Despite the piracy of the Buvuma islanders noted by Stanley in 1875, goods passed from one end of the lake to the other; the salt trade between the east side of the lake and Buganda has been mentioned already; in the late nineteenth century the Sukuma were supplying hoes and other iron goods to Busoga. Recent research there has shown that southern Busoga was traditionally an important centre of trade from the Sesse and Buvuma islands and the coastal parts of Buganda, dealing in white ants, dried fish and bananas, canoes, pots, hoes, livestock, and poultry. As the

[1] G. Casati, *Ten Years in Equatoria*, 2 vols., London, 1891, II, 54; S. W. Baker, *Albert N'yanza*, 2 vols., London, 1866, II, 54–5; J. H. Driberg, *The Lango*, London, 1923, 30, 81; Junker (1892), 471, 479; J. C. D. Lawrance, *The Iteso*, London, 1957, 148; D. A. Low in (eds.) R. Oliver and G. Mathew, *History of East Africa*, I, Oxford, 1963, 327.

[2] Tribute in the sense that no commercial exchange, however indirect, was involved, the transaction being essentially political. For an example, see above, p. 105.

[3] Kiwanuka (1965), 452.

political influence of Buganda expanded along the lakeshore, her share in this trade probably increased; at any rate, Carl Peters believed that 'in estimating the political and commercial affairs of East Africa too little stress is laid on this internal trade among the tribes. . . . The barter trade of [B]Uganda along the coast defies all direct calculation.'[1]

The centres of trade which attracted the notice of Europeans were probably not the only ones; indeed they may not have been the most important. But plainly such centres existed. To what extent were they under royal control? Here the evidence is particularly slender. Often important markets were sited at the royal residence: Mpara Nyamoga, for example, was Kabarega's capital in the 1870s. This suggests that the king was either a trader on his own account or else imposed some form of tax. In Buganda, market-places in and around the capital were supervised by a special chief who levied dues of 10% on all transactions for the Kabaka. More stringent controls must have operated at the Kibero salt-mines which Junker described as 'being largely in the hands of Kabarega'; in 1894 during the British campaign against Bunyoro, Colonel Colvile saw the mines as 'Kabarega's chief source of wealth and means of procuring arms and ammunition'.[2] But it is hard to say whether this high degree of political control over trade was long-standing, or whether it was a reaction to the growth of long-distance trade which presented a more obvious challenge to the stability of the interlacustrine states.

The almost total lack of contemporary evidence renders any reconstruction of traditional trade distorted and incomplete, but some attempt must be made if the impact of the long-distance caravans is to be understood. Certainly, the apparatus of traditional trade was primitive enough. As far as can be seen, there was no currency nor professional trading, and the number of specialist producers was small. Nevertheless exchange seems to have been a highly significant feature of the interlacustrine economies, not only because it was the principal means of distributing such essentials as salt and iron, but also because it transcended political divisions. The inhabitants, and especially their rulers, were familiar with a commercial system which was relatively advanced in scale, if not in methods. Without this experience Africans

[1] Stanley (1878), I, 223; Roscoe (1911), 438; C. Peters, *New Light on Dark Africa*, London, 1891, 391–2; D. W. Cohen, personal communication.

[2] Roscoe (1911), 452; Junker (1892), 524; Foreign Office Confidential Print 6557/147, Colvile to F.O. from Kibero, 5 Feb. 1894.

could not have exploited as they did the opportunities created by long-distance trade. The coastal traders provided an indispensable stimulus from the 1840s onwards, but they did not take control of the commercial life of the region. Instead, Africans dominated every stage of the commercial process save the actual transport of goods to and from the coast.

Their capacity to do so was greatly enhanced by the fact that long-distance trade goods preceded the long-distance caravans by over fifty years. We know this from the oral traditions of Buganda set down by Apolo Kagwa; excavations in Ankole have also uncovered a few coastal trade beads from the eighteenth century.[1] Taken together, the evidence suggests a process of filtration in which the Nyamwezi possibly took a prominent part. Cups and plates first appeared in Buganda during the reign of Kabaka Kyabagu in the latter half of the eighteenth century.[2] His son, Semakokiro, took an active interest in the new trade: he amassed great quantities of copper and cowrie-shells, bought cotton cloth in Karagwe, and sent his own traders to Kiziba with ivory; when one of them was killed by the Baziba, Semakokiro dispatched a punitive expedition. As the volume of trade increased, so Buganda strove to expand down the western side of Lake Victoria and to monopolize all long-distance trade. Semakokiro's predecessor, Junju, had conquered Buddu, and during the nineteenth century Buganda's sphere of influence was extended to Kiziba and Karagwe.[3] This interim period of filtration gave Africans invaluable experience in handling new problems of supply and demand and strengthened the indigenous commercial system. The coastal traders found a ready-made demand for their luxury goods as well as surpluses of ivory available for export. They did not have to create a new commercial infrastructure, for the existing one served their needs adequately enough.

The Arab and Swahili caravans followed the same route up the west coast of Lake Victoria to Buganda as the earliest trade goods had done. They established their main base in Karagwe, where by 1855 they had a settlement at Kafuro near Bweranyange, the Mukama's capital. There was also a large Arab colony at Kitangole in northern Karagwe, close to the Kagera river and the frontier with Buganda. Some Arabs

[1] Posnansky (1961), 193.

[2] Kiwanuka (1965), 658, estimates that Kyabagu's reign fell towards the end of the period 1744–1771 (±36); his calculations follow the method suggested in R. Oliver, 'Ancient Capital Sites of Ankole', *Uganda J.*, 23 (1959), 51–2.

[3] A. Kagwa, *Basekabaka be Buganda*, translated in Kiwanuka (1965), 341, 343–4, 450, 459.

stayed in Karagwe for years at a time; when Stanley met him in 1876, the famous Ahmed bin Ibrahim had been there for twelve years and had amassed large quantities of livestock.[1] Once in Karagwe, the Arabs had no difficulty about provisions and they found comparatively civilized conditions in which to live. All this no doubt contributed to the preference the Zanzibaris had for Karagwe as against any other route. The Kavirondo route was never favoured: Speke was told in 1861 that a caravan approaching Buganda from the east had been turned away shortly after Suna's death in 1856; when Emin enquired of a Zanzibari in Buganda whether people ever arrived from Masailand, 'there was a decided negative' in reply. In later years, considerable use was made of the route across Lake Victoria once dhows had been constructed on its southern side; in 1882 the missionary Robert Ashe found the port of Kageyi full of Arabs whose dhows were sailing from Buganda laden with ivory and slaves.[2]

It was of the greatest significance that the early Zanzibari traders went without exception to Buganda. This was the beginning of the process whereby the Baganda cornered the attention and sympathies of the many non-African agencies interested in the region. The Arabs' slowness to penetrate the other kingdoms was partly due to the open-handedness of the Kabakas, who made a policy of attracting strangers to their court and keeping them there. Burton at Tabora in 1858 found the Arabs praising Suna's 'gifts and attention'; with a characteristic eye for the exotic, he recounted the case of Isa bin Hussein who had been given by Suna a harem of 200 or 300 women; perhaps this was an exaggeration, but it illustrates the Kabaka's attractive reputation at Tabora.[3]

For many years Suna and his successor Mutesa were able to prevent the Zanzibaris from visiting the rival kingdom of Bunyoro. It was not until 1877 that two Arabs arrived there from Karagwe 'without touching [B]Uganda', though parties of Banyoro had been travelling to Kafuro in the '60s to sell ivory. The Banyoro were no less anxious than the Baganda to profit from the coastal traders, but their enthusiasm was not shared by all states. As late as 1878 Ankole was 'inaccessible to

[1] J. Ford and R. de Z. Hall, 'History of Karagwe', *Tanganyika Notes and Records*, 24 (1947), 9; Stanley (1878), I, 453. For further details of the Arab penetration see J. M. Gray, 'Ahmed bin Ibrahim—the first Arab to reach Buganda', *Uganda J.*, 11 (1947), 80–97.

[2] J. H. Speke, *Journal of the Discovery of the Source of the Nile*, London, 1863, 187; (ed.) J. M. Gray, 'The Diaries of Emin Pasha [hereinafter D.E.P.]—Extracts III', *Uganda J.*, 26 (1962), 80; R. P. Ashe, *Two Kings of Uganda*, London, 1889, 39.

[3] Burton (1860), II, 193.

traders', though by 1885 Zanzibaris could go there. Rwanda was always hostile; both Grant and Stanley found Arab traders loudly abusing the Banyaruanda for refusing to admit them to their kingdom.[1]

The Zanzibaris seem to have had few illusions about their position; when they were prohibited entry into a kingdom, they obeyed. They were confronted by a well-established state system which was for the most part confident of containing the social and economic effects of long-distance trade. Few in numbers and far from their base, the coastmen were ill-equipped to challenge the status quo; their interests lay in accepting the protection which it offered. Generally they avoided giving provocation. Their temporary exclusion from Buganda in the 1850s was probably, as J. A. Rowe has suggested, intended not as punishment but to prevent foreign interference in the aftermath of Suna's death; once Mutesa was secure, they were welcome as before. The interlacustrine rulers in their turn kept close watch on the Arabs, and usually restricted them to the capital or its immediate vicinity, as at Mpara Nyamoga, Rubaga, and Kafuro. Moreover, the Arabs did most of their business with the rulers rather than the ruled. In Bunyoro and Buganda, Emin noted that it was the practice for each trader to present about half his goods to the king, and to receive on his departure a gift of ivory in return; in the meantime he had at his disposal house, garden, and provisions. Hence the Zanzibaris, prosperous though they might be, seldom exercised political influence. Only once was their intervention decisive: this was on the death of Ndagara of Karagwe about 1855 when they helped Rumanika and bribed Suna of Buganda to attack the rival claimant. On the whole the coastmen behaved as passive recipients of royal patronage.[2]

But however much diplomatic support the Zanzibaris received from their hosts, their trade with the region remained a costly and chancy business, mainly because of porterage and transit charges. The whole venture only paid off because ivory was so highly prized overseas and because such generous terms of exchange obtained. Emin observed that when Arabs traded with the rulers of Buganda and Bunyoro they usually left with ivory worth five times the value of the goods they had brought. Grant on his visit to Buganda in 1862 recorded the case of the

[1] Schweinfurth (1888), 67, 115; Speke (1863), 242; 'D.E.P.—Extracts III', *Uganda J.*, 26 (1962), 85; 'D.E.P.—Extracts V', *Uganda J.*, 27 (1963), 11; Grant (1864), 161; Stanley (1878), I, 454.

[2] J. A. Rowe, 'Revolution in Buganda 1856–1900: Part One', Wisconsin Ph.D. thesis (1966), 50 (microfilm in Rhodes House Library); Schweinfurth (1888), 115; Ford and Hall (1947), 10; Burton (1860), II, 183.

trader Jumah who was asked by Mutesa to surrender clothing, brass wire, beads, and two flint-locks, and in return was later given 700 lbs. of ivory, seven women, and fifty cows, together with the same two flint-locks.[1]

In stark contrast was the reputation of the Khartoumers who arrived from the north in the 1860s. Grant was well aware of the difference between Zanzibaris and Khartoumers; the latter plundered cattle with which to pay porters and purchase ivory, and they refused to pay taxes. It was in the country north of the interlacustrine region that the impact of the Khartoumers was most devastating. But their activities also impinged on Bunyoro, where they were 'trading' during the reign of Kamurasi; when Baker paid his first visit to Bunyoro in 1864, his arrival was greeted with suspicion because a few months previously a party of Sudanese had abused the Mukama's hospitality and killed 300 Banyoro. Kamurasi's son, Kabarega, owed his throne to the Khartoumers and was himself much troubled by their machinations until the severing of communications with the north by the Mahdists in 1883 weakened them.[2]

The impetus for economic growth came, of course, not from the Khartoumers but from the Zanzibaris. Direct contact with the East African coast greatly increased the flow of long-distance trade goods into the interlacustrine region. As the import-export trade expanded, so indigenous trade was invigorated by the more advanced commercial practice of the Arabs. This process must now be examined a little more closely.

From the African point of view the most obvious change wrought by the Arabs must have been the introduction of firearms. There is no evidence that this event occurred in the period of filtration. In the 1840s coastal traders were helping Buganda with guns in a raid on Busoga. One of the Kabaka's reasons for keeping them at his court was to prevent arms going to Bunyoro. Even Kigeri of Rwanda did business with the Arabs in order to obtain guns. By the 1880s all three of these powerful states had large numbers of troops equipped with firearms.[3]

Apart from guns, the Arab traders chiefly brought luxury goods. As we have seen, cups and plates were among the earliest imports to

[1] Schweinfurth (1888), 115; Grant (1864), 163.

[2] Grant (1864), 163–4; Baker (1866), II, 24; Baker (1874), II, 138.

[3] J. M. Gray (1947), 81; A. Pagès, *Un Royaume Hamite au centre de l' Afrique,* Brussels 1933, 164.

Buganda, and they later spread to the rest of the region; in 1880 Emin found that such things as spoons, glasses, and china dishes had become indispensable to the rebel Munyoro chief Mupena. Cotton cloth, which first arrived in Semakokiro's time, became the regular apparel of the Baganda ruling classes. But the trade goods with the most general appeal were brass and copper ornaments; these were within the reach of ordinary folk like the Jopalwo women whose husbands were travelling to Karagwe in the 1860s to purchase brass wire for them.[1] The everyday economy was also affected in some areas by new food crops. Maize was being grown in Buganda by 1862, cassava by 1875, and rice three years later.[2]

Both the Khartoumers and Zanzibaris were chiefly interested in acquiring ivory, which now became for the first time a prominent article of trade. Ivory appears to have been exploited hardly at all until Semakokiro began sending it to Karagwe in exchange for coastal goods. In the early days of Arab penetration, Karagwe seems to have had the highest reputation for ivory; Burton was told at Tabora that the tusks there were 'the whitest and softest, the largest and heaviest in this part of Central Africa'. Later, the Zanzibaris relied on supplies from Bunyoro and from outside the interlacustrine region altogether. Something of the scope of this trade is conveyed by Emin's comment in 1883: 'Ivory is still the chief export of the equatorial countries for hitherto scarcely any attention has been paid to many other products.'[3]

The only other export of note was slaves. The interlacustrine region was not nearly as badly affected by this menace as other parts of tropical Africa. Even the Khartoumers were not so blameworthy as some English contemporaries supposed. The Zanzibaris were often interested in taking female slaves: Emin reported that all caravans travelling south from Bunyoro and Buganda were well supplied, especially with the much-prized BaHima girls. But the implication is that slavery was not the main business of these caravans, and the small proportions of the trade are indicated by Ahmed bin Ibrahim's statement to Stanley in 1876 that he had one hundred slaves at Kafuro: for a man who after twelve years in Karagwe was doyen of the Arab com-

[1] Schweinfurth (1888), 284; Kagwa, *Basekabaka* in Kiwanuka (1965), 341; Grant (1864), 307–8.

[2] Grant (1864), 237; Stanley (1878), I, 383; Schweinfurth (1888), 86.

[3] Kiwanuka (1965), 343; Burton (1860), II, 184; Schweinfurth (1888), 117. For the nineteenth-century ivory trade, see R. W. Beachey, 'East African Ivory Trade in the nineteenth century', *J. African Hist.*, 8 (1967), 269–90.

munity there, this number seems modest enough. There was, in short, no serious drain on the human resources of the region.[1]

The passage of goods to and from the coast did not remain exclusively in Arab hands. In 1870 Mutesa of Buganda sent a trading mission with ivory and a young elephant to Zanzibar; it returned two years later with firearms, gunpowder, soap, and spirits; other expeditions followed in 1877, 1879, and 1882.[2] But this initiative was not emulated by other rulers. Africans could make profits just as easily by organizing the local distribution of luxury goods. The network of distribution was certainly far-flung; as early as 1851 the Pari in the heart of the southern Sudan were receiving a trickle of trade goods from Acholiland which derived ultimately from Zanzibar. Equally, the ivory taken to the coast was collected in the first instance by Africans. In Bunyoro a class of professional elephant-hunters emerged. Admittedly, some of the ivory was acquired by plunder, particularly by the Baganda who had little of their own. But much of it was obtained by normal commercial means. Banyoro caravans used to barter for ivory among the Acholi, and the Lango and Iteso relied to some degree on ivory in order to purchase ironware from the Banyoro. Sometimes distribution and collection were parts of the same process; in the early eighties the Acholi were supplying Mutesa with ivory in exchange for brass, using Kabarega's rival, Rionga, as middleman.[3]

However, the most effective way in which the Arabs invigorated indigenous trade was by the introduction of a convenient currency in the form of cowrie-shells. Cowries arrived in Buganda along with the earliest long-distance trade goods; Semakokiro was said to have acquired considerable quantities, but their number was probably fairly limited until the coastmen themselves began coming regularly. Grant came away from Bunyoro in 1862 with the belief that 'cowries were the chief coin of the country', and he quoted prices for spear-heads and flour. But it is difficult to tell how soon cowries were accepted as currency strictly speaking, since they had an ornamental value and probably fitted into a barter system for many years. This indeed is the impression given by this passage from Baker, recording his experience in Bunyoro in 1864:

[1] R. Gray, *History of the Southern Sudan 1839–89*, Oxford, 1961; Schweinfurth (1888), 116–17; Stanley (1878), I, 453.

[2] D. Livingstone, *Last Journals*, 2 vols., London, 1874, II, 176; Rowe (1966), 210.

[3] R. Gray (1961), 38, 146; Roscoe, *The Bakitara*, London, 1923, 315; Schweinfurth (1888), 278; Lawrance (1957), 19.

Every morning shortly after sunrise, men might be heard crying their wares throughout the camp—such as, 'Tobacco, tobacco; two packets for either beads or simbis!' (cowrie shells). 'Milk to sell for beads or salt!' 'Salt to exchange for lance-heads!' . . .

The fullest and probably most reliable description of cowrie currency is Emin's of 1883. He tells us that in Buganda cowries were widely current and even the smallest transactions could be made with them—salt, indeed, could only be bought with cowries. But in Bunyoro, according to Emin, the majority of the people stuck to barter even after the Zanzibaris arrived. A few years later, Casati, after his long detention in Bunyoro, was more positive about the impact of cowries there. 'The merchants of Zanzibar', he wrote, 'have greatly contributed to develop the commercial tendencies of the natives, and the introduction of cowries has facilitated and extended business.' Casati's observations carry less weight than Emin's, but they do suggest that on the eve of the colonial era Bunyoro was in this respect beginning to follow the same path as Buganda.[1]

It is doubtful whether the bigger volume of trade caused a major improvement in the general standard of life. This is because such a large proportion of the trade was in the hands of the rulers, who squandered their resources on firearms. In particular, the ivory trade was generally a royal monopoly. In Buganda, Ankole, and Bunyoro, the king retained one tusk in every pair collected and had purchasing rights to the remainder; only the Mukama of Karagwe seems not to have availed himself of this privilege. In Bunyoro, in Baker's day, 'no trade could be carried on with the natives, all business being prohibited by Kamrasi, who himself monopolized the profits'; Kabarega forbade on pain of death the free trade in ivory which Baker so earnestly desired, and he dealt directly with the Lango who came to his court to trade ivory.[2] In Buganda there was something of a commercial bureaucracy. The Kabaka had his own ivory-hunters who were paid in cattle and women. Certain chiefs had special responsibilities for collecting the royal ivory and were issued with guns for the purpose; Semei Kakungulu began his career in one such post in Buddu. Yet the monopoly needed tight control at the centre; in his last years Mutesa's

[1] Kagwa, *Basekabaka*, in Kiwanuka (1965), 341; Grant (1864), 271, 295; Baker (1866), II, 182; Schweinfurth (1888), 114–16, 122; Casati (1891), II, 56.

[2] Beachey (1967), 275; Grant (1864), 159; Baker (1866), II, 248; Baker (1874), II, 251–2; Schweinfurth (1888), 113.

grip on affairs was weakened by illness, and his chiefs took to trading ivory on their own account in exchange for firearms and fine clothes.[1]

The full political repercussions of the growth in trade lie outside the scope of the present study, which has been mainly concerned with economic life. The picture here presented can hardly be a balanced once, since the total volume of evidence is so small and so taken up by Bunyoro and Buganda at the expense of the other kingdoms. The European accounts describe, in effect, an indigenous commercial network closely related to subsistence needs but overlaid by the effects of long-distance trade. The history of nineteenth-century interlacustrine commerce mainly concerns the interaction between these two elements. On the one hand, the Africans provided the infrastructure on which the Arabs relied for the collection and distribution of merchandise; on the other hand, the Arabs with their more advanced economic system expanded the traditional avenues of trade. The resultant commercial structure was still very elementary, and it is easy to dismiss it as irrelevant to the future development of the Uganda economy. Yet in Buganda, where substantial inroads had been made into the subsistence pattern, two growing-points can be identified. In the first place, the professional ivory-hunters, although exploiting a diminishing asset, were nevertheless specialists who were perhaps more likely to take up other entrepreneurial activities than to return to subsistence farming. Still more important, among the Baganda chiefs and their dependants the taste for imported luxuries was by the end of the century sufficiently developed to stimulate new forms of production when the ivory trade declined; the initiative for the peasant cultivation of cotton after 1904 came to a large extent from the Baganda themselves.[2] The Arab influx and the subsequent European intervention were obviously turning-points in the economic history of the northern interlacustrine region. But the active participation of Africans themselves should not be ignored. It provided far more than a colourful 'native' back-cloth to the activities of Arabs, Europeans, and Asians.

[1] Roscoe (1911), 447; M. J. Twaddle, 'Politics in Bukedi 1900–1939', London Ph.D. thesis (1967), 81; Rowe (1966), 152.

[2] Wrigley (1959), 14–18. See also, A. T. Matson, 'Baganda Merchant Venturers', *Uganda Journal*, 32, 1968, 1–15, for the Baganda attempt to enter the coastal caravan trade in 1898–9.

6

Southern Ethiopia

M. ABIR

Ethiopia's traditional exports, gold, ivory, precious skins, spices, and incense, were known to the people of the Mediterranean civilization from ancient times. Some of the earliest expeditions sent by the Pharaohs southwards are thought to have gone to Ethiopia, and colonies of foreign merchants, Greek, Egyptian, Arab, and possibly Indian, are known to have existed on the Ethiopian coast as early as the first millennium B.C. As most of Ethiopia's luxury products came from the southern and western parts of the plateau, the caravan trade between these areas and the north of Ethiopia must have been developed at an early date. To some extent the growth and development of Axum and its sister city-states in northern Ethiopia are attributable to their having been centres of caravan trade and to their domination of the most important routes connecting the coast and the interior.

The trading activity of Axum, and its contact with the outside world, were probably responsible for the early coining of money in northern Ethiopia. But even more important for the commercial development of the country was the early use of blocks of salt (*Amoleh*) as currency which had a far wider circulation in the plateau than coined money.[1] The use of salt as currency was a common phenomenon in Africa and can be explained by a general scarcity of salt which also affected the Ethiopian plateau. The coastal salt-plains of northern Ethiopia were probably therefore an important asset to the people of Axum and helped to foster their commercial activity and sponsor caravan trade with the interior.

The early Muslim trading towns and principalities on the western

[1] (ed.) J. W. McCrindle, *The Christian Topography of Cosmas*, London, 1929, 52–4. Also M. Abir, 'Salt, Trade and Politics in Ethiopia in the "Zamana Masafint"', *J. Ethiopian Studies*, IV, 1966.

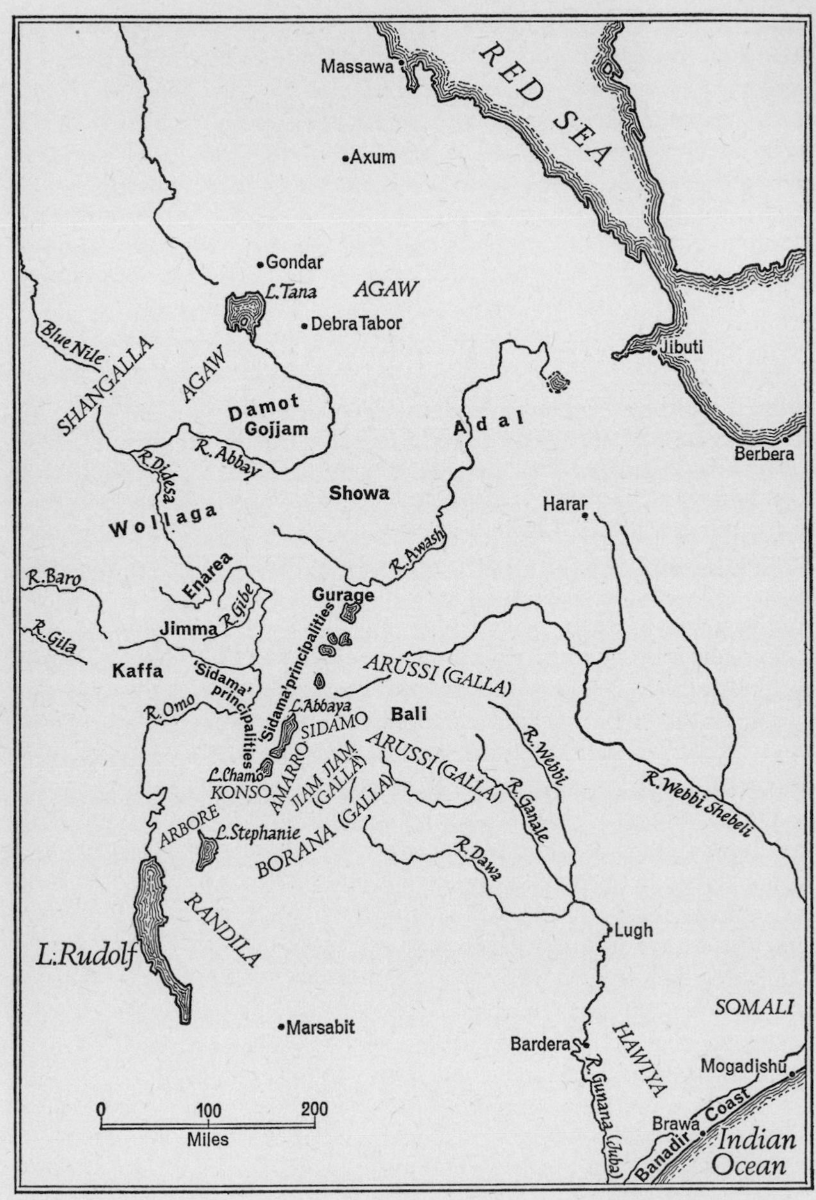

Map 7. Southern Ethiopia

coast of the Red Sea and in the Gulf of Aden began to expand along the Harar plateau at the end of the first millennium A.D. This expansion was probably in part an attempt by the Muslim coastal communities to open a new route by which to tap the rich trade of the south and bypass the Christian north which was sinking into chaos. By the beginning of the second millennium A.D. this expansion of Islam, described by the geographers, travellers, and historians, had led to the founding of Muslim sultanates among the Kushitic peoples of the southern plateau. Although a lively trade clearly existed between these sultanates and the coast,[1] the Muslim scholars throw but a meagre light on its extent, organization, and character.

In the twelfth and thirteenth centuries, after the fall of the Axumite empire, northern Ethiopia was ruled by the Zagwe dynasty. This Kushitic dynasty left the central and southern plateaux undisturbed and concentrated its efforts on uniting the northern parts of the country, but the new Solomonic dynasty, which came to power about 1270, was to some extent based on the central plateau and was far more aggressive in its external relations, especially regarding the rich south. From the thirteenth to the sixteenth century the Solomonic emperors defeated and gradually annexed the Muslim and pagan Kushitic sultanates and principalities, and the authority of the King of Kings was extended as far as Lake Abbaya (Margherita) to the south and beyond Enarea to the south-west.

Although Christian Ethiopia had succeeded in conquering most of the southern parts of the plateau and had defeated time and again the important Muslim sultanate of Adal, it seems that caravan trade on the plateau remained to a large extent in the hands of the Muslim elements.[2] Echoes of the commercial activities of this period reach us through the writings of the Portuguese, and we even hear of large caravans from one part of the plateau to another. If the caravan trade was not more extensive than it appears to have been, this was due not to lack of demand for Ethiopia's luxury products and slaves but to the continuous wars and the insecurity of travelling over the plateau.[3] *Amoleh* salt money, mined in the salt-plains on the coast of northern

[1] See for example Abū'l Fidā, *Kitāb Taqwīm al-Buldān*, Dresden, 1846, 283, quoting Ibn Saīd regarding the exportation of slaves.

[2] C. F. Beckingham and G. W. B. Huntingford, *The Prester John of the Indies*, Hakluyt Society, Cambridge, 1961, II, Ch. CXXIV.

[3] Beckingham and Huntingford (1961), I, 193; C. F. Beckingham and G. W. B. Huntingford, *Some Records of Ethiopia*, Hakluyt Society, London, 1954; Manoel de Almeida, *The History of High Ethiopia or Abassia*, S.O.A.S. Library MS., 146.

Ethiopia, was in use over large parts of the plateau as far as the kingdom of Damot in the south-west. In the more northerly Sidama[1] principalities *amoleh* salt and pieces of iron served as currency also, but barter was more common. In the more remote regions trade was only by barter, and gold, for instance, was exchanged against cattle, beads, and other imported goods. The kingdom of Enarea, in the Kushitic south-west, appears to have been the key to the trade of the whole region at this time, since it was not only a producer of luxury goods but was also situated in a most advantageous position *vis à vis* the other producing areas of the south and west.[2]

The period of northern colonization came to an end in the second quarter of the sixteenth century when the south was swept by a *jihād* led by *Imām* Ahmad Grañ. Grañ's forces, composed mainly of Somali and Afar nomads, had no qualms about sacking and burning the rich agricultural areas which they overran; the economy of the Sidama countries, and their caravan trade, were completely disrupted.[3] This disruption was followed by the final death-blow to the close commercial and cultural contacts between the people of the south and the people of northern Ethiopia which the Galla invasion dealt to the country.

Throughout the sixteenth and seventeenth centuries the Galla succeeded in overrunning many parts of the central plateau. The rich south-western regions of Ethiopia were gradually penetrated, and by the beginning of the eighteenth century the kingdom of Enarea was also conquered. The Galla pastoralists were not used to trade, and in any case the situation of chaos and insecurity which prevailed was not conducive to commerce. It would be incorrect, however, to think that commercial activities on the Ethiopian plateau stopped altogether. Salt was always needed for human consumption and for cattle-rearing, and, as it was not available from local sources, it was probably brought to the Galla areas to be exchanged against gold, ivory, incense, and slaves, which were always in demand on the coast. Such trade might

[1] Beckingham and Huntingford (1961), I, 179–82; de Almeida, 44–5. The term Sidama, a general name in use for most of the Kushitic peoples of the southern plateau, is questionable, but will be used nevertheless in this chapter for the sake of convenience. However, one must differentiate between Sidama and Sidamo, the latter being the name of one tribe. The term Sidama lakes will be also used for the sake of convenience and indicates the chain of lakes in the rift valley in the southern parts of the Ethiopian plateau.

[2] de Almeida, 42, 146, 149–50.

[3] For a contemporary work describing the *jihād* see Shihab ad-Din, *Futūh al-Habasha*, ed. René Basset, Paris, 1897–1901.

have been conducted as was that between the Agaw and Shangalla described by Bruce:[1] 'The way this trade, though much limited, is established, is by two nations sending their children mutually to each other; there is then peace between those two families which have such hostages; these children often intermarry; after which that family is considered to be protected, and at peace. . . .' However, Bruce adds that such cases were very rare because the natural tendency of the people was to raid each other.[2] It is not surprising therefore that reports on the trade of the Red Sea in the second half of the eighteenth century dismiss the trade of the Ethiopian coast as negligible.[3]

By the second decade of the nineteenth century it seems that the trade of Ethiopia had begun to revive and merchant caravans were pushing again further into the interior in search of the luxury products which were highly in demand on the coast. As in the past, trade in Ethiopia, especially caravan trade, was practically monopolized by the Muslim Ethiopians (Jabartis) and their co-religionists from neighbouring countries. Amhara and Tigre Christian society had always looked down on commercial activities and crafts. Moreover, as a result of the unceasing wars, slaves were the commodity most available in the Galla and Sidama areas, whereas gold, musk, and ivory were scarce. At the same time the demand for Ethiopian slaves, especially young females, in the markets of Arabia had grown by leaps and bounds as a result of the revival of the *Hajj*, coupled with British interference with the slave trade in East Africa. Thus Christian merchants, forbidden to deal in slaves, had no hope of competing with the Jabartis in the markets of the interior, while on the coast they were also at a disadvantage as the Muslim authorities and Muslim merchants gave preference to their co-religionists.

On the central plateau the rulers of the new kingdom of Showa had brought within the borders of the kingdom, since the end of the eighteenth century, some of the most important caravan routes and markets connected with the trade of the south. Consequently they tried to attract caravan trade to their country. Besides the security to body and property which existed in their dominions, the rulers of Showa gave special treatment to foreign merchants visiting their country. At

[1] J. Bruce, *Travels to Discover the Sources of the Nile*, London, 1790, III, 737.

[2] Amha Yesus to Bruce regarding the decline of the trade of Showa with the coast as a result of the Galla overrunning the intermediate countries: Bruce (1790), IV, 98.

[3] India Office Archives, Marine Miscellaneous, Vol. 891, report from 15.8.1790; I.O.A., Factory Records, Egypt and Red Sea, Vol. VI, No. 393, 'A sketch', etc.; ibid., Murray report from 6.10.1799.

the same time, however, merchants from the north, from Harar and from the coast, were not permitted to advance beyond certain markets of the kingdom,[1] which were supplied by Galla and Sidama merchants coming from the south and south-west; these latter traders never themselves travelled to the coast. By this arrangement the rulers of Showa in the nineteenth century succeeded in turning their country into an important trading centre and greatly multiplied their revenue from trade. With this revenue, and with firearms acquired from the merchants, the rulers of Showa strengthened their country until it became the centre of the new Ethiopian empire in the last quarter of the nineteenth century. Indirectly the rulers of Showa thus fostered not only the development of caravan trade between the Sidama and Galla principalities and the markets of Showa, but also the growth of a Galla and Sidama merchant class in the southern parts of the plateau.

In south-western Ethiopia itself, however, the situation regarding the caravan trade was quite different. At the beginning of the nineteenth century this area was divided up among numerous Galla and Sidama principalities and tribes, with varying attitudes towards trade, caravans, and foreign merchants. The pastoral Galla tribes, who were gradually becoming agriculturalists, were still not accustomed to trade and looked with great suspicion upon the passage of trading caravans through their countries. If caravans were allowed to cross Galla territories at all, it was because the Galla coveted the goods carried by the caravan merchants. The lack of central authority among the Galla tribes, together with the chaos and continuous wars in their areas, were a great hindrance to the redevelopment of caravan trade in the richest parts of the plateau. The passage of caravans through Galla territories necessitated infinite patience and long months of haggling over presents which were to be given to different protectors (*mogassa* or *gofta*) and to the different clans along the route. Even then it was not unusual that a whole caravan would be wiped out without apparent reason.[2] Because of this insecurity, only the most daring entrepreneurs at first joined the small caravans which penetrated the Galla areas; the profits

[1] Each group of merchants was allotted a village in which the merchants were to live while in Showa. Sir W. C. Harris, *The Highlands of Aethiopia*, London, 1844, I, 484; C. Johnston, *Travels in Southern Abyssinia*, London, 1844, II, 18–19; India Office Archives, Bombay Secret Proceedings, Lantern Gallery, Vol. 185, No. 1440, Barker, 7.1.1842.

[2] Describing the complete chaos and insecurity in Wollaga, a native merchant told the traveller Antoine d'Abbadie in 1843 that the situation resembled that of Enarea at the beginning of the nineteenth century: Bibliothèque Nationale, Paris, Catalogue France Nouvelle Acquisition, no. 21303, 344, para. 166; see also 314, para. 302, December 1845.

were so great, however, that the number of Jabartis involved in the south-west trade grew from year to year.

By the beginning of the nineteenth century Galla monarchies began to emerge in the area between the Didesa and the Gibe, the source of most of Ethiopia's luxury produce. The emergence of these monarchies was undoubtedly the culmination of a long and complex social process;[1] it is surely significant, however, that the Galla turned from a democratic social organization to absolute monarchy in precisely the area which was most crucial to the trade of Ethiopia, and did so, moreover, at the moment when the demand for Ethiopian products was greater than ever before and when increasing numbers of Jabarti merchants were reappearing in the area. The evidence shows that foreign merchants were on the whole well treated in the Galla monarchies. Some rulers went out of their way to attract merchants, and it was not long before merchant villages (*mander*) sprang up near the most important market-places in south-western Ethiopia. From centres such as Bonga in Kaffa, Sakka in Enarea, and Jiren in Jimma, the caravan merchants tapped the trade of the whole region.

The presence of foreign merchants in the Galla countries of the south-west and, even more so, in the markets of the Amhara areas bordering on the Galla countries, enhanced the demand for the products of the south, and, as was only to be expected, intensified the production and collection of luxury trade items. Many more people, most of them slaves, were employed panning gold from rivers in the gold-producing areas. The hunting of elephants, which in the past was just an act of bravery, became more and more of a profession (especially with the introduction of firearms).[2] The ivory, which in some remote districts had been left to rot, was now carefully collected. Plants such as coffee and coriander which grew wild in some areas, were now cultivated and their fruits sold to the passing merchants. The musk of the civet cat, which had been gathered sporadically from among the rocks inhabited by the civet cats, now became the basis for an 'industry'. Hunters captured male cats for growers who set up civet cat farms. In these farms the cats were kept in specially constructed cages, with attendants who fed them and milked them daily by a special method

[1] M. Abir, 'The Emergence and Consolidation of the Monarchies of Enarea and Jimma in the First Half of the Nineteenth Century', *J. African Hist.*, VI, 2 (1965).

[2] Abbadie, F.N.A. 21300, 638; 21303, 364; C. T. Beke, *On the Countries South of Abyssinia*, London, 1843, 12; M. G. Lejean, 'Note sur le royaume de Koullo', *Bull. Société de Géographie*, Paris, 5th series, 8, 1864, 390; E. Cecchi, *Da Zaila alle frontiere del Caffa*, Rome, 1885, II, 516, 556–7.

which yielded a few drops of precious musk.[1] This growth of trade had the blessing of the local rulers, and some of them participated in the profits by declaring gold, ivory, and other products a royal monopoly, and by being the owners of large plantations of coffee, coriander, and other agricultural products.

As a result of their growing revenue from trade and other sources, Galla rulers began to accumulate wealth in kind and in *amoleh*.[2] To some extent this wealth was used to foster relations with neighbours, with local dignitaries, and with famous warriors. It also helped to pay for the upkeep of a small standing army and a handful of northern gunmen who were the pride of each ruler. Most of all, however, the newly acquired wealth was used for the enlargement and embellishment of the rulers' courts and palaces, and it was not long before the different *mander* developed groups of craftsmen employed in most cases by the rulers and producing goods for them.[3] As a Galla monarch became more dependent on his income from trade and more addicted to foreign fineries, he realized the importance of maintaining his country as a centre of trade and of preventing its benefit from going to his enemies. Galla kings consequently forbade foreign merchants from advancing beyond their countries, as did some Sidama rulers.[4]

Another most significant outcome of the growing demand for the produce of the south was the emergence of a Galla merchant-class called *Afkala*. The *Afkala* were in many cases ex-slaves or ex-servants of northern merchants; but they also comprised younger sons who did not share the inheritance of their fathers 'according to custom in the Galla and Sidama areas'.[5] Probably these 'younger sons' had been born after their fathers had completed the full cycle of five *Gada* (40 years) in which the Galla were organized in each tribe. Such offspring found themselves in the awkward position of being left out of the traditional tribal organization, because, according to custom, only sons who were born while their father was an active member of a *Gada*, could them-

[1] (ed.) N. N. Halls, *The Life and Adventures of Nathaniel Pearce*, London, 1831, II, 9; Abbadie, F.N.A. 21300, 642; Cecchi (1886), II, 515–16, and G. Massaia, *In Abissinia e fra i Galla*, Milan, 1880, 230, for the musk industry in Enarea and Kaffa.

[2] Abbadie, F.N.A. 21300, 797; Cecchi (1886), II, 182—regarding old *amoleh* in Enarea's treasury.

[3] Cecchi (1886), II, 527—Abba Mizan responsible for royal workshops; Beke (1843), 6; Abbadie, F.N.A. 21300, 637; 21303, 365, para. 191.

[4] P. V. Ferret and J. G. Galinier, *Voyage en Abyssinie*, Paris, 1847, II, 243; Abbadie, F.N.A. 21300, 797–8, April 1848; Beke (1843), 13.

[5] Abbadie, F.N.A. 21300, 633.

selves be initiated into the first *Gada*. These pariahs of each Galla tribe were, therefore, probably the first to turn to trade.

Although in most cases the capital of the *Afkala* merchants was quite limited, their most important asset was that they belonged to the country and had relatives or other connections in the surrounding areas. They could travel swiftly from one place to another and reach the remotest markets. While travelling they stayed with their kinsmen and were protected by them. As their expenses were minimal they did not mind going out of their way to buy merchandise whose quality and quantity would not interest the Jabarti merchants.[1] In fact the limited scale of their commerce enabled the *Afkala* to terminate their affairs quickly in each market and, when they exhausted their stock of goods, to travel swiftly to one of the main commercial centres of the south or to the markets on the verges of the Amhara areas.[2] Whereas Jabarti merchants could only undertake one trip to the south-western markets each season, or if they brought a large quantity of goods, might even take two or three seasons to dispose of their merchandise,[3] the *Afkala* could travel several times a year to the northern markets and back.

It was not long before the Jabarti merchants began to feel the competition of the *Afkala* and were obliged to limit their activities to the more important trading centres in the south-west.[4] It seems that by the middle of the nineteenth century a majority of the caravans travelling between the southern markets and the markets on the verges of the Amhara areas, although not necessarily the most important ones, were organized by *Afkala* merchants.[5] Nevertheless much of the larger-scale trade was still conducted by the Jabartis, some of whom settled in most important commercial centres in the south-west.

While foreign caravan merchants were generally welcomed in most of the Galla kingdoms and principalities, this was not so in the Sidama principalities of southern Ethiopia. Even after the Sidama were severed from the north by the Galla migration, commercial activities and caravan trade on a limited scale probably continued between the Sidama areas and Harar, between the Sidama principalities themselves,

[1] Massaia (1880), 227–8. [2] Abbadie, F.N.A. 21300, 357–8.

[3] Cf. the case of Omar Baduri who came from the coast to Jimma with 20 loaded mules, worth in Gondar about 1,000 thallers, and who was obliged to stay for two years in the south-west before he disposed of all his stock: A. d' Abbadie, *Athenaeum*, 1848, 1105.

[4] A. d' Abbadie, *Géographie de l'Éthiopie*, Paris, 1890, 9; id., F.N.A. 21300, 357–8, 386.

[5] According to Abbadie (F.N.A. 21300, 179), the caravan with which he travelled to Enarea in 1843 was made up mainly of Galla merchants. See also C. T. Beke, *Letters on the Commerce and Politics of Abyssinia*, London, 1852, 7, 16; P. Matteucci, *In Abissinia*, Milan, 1880, 263–4.

and possibly even with the non-Kushitic areas to the south and south-west. When trade with the north was reopened in the nineteenth century, the Sidama merchants had no intention of surrendering their trade to the newcomers from the north. In this they were helped by the rulers of Showa and some Galla principalities, who prohibited foreign merchants from penetrating beyond their countries.[1] Even as late as the third quarter of the nineteenth century it seems that the north Ethiopian caravan system did not extend its direct activities much beyond Showa and the upper reaches of the Omo river, and this was roughly also the southern limit of *amoleh* salt-money diffusion in Ethiopia until about the last quarter of the nineteenth century.

European travellers who visited central Ethiopia until the 1870s were, therefore, not able to gather much information about the Sidama principalities from the Jabarti merchants whom they interrogated. However, the Jabarti and Galla merchants who visited the markets of the central plateau reported that the areas beyond those in which they themselves operated were visited by what appeared to be another set of foreign merchants. In some cases it was said that they came from the general direction of the Sudan and in other cases from that of the Indian Ocean. In most cases they were said to have come in boats along navigable rivers. The scholar Charles Beke, who visited Showa and Gojjam in the 1840s and who collected information from Jabarti merchants active in the trade of southern Ethiopia, became convinced that there was a direct commercial contact between southern Ethiopia and the Indian Ocean.[2] His conviction was based mainly on the fact that the salt powder in use in the far south was said to come from the shores of the great sea of the Banians. Similar rumours also reached the ears of Antoine d'Abbadie, who penetrated to Enarea and Kaffa in the 1840s. Other Europeans were convinced that the upper reaches of the Omo were in fact the upper reaches of the Juba (Webi Gunana), and that Somali merchants were using this waterway to trade with southern Ethiopia.[3] This belief was further strengthened by information about the extent of Somali trading activities, publicized about the middle of

[1] Abbadie, F.N.A. 21300, 366; 21303, 342, para. 164; Beke (1843), 13. The direct Harari trade with the Sidama and Galla markets had been stopped by the nineteenth century, as a result of disturbances around Harar and the expansion of the kingdom of Showa. See M. Abir, *Ethiopia: The Era of the Princes*, London, 1968, Ch. 1.

[2] Beke (1843), 11.

[3] Abbadie, F.N.A. 21303, 247, para. 96; Léon des Avanchères, *Bull. Société de Géographie*, 1866, 169; L. Krapf, *Travels and Missionary Labours in East Africa*, London, 1860, 56; India Office, Bombay Secret Proceedings, Lantern Gallery, 206, 1612, Harris, 5.5.1843.

the nineteenth century by Europeans who visited the East African coast.

Very little was known of Somali caravan trade until this period. Somali and Arab merchants in the Banadir towns apparently did not record their experiences, and the Portuguese, who failed to get a foothold on the Somali coast, hardly mention it in their books. True, the Jesuits, when trying to reach Ethiopia in the sixteenth century, were told in Goa, presumably by local merchants, of the existence of commercial contacts between the Banadir coast and southern Ethiopia. However, this information proved to be false when two of the Jesuit fathers actually tried to penetrate Ethiopia from this direction.[1] It is possible that such commercial contacts did exist before the *jihād* of Ahmad Grañ when the kingdom of Hadya stretched, it was said, as far as Mogadishu. However, those connections, if they ever existed, were completely disrupted by the Galla invasion of Ethiopia.[2]

About the middle of the nineteenth century, European missionaries, travellers, and government agents heard that merchants from the Banadir coast, especially from Brawa and Mogadishu, together with Somali tribesmen from the interior, were actively engaged in long-range caravan trade with present-day northern Kenya and southern Ethiopia.[3] In the 1840s Commandant Guillain obtained information from some Banadir merchants regarding the peoples and the countries of the interior including the Randile, the Borana, the Amarro and Konso (the last two near Lake Chamo) of the provinces of Bali and Gurage, and possibly even the Kere on the lower Omo. Léon des Avanchères, a Catholic missionary in the 1850s, collected information in the Banadir towns regarding a vast area in the interior. He was even given details of a trade-route which allegedly existed between the coast and Kaffa in south-western Ethiopia.[4] Charles New, another European missionary, heard from dismayed Zanzibari merchants who reached Reya near Marsabit in northern Kenya about 1870, that the whole region as far as Lake Rudolf had been for some time

[1] Jerome Lobo, *A Voyage to Abyssinia*, London, 1789, 29–31; Beckingham and Huntingford (1954), 191–3.

[2] Beckingham and Huntingford (1961), II, 452–4; Lord Stanley of Alderley (tr.), *Purchas His Pilgrims*, Glasgow, 1905, VII, 360; Bruce (1790), IV, 98.

[3] India Office, Lantern Gallery (L.G.), 209, 2336, Christopher, 8.5.1843; Krapf (1860), 112; C. New, *Life, Wanderings, and Labours in East Africa*, London, 1847, 460; R. F. Burton *Zanzibar, City, Island and Coast*, London, 1872, II, 45–6; C. Guillain, *Documents sur l'histoire, la géographie*, etc., Paris, 1856, II, 173, 175–6; Léon des Avenchères, *B.S.G.*, letters from 1857 and 1858.

[4] Guillain (1856), II, 534, 537; id., III, 45, 51, 53; Avanchères, *B.S.G.*, 17, from 1859.

frequented by Somali caravans which were said to come from Brawa.[1]

It is not surprising, therefore, that James Christie traced the cholera epidemic which broke out on the East African coast in October 1869 to an outbreak reported in Debra Tabor in July 1866. In arguing his case, Christie assumed that direct and frequent trade connections existed between the Somali and Enarea in south-western Ethiopia and that the epidemic was brought by Somalis to the Boran area in 1869 and was carried from there by Masai raiders to the coast of East Africa.[2] Christie's theory, however, does not convince. In the first place it is strange that an epidemic would take more than three years to cross from Ethiopia to the East African coast if extensive caravan relations did exist between south-western Ethiopia and the Somali coast. Moreover, it seems that Christie was ignorant of some basic facts regarding caravan trade in Ethiopia, such as caravan seasons and routes.[3]

It was in fact the ignorance of the European travellers which led them to believe that the Banadir merchants were engaged in long-distance caravan trade which took them as far as Kaffa and beyond Lake Rudolf. It was not difficult to accept such ideas as true in view of the success of the Zanzibari trading system in penetrating the African interior from the coast to beyond Lake Tanganyika. Indeed, the presence of Somali merchants in Bali, and as far as the borders of the country of the Arussi Galla and in present-day northern Kenya, is reported by various sources. But the same sources stress that the Somali merchants were prevented by the Borana from penetrating beyond their country and that the Arbore, Konso, Arussi, and 'Jiam Jiams' were opposed altogether to their penetrating their country.[4]

The trading activities of the Banadir coast probably resembled what might have been the situation on some parts of the East African coast in the centuries before the nineteenth. The trade of the coastal towns was fed by relays of indigenous trading systems passing the trade goods

[1] New (1847), 460.

[2] J. Christie, *Cholera Epidemics in East Africa*, London, 1876, 169, 191, 233.

[3] He absurdly says in connection with the trade-route between the Somali and Ethiopia: 'It is indeed in this direction that the pilgrims' route to Massuah lies': ibid., 191; see also 170. It would have been far simpler to assume that the cholera was carried by merchants from one of the Banadir ports to which it was brought by an Indian or Arab boat, as was the case in the past. See Guillain (1856), II, 526.

[4] Avanchères, *B.S.G.*, 4th series, 16, 1858, 362–3; ibid., 1859, 162; L. Vanutelli and C. Citerni, *Seconda espedizione Bottego,* Milan, 1899, 142, 158, 168–9, 199, 214, 355; A. Donaldson Smith, *Through Unknown African Countries*, London, 1897, 177–8, 185, 206, 229; U. Ferrandi, *Lugh, Emporio commerciale sul Giuba*, Rome, 1903, 133, 353; L. von Höhnel, *The Discovery of Lakes Rudolf and Stephanie,* London, 1894, II, 167, 187.

of the far interior from one set of trading people to another until they finally reached the coast. The outstanding difference, however, was that the continuous close contacts between the Somali and the Arabs in the Banadir towns, together with the political hegemony of the Somali tribesmen in the area, gave birth to a more developed trading system among the nomadic Somali tribes of the interior. Centres of trade, which could be considered emporia, emerged at advantageous points along the rivers and the caravan routes in the interior. At such centres as Bardera and Lugh on the Gunana (Juba) caravans were organized to go to different parts of the interior or to the coast and incoming caravans from the interior were met by coastal and local merchants. Somali commerce reached such a sophistication that at Lugh, for example, there was a highly developed system of weights and measures; credit was available, and ways were even formed to bypass the Islamic prohibition on interest. Written contracts were signed between merchants and caravaneers who carried their merchandise into the interior, and the court of the local *Qadi* dealt with commercial disputes.[1] The Sultan and Gasar Gudda aristocracy of Lugh did their best to develop trade in their town. They seldom engaged in the actual caravan trade which was left to the professional caravaneers, but they practically monopolized the compulsory, yet well regulated, system of brokerage which existed in Lugh. Merchants of the Banadir towns did send caravans into the interior, but those caravans usually travelled only as far as the trading centres of the Somali tribesmen in the interior. The coastal merchants travelled from time to time with their caravans and in some cases even settled in places such as Lugh and Bardera. However, this was the exception and in most cases they entrusted their merchandise to their slaves or to a representative (*Wakil*) who was usually a professional caravaneer from among the Somali tribesmen.[2]

The trade of present-day northern Kenya and south-eastern Ethiopia was mainly in the hands of a number of Somali tribes, the most outstanding of which were probably the Gara, who dominated the caravan trade between Lugh and the interior.[3] The Gara absorption in caravan

[1] V. Bottego, *Il Giuba Esplorato*, Rome, 1895, 440; Ferrandi (1903), 345–8. While Lugh was strongly connected with Mogadishu, Bardera had its ties especially with Brawa. Guillain (1856), II, 531–2; Ferrandi (1903), 321; Bottego (1895), 479–80.

[2] Ferrandi (1903), 26, 341, 343, 351; Bottego (1895), 348, 389–92; Guillain (1856), II, 354; ibid., III, 2.

[3] Bottego (1895), 355; Ferrandi (1903), 353–5. See also Ugaden Somali using the services of Lugh's caravaneers: C. J. Cruttenden, *Memoir of the Western Edour Tribes*, Bombay, 1848, 198.

trade, as was the case with some Hawiya and other Somali groups, could probably be attributed to the fact that Gara groups lived all the way from the Banadir coast to the upper reaches of the Gunana and the Shebeli while Gara families lived among, and intermarried with, other Somali and Galla tribes.[1] It is thought that Somali penetration of the area between the middle Gunana and Shebeli had not started before the eighteenth century; but by the nineteenth century the Somalis had become the masters of most of the area. The Somali itinerant merchants made good use of their connections, but the extent of their penetration into the interior was determined mainly by the willingness of other people to permit them to go through their countries, and by the availability of water. These factors confined their main area of activity to the upper reaches of the Gunana and the Shebeli, and although the Somali trading sphere touched on southern Ethiopia east and south-east of the Sidama chain of lakes, it was not permitted to expand to the areas west and south-west of those lakes. The indigenous merchants who tapped the trade of southern Ethiopia were too astute to allow Somali competitors to penetrate westwards beyond their countries. Somali itinerant merchants therefore had to wait in Borana country or in Bali for the Borana, Konso, Arbore, and Sidamo merchants who collected ivory and other luxury products from all the area to the west, south, and south-west of the Sidama lakes.[2]

It is clear that overseas trade, especially from Arabia, had a noticeable impact on the Somalis. This was not a momentary affair but a continuous process which had greatly influenced Somali society and culture. On the other hand, the extent of the impact of overseas trade channelled by the Somalis to their Galla neighbours is more difficult to determine. One may safely assume that the Galla tribes in the period immediately following their irruption into the Ethiopian plateau were not engaged in trade above the local barter of basic commodities; but by the nineteenth century there is ample evidence that the Borana Galla served as the link between the Somali caravan system and the trading systems which were then operating in present-day southern Ethiopia, while by the end of the nineteenth century Boran was the commercial lingua franca in Lugh.[3]

[1] Guillain (1856), III, 176–7; Ferrandi (1903), 316; Vte du Bourg de Bozas, *De la Mer Rouge à l'Atlantique*, Paris, 1906, 91–2; Vanutelli and Citerni (1899), 355.

[2] Vanutelli and Citerni (1899), 168–70, 199, 214; Donaldson Smith (1897), 206, 230, 239; Avanchères, *B.S.G.*, 1859, 162–3; Ferrandi (1903), 133, 352–3.

[3] Vanutelli and Citerni (1899), 82.

Initially the Borana, who made use of the salt deposits found in different parts of their country, began to exchange their salt for agricultural and other products of their neighbours. By the nineteenth century Borana salt and natron of soda were sold not only in southern Ethiopia but also on the Banadir coast, where it was used for human consumption and for rearing cattle.[1] Thus probably originated the rumours referred to above, which the European travellers reported from Ethiopia regarding salt coming to southern Ethiopia from the Indian Ocean. At some unknown time the Borana must have also realized the advantageous position of their country in relation to the caravan trade between the Indian Ocean coast and the rich countries of southern Ethiopia. At first they may have merely exacted 'passage dues' from caravans, but later on they began to participate in this trade. This process was probably helped by the special relationships which must have existed for a long time between the Konso, the Amarro, and the Borana.

This special relationship, which still exists between the Borana and the Konso, may well have grown out of the need of the pastoral Borana for the services and products of the Konso, while the Borana for their part protected the Konso, supplied them with the much-needed salt, and diffused the Konso products. Borana tradition claims that in times of famine the Konso would exchange their children for meat and animal products, these children being adopted into Borana society. Many Borana took Konso wives and Konso artisans live among the Borana.[2]

Responding to the increased demand for the produce of southern Ethiopia, which had brought about the intensification of Somali mercantile activity, Borana caravans by the end of the nineteenth century were busy collecting ivory, slaves, and other products from the areas of their neighbours. Moreover, the Borana at this time demanded and received permission to send caravans to Lugh in exchange for permission to Somali caravans to trade in their country.[3]

In contrast to the impact of the Jabartis, it is doubtful if the active

[1] Guillain (1856), III, 172–3; Vanutelli and Citerni (1899), 161, 196, 211–12; Ferrandi (1903), 360; Donaldson Smith (1897), 197 n.1; Abbadie, F.N.A., 21303, 247, para. 96; 345, para. 167; Beke (1843), 11. Natron salt together with tobacco was used as snuff and purgative.

[2] I am indebted to Dr. P. Baxter of Manchester University for some of the above material. See also A. E. von Jensen, *Altvölker Süd-Äthiopiens*, Stuttgart, 1959, 148–9; Vanutelli and Citerni (1899), 196; Donaldson Smith (1897), 230.

[3] Ferrandi (1903), 135, 350.

participation of the Borana in the trade of the interior, a process which had probably started before the nineteenth century, actually produced many noticeable changes in Borana society and way of life beyond the fact that some Borana tribesmen were occasionally occupied in trading ventures of limited scale. It is even more doubtful if the intensification of caravan activity based on the Banadir coast had directly changed the trading patterns and the lives of the different peoples who lived in the heartlands of southern Ethiopia. Somali caravans did not even reach the Sidama lakes area and could not exert therefore any direct influence on the Sidama people and on their Galla neighbours. Moreover, it seems that in the first half of the nineteenth century the trading systems within the Sidama and Galla areas of southern Ethiopia were already more and more oriented to the Jabarti trading system rather than to that of the Somali *Safara*.[1] It is a fact that the Banadir ports never became outlets for Sidama and Galla (excluding Borana) slaves, as were the ports of the Ethiopian coast in the nineteenth century.[2]

As for the area to the extreme south of Ethiopia it escaped to a large extent even the limited social, cultural, and economic impacts of the Christian north or the Muslim coast in their heyday in the Sidama areas. This remote area, where the plateau gradually falls towards the sterile volcanic country around Lake Rudolf, is partly desert, partly savanna, partly swampland, and partly forest and bush country. Here a multitude of small tribes lived until the second half of the nineteenth century in nearly complete isolation and preserved to a large extent their ancient cultures. Some of the people living in the area could be classified as hunters and gatherers, some as primitive agriculturalists, and some as pastoralists. Outstanding exceptions were the Konso, the Amarro, and Burji with their relatively sophisticated material and spiritual culture. These people, the most industrious and interesting peoples on the southern verges of the Ethiopian plateau, had advanced far beyond the level of local subsistence and barter. Their highly developed terrace agriculture produced cereals, cotton, coffee, and tobacco, which supplied all their needs and left surpluses for trade with neighbouring peoples. They were renowned as builders, weavers, and metal-workers. Even recently Konso blacksmiths were still supply-

[1] Abbadie, F.N.A. 21300, 419–20, para. 277, Sakka, September 1845; Cecchi (1886), I, 490, 539; ibid., II, 60; Public Records Office, Foreign Office Abyssinia 1/3, 54, Krapf, 3.7.1840; L.G., 189, 2060 G, paras. 23, 24, Harris, 5.1.1842.

[2] See for instance *Church Missionary Recorder*, Church Missionary Society, London, 1845, letter from Krapf, 25.12.1843.

ing iron utensils and weapons to the Borana and to other peoples in the area, and Konso cloth was preferred by the Borana for ritual wear.[1]

It is only to be expected that an exchange of basic commodities between hunters, agriculturalists, and pastoralists went on in the region from ancient times. There are signs that caravan trade on a limited scale also existed in those remote and extremely poor areas before the nineteenth century. This trade, which was centred around basic commodities such as foodstuffs, domestic animals, salt, and iron, was also accompanied by a limited trade in locally manufactured cloth, iron utensils, ornaments, and weapons, and in very small quantities of imported goods. These included specific types of beads and cloth as well as copper, which were paid for mainly with salt and occasionally with ivory.[2] However, as the needs of the people of the area were very small, most of them being very poor or self-sufficient, the volume of such trade must have been negligible and the contact with the larger caravan systems of neighbouring peoples was minimal. A change of a sort probably occurred some time in the nineteenth century as a result of the intensification of caravan activities among the Somali, Sidama, and Galla. Tribes such as the Arbore, north of Lake Stephanie, who were engaged in caravan trade in the past, now combed the whole area as far as the lower Omo for ivory and other luxury items which were not so much in demand in this area in the past. It appears also that merchants from the Sidama and Galla principalities extended their activities more southwards, even as far as Lake Rudolf, in search of ivory and salt, but it seems that these new contacts had the character of raiding parties rather than trading ventures.[3]

[1] I am indebted to Dr. P. Baxter of Manchester University for this information. Konso cloth was produced from Konso-grown cotton: Bourg de Bozas (1906), 257. For further reading on the area: E. von Haberland, *Galla Süd-Äthiopiens*, Stuttgart, 1963; Jensen (1959); H. von Straube, *Westkuchitische Völker Süd-Äthiopiens*, Stuttgart, 1963; Ernesta Cerruli, *Peoples of South-West Ethiopia and its Borderland*, London, 1956; G. W. B. Huntingford, *The Galla of Ethiopia*, London, 1955.

[2] Avanchères, *B.S.G.*, 5th series, 12, 169–76; M. Lejean, *B.S.G.*, 5th series, 8, 1864, 388–9; Höhnel (1894), II, 157, 167–8, n. 1; Donaldson Smith (1897), 351; W. A. Chanler, *Through Jungle and Desert*, London, 1896, 91–3; Haberland (1963), 141; Jensen (1959), 252–4; A. K. Bulatovich, 'Dall'Abissinia al Lago Rudolfo per il Cafa', *Bull. Società Geografica Italiana*, serie 4, I, 1900, 132.

[3] J. Borelli, *Ethiopie méridionale*, Paris, 1890, 344, 346, 349; Cecchi (1886), II, 516; Vanutelli and Citerni (1899), 323, 328–9; Höhnel (1894), II, 166–7; Abbadie, F.N.A. 21303, 346, para. 190; Avanchères, *B.S.G.*, 1866, 171; Lejean, *B.S.G.*, 5th series, 8, 1864, 390–91.

Thus the course and consequences of caravan trade in southern Ethiopia depended not merely on the fluctuation of external demand but on the response of the local communities and the character of the principal intermediaries. The peoples of the Horn of Africa were exposed to foreign trade from an early date as a result of the nature of the products of their area and its proximity to old-established world trade-routes. The demand created by external trade was, however, insufficient by itself to foster the development of extensive caravan trade into the interior. The growth of local trade and economic specialization was essential for the development of external trade, but although contact with foreign trading systems was sometimes enough to bring major changes to the societies involved, in most cases it only accelerated social and economic processes which had begun earlier. The extent of the influence exerted by the external trading systems depended on the cultural background of the merchants engaged in the caravan trade: the impact of the more sophisticated Jabarti system was far more significant than that of the Somali *Safara*. Yet in both cases the contacts with external trade either intensified the activities of those indigenous elements already engaged in commerce or, where such elements did not exist, led to the emergence of a new class of local merchants. The more profitable the trade of the south became, the more unwilling were its own trading peoples to allow foreign merchants to penetrate into, or beyond, their areas. In Africa as a whole caravan trade was often a vehicle by which Islam was carried into the interior. The fact, therefore, that the spread of Islam in the Horn of Africa in the nineteenth century roughly corresponds with what seems to be the extent of the penetration of the Somali and Jabarti merchants into southern Ethiopia, with a borderline running from Borana in the extreme south, northwards to Bali and Gurage, and from there westwards to the Gibe and to the eastern parts of Kaffa, bears dramatic witness to the initiative and resilience of the local trading communities in the south. Jabarti, Harari, and Somali caravans were too small and too weak to challenge the traders of the Sidama principalities of the Borana, or of other peoples who stood in their way. The *Jalaba* merchants from the Sudan were not permitted to penetrate Ethiopia beyond Gondar and the peripheral areas of present-day north-western Ethiopia until the last decades of the nineteenth century,[1] and the 'Zanzibari' caravans did not reach the northern shores of Lake Rudolf

[1] Abir (1965), 205.

until about 1890. Thus the heartland of southern Ethiopia remained, until the great southward expansion of Amhara in the last decades of the nineteenth century, the watershed between the important caravan systems which operated in the Horn of Africa.[1]

[1] I wish to thank the Friends of the Hebrew University of Jerusalem for their research grant which made possible the writing of this essay.

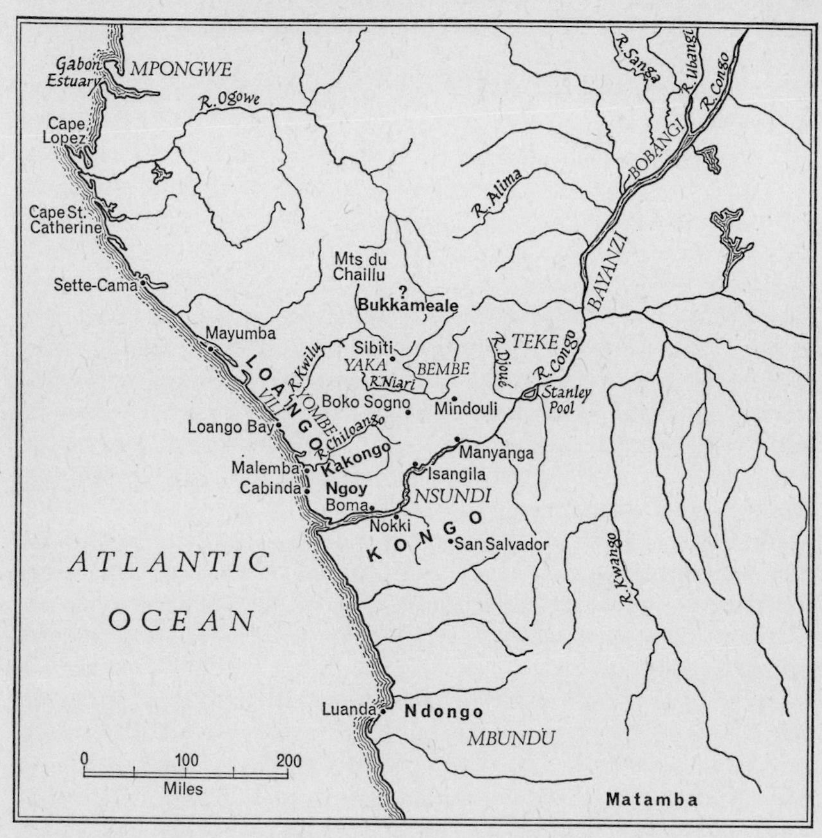

Map 8. West Central Africa

7

The Trade of Loango in the Seventeenth and Eighteenth Centuries

PHYLLIS MARTIN

The Vili of Loango began their first regular trade with the Portuguese in the 1570s. Although Portuguese traders must have visited Loango before this time, they seem to have confined their main activities to the Kongo and Ndongo kingdoms, south of the Congo river. A regular trade was started between Loango and Luanda after the founding of the latter in 1576.[1] Portuguese ships sailed to the Loango coast with cargoes of European manufactured goods—cloths, rugs, mirrors, and beads. These the Vili exchanged for ivory, elephants' tails, palm-cloth, redwood, and skins.[2] These products, together with copper, remained the staple exports of Loango in the first half of the seventeenth century.

Ivory, the most important Portuguese export from Loango, was sent first to Luanda and then to Europe. The trade in the high-quality Vili palm-cloth, redwood, and elephants' tails, was the result of African tastes. In order to obtain slaves from the Mbundu states east of Luanda, local trade goods as well as European products were necessary. Among African products the redwood of Mayumba and the cloth of Loango seem to have been in great demand.[3] Palm-cloth, in particular, was the means used by the Portuguese to pay their soldiers in inland forts such

[1] P. Broecke, *Reisen naar West Afrika (1605–1614)*, ed. K. Ratelband, The Hague, 1950, 66 n.2, 71.

[2] Broecke (1950), 72; A. Battell, *The Strange Adventures of Andrew Battell in Angola and the Adjoining Regions,* ed. E. Ravenstein, London, 1901, 9; F. Pigafetta and D. Lopez, *Description du Royaume de Congo et des Contrées Environnantes (1591)*, ed. W. Bal, Louvain, 1963, 32.

[3] The significance and size of this local trade is made clear by Dutch reports when they occupied Luanda, 1641–8. They quickly discovered the complexities of the trade network which they had inherited from the Portuguese. An early report said that without supplies of palm-cloth and *nzimbu* shells, the slave trade 200–300 miles in the interior could not go on. OWIC, 57, Loango to Brazil, 26.2.1642; 56, Luanda to Brazil, Sept. 1642; 46, Zegers to XIX, 1643. (For abbreviations of sources see p. 161).

as Massangano; there the soldiers were able to exchange the cloths locally for food and supplies.[1] Every year two or three ships were sent from Luanda to Loango to fetch cargoes of 6,000–7,000 pieces of palm-cloth.[2] The main source of supply for the trade in redwood was the two northern provinces of Loango, Sette-Cama and Mayumba. Redwood, called *tacula* by the Portuguese, was in great demand along the whole coast from Cape Saint Catherine to Benguela. For example, it could be exchanged in Ngoyo for palm-cloth, in the Congo river for ivory, or taken to Luanda and exchanged for slaves.[3]

An important extension of Loango's external trading contacts came with the arrival of the Dutch in the area in the closing years of the sixteenth century. In the first decade of the seventeenth century, they set up factories at Loango Bay and at Mayumba, the two principal ports of the kingdom. Dutch traders were also active in the kingdoms of Kakongo and Ngoyo, Loango's southern neighbours on the Atlantic coast north of the Congo river.[4] Whereas Portuguese trade in Loango remained secondary to their interests in Kongo and Angola, Loango became the centre for Dutch interests in West Central Africa.

The Dutch, like the Portuguese, participated in the local trade in palm-cloth and redwood, but their main trade in Loango was in ivory. Pieter van den Broecke, who made three visits to Loango between 1608 and 1612, reckoned that during these years the Dutch alone were exporting 50,000 lbs. of ivory annually. At the same time he was much impressed by the fine red copper that he saw in Loango,[5] although the Dutch do not seem to have discovered the commercial possibilities of exporting Loango copper to Europe until a decade later; by the 1620s copper had become one of Loango's main exports.[6]

These new trade contacts of Loango, starting with the Portuguese in the last decades of the sixteenth century and expanding with the Dutch in the first half of the seventeenth century, brought a great stimulus to the Vili economy. It seems, however, that the trade expansion brought an intensification of the existing trade activities of the Vili, rather than a completely new pattern of trade.

[1] Broecke (1950), 45.

[2] D. Birmingham, *Trade and Conflict in Angola*, Oxford, 1966, 79, cites the report of Pedro Sardinha on the palm-cloth trade in 1611.

[3] Broecke (1950), 72; OWIC, 9, XIX to Luanda, 6.10.1645.

[4] Broecke's journal records the development of these Dutch trading interests.

[5] Broecke (1950), 64, 70.

[6] P. Heyn, *De West Afrikaanse Reis van Piet Heyn, 1624–1625*, ed. K. Ratelband, The Hague, 1959, xcii n.2.

In the first place, Europeans were dealing in Loango products that were already part of traditional commerce and were in local circulation. Andrew Battell, writing towards the end of the sixteenth century, described the market of Buali, the Loango capital, as follows:

... and there is a great market every day, and it doth begin at twelve of the clock. Here there is a great store of palm-cloths of sundry sorts, which is their merchandizes; and a great store of victuals, flesh, hens, wine, oil and corn. Here is also very fine logwood, which they use to dye withall ... and molangos [bracelets] of copper. Here is likewise a great store of elephants' teeth, but they sell none in the market place. ...[1]

Although this account was written some twenty years after regular trade was started by the Portuguese at Loango, it seems reasonable to suppose that such a market flourished before there was much European contact. The palm-cloth industry was essential for clothing and currency. Cloth was traditionally standardized according to quality and pattern and four different varieties could be distinguished.[2] The hairs from elephants' tails and copper rings were much prized as jewelry. Copper was a sign of wealth and Vili women could be seen wearing rings up to fourteen pounds in weight.[3] Ivory was used for personal ornamentation, for musical instruments, for knives at table, and in religious ritual.[4] Redwood was essential in Vili life as a dye and a cosmetic.[5]

Although farming remained the basis of economic activity, the Vili of Loango had clearly developed, by the end of the sixteenth century, a commercial system which had advanced from a subsistence-oriented economy. The first Vili, according to some traditions, were farmers who broke away from other Kongo groups on account of a land shortage in the interior. They passed through the Mayombe region and settled in the coastal plain between the Kwilu and Chiloango rivers. This almost certainly took place in the thirteenth or fourteenth centuries.[6] The growth and consolidation of the Vili kingdom of

[1] Battell (1901), 43–4.

[2] Broecke (1950), 67; O. Dapper, *Naukeurige Beschrijvinge der Afrikaensche Gewesten*, 2nd edn., Amsterdam, 1676, 149.

[3] Broecke (1950), 67, 70; S. Brun, *Samuel Brun's Schiffarten (1624)*, ed. Naber, The Hague, 1913, 12–13.

[4] Battell (1901), 47, 51; Brun (1913), 12; Dapper (1676), 151.

[5] Brun (1913), 22; Dapper (1676), 155, 200.

[6] Some of the traditions concerning the origins of the Vili of Loango have been published by the following: R. Lethur, *Étude sur le Royaume de Loango et le Peuple Vili*, Pointe-Noire, 1952, also published as *Les Cahiers Ngonge*, II, Lovanium, 1960, 21–2; K. Laman,

Loango which had taken place by the sixteenth century, must have been accompanied by considerable economic expansion and specialization. This specialization seems to have been possible both in terms of regional production and in terms of occupation. Certain Loango provinces were famous for their special products and the description of Buali market suggests that some form of organization had developed to allow the transport and exchange of products at central markets—redwood and ivory from Sette-Cama and Mayumba, palm-oil from Loangomongo (a province probably situated in the Mayombe foothills), fish and salt from the coastal province of Loangeri.[1] At the same time copper was imported from beyond Loango's boundaries and salt was carried to the interior. Specialized occupations such as those of palm-cloth weavers and coppersmiths were highly respected.[2]

The development of a palm-cloth currency also seems indicative of an economy of some sophistication. P. Bohannan suggests that money may be the most important single item in the changing of an economy. A general-purpose money, such as the Loango palm-cloth, might do at least three things. It could be a method of evaluating and comparing goods of different kinds; in the Loango context, by the end of the sixteenth century, these goods would include copper, ivory, and redwood as well as salt and the produce of farming, hunting, and fishing. It could be a means of payment; this factor would be increasingly important in an economy where there was specialization of occupations such as those of an ivory porter or a smith's helper. It could be a means of facilitating exchange.[3]

Palm-cloth, like cowries or *nzimbu* shells, had the additional advantage of being a comparatively non-perishable substance which could be stored. At his court at Buali, the king had houses full of palm-cloth, ivory, and copper.[4] This suggests firstly that palm-cloth was a means of storing wealth, and, secondly, that the Maloango, who presumably only kept the finest palm-cloth in the kingdom, could control its current value. The Loango ruler was probably the chief guarantor of the value of the palm-cloth. The wide circulation of this indigenous money has already been referred to.[5] It was current in

---

The Kongo, Stockholm, 1953, I, 17; II, 137; J. Cuvelier, 'Traditions Congolaises', *Congo*, II, Brussels, 1930, 470–72; A. Doutreloux, *L'Ombre des Fétiches: Société et Culture Yombe*, Louvain, 1967, 34–7.

[1] Accounts of Loango provinces are given by Battell (1901), 52–9, and Dapper (1676), 143–7, 159.

[2] Brun (1913), 13.

[3] P. Bohannan, *Africa and Africans*, New York, 1964, 218.

[4] Broecke (1950), 64.

[5] See above, pp. 139–40.

Loango, Kakongo, and Ngoyo (where it was also manufactured), and also in the coastal regions of Kongo such as Bemba province, and among the Mbundu.[1] Considering the greater accessibility of the Luanda island *nzimbu* shells, it is remarkable to find Loango palm-cloth so widely used. The fine quality of the cloth was probably an important element in its popularity. It may not be going too far, however, to deduce that at the beginning of the seventeenth century this was a 'hard currency'; that the strength of Loango palm-cloth reflected the status of the Maloango, not only internally, but among other peoples of West Central Africa.

Perhaps the best example of a developed pre-European trade organization was the trade in copper. Europeans remarked on the quantities of fine copper jewelry worn by the Vili, long before they themselves began to export the mineral. Dutch traders in the Gabon estuary in the last decade of the sixteenth century also remarked on the quantities of copper jewelry worn by the Mpongwe peoples.[2] The source of Vili copper was the great metalliferous region between Boko Songo and Mindouli in the Niari basin. This area at the beginning of the seventeenth century was in Teke hands, but later in the century it was occupied by the Kongo Nsundi who crossed into the region from the south bank of the Congo river.[3] It seems likely that the copper seen in Gabon was also from this area. There is no important local source of copper in the Gabon region, and it could have reached the Mpongwe via the Teke and traders on the Ogowe river, or, more likely, via the Vili who carried it to Loango whence it could be transported north along the coast.

By the 1660s the mining, smelting, and transporting of the copper on sale at Loango was a highly organized operation and in Vili hands. Large caravans of smiths and traders, with their slaves, left Loango for the mining regions in September. There the slaves brought the copper from the mines to centres where it was moulded by the smiths into the shapes in which it was brought to the coast. They remained until May when the dry season began and wars often broke out. Then they returned to the coast with the smelted copper.[4] The whole operation

[1] Brun (1913), 22; Broecke (1950), 45; Dapper (1676), 157–8, 194, 233.

[2] Paludanus, *Beschrijvinge van de Gantsche Cust van Guinea, Manicongo, etc.*, ed. C. P. Burger and F. Hunger, The Hague, 1934, 7.

[3] Broecke tells of Loango copper coming from the *Insiques* (the Teke kingdom elsewhere referred to as *Ansiko*), Dapper refers to the copper mines of *Sondy*: see Broecke (1950), 70; Dapper (1676), 158.

[4] Dapper (1676), 158.

had doubtless grown in size by the 1660s under the impetus given to trade by European demand. Yet it seems probable that the organization of the copper trade may have been similar at a much earlier period, although on a smaller scale. The Teke who occupied the region may have allowed the Vili to work the mines in return for some arrangement over mining rights. The Vili could also offer the Teke goods such as salt and redwood.

The European demand for ivory caused a considerable extension in the external trade contacts of the Vili. While caravans probably continued to be organized in the traditional manner, they must have increased in number. The need to equip a caravan to cover distances of over a hundred miles must also have demanded greater organization. Unfortunately the contemporary sources have little to say on how this was done in the seventeenth century; but by 1642 the Vili traders had won a reputation among the Dutch as being skilled men of business who could always remain calm in a situation where there was a profit to be made.[1]

As long as the demand was limited to local needs, the elephant population, for example in the Mayombe region to the east of the coastal plain, would have supplied Vili requirements. Following the great increase in demand, stimulated by the Portuguese and the Dutch, it was necessary for the Vili to go further inland as the more accessible sources of ivory became exhausted. At the end of the sixteenth century, Mayumba, Sette-Cama, and regions in the Mayombe remained the main sources of supply.[2] By 1642, however, ivory was being brought by the Vili from Teke markets at what is now Stanley Pool, and Vili caravans were crossing the Congo river into the Kongo kingdom, going as far as Luanda itself. The Teke markets were reached by a trade-route that left the Loango capital, passed through the difficult Mayombe mountains and forests, and then had a relatively easy passage along the Niari and Djoué valleys to Stanley Pool. Tusks weighing between eighty and ninety pounds were carried back to the coast in caravans that might number fifty men and more.[3]

By the 1660s, Bukkameale, a region also known as 'the Mountains of Ivory', had become the main source for the Loango ivory trade. The province was situated on the borders of the Vili and Teke kingdoms,

[1] OWIC, 46, Cappelle to XIX, March 1642. Part of this document has been published by L. Jadin, 'Rivalités luso-néerlandaises au Sohio, Congo, 1600–1675', *BIHBR*, XXXVII, Brussels, 1966, 85–101.

[2] Battell (1901), 52, 58–9.

[3] OWIC, 46, Cappelle to XIX, March 1642.

possibly in the region of the present-day du Chaillu Mountains between the upper Ogowe and Niari rivers. The journey from the Loango coast was long and arduous; it took three months to go and return. The Vili carried baskets of salt, palm-oil, locally made knives, cloth, and trinkets. These they exchanged for ivory which the people of Bukkameale obtained from pygmy hunters who killed elephants with poisonous darts. The Maloango seems to have concluded some sort of agreement with the Bukkameale ruler, perhaps as a result of his trading interests there. Bukkameale provided soldiers for the Maloango's army, thus being a useful ally on the eastern boundaries of the Loango kingdom.[1] On the other hand, Bukkameale also benefited from the association since the Vili were prepared to come the long distance from the coast with salt and carry back Bukkameale ivory.

The Maloango seems to have maintained a considerable degree of control over the economic affairs of his kingdom, through a hierarchy of royal officials. Administration of the six coastal states was in the hands of officials appointed by the king in villages, towns, and provinces. These were responsible for justice and the collection of tribute.[2] This tribute may have been in the form of redwood, ivory, or food, depending on the region. One example of a royal tax was the 10% duty which the people of Sette-Cama had to pay to the Governor of Mayumba province when they brought their redwood to sell at Mayumba.[3] The fact that there was no ivory for sale at Buali market, and yet houses full of ivory at the royal palace, suggests the possibility of a royal monopoly or at least some limitations on its general marketing.[4] The Maloango himself and his nobles were apparently the main beneficiaries of Loango's thriving economy.[5]

The extent of the royal authority was also exemplified in the experience of early Europeans on the coast. It was necessary to have royal assent to open trade at Loango Bay or at Mayumba.[6] The fact that the Maloango lived only a few miles from the main trading point at Loango Bay must have aided him in controlling trade. In this respect, he was much better placed than the Manikongo at his inland capital of San Salvador. The Maloango early established the principle of free trade for all Europeans and this made possible the establishment of

[1] Dapper (1676), 158, 216, 219; J.-B. Labat, *Relation Historique de l'Éthiopie Occidentale*, Paris, 1732, III, 415.

[2] Dapper (1676), 159–60; L. B. Proyart, *Histoire de Loango, Kakongo et autres Royaumes d'Afrique*, Paris, 1776, 126–7.

[3] Dapper (1676), 146.

[4] Battell (1901), 44; Broecke (1950), 64.

[5] This question is further discussed on p. 157, below.

[6] Broecke (1950), 29–30, 44.

Dutch interests in face of Portuguese opposition. There were obvious reasons why the Maloango should welcome Dutch traders. In the first place, they brought European goods which were denied the Vili in large quantities as long as the Portuguese traded mainly with Luanda. Also, he was doubtless aware of the fate of the rulers of Kongo and Ndongo under Portuguese domination. Two incidents serve to illustrate the Maloango's attitude.

Shortly before 1608, some Portuguese captains plotted the death of some of the leading Dutch traders in Loango harbour. The Vili traders were infuriated by the plot and with the approval of the Maloango beat one of the Portuguese to death with ivory tusks and made the others pay a large fine.[1] In 1624, the Portuguese governor of Luanda again tried to counter Dutch influence at Loango by writing to the Maloango exhorting him to close the Dutch factories and only to trade with the Portuguese. He also offered to send missionaries to Loango. The Maloango refused the missionaries and replied that he intended to trade with the Dutch and the Portuguese on equal terms.[2]

A striking feature of the trade of Loango until about 1670, especially when compared with the trade of Luanda in the same period and with that of Loango in the eighteenth century, was the small volume of the slave trade. At first the Portuguese seem to have concentrated on exploiting their Angola sources, while the Dutch, before 1630, had no territories which demanded a supply of slaves. In the 1630s, however, the situation changed. Between 1630 and 1636, the Dutch captured Pernambuco and Paraibo in north-eastern Brazil where the expanding sugar industry created a huge demand for labour. Loango was now viewed as a potential source of slaves. A Dutch factor was appointed to the Loango factory in 1637 with special responsibility for increasing the slave trade there.[3] Portugal also seems to have become interested in the possibilities of opening up a trade in slaves at Loango. From 1636 to 1644, an asiento contract was issued for the slave trade in 'Angola, Congo and Loango'.[4]

These efforts met with little success. In 1639, the Dutch agent reported to the West India Company directors that only about two hundred slaves could be acquired annually at Loango, and about one hundred in Kakongo.[5] Since the Dutch were in a much stronger

[1] Broecke (1950), 28–9.
[2] Heyn (1959), lxxxii, xcii.
[3] OWIC, 23, Minutes of the Zeeland Chamber, 5.1.1637.
[4] F. Mauro, *Le Portugal et l'Atlantique au XVIIe siècle, 1570–1670*, Paris, 1960, 161.
[5] OWIC, 8, XIX to Elmina, 28.11.1639.

position than the Portuguese in Loango, it is unlikely that the Portuguese did any better. Records of Dutch cargoes in the 1640s and 1650s suggest that the slave trade continued to be sluggish, and that ivory and copper remained important items in Dutch trade from Loango.[1]

Given the strength of Dutch demand and the fact that the Vili had a considerable reputation as astute traders, one is led to ask why so few slaves were available at Loango in this period. Clearly the Loango situation seems to disprove any theory that it was sufficient for European traders to appear on the African coast with cheap manufactured goods, in order to obtain a plentiful supply of slaves. The African response was by no means automatic, and in Loango, at least, the initiative in the trading situation was apparently on the African side. To be certain of the attitudes and motives of the Loango government is, however, difficult, due to the lack of source material for this crucial period.

It is possible that the sources that the Vili tapped for ivory and copper could not supply slaves. The hinterland of Loango was probably not thickly populated before about the middle of the seventeenth century, and slave raids in the Mayombe region and in the Niari valley beyond would not have proved very fruitful. It was only in the course of the seventeenth century that Kongo groups started to move into the area of the Niari valley and occupy the borderlands between the Vili and Teke kingdoms.[2] It may have been necessary for the Vili to forge new trade links in order to acquire slaves; this would take time. This may have been especially true of areas south of the Congo river, which were a major source of slaves in the eighteenth century. In terms of extending trade, slaves were a 'commodity' akin to ivory.

Another possible explanation for the paucity of Loango slaves was that the Maloango may have resisted the introduction of the slave trade with Europeans; and in this period his power was probably strong enough to maintain the policy. There were close contacts, both traditional and commercial, between the kingdoms of Kongo peoples north and south of the Congo river. The ruler of Loango must have

[1] References to Dutch trade with Loango can be found in the Journal of Louis Dammaert, under-factor on the Guinea Coast, 1652–1656 (ARA, Aanwinsten, 1898, XXII); also OWIC, 8, 10, 55, 56.

[2] G. Sautter, *De l'Atlantique au Fleuve Congo, une Géographie du Sous-Peuplement*, Paris, 1966, II, 620–21; Sautter discusses the question of pre-Kongo inhabitants of the Niari valley in the light of oral traditions collected in the area. For the arrival of the Kongo in the area, see also M. Soret, *Les Kongo Nord-Occidentaux*, Paris, 1959, 21, and J. Cuvelier, *Documents sur une Mission Française au Kakongo (1766–1776)*, Brussels, 1953, 8.

been well aware of the adverse effects of the slave trade in the kingdom of the Manikongo. Reports of a Capuchin missionary who worked in Loango in 1663 suggest that the Maloango still had considerable influence internally in enforcing his will on his subjects.[1] In relation to European traders the Loango government also seems to have retained the initiative. The Dutch factory at Loango in 1670 was only allowed to exist 'subject to the African government', which contrasted with the more secure tenure of the Gold Coast forts.[2]

Gradually, however, the slave trade at Loango grew in volume. By the 1660s, Vili traders were finding it was more profitable to trade in slaves than in ivory and were bringing ivory to the coast in smaller quantities.[3] They may also have consolidated their contacts south of the Congo river. By 1651 they were regular visitors in San Salvador.[4] Besides, by the 1670s, the Dutch at Loango had been joined by the English and the French, whose primary interest was the trade in slaves for their New World colonies. The Maloango may have either bowed to these pressures or found it politic not to resist them.

By 1670, the Dutch West India Company factory at Loango was exporting three thousand slaves annually.[5] In 1680, the Directors of the new Royal Africa Company were sufficiently interested in the prospects of the Loango Coast trade,[6] to discuss the possibilities of setting up a factory there.[7] In 1686, a French report estimated that the king of Loango could provide five hundred slaves per month.[8] A new phase in the development of the trade of Loango and her southern neighbours had begun. Although slave ships continued to trade in small quantities of ivory, copper, and redwood, especially at the northern port of Mayumba, the trade in slaves began to dominate all other activities.

[1] Labat (1732), III, 421–5.

[2] GAR, 802, Report on the Trade of the West India Company.

[3] Dapper (1676), 158.

[4] J. Cuvelier, 'Contribution à l'Histoire du Bas-Congo', *BIRCB*, XIX, Brussels, 1948, 895–921; Cuvelier quotes Father Antonio de Monteprandone, who in 1651 wrote of 'the pagans from Loango many of whom come every year to San Salvador to trade and very often I preach to them at that capital'.

[5] GAR, 802, Report on the Trade of the West India Company.

[6] In discussing the slave trade period at Loango, it is useful to consider it within the wider context of the slave trade on the coast north of the Congo river and south of Mayumba. The term Loango Coast can be conveniently used in this wider sense, meaning the coasts of the three kingdoms of Loango, Kakongo, and Ngoyo, with their three ports of Loango Bay, Malemba, and Cabinda.

[7] T70/78, fos. 113, 114.

[8] BN, PIII, Div. 2, 12/1. The figures are given on a manuscript map by de Monségur.

By the 1740s, competition had reached considerable proportions. The French ship the *Flore* arrived on the Loango Coast in 1742 and found fourteen other ships. It took four months to collect a cargo of 362 slaves at Loango Bay.[1] A Dutch ship from Middelburg, arriving at Malemba in 1749, found eighteen competitors, seven at Malemba, six at Cabinda, and five at Loango. After nine months it had bought 348 slaves, and already eighty-three had died before it set sail for Surinam.[2] Apart from a lull during the Seven Years' War (1756–63), this competition seems to have continued and increased.

In the years 1765–75, it was normal to find about twenty ships trading on the Loango Coast. Taking as an average a cargo of four hundred slaves and an average trading time of six months, the number of slaves obtained per year on the Coast would be in the region of 16,000.[3] This if anything would be a conservative estimate, since many of the French ships could carry more than four hundred slaves. A French report of the trade of the Loango Coast for the years 1762–78 estimated the French trade at 10,000 slaves per year, the English trade at 1,000, and the Dutch trade at 1,500.[4] While the estimate for French trade may be accurate, the figures for the trade of their rivals seem very low, especially when compared with Dutch reports on the number of ships to be found on the Coast. In 1786–7, Degranpré estimated French trade alone at 15,000 slaves annually, this being the lowest estimate he thought possible.[5] A Portuguese report of the 1770s put the Loango Coast trade at 20,000 slaves per year,[6] while reports to the Committee of Inquiry into the Slave-Trade which met in England in 1789 suggested a figure of 13,000 to 14,000 for the slave trade at Loango Bay, Malemba, and Cabinda.[7] Taking these figures together, a figure in the region of 14,000 to 18,000 may be suggested as an average for the export of slaves from the Loango Coast in the years 1765–90.

Most of those slaves were brought in caravans to the coast from long distances in the interior. One of the best contemporary sources on the Loango Coast slave trade is the book written by the Frenchman

[1] AMM, 4JJ, 71/35, Journal of the *Flore*.

[2] MCC, 459, letter from Malemba, 12.2.1749.

[3] The figure is based on the journals, letters, and account books of the ships of the MCC which visited the Loango Coast in these years.

[4] AC, C6/24.

[5] L. Degranpré, *Voyage à la Côte Occidentale d'Afrique . . . 1786 et 1787*, Paris, 1801, I, xvii.

[6] Birmingham (1966), 157.

[7] E. Donnan, *Documents Illustrative of the Slave-Trade,* Washington, 1931, II, 597–8.

Degranpré, who himself traded in slaves in the area for thirty years. He suggests that the traders of Loango, Kakongo, and Ngoyo were both exploiting old trade-routes used in the copper and ivory trade in the sixteenth and seventeenth centuries, and also developing new trade-routes.

There were different categories of slaves on sale at the three ports. At Loango Bay were to be found *Monteques, Mayombes,* and *Quibangues*; at Malemba were *Mayombes* and *Congues*; at Cabinda were *Congues*, *Sognes,* and *Mondongues.*[1] These names did not, however, indicate the exact source of the slaves; rather they derived from the peoples who supplied the slaves or across whose territory the slaves had passed en route to the Loango Coast.[2] This would explain, for example, why Mayombe slaves figured prominently at Loango Bay and Malemba. These were not necessarily the Yombe inhabitants of the Mayombe region. They were rather given this name since the caravans going to Loango Bay or Malemba would pass through this region. The same would be true of the many *Congues* on sale at Malemba and Cabinda. This would be a general term for all slaves provided by the Kongo south of the river Congo, or for slaves which passed through Kongo territory on the long journey to the Atlantic coast.

Many Loango caravans continued to follow the old caravan route to the Teke markets at Stanley Pool. A quarter of the slaves on sale at Loango Bay were Teke (*Monteques*) while a sixth were known as Boubangui (*Quibangues*).[3] The latter name is particularly significant since it suggests how far inland the trade contacts from the coast had been extended by the second half of the eighteenth century. French explorers who went up the Congo river beyond Stanley Pool in the nineteenth century, found that the term Boubangui was a very broad one; it was used to designate different peoples who lived along the banks of the Congo, Alima, Sanga, and lower Ubangi rivers. Peoples who were individually referred to as Bayanzi, Apfourou, and Bobangi were all part of a larger Boubangui group. They had many common characteristics, including the same language, customs, and tribal marks. The Boubangui originated on the upper Ubangi river, and according to their traditions were pushed down the river by new arrivals. They were also attracted to the Congo river by the European goods arriving in the area from the Teke at Stanley Pool. They continued their advance to Stanley Pool and were only stopped by the

[1] Degranpré (1801), II, 12–13, 25, 37. [2] ibid., I, xxvi. [3] ibid., II, 14.

Teke after they had reached the stretch of the Congo river immediately upstream from Stanley Pool. This seems to have happened about the year 1840.[1] From Degranpré's comments, it seems that by the second half of the eighteenth century, the Teke already had contacts with the Boubangui. Pechuel-Loesche also found confirmation that the slaves who reached Loango included Teke and Yanzi.[2]

Another trade-route led from Loango in a north-easterly direction, crossing the Niari river and climbing the Sibiti plateau to the Yaka. These were probably descendants of the Jaga who had ravaged the Kongo kingdom in the sixteenth century.[3] From there routes communicated with peoples on the upper Ogowe and the upper Alima, bypassing the Teke plateau to the south-east. De Brazza, who crossed from the upper Ogowe to the Alima river in the 1870s, found that the people of that area received salt, guns, and cloth from the Loango Coast. In return they sent slaves to the coast.[4] A trade-route may also have reached the coast at Mayumba, having followed the Nyanga river. From Mayumba, slave caravans went south to the three main ports.[5] Although these connections between the upper Ogowe regions and the Loango Coast were not documented before the nineteenth century, they probably existed from a long time previously. Bukkameale, the seventeenth-century source of ivory, was probably situated in the same area.

By the second half of the eighteenth century, Loango had lost the initiative in the slave trade to her rivals, Kakongo and Ngoyo. Degranpré states that the best-quality slaves, and also the greatest quantity, were to be had at Malemba.[6] The two attempts that were made to monopolize trade on the Loango Coast in the eighteenth century were made at Cabinda, where first the English and then the Portuguese attempted to erect forts.[7] Not only did Cabinda have the

[1] E. Froment, 'Trois Affluents Français du Congo: Rivières Alima, Likouala et Sanga', and 'Un Voyage dans l'Oubangui', *Bulletin de la Société de Géographie de Lille*, VII, Lille, 1887, 458–74, and XI, 1889, 180–216; C. de Chavannes, *Un Collaborateur de Brazza*: *Albert Dolisie. Sa Correspondence avec l'Auteur*, Paris, 1932, 102. Chavannes quotes a letter from Dolisie dated 19.5.1885; C. de Chavannes, 'Exposé Sommaire d'un Voyage dans l'Ouest Africain', *Bulletin de la Société de Géographie*, Lyons, VI, 1886, 65–96.

[2] E. Pechuel-Loesche, *Volkskunde von Loango*, Stuttgart, 1907, 4.

[3] M. Plancquaert, *Les Jaga et les Bayaka du Kwango*, Brussels, 1932, 72–4.

[4] P. S. de Brazza, 'Voyage dans l'Ouest Africain, 1875–1887', *Le Tour du Monde*, Paris, LIV, July-Dec. 1887, 289–336, and LVI, July-Dec. 1888, 1–64; Sautter (1966), II, 622.

[5] Degranpré (1801), II, 5. [6] ibid., I, xxiv.

[7] An English fort built in 1722 was destroyed by the Portuguese in 1723; a Portuguese fort built in 1783 was destroyed by the French in 1784.

best harbour on the coast, but its position near the mouth of the Congo river gave it a favourable situation in the slave trade to the south; it was also within easy reach of Malemba, only a few miles along the coast. The thriving trade of Malemba and Cabinda was due to the fact that the trade-routes from the south crossed Kakongo and Ngoyo, and their rulers could simply prevent the caravans going further north to Loango. An important route led to San Salvador from Nokki, which could be easily reached from Boma on the north side of the Congo river. Another possibility was upstream beyond the Yellala cataracts at Isangila where the river becomes navigable as far as Manyanga. The *Mayombes, Congues, Sognes,* and *Mondongues* may all be references to slaves who arrived at Malemba and Cabinda from a southerly direction. Although the situation was much regretted by the king of Loango, he lacked the power to gain trade by force and had to watch the lucrative Kongo trade passing to his rivals.[1] By 1683, traders who crossed the Kongo kingdom from the Loango Coast had reached the Mbundu state of Matamba on the west side of the upper Kwango river. They aroused the attention of the Portuguese since they offered firearms and gunpowder in exchange for slaves.[2] In the eighteenth century, the Portuguese became even more alarmed by the activities of these traders from the north since they were siphoning off trade that might otherwise have reached Luanda. It is probable that some of the slaves reaching Malemba and Cabinda from the south had come from places as distant as the Lunda empire.

These traders from the Loango Coast had a formidable advantage over their Luanda rivals, for the English, French, and Dutch on the Loango Coast attracted trade by offering higher prices than the Portuguese in Angola and by selling firearms without restriction.[3] Comparing the number of guns contained in each slave ship's cargo on the outward voyage with the number of slaves bought, one finds that about two or three guns were unloaded by the Dutch for every slave acquired.[4] Since the French were offering better prices than the Dutch,

[1] Degranpré (1801), I, 166.

[2] Birmingham (1966), 131–2. The traders from the Loango Coast were often referred to as *Mubires*. See L. Jadin, 'Aperçu de la Situation du Congo . . . d'après le Père Cherubino de Savona', *BIHBR*, XXXV, Brussels, 1963, 408; the word is probably derived from *Muvili,* meaning 'a Vili', since a 'b' and a 'v', and an 'r' and an 'l', are frequently interchangeable in Bantu languages.

[3] Birmingham (1966), 133–4, 137.

[4] The figures are based on the account-books of sixteen ships of the MCC which traded on the Loango Coast between 1757 and 1795.

it is probable that at least three guns changed hands for every slave sold. If one takes the figures of 14,000 to 18,000 as the number of slaves sold on the coast per year, it would mean that something in the region of 50,000 guns may have arrived on the Loango Coast each year in the second half of the eighteenth century. From there they were probably widely dispersed through West Central Africa.

The organization of the slave caravans was a highly specialized business. The dry season saw the peak of caravan activity. The main problem was to ensure an easy passage through the various small chieftaincies through which the caravans passed, especially in the Mayombe region after Loango power had shrunk, among the various Kongo groups who had settled between the Yombe and the Teke, and in the old Kongo kingdom which had disintegrated into many small chieftaincies by the eighteenth century.

Supplies of slaves at the coast could dry up completely if chiefs in the interior decided to close the roads to the passage of caravans. Although there were no fixed duties that a caravan had to pay for such privileges as the right to pass through a chief's land, or the use of bridges, the rate was generally calculated according to the worth of goods in the caravan. Ivory incurred the heaviest tax.[1] Chiefs were, however, strongly placed to exploit their position by raising duties, or even, on some pretext, seizing the trade-goods carried by a caravan. There were certain points where a chief could extort special terms from a vulnerable caravan leader. For example, the roads from Loango to the interior had to pass through the treacherous Mayombe region where the good paths were few and the routes passed along the sides of mountain slopes, by deep precipices, and through dense tropical forest. Here, there was little choice of route, and chiefs had a strong hand in levying customs. They erected barriers across the path and appointed watchmen to keep a look-out for caravans that could be stopped to pay duties. Ferry-places were other lucrative points which chiefs put in the hands of their most trusted followers so that tolls would be collected. Usually the position of ferryman was passed down in certain families.[2]

The caravans that left the Loango Coast were accompanied by guards armed with guns. These seem to have been more to prevent rebellious slaves from running away than to deal with opposition en route.[3] The Loango Coast caravans do not seem to have depended on gunpowder to force a passage through the lands of unco-operative

[1] Pechuel-Loesche (1907), 219. [2] ibid., 221. [3] Degranpré (1801), II, 48–9.

chiefs. If guns were widely spread through West Central Africa, they would probably have been foolish to attempt to do so, especially when they were not on their home ground. The safe-passage of caravans was due, rather, to the skill of the caravan leader who was usually a far-travelled and intelligent man from the coast.[1]

The caravan leaders were, above all, specialists in the art of negotiation; men who knew the customs and duties that had grown up round the passage of caravans in the course of years in the various regions. They had to be able to negotiate prices with difficult chiefs although this might take days to achieve; they had to know when to call a chief's bluff by threatening to turn back, when to give in and pay, and the possibilities of alternative routes. Chiefs always had the fear that if they abused the traders too much, the caravans might stop using the route through their territory and the revenue from customs might dry up. Clearly, a skilled caravan leader had some cards to play, too. Another problem for the leader was that of inexperienced porters and guards. He must be able to discipline them and prevent them from being enticed off the road by the comforts of a village or from being frightened by the fear of some fetish on the road.[2]

Once the duties had been paid to a chief or his representative, he would send one of his officials before the caravan. This man would sound the chief's bell and escort the traders as far as the next district, so that they were not molested; and so the caravan progressed from region to region.[3] As trade expanded, the occupation of a caravan leader must have become both a lucrative and a highly skilled profession.

Once the slaves had arrived on the coast, their sale was also a highly organized affair. In each of the three ports of Loango Bay, Malemba, and Cabinda, a similar system of administration was evolved to deal with the great volume of the eighteenth-century slave trade. The chief official at the port was the Mafouk. He was appointed by the king as a sort of Minister of Commerce and was one of the most important members of the royal council. No trade, either on the European or on the African side, could be commenced without his consent. On arrival in port, the European captain had to go ashore to arrange for the building of a temporary trading-house and to discuss the terms of trade. The latter included such matters as the price of slaves, the duty that must be paid to the king and the royal officials, and the fees for the

[1] Pechuel-Loesche (1907), 222. [2] ibid., 221–2. [3] ibid., 222.

brokers who were the middlemen between the caravan merchants and the European buyers.[1] On the African side, no merchant could trade directly with a European captain, but only through the brokers appointed by the Mafouk. All trade regulations laid down by the king and the Mafouk had to be obeyed.[2]

In this situation, the Africans of Loango and her neighbours seem to have retained the initiative on most occasions, especially in the second half of the eighteenth century when trade reached its peak. For demand seems generally to have outstripped supply in this period, and no European nation was able to build a permanent base and gain a trade monopoly on the Loango Coast. The attempt by the Portuguese to fortify the port of Cabinda (1783–4) and monopolize trade, failed, not only because of the hostile reactions of the French but also because of the African response to their efforts.

The French version of the incident, which claimed that the Mambouk[3] of Cabinda had agreed to the building of a Portuguese fort only after he was taken on board a Portuguese frigate and put under considerable pressure, seems verified by the events that followed.[4] When the Portuguese soldiers started to build their fort, the Cabindans adopted a policy of passive resistance. The brokers, merchants, and those who generally worked as servants of European traders, ran away into the interior and refused to co-operate.[5] Trade almost ceased, and any Portuguese who ventured from the fort did so in danger of his life. When a French expedition arrived the following year to destroy the fort, the Mambouk of Cabinda promised eight hundred African soldiers to help the French eject the Portuguese and declared that the Cabindans favoured free trade.[6]

It seems likely that if a similar situation had arisen at Loango and Malemba, the African response would have been the same. The lack of a permanent base certainly made the work of European captains more difficult. Time was a vital factor in their trade negotiations. The outward voyage to the Loango Coast could take from two to six months,

[1] This account is based on the journals of the ships of the MCC.

[2] Proyart (1776), 150.

[3] The office of Mambouk was traditionally in the hands of the man second in line in the succession to the throne; see Battell (1901), 50, and Dapper (1676), 161. At Cabinda, the Mambouk seems to have retained important functions. He was the royal official in charge of negotiations with the Portuguese in 1783.

[4] AMM, B4/267, Journal of the *Usbele*, 23.7.1783–23.8.1783.

[5] AC, C6/24, Report of S. Marois, 1784.

[6] AMM, B4/267, Journal of M. Marigny, 1784.

and if competition was severe, a captain must reckon another six months or more on the coast in order to acquire a cargo of slaves. Yet trade had to be concluded in the shortest time possible, if the crew and slaves were to survive the Atlantic crossing. In this situation concessions often had to be made to African brokers. The few attempts at price-fixing agreements among European captains were abortive because of the degree of competition. European merchants were generally prepared to work within the trading system which was essentially an African-initiated one.

European competition was reflected in the rise of Loango's rivals, and by the end of the eighteenth century the external authority of Loango had shrunk drastically. At the beginning of the seventeenth century, the Loango kingdom had dominated the whole area of West Central Africa from the Congo river to Cape Saint Catherine. Ngoyo and Kakongo recognized Loango's superior military strength and accepted the Maloango's mediation in their disputes.[1] A very different picture was presented just under two centuries later. Loango had declined so much that the kingdom was smaller than that of Kakongo or Ngoyo. Since Loango continued to have a longer coastline than Kakongo or Ngoyo, the inference is that she had lost territories in the Mayombe region. Although the Maloango was still recognized as suzerain over her two southern neighbours, their kings did not go in person to pay tribute to the Maloango but sent princes of the royal blood.[2] In the north, Mayumba, once a province of Loango, had its own ruler by the end of the eighteenth century; like Kakongo and Ngoyo, the Mayumba ruler sent an envoy to pay homage to the Maloango.[3]

Loango, therefore, had shrunk, in terms of real power, to a coastal strip from the Chiloango river in the south to just north of the Kwilu river. It seems certain that this was due to the effects of the slave trade. It has already been suggested that Kakongo and Ngoyo won a bigger share in the eighteenth-century slave trade than did Loango.[4] This must have led to a greater confidence on the part of the southern kingdoms and affected their dealings with their traditional overlord. At the same time, Loango itself was shrinking. The temptation to try and dominate the caravan routes through the Mayombe may have caused the Yombe chiefs to end their allegiance to the Maloango. Although Mayumba was not much concerned in the slave trade, English and Portuguese ships continued to call for ivory and redwood.

[1] Pigafetta and Lopez (1963), 31; Battell (1901), 42; Dapper (1676), 159.
[2] Degranpré (1801), I, xxvi-xxvii, 166. [3] ibid., I, 166. [4] See p. 151, above.

The Mayumba ruler may have felt strong enough to follow the example of other break-away states. All this, the Maloango was powerless to resist because of domestic problems, also in part brought by the slave trade. At the same time, the weakening of external authority may have created a loss of respect for the Maloango's political authority at home, and exacerbated existing internal tensions.

The slave trade caused fundamental changes in the political and social structure within the Loango kingdom. Its main effect was to undermine the traditional system by creating new opportunities for advancement quite independent of it. Those with a vested interest in preserving the traditional structure were unable to resist the new pressures.

Power in seventeenth-century Loango society seems to have rested firmly in the hands of the king and nobles. These 'nobles' or 'princes', who figure prominently in most seventeenth-century accounts, probably originated in certain families who were the leaders of Vili clans which united to form the Loango kingdom. The privilege of belonging to the class was passed on by matrilineal inheritance.[1] Only those whose mothers were princesses or who had married a princess could claim the traditional prerogatives that belonged to the princely class.[2]

Since the Maloango appointed his royal officials in provinces and districts from this same class, they were able to exploit both their traditional and administrative positions in Vili society.[3] Traditionally, the common people were bound to work in the fields of the nobles at certain times of the year, just as they worked in the fields of the king.[4] The nobles meted out justice and collected tribute on behalf of the Maloango. As has already been suggested, the early European trade in ivory, redwood, copper, and palm-cloth, may have been administered through this same system.[5] Thus it was the king and nobles who most benefited from the early trade contacts with Europeans. This was indeed evidenced by their enormous wealth; the nobles imitated the king in the details of their daily life, living in splendour, dressing finely, possessing quantities of servants and slaves, and receiving the great respect traditionally shown to them by the common people.[6] At the other end of the social scale were the freemen and slaves, with little to

[1] J. Pouabou, 'Le Peuple Vili ou Loango', *Liaison*, LIX, Brazzaville, 1957, 57–9.
[2] Degranpré (1801), I, 109; Proyart (1776), 128.
[3] Dapper (1676), 159. [4] ibid., 167. [5] See p. 145, above.
[6] Broecke (1950), 66; Brun (1913), 13–14; Dapper (1676), 149, 169.

distinguish them except that the former could move freely about the country.[1]

The main effect of the great volume of the eighteenth-century slave trade was to broaden the base of political, economic, and social power. Vili society became more open, and men outside the class of nobles could find opportunity for advancement. In the first place, the system that evolved to deal with the slave trade involved a greater number of people than under previous trading conditions—brokers, merchants, caravan leaders, interpreters, surfboatmen, water-carriers, personal servants for Europeans, and so on. Power came to be measured less in terms of traditional rights and more in terms of a man's place in the slave-trading system and the wealth he amassed from his position. Those new opportunities cut across the traditional distinction of noble or commoner. In many cases nobles become involved in the slave trade as brokers and merchants. At the same time, common people found new opportunities open to those with business acumen.[2] Even slaves were able to enrich themselves, perhaps at first as the servants of a rich broker and, later, for the personal reputation they had acquired. Technically, a man might remain a slave but he was protected by his new wealth.[3]

The Maloango himself may have initiated changes in the administrative system to deal with the demands of the slave trade. In the seventeenth century, the most important members of the royal council were provincial governors.[4] By the eighteenth century, however, these seem to have been less important. The principal members of the royal council were officials who had direct dealings with Europeans, for example, the Mafouk, and the Mangova and Manpoutou who were responsible for foreign affairs and the introduction of strangers at court.[5] The Maloango retained the power to appoint these officials, but instead of appointing those of noble birth, he tended to sell these lucrative offices to the highest bidder.[6] This may have been an attempt to bolster up his own economic position in relation to those of his subjects who were benefiting from their role in the slave trade. Yet he was merely exalting the status of these 'nouveaux riches' further, for they were the very ones who were able to pay large sums and take over

[1] Dapper (1676), 169.

[2] The account-books of ships of the MCC give the names of brokers who supplied slaves. These include the names of members of the royal council, princes, and common people.

[3] Degranpré (1801), I, 105, 107.

[4] Dapper (1676), 159–60.

[5] Proyart (1776), 126.

[6] ibid., 126–7.

office. Once in an important administrative post, this same class was able to exploit their office by extorting tribute from the common people in proportion to their land, cattle, and slaves.[1]

The king, however, was not a pauper in relation to the 'nouveaux riches'. Not only did he continue to retain traditional powers that went with his office, but also he was able to benefit financially from the slave trade. The captain or officers of every ship that traded at Loango visited the Maloango at his capital and gave him considerable presents.[2] More important was the sum of money paid by every ship for the right to trade freely. The combined value of this duty and the presents gave the Maloango an income equal to that of most of the brokers, although he seldom made as much as the Mafouk.[3] Yet although not poor, he was now economically one among his equals.

One of the most striking changes in the system of government in Loango by the end of the eighteenth century concerned arrangements for the succession of a new Maloango. In the seventeenth century, the succession was based on the hereditary principle. When the king died he was succeeded by his sister's son. The king's nephews were appointed in his lifetime to four lordships with the titles of Manikaye, Manibock, Manisalag, and Manicabango. When the Maloango died the Manikaye became the new ruler, the others were promoted, and a new Manicabango was appointed.[4] At the same time, there was by the 1660s some friction among the claimants to the throne and possibly the issue was not as cut-and-dried as the description makes it seem.[5]

By the end of the eighteenth century there was a definite deterioration in the working of the system. The king nominated his successor, the Manikaye, but almost always the appointment was disputed. In this case a Regency Council consisting of the chief ministers took over power and elected a successor.[6] This council, with full political authority in its hands, sought to perpetuate the interregnum in its own interests.[7] Since the chief ministers were generally those that had bought their offices, one can see the important role that the slave trade had in influencing the system of Loango government. The new Maloango usually bribed his way into office. Still, once in power, his traditional authority remained, and he was in the position of having

[1] Proyart (1776), 126.

[2] This is clear from ships' journals. Visits to the Maloango and the Manikakongo are mentioned in MCC 215, 487, 800, 803, 825, 989; and in AMM, 4JJ, 73/66.

[3] Account-books of MCC ships; e.g., 456, 795, 803, 809, 825.

[4] A. Battell (1901), 50; Dapper (1676), 161.

[5] Dapper (1676), 161.

[6] Proyart (1776), 128–31.

[7] ibid., 173.

powers of life and death over those who had just elevated him to the throne.[1]

In conclusion, one can agree with Jan Vansina's view that the changes in Loango society brought about by the trade contacts of the seventeenth and eighteenth centuries should be viewed, not in terms of decay, but in terms of mutation, an adaptation to a new set of circumstances.[2] Seventeenth-century Loango was apparently a vigorous kingdom which had the ability to adapt to the new trade contacts. The result was a greater diversification in the means of climbing the economic and social ladder. Politically, there was a sharing of power between the traditional repositories, the Maloango and the nobles, and the new-type politicians who had gained their position through trading connections.

The real fragmentation of central authority in Loango seems rather to have been associated with events in the first half of the nineteenth century. During the Napoleonic wars and with the influence of the anti-slave trade movement, the slave trade of Loango declined.[3] This was a blow which the already weakened central authority could hardly adapt to. When the slave trade at Loango partially recovered after the war, due to the influence of Portuguese, Spanish, Brazilian, and American traders, it was organized in a different fashion. The whole object was to escape the surveillance of anti-slave trade cruisers; this demanded many small trading-points along the coast.[4] By this period, the slave trade was practically the only means of making a living known to the coastal merchants. Mafouks sprouted all along the coast. It seems that this new generation of mafouks were recognized as having political authority, and not just as the chief commercial agents of the king, as had previously been the case.[5] Elaboration of this point, however, must await further research on nineteenth-century Loango history.

[1] Degranpré (1801), I, 173.

[2] J. Vansina, *Kingdoms of the Savanna*, Madison, 1966, 194.

[3] AMM, BB4/252, Report of Linois, 20.5.1806. Linois found that French trade at Loango had virtually stopped. See also J. K. Tuckey, *Narration of an Expedition to Explore the River Zaire,* New York, 1818, 126. Tuckey, who visited Malemba in 1818, was told that only one ship had visited that port in the previous five years. Only at Cabinda did the slave trade thrive under Portuguese influence.

[4] E. Bouet-Willaumez, *Commerce et Traite des Noirs aux Côtes Occidentales d'Afrique*, Paris, 1848, 191, 197.

[5] W. F. W. Owen, *Narrative of Voyages to Explore the Shores of Africa, Arabia and Madagascar*, New York, 1833, II, 165, 171, 175. Owen refers to meetings with *Mafulas* in the Congo river, at Cabinda, and at Loango Bay. A *Mafula* he defines as 'a title bestowed on the governor of a district, or town, appointed by the king'. It seems probable that this is the same word as Mafouk, also sometimes referred to as Mafouka.

Abbreviations in the Footnotes

AC	Archives Coloniales, Paris
AMM	Archives du Ministre de la Marine, Paris
ARA	Algemeen Rijksarchief, The Hague
BIHBR	*Bulletin de l'Institut Historique Belge de Rome*
BIRCB	*Bulletin de l'Institut Royal Colonial Belge*
BN	Bibliothèque Nationale, Paris
GAR	Gemeente Archief, Rotterdam
MCC	Middelburgsche Commercie Compagnie, Middelburg
OWIC	Oude (Old) West Indische Compagnie, The Hague
T70	Treasury Records, Public Records Office, London
XIX	Governors of the First (Oude) Dutch West India Company

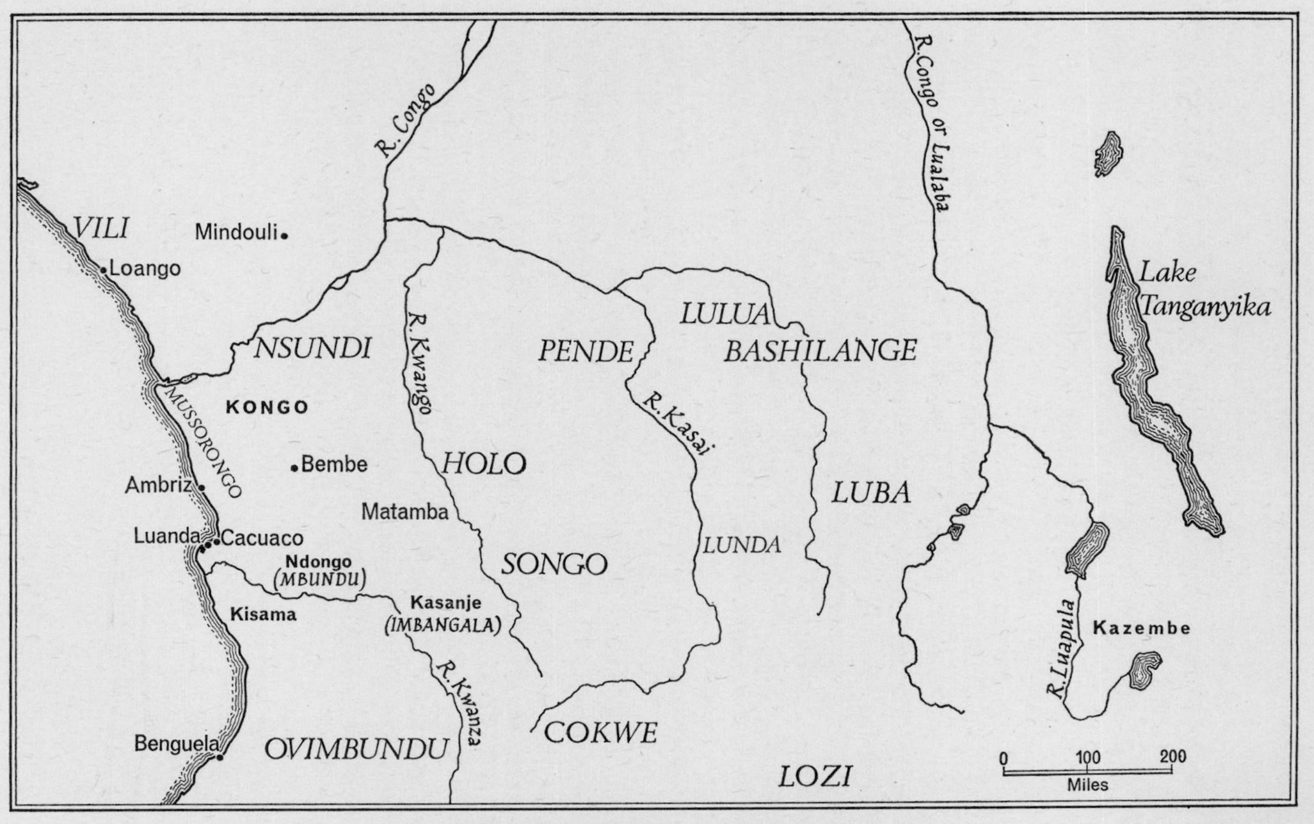

Map 9. Angola and its Hinterland

8

Early African Trade in Angola and its Hinterland

DAVID BIRMINGHAM

When the Portuguese first arrived on the coast of Angola in the last years of the fifteenth century they were seeking trade. It has often been assumed that at this early date they were already wedded to the slave trade. This was clearly not the case. They were interested in any economic pursuit which could show a profit. It has also been claimed that their second preoccupation was with precious metals. This too is an over-simplification. Certainly the discovery of precious metals was the fastest and surest way of attracting investment from mercantilist entrepreneurs of the sixteenth century, but the early Portuguese explorer-traders were quite willing to espouse any commercial undertaking which could show a profit after covering the enormous expenses of reaching out from Europe to the coast of Central Africa. In order to succeed, these early European investigators had to gain as much detailed information as they could about African business enterprise. They had to seek out trading situations in which their skills and products could be offered. On the whole the Portuguese had more entrepreneurial and technical skills than material products to offer to their African counterparts. In particular they had the navigational skills capable of organizing coastal shipments on a larger and more economic scale than was previously possible. Illuminating examples of how the Portuguese insinuated themselves into the African trade pattern can be found among their early activities before they had reached the Angolan coast. In Upper Guinea, for instance, they were able to use African labour and African skills in textile manufacture to set up a new cotton-growing and cloth-weaving industry in the Cape Verde Islands. The Portuguese contribution consisted of a small initial investment, partly in iron bars, and the erection of a sea-borne collection and distribution network which brought the labour to the islands and redistributed the finished cloth among the coastal ports. The profits which the Portuguese made out of this venture could then be converted into African produce saleable in Lisbon such as gold, wax, wood, slaves, and pepper.[1] This situation, in which profit was derived from a very small amount of capital and a rather larger amount of entrepreneurial skill, was often to be repeated in the heyday of the colonial period four hundred years later. Another striking example of the way in which the Portuguese were able to use their trading facilities to insinuate themselves into an existing commercial system and stimulate innovations can be seen on the Mina coast of modern Ghana. Prior to the 1470s it is likely that most of the gold exported from this region travelled north to the Sudanese markets, notably Jenne. If any trade took place with the lower Niger region it probably did so in small canoes along the tortuous creeks behind the coast. When the Portuguese and their European rivals arrived they soon discovered that one of the pressing needs of the Akan mining communities was labour. With their sailing ships these Europeans found that they could obtain labour more easily, and transport it from further afield more cheaply, than rival customers for the gold, and were thus able to cut a slice of the trade for themselves. They also found that Benin cloth, food, and beads were in great demand on the Mina coast and that they could carry these more cheaply and efficiently than African canoemen. Thus the Portuguese appear neither to have inaugurated a new trading system, nor to have introduced new material possessions in any quantity, but to have gained their *entrée* with novel skills in the field of transport.[2]

The most important pre-European trade which the Portuguese found when they moved on down the coast to Angola was probably the trade in salt. As several of the essays in this book have shown, salt is one of the first commodities which communities endeavour to obtain when they begin to supplement subsistence living with goods exchanged outside. The salt mined in Kisama, south of the Kwanza river and some thirty miles inland from the sea, was of exceptional quality. It was quarried in square slabs some two feet across, which were easily transportable and whose regular size made their sale easily negotiable. In the neighbouring kingdom of Ndongo, and perhaps

[1] Walter Rodney, *A History of the Upper Guinea Coast 1545–1800*, Oxford, 1969.

[2] Milan Kalous, 'Contribution to the problem of the hypothetical connection between Ife and the Gold Coast before the fifteenth century', *Archiv Orientalni*, 35, 1967; D. Birmingham, 'The Regimento da Mina', *Trans. of the Hist. Soc. of Ghana*, forthcoming.

further afield as well, these slabs seem to have been used as a currency; one block of salt would buy half a dozen chickens, three blocks a goat, and about fifteen a cow.[1] This use of Kisama salt as a currency both in Angola and in the hinterland was still common in the nineteenth century. The finish of the salt bars had been somewhat refined and they were by then presented in tapering hexagonal bars nine inches long and one inch thick. To improve their handling qualities as a currency the bars were enclosed in closely woven canework cases.[2] Salt presumably fulfilled not only the first function of a currency, that is of providing a regular comparative scale of values, but also the second, of providing a durable means of storing wealth. Most subsistence produce, mainly foodstuffs, cannot be kept for long periods, but blocks of rock salt can be stored away as a token of one's affluence and as an insurance against a lean year. The large Kisama supply of most valuable salt probably formed the basis of an important commercial system. Certainly the Jesuit Gouveia, writing about the trade in 1563, described salt as the main richness of Angola and said that traders came from many nations in the interior to purchase it. He referred to a people called Dambia Songe—possibly the Songo—who lived in a large kingdom seventeen days beyond Angola and came to buy salt; they appeared to be very familiar with regions beyond their country in the far interior.[3] A hundred years later Cadornega described Lunda traders who came to the fringes of Angola in order to buy salt, which still remained an important export.[4]

In view of the importance of Angolan salt-production it seems likely that the salt trade was one of the major factors which attracted the Portuguese to Angola. They showed considerable skill elsewhere in Africa in siting their settlements at key-points on existing commercial networks such as Sofala and Elmina, and it seems unlikely that their business acumen was any less accurate in assessing the potential of Angola. African accounts of Portuguese activity certainly emphasize the loss of the coastal salt-pans as being the noteworthy feature of the Europeans' arrival: 'the white men spat fire and took away the king's salt-pans'.[5] Although the foreign encroachment was resisted, it would seem that the coastal salt supplies were not as vital to the economy of

[1] António Mendes, 'Letter from the Court of Ndongo, 9 May 1563' in A. Brásio, *Monumenta Missionaria Africana*, Lisbon, 1952–68, II, 495–512.
[2] J. J. Monteiro, *Angola and the River Congo*, London, 1875, II, 148.
[3] Francisco Gouveia, 'Letter from Angola, c.1563' in Brásio (1952–68), II, 518–21.
[4] A. de O. de Cadornega, *História das Guerras Angolanas*, Lisbon, 1940, III, 219.
[5] G. L. Haveaux, *La Tradition Historique des Bapende Orientaux*, Brussels, 1954, 47.

Angola as the rock-salt mines further inland, and their loss was not an irreparable calamity which had to be prevented at all cost. When at a later date the Portuguese tried to move inland and gain control of the mines, resistance forces of a far greater magnitude were mobilized. In the last quarter of the sixteenth century several major engagements were fought on the south side of the lower Kwanza, which dramatically demonstrate the determination of those who controlled them to defend the salt-mines and the trade-routes into the interior. In all these engagements the Portuguese lost, though precisely to whom they lost is not always clear; it may be that the African control of the trade was changing hands at the time; whoever was in control, however, was certainly able to prevent Portuguese encroachment south of the river and only allowed them to penetrate along the north bank, albeit slowly and painfully even there. This defence of Kisama and exclusion of foreign enterprise was preserved well into the nineteenth century when Lopes de Lima referred to the salt trade controlled by the 'barbarous powers' as one of the greatest riches of the area.[1]

Salt was undoubtedly the most important Angolan produce geared to market production. Other minerals were of limited scope. The Portuguese spoke frequently of silver in trying to encourage settlement and investment in their Angolan venture, but little or no silver existed and it is hard to believe that such hard-headed businessmen as António Dias and his son Paulo would have put so much capital into a non-existent will-o'-the-wisp. Indeed, the charter which was accorded by the Portuguese crown to Paulo Dias for the conquest of Angola indirectly recognized the prime importance of salt—for all the talk of silver—and awarded the *donatário* a monopoly in the trade of both dried and excavated salt, a monopoly which he and his successors were permanently debarred from enjoying by the prior claim of African entrepreneurs.[2]

Copper was another mineral in great demand. The Portuguese saw it in frequent use, especially as bracelets, from an early date and made great efforts to find and control the source of supply. The colony of Benguela was founded in 1617 for the express purpose of exploiting the local copper deposits, but these always proved very disappointing, ore usually being found in small water-borne deposits containing only a few tons of ore each. The only large copper-bearing region was in

[1] J. J. Lopes de Lima, *Ensaios sobre a Statistica das Possessões Portuguesas*, III: *Angola e Benguela*, Lisbon, 1846, 24.

[2] 'Carta de doação a Paulo Dias', in Brásio (1952–68), III, 36–51.

Bembe, in southern Kongo, where copper malachite was found at the bottom of a deep valley about a mile long. The ore was extracted by digging irregular pits about three feet across and up to 30 feet deep in the floor of the valley. The process was extremely hazardous, especially as the pits were dug very close together in the more favourable areas and often collapsed into each other, killing the miners. No mining could be conducted during the wet season and each dry season the pits had to be dug anew as they rapidly silted up. The villages which controlled the area allowed some neighbouring peoples in to work the mines on payment of a fee, but others such as the Ambriz were excluded from the area and had to buy the malachite in basketfuls at the crossing on the Luqueia river.[1] Whether this small copper-mine which flourished in the nineteenth century was large enough or old enough to have supplied the whole Angola region in former centuries is doubtful. It seems possible that the copper which early Portuguese visitors saw had often been obtained by trade over long distances. The nearest major copper-mine lay north of the lower Congo river at Mindouli and was probably operated by the Vili from the Loango Coast and by the Nsundi from south of the river. It is not unlikely that some of this copper found its way by commercial exchanges into Angola to supplement the meagre local deposits. By the nineteenth century, at least, Katanga copper in the distinctive cross form was reaching the west coast at Benguela via Lunda agencies.[2] If much of the copper seen in Angola was imported this might explain the Portuguese failure to find viable copper-mines in the seventeenth century. At the same time the failure of the Portuguese to penetrate the Bembe area before the nineteenth century may have been due to effective defence of the copper-mines by the Mussorongo or other interested peoples who generally kept the Portuguese fairly closely confined to Luanda on the north side.

In addition to copper, iron was of course an important mineral sought in Angola. The richest deposits seem to have been along the edge of the plateau a hundred miles inland from Luanda. They had formed the basis of an important industry since before the arrival of the Portuguese. The traditions of origin of the ruling dynasty of Ndongo, whose capital sites mostly lay in this region on the plateau edge, refer to a founder who had gained wealth and prestige from ironworking.[3] The quality of the ores was such that in the eighteenth century the

[1] Monteiro (1875), I, 189–97. [2] Monteiro (1875), II, 190–91.

[3] D. Birmingham, *Trade and Conflict in Angola*, London, 1966, 19.

Portuguese built two iron foundries in the area and brought Basque smelters to operate them, though never with any great success owing to labour shortage and high European mortality.[1]

In the sixteenth century the Portuguese were not the only people to be actively exploring the economic potential of Angola. In the middle years of the century a series of Imbangala groups from the Lunda territory were exploring the region at least as thoroughly, and possibly a great deal more thoroughly, than the Portuguese. There has been a tendency to examine the Imbangala migrations in terms of the forces which drove them out of their original homeland. They have been seen as outcasts wandering across the Central African plateau in search of new land, as refugees unwilling to tolerate the burden of Luba over-lordship which the hunter-king Kibinda Ilunga had brought to their country. It may perhaps be more realistic to examine the Imbangala movements in terms of what attracted them to Angola rather than what drove them out of Katanga. A first reason for the Imbangala interest in Angola might have been the presence there of the Portuguese. The interrelationship of the arrival of these two sets of peoples needs careful chronological investigation. It is known with some certainty that the Portuguese were trading at the mouth of the Kwanza river by about 1500; on the other side there is no evidence that the Imbangala reached Angola before the mid-sixteenth century and some authorities put it later still.[2] These dates give at least fifty years for news of the Portuguese to have travelled to the Kasai basin and for Imbangala investigators to have followed up the information by moving down to the coast. Such a time-schedule is not impossible. It does not imply that regular caravans were plying between Angola and the Kasai, but simply that commercial news was exchanged between neighbours, including perhaps news about firearms which the Portuguese introduced for the first time.[3] The question of interaction between the Portuguese and the Imbangala movements does, however, raise wider questions. The migrations of the Imbangala were part of a major upheaval in the political alignments of Katanga; could this whole process, which finally

[1] Ralph Delgado, 'O Govêrno de Souza Coutinho em Angola', *Studia*, 1960–62.

[2] A more detailed discussion of this dating will be seen in D. Birmingham, 'The African Response to Early Portuguese Activity in Angola', paper presented to the University of California colloquium on Africa and Brazil, to be published under the editorship of R. H. Chilcote.

[3] This spread of commercial information may be compared to the speed and subtlety with which the peoples of south-east Africa responded to changing trade situations at Delagoa Bay, as depicted in Ch. 13, below.

resulted in the rise of the greatest of all the Central African empires in Lunda, be attributed to the new circumstances which Portuguese overseas trade had created? The answer is probably that it could, but not as quickly as the traditional sources suggest. The somewhat telegraphic style of oral tradition implies that a revolution took place overnight in the Kasai-Katanga territories. This is misleading. It is, however, likely that the opening to the west was initiated or widened in the sixteenth century and that this new factor gradually had far-reaching effects over the next three centuries, beginning with the Luba movements which brought new political ideas and leadership to their western neighbours. These changes led, by the eighteenth century, to the growth of the full-fledged Lunda empire which owed much of its power to its several links with the trade of the west coast.

Another factor which might have influenced the Imbangala movements may have been the salt trade already discussed. Certainly the Lunda country from which they came suffered from a severe shortage of salt. Early phases of the expansion of the Lunda empire after its rise to power seem to have been associated with the search for salt, for instance during the Kazembe migrations to the east. Later, in the nineteenth century, caravans into the Lunda, Cokwe, and Bashilange regions carried salt, among other things, with which to buy ivory, rubber, and slaves.[1] The proven need for salt in the lands east of the Kwango and the known richness of Angolan salt combine to make one suspect that the trade may have played a role in the Imbangala explorations. The earliest traditions of the Luba arrival in Lunda claim that the Luba hunters were moving westward in search of salt, salt which could conceivably have been coming from Angola even at such an early date.[2] The existence of such a trade would reinforce the theory that news of the Portuguese arrival on the coast could have penetrated to the Kasai fairly quickly and caused exploratory expeditions to set out.

The impression that the Imbangala were particularly interested in supplies of salt is reinforced by the early documentary references to the Imbangala leaders. The most detailed description of the Imbangala associates them with the Kisama region. The chief who most definitively defeated the Portuguese governor Coutinho in his 1602 campaign to reach the salt-mines was called Kafushe, a name associated with the Imbangala leadership. Other accounts of the Imbangala describe their

[1] P. Pogge, *Mittheilungen der Afrikanischen Gesellschaft in Deutschland*, IV, 186–90, refers to Imbangala salt reaching the Lunda.

[2] Dias de Carvalho, *Ethnographia e história tradicional dos Povos da Lunda*, Lisbon, 1890, 67.

success in driving the Mbundu away from Cacuaco, a still flourishing salt-drying village on the coast. This incident again suggests a keen Imbangala interest in salt supplies. Finally, when the Imbangala under the leadership of a later Kasanje retired from Angola to found their own kingdom in the 1630s, they did so partly in order to take possession of the salt-pans of the Holo people on the Kwango river and drive away the Pende, who had earlier gained possession of them when expelled from Angola. It was in this area that Cadornega described Lunda traders coming to fetch salt in the second half of the seventeenth century.[1]

The presence of the Portuguese on the Angolan coast may have stimulated the Imbangala to move there, but the arrival of the Imbangala may in its turn have increased the Portuguese interest in Angola. If the Portuguese were aware that these people came from several hundred miles inland, it would have greatly enhanced the potential value of Angola by opening the prospect of a route into the far interior. The Portuguese had hitherto been conspicuously unsuccessful in gaining entry to the African interior everywhere except on the Zambezi, and their progress even there was strongly opposed. It may therefore be that in deciding to attempt the conquest of Angola from 1575 onwards their prime objective was a route into the hinterland to find out for themselves about the inland resources of Africa.[2] If the Kwanza valley was the highroad used both by old-established salt-traders and by new immigrants of Lunda–Imbangala origin, their choice of a route was clearly not a bad one—at least in theory. The snag of course lay in the effectiveness of the resistance they were to meet. This resistance was both commercial and military.

On the commercial plane the Portuguese were much less successful than they had been in Upper Guinea or in the Bight of Benin in insinuating themselves into the existing trading pattern and supplying a new ingredient which made them welcome to the local people. The best they could do was to initiate, or take from others, the coastal trade in palm-cloth. This cloth was manufactured in the wetter, palm-growing regions north of Angola, and most attractively in Loango. The Portuguese bought it there and retailed it in Angola, where it was in demand not only as clothing but also as a currency which the Portu-

[1] Birmingham (1966), 62, 66–7, 69, 98.

[2] In 1586, for instance, Father Diogo da Costa reported that Monomotapa was very close and that 2,000 armed men could easily establish communication across the two small intervening kingdoms: Brásio (1952–68), III, 339.

guese themselves adopted and used for many years.[1] In other forms of local trade the Portuguese had less to offer. The Kwanza was not readily navigable and they could not provide an effective river-transport system to compete with traditional head-porterage, which therefore remained the means of transport until the twentieth century. The foreign imports which they brought to Africa were also not as helpful to trade as might have been expected. Their supply was limited and they were extremely expensive. Cloth and beads were not manufactured in Portugal in adequate quantities and therefore had to be imported from Northern Europe, the Mediterranean lands, or India, before Lisbon could re-export them in the African trade. In their early association with the Kongo kingdom, the Portuguese had overcome this difficulty by offering their services to the court as clerks, masons, accountants, teachers, and even domestic science specialists, in part payment for the produce and slaves which they received. In Angola attempts were made to establish a similar relationship with the king of Ndongo, although never with the same degree of success on the Portuguese side.

By 1575 the Portuguese had been on the Angolan coast for nearly a century without any dramatic success in establishing themselves as traders. The inauguration of the wars of conquest in that year might then be interpreted as a radically new policy to establish the profitability of the Portuguese presence. They might have decided that the only way to extract a return was by imposing their suzerainty in order that a system of tribute payments could be instituted. The accumulation of commodities through a hierarchy of tributary payments from the subject to the chief, then to the paramount chief, and finally to the king was a central feature of both the Kongo and Ndongo kingdoms. When the Portuguese sought to obtain produce from these regions they obtained it from the kings, who had accumulated both goods and slaves in this manner. The Portuguese, faced with the difficulty of paying for such goods, and unable to earn part of the proceeds by offering skills and services, may well have decided that their only hope was to set up their own political structure which would accumulate tribute in the African manner directly for their own benefit. When the wars of conquest started, therefore, they awarded to their army captains the chiefs who were conquered. These chiefs and their subjects had to keep the captain supplied with all his needs and with a tax in slaves who could later be redeemed for credit-notes drawn on the office

[1] See the account of the Loango trade, Ch. 7, above.

of the slave trade contractor who held the monopoly of the export of slaves. For some fifty years the payment of tribute to a military government was the major means of obtaining slaves in Portuguese Angola.

In the long run, military methods proved little more effective than previous attempts at cooperation in obtaining for the Portuguese a position in the economic structure of Angola. Their initiatives met with increasingly effective military resistance, first from the kingdom of Ndongo and, when that began to collapse in the 1620s, from the new and more powerful kingdoms of Matamba and Kasanje. Their dreams of a highroad into Africa, even a short-cut to the Indian Ocean avoiding the perilous Cape of Good Hope, were rapidly destroyed. Once again Portuguese policy had to be changed, and this time increasing emphasis was put on trade. By now Brazil contained a flourishing series of colonies and the Portuguese were relatively well stocked with goods which satisfied African demands. Rum and thick ropes of Brazilian tobacco cured with molasses were especially useful in building up trade once the limits of raiding and military conquest had been reached.

On the African side the response to the seventeenth-century trade developments was even more interesting than the earlier response to the attempts at foreign conquest. It was perhaps not surprising that the Mbundu had been able to erect military barriers of considerable effectiveness when faced with an all-out challenge to their very existence; even so the armies, occasionally reported to number tens of thousands, were massive affairs which must have required considerable ability to organize, even if no central system of supplies was provided and the campaigns lasted only so long as the forces could live off the land. More spectacular than these military achievements, however, was the response offered to the commercial innovations of the seventeenth century. The trading barriers that were erected by Matamba and Kasanje were more sophisticated and effective than any of the old military resistance had been. They triumphantly succeeded in preventing any spread of Portuguese commercial undertakings and initiatives beyond Angola. At times there was a Portuguese commercial factor resident at the Kasanje court, but he had little power other than to settle disputes between rival traders, and if his activities appeared to be contrary to the interests of Kasanje, he was unceremoniously dispatched back to Luanda. Behind the barrier of the Kwango valley states a commercial network was gradually built up which collected the exportable goods from a large sector of Central Africa and redistributed in return foreign goods brought up from the coast. It is this response to the new opportunities of the seventeenth century which appears so remarkable. African trading entrepreneurs succeeded both in excluding foreign rivals and in meeting the demands put upon them to supply the goods. Furthermore they were able to evolve a degree of flexibility in their system so that it could meet changing conditions. When in the later seventeenth century the demand for slaves was rising on the Loango Coast, it was possible for supplies to be diverted there from the traditional lines of communication to Luanda, firstly across the old Kongo kingdom, and later, perhaps, by more direct routes.

From this speculative reassessment of familiar sources relating to the history of Angola it would seem that trade may have played a larger role at an earlier date than has previously been realized. By the sixteenth century at least the people of Angola were using a form of currency which, if not quite as sophisticated as the Kongo shell currency, was still a major step forward in economic development. The country also had, or rapidly developed, the necessary diplomatic and military services to protect its resources and commercial undertakings from foreign intrusion from whatever quarter it might come. Most important of all, however, some of the Angolan people were able to adapt their political and economic systems in order to carry on a flourishing trade without being destroyed by it. As yet far too little is known about the way in which the slave trade operated from the middle of the seventeenth century. The relative importance of the Portuguese *pombeiros* and the Kasanje entrepreneurs in raising credit, negotiating profit margins, competing for trade-routes, is not yet known with any clarity. Even less is known of the specific impact of the trade on communities further afield, about who succumbed and went to the wall and who survived to become masters of the system. All that is clear is that those who emerged on top to control the trading states must have had very considerable commercial acumen. These skills were probably rooted in a long tradition of growing trade specialization and showed themselves capable of adapting to changing economic conditions over several centuries.

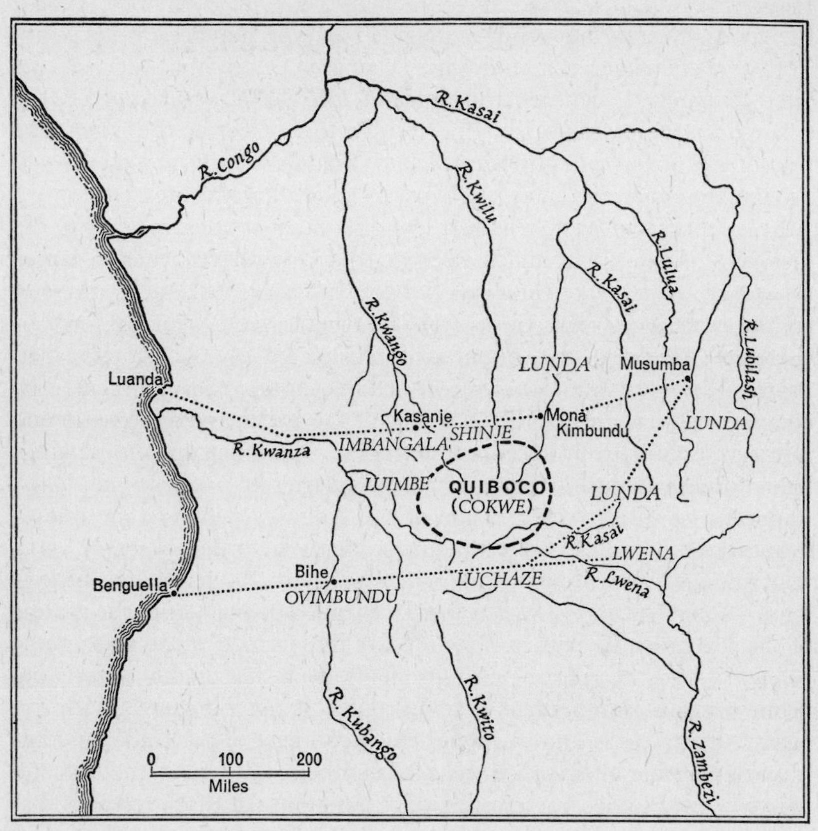

Map 10. The Original Cokwe Territory: Peoples, Places, and Trade-Routes before 1850

9

Cokwe Trade and Conquest in the Nineteenth Century[1]

JOSEPH C. MILLER

In the 1830s and 1840s, a shift in European demand for African products along the Angola coast produced changes in the pattern of long-distance trade in the interior and altered the fortunes of many of the peoples of eastern Angola and the south-western Congo. The expansion of the Cokwe people, an important component of the new situation, challenged the power of the Lunda empire, confronted experienced Imbangala and Ovimbundu traders with a strong commercial rival, and helped to determine the shape of the modern ethnic and political map of the region. Existing Cokwe social and economic institutions provided the basis for the growth of Cokwe power and wealth, but at the same time Cokwe chiefs and traders creatively modified their customary patterns of behaviour in order to profit from changing circumstances.

Although the eighteenth-century slave trade largely passed the Cokwe by, they managed to establish themselves as producers of a few slaves, and some wax and ivory. Here, the Cokwe had special advantages: they were the best hunters in the interior and they lived in an area where elephants abounded. Their forests swarmed with bees, which the Cokwe supplied with artificial hives and then robbed for honey and wax.[2] They were exporting these products through Bihe

[1] I wish to express my gratitude to Professors Philip Curtin and Jan Vansina for their valuable criticism of an earlier version of this paper. Any remaining errors are, of course, my own.

[2] In 1960, the district of Moxico, the former Cokwe homeland, was the most important wax-producing region of Angola; it accounted for some 50% of the total production of Angola, almost entirely by traditional methods. The African bee, *apis mellifera adansoni* Latr., is found throughout Angola but is most abundant on the interior plateaux which are covered by dry forest. See José Filipe Rosário Nunes and G. C. Tordo, *Prospecções e ensaios experimentais apícolas em Angola*, Lisbon, 1960, 85, 163, 165, and passim.

and Kasanje by 1803, when the Cokwe chief Mushiko detained the *pombeiros* Amaro José and Pedro João Baptista because he wanted payment for products he had sent out through Kasanje some time previously.[1] That same year, an unidentified *sertanejo* reported in Benguela that he had traded in the lands of 'Quiboco'.[2] But slave exports dominated the economy of Angola at that time and relatively few buyers appeared for the ivory and wax which the Cokwe produced.[3] Prices on the coast were too low to make exports from so far inland very profitable, and quantities consequently remained low.

The Cokwe nevertheless imported a significant number of guns by concentrating on importing firearms. As excellent blacksmiths, they had little need of European knives and other metal products, and they seem to have preferred their home-made mead to European intoxicants. Even cloth, the staple of the trade to many parts of central Africa, may have been less important for the Cokwe: in the middle of the nineteenth century European fabrics were conspicuous by their absence in Cokwe villages.[4] This relative independence of the standard trade items left the Cokwe free to use their export earnings to buy guns. Once they obtained the guns, they had enough skill in ironworking to repair any part of a damaged weapon, except the barrel.[5] They could use the few guns they had for many years rather than replacing them as their less talented neighbours had to do. Thus the Cokwe began to build their arsenal of firearms even before they entered the long-distance trade on a large scale.

The Ovimbundu possessed firearms as early as 1661, and they had spread them all over the Bihe Plateau by 1700.[6] They thus could have provided the Cokwe with guns as soon after this as trade began. The first gun obtained by the Cokwe, and the one they preferred up to the present century, was the flintlock musket. Europeans first sent this type of weapon to Africa in 1635 and ceased making it around 1820.[7]

[1] R. F. Burton, *The Lands of Cazembe: Lacerda's Journey to Cazembe*, London, 1873, 199.

[2] A. Teixeira da Mota, *A cartografia antiga da África central e a travessia entre Angola e Moçambique*, Lourenço Marques, 1964, 122. *Sertanejos* were African or mulatto agents or caravan leaders in the employ of Portuguese merchants, who lived at the coast or in Bihe.

[3] Allen Isaacman, 'An Economic History of Angola, 1835–1867', Wisconsin M.A. thesis, 1966, 14–15.

[4] Joaquim Rodriguez Graça, 'Expedição ao Muatayanvua', *Boletim da Sociedade de Geografia e de história de Lisboa*, IX (1890), 416.

[5] A. Petermann, 'Ladislaus Magyar's Erforschung von Inner-Afrika. Nachrichten über die von ihm in den Jahren 1850, 1851, und 1855 bereisten Länder Moluwa, Moropu, und Lobal', *Petermann's Geographische Mittheilungen*, Gotha, 1860, VI, 228.

[6] Gladwyn Childs, *Umbundu Kinship and Character*, London, 1949, 7, 195.

[7] Marie-Louise Bastin, 'Tshibinda Ilunga: Héros civilisateur', Université Libre of

This almost certainly dates the arrival of firearms among the Cokwe to the eighteenth century at the latest, perhaps as early as 1700, certainly by 1750 or so. In mid-century Portuguese smugglers were importing as many guns through Benguela as the British and French were selling north of the Congo, and the Portuguese government authorized a limited legal importation of guns in 1767.[1]

Availability of firearms therefore presented no problem to the Cokwe, but the relative unprofitability of Cokwe wax and ivory before 1840 meant that they had few guns before the middle of the nineteenth century. The fact that they could still hunt elephants in their own lands as late as 1850 confirms the hypothesis; with any large quantity of guns, the Cokwe would have exterminated the elephants long before, as they did in the following five years. At an unknown date, but probably in the late eighteenth or early nineteenth century, the Ovimbundu were therefore able to raid the Cokwe for slaves, and to capture enough of them to produce an identifiable Cokwe population in Brazil.[2]

As long as slaves dominated Angola's economy, the Cokwe could not profit from long-distance trade to the coast. The Cokwe got their chance of success in the 1830s, however, when the Portuguese abolished slavery in Angola, thus beginning the end of the 'golden age' of the slave trade.[3] This end of the slave trade was hastened in 1850 when Brazil closed her ports to slave-traders, thus closing the major market.[4] By 1854 the trade had fallen so drastically that Luanda suffered from a severe economic depression. The price of a slave youth had fallen from \$70–\$80 to a mere \$10–\$20.[5] The Portuguese officially

Brussels dissertation, 1966, 125; Leon Duysters, 'Histoire des Aluunda', *Problèmes de l'Afrique centrale*, 40 (1958), 84; G. Tylden, 'The Gun Trade in Central and Southern Africa', *Northern Rhodesia Journal*, II, 1 (1953), 47.

[1] David Birmingham, *Trade and Conflict in Angola*, London, 1966, 147.

[2] José Redinha, *Etnossociologia do nordeste de Angola*, Lisbon, 1958, 53; W. D. Hambly, *The Ovimbundu of Angola*, Chicago, 1954, 113. Redinha, unfortunately, did not cite his reference to Cokwe in Brazil, but Coelho de Senna Nelson, *Africanos no Brasil*, Bello Horizonte, 1938, 122ff., gives a list of names of African ethnic groups appearing in literature dealing with Brazil. The Cokwe appear as 'Kiôcos', 'Maquiôcos', 'Makiôcos', 'Maquiôcas or Makiôcas', and 'Quiôcos'.

[3] Jan Vansina, 'Long-distance Trade-routes in Central Africa', *J. Afr. Hist.*, III, 3 (1962), 385.

[4] Mary Karasch, 'The Brazilian Slavers and the Slave Trade, 1836–1851', Wisconsin M.A. thesis, 1967, 38ff., establishes that the important date for the slave trade from Angola was 1851, not 1836. After 1836, the bulk of the trade left the hands of the Portuguese merchants in Luanda and thrived under those of slavers from other nations who called at Ambriz, Ambrizette, and other ports in Angola.

[5] David Livingstone, *Family Letters, 1841–1856*, London, 1959, I, 252–3.

closed all trade in slaves in 1878, although it did not disappear until the second quarter of the twentieth century.[1]

From the 1830s on, the Portuguese government looked for products to replace slaves at Luanda and Benguela. Wax and ivory benefited first. The government abolished its monopoly on ivory in 1836, and the artificially low price shot up by 300%. Higher prices meant profits for both the merchants on the coast and the peoples in the interior, whose ivory could now bear the expense of transportation to the coast. Legal ivory exports at Luanda reflected the expanded range of ivory production in the interior as they rose from 3000 pounds in 1832 to 105,000 pounds in 1844.[2] The Cokwe almost certainly entered a period of unprecedented prosperity. Ivory exports rose another 80% from 1844 to 1859 at Luanda, and these statistics suggest the trend at Benguela where the Cokwe sent most of their production.[3]

Wax had been a more important export than ivory at Benguela since the seventeenth century. Before 1832, it was the only product of any importance besides slaves.[4] After the slave trade declined in the 1850s wax exports increased even more dramatically than those of ivory. At Luanda, quantities exported rose from 52,690 pounds in 1844 to 1,698,248 pounds in 1857.[5] The magnitude of the change suggests its effects on the Cokwe. By 1846 wax was the only plentiful commodity in Cokwe country and the chief Kanyika was exporting great quantities of it through Kasanje and Bihe. The Cokwe and Luchaze were responsible for the production of most of the wax received at Luanda and Benguela.[6] By 1851 wax from Quiboco enjoyed a reputation as 'the best in southern Africa' and in 1855 it was the major export of the region.[7]

The Cokwe acquired their dominant position in the wax trade between 1830 and 1850 partly by virtue of their advantageous geographical position. Other areas farther away from the coast could have produced much more wax than relatively small Quiboco, but they lay so far inland that transportation costs made it prohibitively expensive to export. The Cokwe and Luchaze lived only twelve days' march east of

[1] Childs (1949), 214.

[2] Isaacman (M.A. thesis 1966), 17–20. The fact that part of this increase came from previously illegal exports and from diversion of the ivory formerly sent through non-Portuguese ports to the north did not affect the order of magnitude of the increase. It was still very great.

[3] Isaacman (M.A. thesis 1966), 96.

[4] Childs (1949), 193.

[5] Isaacman (M.A. thesis 1966), 96.

[6] Graça (1890), 409.

[7] Petermann (1860), 227–9; David Livingstone, *African Journal,* London, 1963, 106.

Bihe so that the Ovimbundu could carry their wax out at much less cost. Others, like the Lwena, began to export wax after 1850 when the demand grew so great that the Cokwe could not possibly satisfy it by themselves. Even then, peoples in areas where elephants still roamed, such as the eastern Lunda empire, did not enter the wax trade because higher ivory prices made ivory exports more profitable.[1]

The Cokwe, however, possessed distinctive advantages which also allowed them to benefit from the opportunities presented by the increased demand for ivory. Their beliefs had always given great prestige to hunting, equal to that of the divining profession. The Cokwe, therefore, easily associated wealth with hunting and accepted the hunters as the legitimate beneficiaries of the rise in ivory prices at the coast. The shift in emphasis from hunting for food to hunting for profit caused no serious disruption in the balance of the Cokwe social structure.

Cokwe hunters killed elephants on a minor scale in Quiboco at least by 1803, the year of the *pombeiros*' visit to Mushiko. Firearms gave them such an overwhelming superiority in relation to their prey that, when the demand for ivory rose and the Cokwe acquired guns in quantity, they quickly eliminated the elephant population of their own lands. Elephants had disappeared from the eastern and northern sections of Cokwe territory by 1854.[2] As early as 1850 declining supplies of ivory at home had forced the Cokwe to wander far afield in search of fresh herds. Small groups of Cokwe hunted along the headwaters of the Zambezi and others searched the forests east and north of the Lunda capital.[3] Ivory prices had risen high enough by then to make exports from these interior regions profitable.

At the same time the Lunda began to need the hunting skills of the Cokwe. The economic structure of the Lunda empire had rested on slave exports. Thus, when the slave market in Angola dropped, the Lunda had to turn to ivory production to sustain their supplies of guns, cloth, and other European articles. This drew in the Cokwe, who hunted the elephants for the Lunda and paid them one tusk from every animal they felled. The Cokwe kept the other tusk and probably sold it to the same Imbangala caravan that purchased the ivory they had given to the Lunda chief. Both parties profited from the arrangement. Exports rose quickly, and by 1850 the value of ivory coming out of Lunda exceeded that of slaves.[4] The Mwata Yamvo consolidated this

[1] Petermann (1860), 231, 234.
[2] Livingstone (1963), 106.
[3] Petermann (1860), 231.
[4] Petermann (1860), 231.

new trade pattern when he decreed that tribute would be collected in the form of ivory rather than slaves.[1] If any Lunda governor had avoided hiring Cokwe hunters up to that point, he was now forced to do so.

The division of labour in the Cokwe village, as well as its lineage structure, made it easy for an elephant-hunting band of six or so men to leave their homes for months at a time. Cokwe villages consisted of a core of matrilineally related males, usually a group of brothers and their nephews. This made the male matrikin a cohesive group capable of efficient economic cooperation. The women in a village came from other clans, often only temporarily from the time of marriage until they ceased to bear children, and the stability and lineage-identity of the settlement was quite independent of them. Economically, once the men had cleared the fields, the women did all the planting and harvesting of most crops, of which manioc was most important.[2] Women also processed the wax.[3] So, carrying their antiquated flintlock muskets, the Cokwe hunting-parties could be absent from the village indefinitely without greatly disturbing its social or economic structure.

They were as independent of the village as it was of them. Nor did the Cokwe hunters depend on the inhabitants of the lands through which they passed. They ate the meat of the elephants they shot and sold the surplus to local villages at liberal prices in exchange for vegetable foods. The Cokwe travelled light and probably sold a portion of their ivory for slaves who transported the remainder. For shelter they constructed the same type of temporary straw hut they made when small groups of male matrikin split off from an existing village to found new settlements.[4] As self-contained economic units, the hunting bands did not inconvenience their Lunda hosts, and they were careful to maintain friendly relations by courteous behaviour.[5]

[1] Bastin (Brussels dissertation 1966), 61.

[2] See Merran McCulloch in Daryll Forde (ed.), *The Southern Lunda and Related Peoples*, London, 1951, 36, for a summary.

[3] Cokwe men made artificial beehives and placed them in trees, harvesting the combs just after the beginning of the rainy season. Women performed all the other steps in preparing the wax for export. See Paul Pogge, *Im Reich des Muata Jamwo*, Berlin, 1880, 46; F. S. Arnot, *Garenganze*, London, 1889, 146; H. Capello and R. Ivens, *From Benguella to the Territory of the Yacca* (trans. A. Elwes), 2 vols., London, 1882, 197; Hambly (1954), 141.

[4] Because each Cokwe male desired to head his own village, village fission was commonplace. Small groups of matrilaterally linked males would split off with their wives and other dependants in a well-developed routine of moving; it was an easy matter to adapt these practices to itinerant ivory-hunting.

[5] Emil Torday, *On the Trail of the Bushongo*, London, 1925, 271.

Profits from the production of wax and ivory began to flow to the Cokwe in the late 1830s and rose steadily thereafter. The Cokwe must have used some of their wealth from the trade to buy more guns in order to increase ivory production, but they spent much of it to acquire women. Although the Imbangala and Ovimbundu slave caravans had passed near Quiboco for years, the Cokwe had lacked the resources to buy many captives for themselves.

A strong demand for slave women had always existed among the Cokwe because of the inherent tensions of their matrilineal social system. Residence patterns tended to isolate the Cokwe male from his wife and children, while the matrilineage as a unit felt the threat of a lack of daughters which could bring an end to the kin-group. Such tensions prompted the Cokwe to utilize an extensive system of pawnship[1] to integrate non-Cokwe women into Cokwe lineages. The pawnship system provided women who were subject to greater control by their husbands and strengthened lineages by the addition of children of the female pawns. Advantages like these created such a tremendous demand for pawn women among the Cokwe lineages that by the early twentieth century observers estimated that 80% of the women in some villages were pawns.[2]

The key influence of the system of pawns for Cokwe expansion came from its application to the women of neighbouring peoples or to slave women in the Imbangala or Ovimbundu caravans which had passed near Quiboco on their way to the coast for many years. Cokwe social structure contained no features which could limit the number of women which the Cokwe might add to their numbers. Marriage was polygynous, so that each male had a right to as many wives as he could obtain. Cokwe villages were based on a core of male matrikin and the presence of a great number of alien women did little harm to the internal stability of the village. Prior to 1830, the Cokwe pawnship system operated on the basis of reciprocity, with lineages exchanging pawns already participating in the system. As a result, there occurred no net population increase. As soon, however, as the Cokwe acquired wealth to purchase, or guns to steal, women from other peoples, nothing remained to hinder the tendency of the Cokwe population to increase. This situation arose in the mid-nineteenth century.

[1] For a discussion of the concept, see Mary Douglas, 'Matriliny and Pawnship in Central Africa', *Africa*, XXXIV, 4 (1964), 301–13. The essence of the pawnship system was the transfer of rights over an individual from one lineage to another.

[2] A. A. Mendes Correa, 'Antropologia Angolense: I Quiocos, Luimbes, Luenas, e Lutchazes', *Archivo de Anatomia e Antropologia*, II (1916), 329.

After 1830, wax and ivory supplied the means to purchase many of these pawn women from passing slavers. Cokwe demand for female slaves complemented nicely the demand for male slaves at the coast. Caravans of slaves bound for Bihe or Kasanje would stop and sell their females to the Cokwe for wax and ivory which the male slaves would then carry on to the coast. The result was an influx of women into Cokwe territory which increased their population dramatically. By the 1840s, reports of low food supplies indicated that Quiboco was already overpopulated,[1] and by 1850 it was 'more densely populated than any other land in *inner-Afrika*'.[2]

Up to this time the Cokwe had left the function of transportation to the Imbangala and Ovimbundu traders who had long before developed large caravans well adapted to carrying slaves, wax, and ivory. They in turn depended on the production activities of the Cokwe. This separation of function disappeared in the early 1860s because of the exhaustion of ivory supplies on the upper Kasai.[3] By the mid-1860s the Cokwe around Mona Kimbundu became quite impoverished as a result of the retreat of the elephant herds beyond Mai Munene in the north. When they reached the edge of starvation, a famous hunter, Mukwadianga, set off in desperation on a hunting-trip to the Bena Lulua and Luba territories north-east of the Kasai. Ivory was still plentiful there, for the Cokwe had never crossed the Kasai to hunt and the Luba as yet had no firearms in that region. Mukwadianga contacted a Bena Lulua chief, Mukenge Kalamba, who needed guns which the Cokwe could

[1] W. D. Cooley, 'Joaquim Rodriguez Graca's [sic] Reise zu dem Muata-jamwo in Inner-Afrika', *Petermann's Geographische Mittheilungen*, II (1856), 311, where he quotes Graça as stating that in Quiboco in 1845 food was 'in no way plentiful at present'. Cf. Graça (1890), 415.

[2] Petermann (1860), 229. Jan Vansina, *Kingdoms of the Savanna*, Madison, 1966, 219, doubts that this population pressure existed, yet Magyar had journeyed through most of West Central Africa and his account seems one of the most reliable for the period. See N. de Kun, 'La vie et le voyage de Ladislaus Magyar dans l'intérieur du Congo en 1850–52', Académie Royale des Sciences d'Outremer, *Bulletin des Séances*, VI, 4, Brussels, 1960. Some confusion may have arisen from Livingstone's comments on his 1854 journey through the northern and eastern fringes of Quiboco, just a few years after Magyar had travelled through its heart. Livingstone wrote, 'The population may be said to be very large when compared with the Bechuana or Griqua country, yet there are large tracts of fine fruitful country lying absolutely waste, for there is no game. . . .' (1963, 102). He found a more populous area in 'Balonda' (Lunda) south-east of Quiboco where 'the numbers of people must be very large. We passed through villages without end, sometimes ten in a single day.' The apparent contradiction stems from the fact that Livingstone never really entered Quiboco, only skirting the edges of the land Magyar found so heavily populated. Magyar was familiar with Livingstone's 'Balonda' but still implicitly ranked the Cokwe lands as more populous.

[3] D. Livingstone, *Missionary Travels*, London, 1857, 281.

supply and who could produce the slaves which the Cokwe wanted.[1] Thus a new trade system sprang up, exchanging slaves, and later rubber and ivory in large quantities, for guns and imports from Europe. The Bena Lulua, unlike the Lunda with whom the Cokwe had dealt previously, hunted and gathered ivory and rubber for themselves. This left only the function of transportation to the Cokwe, and so they emerged as middlemen in competition with the caravans of Bihe and Kasanje.

After 1875, nearly all the caravans operating in the interior of Angola used the new north-south trade-route from Mona Kimbundu to the Bena Lulua. A major market-place grew up at Kalamba's capital where the Cokwe predominated in the trade. In a fourteen-month period in 1882–3 four Cokwe caravans arrived there in addition to one each from Bihe, Pungo Andongo, and Kasanje.[2] In 1880, the major export from Kalamba's market to the Cokwe was women and children. The Cokwe valued women according to their corpulence and would pay up to a large tusk of ivory for one they liked.[3] Children sold for four or six to the tusk and men for even less, although prices varied greatly according to the skill of the individual trader. Other 'typical' prices included a girl sold for a musket or twenty-four yards of calico, a woman for a four-pound keg of powder plus eight yards of calico, and an eight- or ten-year-old child for sixteen yards of calico.

The emergence of Kalamba's market meant a shift from the old pattern of two parallel trade-routes leading inland from Bihe and Kasanje to a new and complex set of sub-systems. Ivory and wax largely replaced slaves on the old trade-routes to the coast, but the volume of the slave trade in the interior continued unabated. From the point of view of the Africans it may even have increased, since the prohibition removed Europeans and their agents from the interior and left the field wide open to African slave-dealers.[4] A demand for slaves appeared among the Kuba and other peoples north-east of Kalamba at about the time that his market opened. This demand may have existed previously, but the decline in prices paid for slaves, triggered by the

[1] Henrique Dias de Carvalho, *O Lubuco: Algumas observações sobre o livro do Sr. Latrobe-Bateman*, Lisbon, 1891, 10–11; A. van Zandijcke, 'Note historique sur les origines de Luluabourg (Malandi)', *Zaïre*, VI, 3 (1952), 232–4.

[2] Paul Pogge, 'Die Wissmannsche Expedition', *Mittheilungen der Afrikanischen Gesellschaft in Deutschland*, IV (1886), 186–8.

[3] Pogge (1880), 51.

[4] M. Büchner, 'Über seine Reise in das Lundareich (1879–1882)', *Verhandlungen der Gesellschaft für Erdkunde zu Berlin*, IX (1882), 78.

price drop at the coast, made it profitable to supply this demand for the first time. Ivory supplies soon declined in Kalamba's lands, and caravans therefore began to carry cloth and guns north to the Bena Lulua where they obtained slaves, whom they took farther inland to trade to the Luba for ivory.[1] The demand for slaves was so strong that some caravans brought captives all the way north from the Lwena to the Kasai.[2] Others sold cloth to the Lunda for slaves and then carried them to these same markets among the Luba.[3]

The emergence of this market for slaves in the far north-east was connected with the disappearance of ivory supplies near the coast. As the Cokwe moved north and east in search of elephants, they finally reached peoples who would accept the slaves which no longer found a market on the coast. In many ways, the new trade pattern amounted to the same exchange of slaves for guns and cloth which had existed for centuries, altered only by the appearance of Luba markets in the Kasai which converted Lwena and Lunda slaves into the ivory demanded by the Europeans. But it also differed from the old pattern in that the Cokwe now acted as middlemen rather than solely as producers.

Before the emergence of the slave and ivory markets north of the Kasai, the Cokwe had no experience in the operation of trading caravans. They modelled their expeditions after those of the Imbangala and Ovimbundu and rapidly became successful.[4] Though they had rarely been seen in Angola before 1877, they began to compete soon afterwards on the trade-routes to the coast, becoming so familiar with prices obtainable on the coast by 1880 that it was almost impossible to bargain with them in Quiboco.[5] Success also brought increased size to the Cokwe caravans. One European traveller had found them 'rather small' in 1878, but four years later Cokwe caravans sometimes exceeded those of the Ovimbundu in size, one in particular numbering some 250 bearers.[6] By the 1890s the Cokwe sent out caravans of several hundred men to the region north of the Kasai.[7]

In addition to sending out their own caravans, the Cokwe often

[1] Carvalho (1891), 55; Arnot (1889), 91.

[2] Arnot (1889), 81. [3] Pogge (1880), 52.

[4] Otto Schütt, *Reisen im Südwestlichen Becken des Congo*, Berlin, 1881, 132.

[5] Capello and Ivens (1882), 225; António F. da Silva Porto, 'Novas Jornadas', *Boletim da Sociedade de Geografia e de história de Lisboa*, V (1885), 168.

[6] Hermann von Wissmann, *Unter Deutsche Flagge: Quer durch Afrika*, 9th ed., Berlin, 1902, 340, 417.

[7] A. van Zandijcke, *Pages de l'histoire du Kasai*, Namur, 1953, 97–100. Perhaps some allowance for exaggeration should be made, since the estimate comes from a Belgian military officer who fought a victorious battle against this particular caravan.

participated in the large parties which set out for the far interior from Bihe and Kasanje. These experiences amounted to apprenticeship for the Cokwe in the arts of managing large groups of slaves. Cameron met one such composite group in the Luba chiefdom of Kasongo where it had gone to raid for slaves. It included over 700 porters, Cokwe, Ovimbundu, and Lwena, in a cooperative raiding venture which pillaged its way through Katanga. Each component retained its separate identity but worked with the others when attacked or when attacking. Such cooperative caravans probably continued to provide a means by which small parties of Cokwe could participate in the trading system even after the larger Cokwe caravans had become important.[1]

The arrival of one of these large caravans at a major market-place occasioned great excitement. One Cokwe caravan which reached Kalamba's market in 1882 announced its approach while it was still some distance away. A standard-bearer ran into the market-place waving a coloured banner for all to see and then raced back to the head of the approaching column of porters, which he led into the town with an exaggerated goose-stepping gait. Behind him marched the leader of the expedition, dressed for the occasion in resplendent fabrics and followed by the rest of the bearers. They entered the market square amidst drumming and firing of guns. All the people of the vicinity gathered to watch Kalamba and his council of advisers welcome the caravan with proper honours. Then they joined in a series of dances and festivities which preceded the opening of business itself.

Once business began, buyers and sellers negotiated at length before they agreed on a bargain. When they finally struck an acceptable price, expressed in terms of small balls of rubber, they sat down on the ground and counted out the required number according to the decimal system. They laid out rows of ten balls until they had ten rows of ten which they made into a pile of one hundred. For larger sales, merchants made ten such piles for a unit of a thousand rubber balls, about the equivalent of a woman or a gun. They broke a small straw into pieces to confirm the completed deal. This rubber currency was subject to inflation as sellers gradually reduced the size of the ball. In 1876, there had been eight to ten balls to the kilogram: by 1882, forty balls made a kilogram. However, the inflation seemed about to halt as traders began to adjust their prices.[2]

Cokwe slave caravans travelled with groups of four to eight slaves

[1] V. L. Cameron, *Across Africa*, London, 1885, 327, 364, 375–6.

[2] Pogge (1886), 187–8.

chained together by their wrists. If the leaders feared revolt or escape, they added ankle chains at night, but they rarely punished their captives because in their weakened condition they could stand little abuse. If a slave died he was cut loose from his shackles and the body was left to decompose by the side of the road.[1] Escapes sometimes occurred, particularly in the vicinity of Cokwe villages, since the slaves knew that they would find a welcome from the headman as pawns for his lineage. Other headmen welcomed escaped slaves but only to try to sell them back to the caravan at a price as high or higher than their original cost.[2] The caravan leaders fed their slaves manioc flour, but they often starved them in the early part of the journey, partly in order not to waste money feeding slaves before they had to fatten them up for sale, but also to weaken them physically and thus lessen attempts at escape. They always did this if food was cheaper nearer their destination. The trader could not destroy his captives without losing money, yet he profited most if he delivered them barely alive, leaving it to their purchasers to incur the expense of restoring the slaves to health. Thus the economics of the slave trade tended to determine its degree of harshness.

The 'rubber boom' in the last third of the nineteenth century reinforced the changes in the pattern of long-distance trade which had begun as a result of the Portuguese demand for wax and ivory. The first report of 'first class' rubber exported from Benguela came in 1869. By 1874 rubber accounted for a significant proportion of total exports and in 1886 its value surpassed the combined total of ivory and wax exports.[3] The Cokwe again occupied a particularly advantageous position. The forests of Quiboco produced most of the early rubber exports because they were the closest rich source to the coast, and rubber-gathering fitted easily into the Cokwe economic pattern of hunting and aviculture.[4] The Cokwe probably controlled the supply of rubber sent to Benguela for the first few years, but they exploited their sources so inefficiently that rubber had disappeared south of Mona Kimbundu by 1875.[5] Because the Cokwe failed to replace the plants

[1] Pogge (1880), 51–3.

[2] Hermann von Wissmann, L. Wolf, C. von François, und H. Müller, *Im Innern Afrikas*, Leipzig, 1891, 60.

[3] Childs (1949), 205, 208. 'First class' rubber came from the sap of creepers and trees and was the only kind exported until 1886. In that year 'red rubber', which came from liana roots, came on to the market and soon replaced 'first class' rubber completely. See Vansina (1962), 386.

[4] Arnot (1889), 81.

[5] Pogge (1880), 46.

killed by tapping their sap, no rubber remained. This process paralleled the destruction of the elephants in Quiboco thirty years earlier. The Cokwe adopted the same strategy they had followed when the elephants had disappeared: they followed the gallery forests north in pursuit of the rubber that remained. The opening of the trade-route to Kalamba's encouraged the movement north, and earlier hunting and trading activities of the Cokwe in the region also helped by providing knowledge of geography and living conditions there, as well as local contacts. The difference between this and previous northward expansion was the fact that women and children could exploit rubber as efficiently as men.[1] This helped to change the character of the movement from small hunting-parties and trading caravans to a migration of entire villages.

Pressures building toward the migration phase of Cokwe expansion had originated in Cokwe purchases of women from Imbangala caravans passing near Quiboco. After 1866 Cokwe traders supplemented the flow of women to Cokwe lands by sending back numerous Lulua women and children from Kalamba's market in the north. Together these sources increased the flow of women towards the Cokwe homeland to a torrent. Quiboco had already contained a dense population in 1850 and, since the Cokwe never sold their own women to outsiders, there was no outflow to release the population pressure.[2] Soon the relatively inefficient agricultural techniques of the Cokwe, combined with the infertile Kalahari sands of their home, could no longer support the increase in population.[3] By the 1870s, overcrowding resulted in the inevitable combination of malnutrition and sickness, probably an epidemic of smallpox.[4]

The nature of the Cokwe social and political systems also contributed to the mass migration. The regularity of Cokwe village fission made it easy for them to pull up stakes and transport entire villages from place to place. As long as plenty of available land surrounded the old village

[1] F. S. Arnot, *Bihé and Garenganze*, London, 1893, 32.

[2] Henry W. Nevinson, *More Changes, More Chances*, London, 1925, 62, confirms for the twentieth century the statement made by Magyar in 1850.

[3] H. Nicolaï, 'Disette à Kahemba: une forme aiguë du problème Kwangolais', *Bulletin de la société belge d'études géographiques*, XXVI, 2 (1957), 315, emphasizes the inefficiencies of the Cokwe agricultural techniques and their vulnerability to excessive drought or dampness.

[4] A. A. de Serpa Pinto, *How I Crossed Africa* (trans. Alfred Elwes), 2 vols., Philadelphia, 1881, I, 271. A severe smallpox epidemic had struck Angola in 1864–5 and had spread up the trade-routes to the interior. The disease was reported still prevalent in 1875. See Douglas Wheeler, 'A Note on Smallpox in Angola', *Studia*, 13–14 (Jan.–July, 1964), 356–7.

site, its successor villages could settle near by. But when overpopulation made land scarce, the absence of vacant spaces for new villages created a volatile situation. Internal village tensions rose until aspiring village headmen began to search for lands beyond the borders of Quiboco.

The migrating Cokwe utilized well-established techniques of moving. Following trails broken by Cokwe hunters and traders, they packed up all their movable property and headed north. Men, women, and children moved together, carrying seeds, pigs, goats, and other equipment needed to settle permanently whenever they reached a suitable location. They lived in the same round straw huts while on the move that they had always used to establish new villages, sometimes pausing long enough on the way to plant fields and reap a harvest. Invariably they brought with them their newly assimilated pawn women as they searched for 'more advantageous conditions'.[1] The migration thus amounted to little more than an extension of previously established internal patterns, now turned outward by the influx of women to Quiboco and by the pursuit of rubber.

Individual villages probably did not migrate very far. A few villages would move just beyond the edge of Cokwe settlement and stop. Then the continued population pressure behind them would produce another wave of emigrants, and these lineages would pass through the frontier established by the last groups to extend again the boundaries of Cokwe settlement. These pulses of movement produced a wavelike effect as tides of migrating Cokwe swept through a region.[2]

The cohesive character of the migration stands in marked contrast to the wide-ranging activities of the hunters and traders who had preceded them, all of whom operated far from other bases of Cokwe power. The migrants maintained continuous contact with one another and none advanced very far ahead of previously settled areas. The villages had a strong sense of loyalty to one another and regarded an attack on one as an attack on all.[3] Cohesiveness gave them the strength which mobility and self-sufficiency provided for the other forms of expansion.

[1] G. Haveaux, *La tradition historique des Bapende orientaux*, Brussels, 1954, 29; Carvalho (1891), 10–11; Leo Frobenius, *Im Schatten des Kongostaates*, Berlin, 1907, 329; Torday (1925), 271.

[2] Leo Frobenius, 'Forschungensreise in das Kasai-Gebiet', *Zeitschrift der Gesellschaft für Erdkunde zu Berlin,* V (1906), 118.

[3] Emil Torday and T. A. Joyce, *Notes ethnographiques sur les populations habitant les bassins du Kasai et du Kwango oriental, Annales du Musée du Congo Belge,* sér. iii, II, fasc. 2, Brussels, 1922, 329.

The migration proceeded as a fragmented movement of many small lineages which could enter an area without upsetting its ecology, with no single mass movement of thousands of Cokwe. The entire Cokwe culture centred around forest dwelling. Their economy originally depended on hunting in the deciduous woods of the plateaux, gathering wax and honey from beehives placed in trees, and the extraction of rubber from vines and roots found in the gallery forests running to the north.[1] The Cokwe preferred to live surrounded by trees, even at the expense of the extra effort required to clear spaces for villages and fields.[2] Their supernatural beliefs emphasized trees, springs, and the rivers which flowed through the gallery forests.[3] Because the Cokwe felt at home in these forests, they followed them north and south from Quiboco, thus helping to give the migration its predominantly north-south orientation. Their Lunda neighbours, moreover, lived in the savannahs and had no objection to Cokwe living in their unused forests, just as they had earlier welcomed Cokwe ivory-hunters to do a job for which they had no skill.[4] Thus, although other peoples lived in the areas into which the Cokwe moved, the first Cokwe arrivals found plenty of room to settle because they preferred to live in the relatively uninhabited gallery forests.

The first Cokwe migrants in an area were very submissive and cautious in their relations with the local inhabitants.[5] The villages near their settlements found their skills as hunters, fetishers, and iron-workers useful additions to the neighbourhood and often started a thriving trade with their guests.[6] The Cokwe would even work for food supplies in the villages of their neighbours. This combination of a vacant ecological niche and the advantages which the first arrivals

[1] For example, see Alfred Schachtzabel, *Im Hochland von Angola*, Dresden, 1923, 134, 143.

[2] O. Schütt, 'Die Schüttsche Expedition', *Mittheilungen der Afrikanischen Gesellschaft in Deutschland*, I (1878–9), 179; J. R. Graça, 'Diários', *Annaes do Conselho Ultramarino*, I (1867) (Parte não official), 145; Pogge (1880), 46, 78; Wissmann *et al.* (1891), 48; A. Monard, 'Notes sur les collections ethnographiques de la mission scientifique suisse en Angola', *Bulletin de la Société Neuchâteloise de Géographie*, XXXIX (1930), 101. Vansina (1966), 218–19, offers the hypothesis of the empty ecological niche, but emphasizes it only in relation to the hunting phase of the expansion. It seems to apply equally well to the migratory phase.

[3] For example, see José Redinha, 'Costumes religiosos e feiticistos dos Kiokos de Angola', *Mensário Administrativo*, 20–21 (1949), 35.

[4] Torday and Joyce (1922), 232; Petermann (1860), 229.

[5] Schütt (1878–9), I, 179; Augostinho Sisenando Marques, *Os climas e as producções das terras de Malange à Lunda*, Lisbon, 1889, 522; Monard (1930), 101–2.

[6] T. Delachaux and C. E. Thiébaud, *Land und Völker von Angola*, Neuchâtel and Paris, 1934, 135; Frobenius (1907), 329; Schütt (1878–9), I, 179.

seemed to offer the local inhabitants allowed them to enter new areas with very little resistance. Only after the Cokwe had increased rapidly by marrying the women of the native villages and by the arrival of additional villages from Quiboco did their hosts discover what they had done. The Cokwe soon controlled the economy of their area and began to crowd out the original residents.

The most destructive Cokwe tactic was to attract the women of the local villages. Lunda women valued the advantages of joining Cokwe villages so much that they offered little resistance to assimilation as Cokwe pawns. The Cokwe invariably treated their pawn women very well and gave them better food than they could have obtained from their own people. The cohesiveness of the dominant lineage in each village hastened their cultural assimilation, and they readily adopted Cokwe dress, hair style, habits, gestures, and language.[1] They accepted Cokwe culture so completely in fact that they raised their children as Cokwe rather than Lunda. Thus, in a single generation, Cokwe society could absorb these women and their descendants so thoroughly that only traces of their non-Cokwe origins remained.

A secondary effect of the Cokwe mass migration was felt by the Cokwe merchant caravans. The exhaustion of home supplies of rubber, along with increasing demand on the coast, supported the conversion of the Cokwe from producers to middlemen. Their slave and ivory caravans could carry rubber with practically no change in organization, and they already had access to the Lulua and other Luba peoples north of the Kasai, who soon became the major exporters of rubber as well as ivory when price rises on the coast made its export profitable. A new trade-route appeared to accommodate the increased traffic to and from this area, running from Kalamba's capital through Mai Munene and south-west to Kasanje. By 1880 Cokwe caravans frequented the route along with the Imbangala and Angolan traders from Ambaca and Pungo Andongo.

Raiding parties constituted a fourth form of Cokwe expansion. They spread over as wide an area as the trading caravans and probably evolved from them, since it was a short step from buying women to raiding for slaves. Some caravans had always functioned more as raiders than as traders,[2] and were distinguishable from pillagers only

[1] Henrique Dias de Carvalho, *Ethnographia e história tradicional dos povos da Lunda*, Lisbon, 1890—cited as Carvalho (1890)—487.

[2] The caravan which Cameron met in Katanga acted as mercenaries for the Luba chief Kasongo and travelled with him on his annual round of tribute collection; in return for this service, the caravan enjoyed general plundering rights: Cameron (1885), 364, 375–6.

in theory. The groups of Cokwe raiders, who made no pretence of legitimate or illegitimate trade, varied in size from very small parties up to 600 and even 2000 men.[1] They lived off the countryside, burning villages and robbing passing caravans for whatever they could get. They were highly versatile and could either mass for defence or spread out for their normal pattern of attack.

When threatened by strong enemy forces, the Cokwe would draw up their men in a circular encampment on the top of a small hill from which they had removed all undergrowth for some distance beyond the limits of the camp itself. They usually made no effort to stockade their position but relied on their mobility and on warning from sentries posted at a distance of an hour's march. When news of an impending attack came, they would remove their prisoners to a safe location in the bush. The Cokwe warriors then waited in the camp for the enemy. As soon as he came into range in the cleared area around the camp, they opened fire in an attempt to drive him back at once. If the enemy survived the first fusillade and managed to storm the camp itself, the Cokwe were unlikely to offer stiff resistance in hand-to-hand combat. Instead they melted into the forest to regroup for another stand elsewhere.[2] These tactics depended on superior firepower and indicated the great number of guns in the hands of the Cokwe. They ensured that the Cokwe raiders could suffer temporary defeat without annihilation and made it very difficult for their enemies to expel them from their lands.

Working from this base camp, smaller bands of raiders roamed the surrounding countryside in search of women and provisions. If they desired supplies, they would appear before a village and fire a volley into the air. They gained such an awesome reputation that this tactic sufficed to chase the inhabitants into the woods, allowing the Cokwe to plunder the village at their leisure before leaving it in flames. If the Cokwe wanted captives, the larger band split up into several groups of thirty or forty men which dispersed over a wide area. These groups then detached patrols of ten men which went out to 'beat the bush', as the Cokwe termed the manœuvre. The men of these patrols often brought back as many as ten prisoners apiece.[3]

In areas like the Kasai where firearms were still relatively scarce, the

[1] Zandijcke (1953), 97–100.

[2] Oscar Michaux, *Au Congo: Carnet de campagne—épisodes et impressions de 1889 à 1897*, Namur, 1913, 152, 155–6, 265.

[3] Carvalho (1890), 472–3.

Cokwe guns so terrified the local residents that the Cokwe could simply requisition women and supplies whenever they needed them. Occasionally they used the device of demanding fines (*milonga*) for fancied insults as a pretext for the demands they made on the people living in the area.[1] The Cokwe held an edge in mobility in the areas where they faced better-armed opponents. Unlike most of their enemies, who travelled encumbered by numerous retainers and camp-followers, the Cokwe always left their women and children at home. They did not hesitate to attack large enemy forces by rapidly encircling them and then moving in for easy victories and many captives.[2]

The Cokwe chiefs who stayed in their villages profited from the caravan trade almost as much as the caravan-leaders and heads of raiding parties. Although they sold whatever wax, ivory, and rubber they might have, their wealth did not depend on the sale of these staples, since many other profitable opportunities arose from the presence of a large caravan near a chief's village. Chiefs therefore tried to force trading expeditions to stop at their villages in order to take advantage of them, using the prospect of trade as an inducement.[3] In order to entice caravans to remain for several days some chiefs developed elaborate ruses to support the illusion that they possessed much greater quantities of ivory or wax than they actually had. In the days when ivory was plentiful in their country, Lunda and Cokwe chiefs had buried a few tusks in the ground and, for years after the elephants had disappeared, they displayed them to traders pretending that they still had vast quantities of ivory to sell.[4]

Hopeful traders engaged in lengthy but fruitless bargaining over the illusory tusks while the villagers systematically milked their caravan. Women and children surrounded the caravan camp and eagerly sold manioc flour, chickens, and other foodstuffs to the bearers. Cokwe blacksmiths repaired broken equipment for a fee. Petty trade in all sorts of charms, weapons, and trinkets flourished between the bearers and the villagers. Some chiefs even furnished women for the pleasure of the men of the visiting caravans.[5] Thus the ordinary villagers participated

[1] Haveaux (1954), 30.

[2] Carvalho (1890), 474–5, 491; Henrique Dias de Carvalho, *Methodo pratico para fallar a lingua de Lunda, contendo narrações históricos dos diversos povos*, Lisbon, 1890, 293.

[3] Silva Porto (1885), 168, 170.

[4] Carvalho (1890), 691.

[5] For example, see Silva Porto (1885), 166; Hermann von Wissmann, 'Reiseberichte', *Mittheilungen der Afrikanischen Gesellschaft in Deutschland*, III (1881–3), 152–4; Büchner (1882), 88; J. O. Ferreira Diniz, *Populações indígenas de Angola*, Coimbra, 1918, 145.

in the long-distance trade system by providing food and entertainment for the traders and their men.

The chiefs kept control of business in the standard trade articles for themselves, since caravan leaders who stopped near Cokwe villages could deal only with the chiefs themselves.[1] Elaborate and lengthy formalities preceded the actual transaction of business, as the chief tried to delay the caravan and the trader tried to win the good graces of his host. The Cokwe had a reputation for prolonging these preliminaries to their own advantage. The chief and the trader exchanged gifts, a potentially profitable transaction for the chief since he often sent modest presents to the trader. His chiefly dignity, however, demanded far more expensive gifts in return, and he could usually get them.[2] He also profited by his right to establish the system of weights and measures. After reaching agreement on these matters and settling the prices to be paid, the chief carefully selected pieces of cloth, checked the powder to make sure that no sand adulterated it, and inspected the guns. He always rejected part of the merchandise as a matter of form and then repeated the entire selection process while the trader and his caravan waited.[3] He could take days to sell a single tusk.

Most of the traders extended credit to the chiefs on whom they called. A wealthy chief could take advantage of the trader by buying as much as he could but paying for only a part of his purchases. This forced the trader to return to collect his debt, at which time the chief simply bought enough more trade-goods to require him to return again. Since these debts were regarded as official and involved the honour of his court, the chief rarely defaulted.[4] However, he usually managed to stay permanently in debt, thus imposing on the trader a kind of debt servitude in reverse.

The Cokwe continued to use the *milonga*, originally developed to tax passing caravans in the early nineteenth century, even after they entered the long-distance trading system as producers of wax, ivory, and rubber. All peoples charged tolls for ferrying caravans across rivers or for the use of a ford, but the Cokwe added fines for fancied violations of local customs which seemed to be designed solely for exploitation of passing traders. European travellers generally resented the system. Livingstone, for example, encountered it in 1854 when a Cokwe chief stopped his party and demanded a fine of a man, a gun, or an ox, because one of his porters inadvertently allowed a drop of spittle to fall

[1] Carvalho (1890), 702.
[2] Frobenius (1907), 325.
[3] Carvalho (1890), 695–6.
[4] Ferreira Diniz (1918), 156–8.

on the leg of a Cokwe. Not realizing that he was expected to negotiate the amount of the fine and to pay it gracefully, Livingstone refused and angered the chief so much that a battle nearly resulted.[1] The Imbangala, on the other hand, accepted the *milonga* as taxes and paid them as an ordinary hazard of doing business with the Cokwe.[2] It served to delay the caravan while the villagers hawked their goods among the porters, as well as to provide revenue for the chief who levied the fines.

Pretexts for *milonga* were often of the flimsiest sort. One chief spread manioc flour along the caravan trail and then sat back on the side of the road to wait for a porter to step on it so he could demand his *milonga*.[3] After an offence was committed, the chief's *ngaji* judges arbitrated the case according to standard Cokwe judicial procedures.[4] Because business relations depended on a satisfactory conclusion of the suit, chiefs had the traders at their mercy. The traders' only defence was to play down their own wealth and importance because those who represented more always paid more.[5] Cokwe chiefs evidently knew how to charge what the traffic would bear.

While these patterns of trade and economics strengthened the Cokwe, the Lunda empire suffered from the same changes between 1830 and 1880. Before 1830 the Lunda had grown wealthy from the export of slaves, but after the slave trade to the coast declined they had had to seek new products. Although they lived too far inland to export wax profitably, they found a temporary substitute in ivory which sufficed to buy the European cloth and guns they needed.[6] The 'rubber boom' provided a brief additional prosperity in the early 1870s, but rubber supplies disappeared some time before 1875, and the supply of ivory played out at about the same date.[7]

Because the Lunda lived at the end of the trading system, they could not become middlemen as the Cokwe had done when their ivory and rubber had run out. So, deprived of a profitable export, the Lunda returned to slave trading. Instead of sending slaves to the coast as formerly, they now supplied the new Luba markets in the north, but even this trade did not halt the economic decline of the Lunda empire.

[1] Livingstone (1963), 92–3, 116–17.

[2] Henrique Dias de Carvalho, *O jagado de Cassange na província de Angola: Memória*, Lisbon, 1898, 388.

[3] Silva Porto (1885), 573.

[4] Hermann von Wissmann (1881–3), 153, has a detailed account of a fine charged against one of his men and the procedure used to settle the issue.

[5] Marques (1889), 501.

[6] Livingstone (1963), 245.

[7] Arnot (1889), 81; Carvalho (1891), 51; Pogge (1880), 237.

European travellers of the 1870s emphasized the visible poverty in its heartland. They described the Lunda as poor hunters and traders, who collected no wax or rubber for export and spent their meagre receipts from slaves on unproductive trinkets which only deepened the economic decline.[1] At this time caravans began to avoid the Lunda capital on the Kalanyi. In order to obtain business the Mwata Yamvo ordered his western governors to force traders to visit his *musumba* or capital.[2] As the Cokwe settled along the trade-route to Kasanje in their northward migration, they broke the connection between the Imbangala and the Lunda which had united the two states for over two centuries. The Imbangala, who had fought the Ovimbundu for the right to trade with the Lunda in the early nineteenth century, now made no effort to keep the trade-route open. Instead they shifted their trading pattern to Kalamba's market and refused to resurrect their sagging commerce with the Lunda.[3]

By the 1880s economic disaster had befallen the Lunda empire. Travellers contrasted the poverty-stricken condition of the Lunda with the prosperous Cokwe in the same area, finding that their caravans could buy plenty of food from the Cokwe villages but none in those of the Lunda.[4] At that time internal dissension was tearing the Lunda empire apart and the contending sides needed weapons to conduct their struggles. They remedied their lack of firearms by calling in the Cokwe, thus resorting to the same strategy that their fathers had used in the 1840s to remedy their lack of ivory. This strategy led directly to the Cokwe conquest of the Lunda empire. Dynastic disputes continually plagued the Lunda empire in the latter part of the nineteenth century, both at the *musumba* of the Mwata Yamvo and at the courts of the provincial governors. Cokwe mercenaries helped install each victorious candidate on the throne and then took his power from him by settling on his lands and taking his women as slaves.[5]

[1] Pogge (1880), 77, 237.

[2] Otto Schütt, 'Bericht über die Reise von Malange zum Luba-Häuptling Mai und zurück, Juli 1878 bis Mai 1879', *Mittheilungen der Afrikanischen Gesellschaft in Deutschland*, I (1878–9), 179.

[3] Henrique Dias de Carvalho, *Memória: A Lunda ou os estados do Muatiânvua*, Lisbon, 1890—cited as Carvalho (*Memória*)—143; Büchner (1882), 10.

[4] Marques (1889), 381; Carvalho (*Memória*), 165.

[5] Büchner (1882), 101; Carvalho (1890), 210, 474, 622, 643, for examples. The problem of dynastic disputes in the Lunda empire seems to have been an inherent weakness of their political system. The Lunda built safeguards against it into their kingship in the form of prohibitions against too numerous offspring of their chiefs. See L. de Sousberghe, 'Les Pende—Aspects des structures sociales et politiques', *Miscellanea Ethnographica*, Tervuren,

Cokwe chiefs and upstarts, rather than the hunters or lineage headmen, led the bands of mercenaries which intervened in Lunda politics. They used the prospect of acquiring pawn wives to muster large numbers of men, since the leader of the raid had the right to distribute the captured women as spoils among his men.[1] A war leader known for his ability to capture numerous slaves would have little difficulty in raising a larger number of men than either the conventional political units, the chiefdoms, or the lineages. The extensive pillaging of the Lunda empire by the latter part of the 1880s provided opportunities for unimportant Cokwe chiefs to rise to positions of considerable physical power, unjustified by their low traditional status in the chiefly hierarchy. Some of these later war leaders may have had no traditional chiefly status and simply assumed traditional titles when their power and influence warranted it. From the point of view of the older Cokwe chiefs, the rise of the new generation of war leaders amounted to a political revolution.[2]

The chronology of the Cokwe expansion paralleled the changes in the economics of trade in Western Central Africa. The Lunda traditional histories remembered the first formal contact of their chiefs with Cokwe ivory-hunters and dated it at about 1840. During the 1840s, one of the new generation of chiefs, Cisenge, attempted to gain control of the main trade-route from Kasanje to the Lunda empire; he failed when the Lunda Mwata Yamvo established a new provincial capital at Mona Kimbundu to exclude the Cokwe from the trade.[3] A decade later, however, population pressure in Quiboco was pushing Cokwe villages into the area around Mona Kimbundu. Simultaneously in the 1850s Cokwe traders reached Mai Munene in the north where they did a thriving business.[4] The Cokwe made their first journey across the Kasai to the Bena Lulua of Kalamba in 1866.[5] This set the pattern for the northward dimension of the expansion, which

1963, 74. There is no demonstrated simple economic cause to tie the economic decline to the political fall of the empire.

[1] Carvalho (1890), 487.

[2] Evidence to support this hypothesis depends on the fact that the Cokwe chiefdoms maintained a system of positional succession and perpetual kinship, under which each succeeding chief in a lineage inherited not only his predecessor's office but also his name and position in the kinship web which united the chiefs to each other. The appearance of new chiefs' names in the 1880s marks them as newcomers.

[3] Carvalho (1890), 556–60; also see Duysters (1958), 90; M. van den Byvang, 'Notice historique des Balunda', *Congo*, I, 5 (1937), 558.

[4] Livingstone (1963), 245.

[5] Schütt (1878–9), I, 181, gives this date. Carvalho (1891), 11, agrees.

depended initially on ivory and later on rubber. The slow progression of Cokwe villages northward into the area around Mona Kimbundu, which was solidly Cokwe in the early 1870s, became stronger and more rapid in about 1875; in the following decade the migration carried as far north as the Pende.[1]

Migration to the south was in full swing by the late 1870s when a traveller encountered numerous Cokwe living among the Luchaze between the Kwito and the Kwanvale. They had begun their southward movement quite a while previously and had reached as far south as the confluence of the Kwito and the Kubango near Dario.[2] This migration may have begun even before its counterpart in the north, motivated by a search for beeswax in the early phases and hastened by overpopulation in the 1860s, but the available evidence does not permit the determination of an exact date of origin. In any case the Cokwe were streaming south in large numbers in 1877.

In 1875 a succession dispute in the Lunda empire first drew Cokwe mercenaries across the Kasai, to the heartland of the Lunda empire. In that year a Lunda pretender to the throne led the Cokwe of Cisenge and Cinyama to the Kalanyi where they installed him as Mwata Yamvo. In return they received gifts for themselves and for their men permission to raid one of the Lunda provinces for slaves. The Cokwe returned home well satisfied with many captives.[3] Other Cokwe chiefs followed this successful precedent and soon Cokwe mercenaries fought for Lunda pretenders in the north as well as in the east, sometimes against each other when both claimants to the throne could enlist the aid of different Cokwe chiefs. By the 1880s fighting was general and had disrupted all trade from the Lunda empire to the coast.[4] The Lunda rulers, realizing how dependent they had become on their Cokwe troops, attempted to break the cycle of fighting by requesting Portuguese aid and by declaring an end to the use of Cokwe troops. These efforts failed in 1884 when another Lunda noble raised an army of Cokwe and successfully installed himself as Mwata Yamvo.[5]

In 1885 Cokwe migration began to cross the Kasai in the wake of the raiders and mercenaries who had been active in the area for several years. This new phase of the expansion stiffened Lunda resistance, and a series of battles between the forces of the Mwata Yamvo and the Cokwe

[1] Schütt (1881), 130; Haveaux (1954), 29.
[2] Serpa Pinto (1881), I, 271.
[3] Carvalho (1890), 599–602.
[4] Carvalho (1890), 626; Pogge (1882–3), III, 146.
[5] Carvalho (1890), 627–43; van den Byvang (1937), 204.

culminated in a crushing defeat for the Lunda. These battles turned the tide in favour of uncontrolled Cokwe pillaging east of the Kasai. They sacked the capital and took its inhabitants as slaves. On the west side of the Kasai, the Cokwe continued to raid Lunda villages for women and took control of vast areas, effectively cutting the former Lunda empire into a number of small enclaves. There a few Lunda governors managed to reach rapprochements with neighbouring Cokwe chiefs by exchanging women with them as wives. Mona Kimbundu and Cisenge achieved peaceful relations in this manner, as did a few others.[1]

The new generation of Cokwe chiefs gained control of the Lunda empire east of the Kasai in 1887 under the leadership of Mawoka. He and the other invaders initiated a reign of terror in the Lunda lands. When they raided villages, they took as many slaves as they could carry with them and killed the rest of the inhabitants by barricading them in huts which they set on fire. The Lunda who managed to escape fled to the Luba kingdoms to the north and east, leaving a virtual desert where the Lunda empire had once stood. Only a few Cokwe villages moved in to settle in its place. Some Cokwe migration filled in the area east of the middle Kasai and many more moved to what is now the south-western corner of Katanga. Cokwe raiders, however, penetrated as far east as Mutombo Mukulu, plundering all over the former Lunda areas. Thus the Cokwe victory in the east came by pillaging, unlike their conquest west of the Kasai by migration.[2]

The expansion of Cokwe raiding and trading reached its zenith in 1890. After that date a series of reverses forced them to curtail their activities and to withdraw west of the Kasai. In Katanga the Lunda reunited under an exiled Mwata Yamvo and by 1896 had driven the Cokwe chiefs out.[3] In the north, Pende, Mbunda, and Kwese cooperated to fight the Cokwe on the Kwilu in 1892 and defeated them soundly with the aid of a downpour which neutralized Cokwe superiority in arms by soaking their powder.[4] Throughout the region claimed by the Congo Independent State European military officers and Congolese troops pursued the Cokwe in an effort to end their economic power and military superiority.[5]

[1] Carvalho (1890), 487, 651–6, 663; van den Byvang (1937), 204.

[2] Duysters (1958), 96.

[3] van den Byvang (1937), 206–7; Duysters (1958), 97.

[4] Emil Torday, *Camp and Tramp in the African Wilds*, London, 1913, 24, 253; Haveaux (1954), 29; I. Struyf, 'Kahemba: envahisseurs Badjok et conquérants Balunda', *Zaïre*, II, 4 (1948), 366.

[5] See, for example, Michaux (1913).

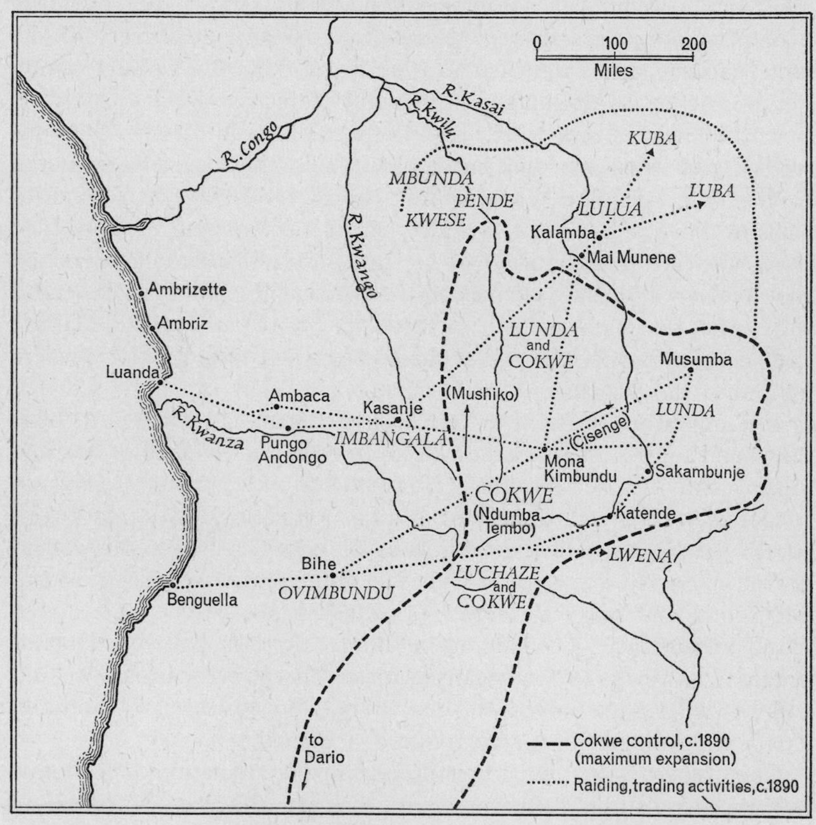

Map 11. Maximum Cokwe Expansion: Peoples, Places, and Trade-Routes, *c.* 1890

The fragility of Cokwe political and military power derived from the nature of the expansion itself. Cokwe ability to mass large bands of fighting men depended on continuing war and the acquisition of captive women; when the total defeat of the Lunda and the growing resistance of European authorities brought an end to the raids, the Cokwe military organization broke down. Former members of the large raiding parties returned to their small villages, unable to unite even for defence against attack. Cultural factors also played a part. The pawnship mechanism, which had served admirably during the conquests, had been the only means by which the Cokwe assimilated neighbouring peoples. When raiding ended, the Cokwe had no other ways of incorporating Lunda and other peoples alongside whom they lived. Instead of becoming Cokwe, the Lunda in particular retained their feeling of separate identity and were thus prepared to rally behind the banner of the resurgent Lunda Mwata Yamvo in 1896. The failure to incorporate peacefully the surrounding villages lay everywhere behind Cokwe defeats in the 1890s.

The migratory phase of the expansion continued unabated in both north and south. Although the Cokwe frontier had stopped advancing, villages still streamed into the Kasai in 1905 to fill in the areas already inhabited by mixed Cokwe and Lunda populations.[1] Migrants continued to arrive in southern Angola as late as 1914. Fewer Cokwe had moved east across the Kasai in the 1880s and 1890s than had gone north and south, and many of these had returned west at the time of the Lunda resurgence. The migration toward the east halted only temporarily, however, and it began again in the 1920s when Cokwe and Cokwe-ized Lunda moved into the Congo and Northern Rhodesia to escape the authority of the Portuguese in Angola.[2]

The Cokwe expansion had resulted from a combination of economic influences radiating from the Europeans on the coast and Cokwe potentialities: the latent responses in Cokwe social, political, and economic institutions. Clearly, the shift from the slave trade to wax and ivory exports in the 1830s and 1840s made the crucial difference in the economic fortunes of the Cokwe. Their geographical location gave them a start in the production of wax and ivory, and their social and economic

[1] Frobenius (1907), 329; this migration continued at a slower pace into the 1930s: see Nicolaï (1957), 318.

[2] Schachtzabel (1923), 144; Duysters (1958), 97; Dugald Campbell, *Wanderings in Central Africa*, London, 1929, 48; C. M. N. White, 'The Balovale Peoples and their Historical Background', *Rhodes-Livingstone Journal*, 8 (1949), 40.

structure made it easy for them to follow the receding supplies of ivory, and later rubber, when their domestic sources ran out. The village social and economic structure tolerated long absences by male hunters and traders, while their skills made them welcome guests in others' lands.

Cokwe values and their social system supplied the key factors in giving Cokwe expansion its unique migratory character. Without them, it probably would have remained a trading system like that of the Imbangala and the Ovimbundu. With them, it acquired slave-raiders and thousands of migrants. The pawnship system allowed the Cokwe to integrate enough alien women to create overpopulation in Quiboco, and lineage headmen easily converted their normal village-moving techniques into methods of migration. Much later, raiding and trading provided more women to fuel the continuing spread of Cokwe settlement.

Cokwe chiefs provided only minimal coordination of the migratory phase of the expansion, but they did lead the assault on the Lunda political system by their repeated intervention in Lunda succession disputes at the request of the Lunda themselves. This request resulted from the economic decline of the Lunda empire which had deprived the Lunda of the firearms which they needed to fight out their internecine struggles, necessitating reliance on Cokwe arms. Thus widespread fighting and disorder created opportunities for a new generation of Cokwe chiefs to rise to power at the expense of the more established rulers.

10

Kazembe and the Tanganyika-Nyasa Corridor, 1800–1890[1]

CHRISTOPHER ST. JOHN

One area with the apparent potential to produce an important professional trade was the 'corridor' between Lakes Tanganyika and Nyasa.[2] The local trade of the corridor involved the exchange over large distances in many directions of a broad range of goods produced by skilled craftsmen exploiting the natural resources of particular localities. On the western border of this region of rich local trade stood the economically and politically sophisticated kingdom of Kazembe, linked with the kingdom of Mwata Yamvo in the west and the Bisa and Yao in the east in a market-oriented trade reaching to both the western and eastern coasts. The corridor, with its highly developed local trade and its position between the trade centres of Kazembe and of the east coast, would seem to have provided an ideal site for the development of professional traders.

The requirements for a 'break-through' from a local trade, tied to subsistence agriculture, to a market-oriented trade are too little known to determine whether the corridor's promise was more apparent than real, whether the peoples left to themselves would have pushed their commerce beyond local and subsistence horizons. But in any case that development was forestalled. The rapid entry of outsiders, at the same time as presenting new commercial opportunities, monopolized the very positions that developing indigenous entrepreneurs might have

[1] I should like to thank Father Aylward Shorter, Dr. Marcia Wright, and Dr. Andrew Roberts for their kind and helpful advice and for permission to use the unpublished results of their research. Lake Nyasa has been renamed Lake Malawi.

[2] While Monica Wilson has defined this 'corridor' in terms of ethnographic similarities, economic connections are more important for the definition of the region as used here. Taking Lake Mweru and Lake Rukwa as boundaries on the west and east, the main peoples included are the Bwile, Tabwa, Lungu, Fipa, Mambwe, Namwanga, Nyiha, Safwa, Bungu, and Nyakyusa. See M. Wilson, *Peoples of the Nyasa-Tanganyika Corridor*, Cape Town, 1958.

filled. None the less, the demonstration of the economic potential of the region, and of the failure of vigorous professional traders to spring from it, may contribute to an understanding of the development of trade in pre-colonial eastern central Africa as well as more positive examples have done.

A description of the economic activity of the region before the influence of coastal trade is hampered by the fact that the earliest observations of the corridor peoples were recorded by David Livingstone in 1867, well after professional traders from outside the region had become common. In a certain sense only oral tradition could yield a true picture of 'unadulterated' pre-professional trade. But traditions are primarily of political content, remembered for their continuing political purposes, and such sparse references to commerce as they contain are not chronologically reliable.[1] But, with the anachronistic nature of the sources borne in mind, wide patterns of exchange may be sketched which probably existed before the advent of professional trade.

To the north-east of Kazembe, on the shores of Lake Mweru and by the swamp Mweru wa Ntipa, the Bena Kabwile and the Tabwa prepared salt. In colonial times salt from these sources was traded as far as Fort Rosebery (in Chisinga and Aushi country well to the south of Kazembe), Mporokoso (in Lungu country), and Kasama (in the Bemba heartland). Fish from Lake Mweru, dried by sun or fire, was of 'great value' to the inhabitants in Livingstone's time, and was 'carried to great distances'. Tabwa men also made mats and baskets which may have been exported in conjunction with fish and salt.[2]

Among the Lungu, the Tabwa's neighbours to the east, Livingstone passed in early 1873 near Chungu 'mines of fine black iron ore' and villages 'with many iron furnaces'. Lungu smiths made hoes, axes, and spears for the Bemba to the south; their goods undoubtedly went in other directions as well. In the eastern chiefdoms of Ulungu some cattle were kept and cotton was cultivated. Livingstone was impressed with

[1] Marvin Miracle's investigations of the Lamba, Senga, and Nsenga suggest that oral tradition may yield—when approached with the goal in mind—much more information about early commerce than so far revealed. The political bias of most traditions recorded may reflect the bias of the collectors as well as that of the authors of the tradition. See M. P. Miracle, 'African Markets and Trade in the Copperbelt', in P. Bohannan and G. Dalton (eds.), *Markets in Africa*, Evanston, 1962, 700ff., and Miracle, 'Aboriginal Trade among the Senga and Nsenga of Northern Rhodesia', *Ethnology*, I, 2, 1962.

[2] R. J. Moore, 'Industry and Trade on Lake Mweru', *Africa*, X, 2, 1937, 145; D. Livingstone, *Last Journals*, ed. H. Waller, London, 1874, I, 267.

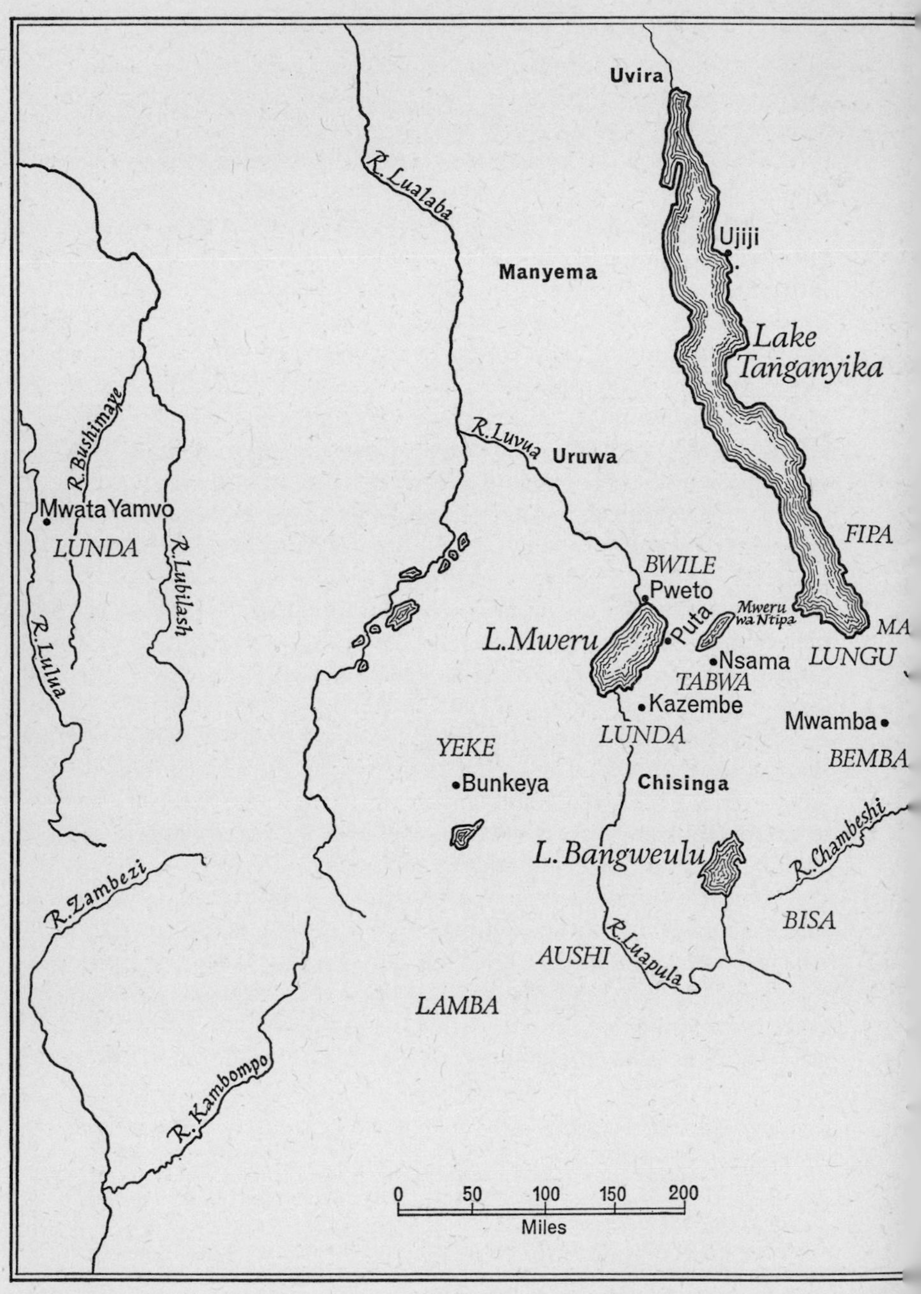

Map 12. Kazembe and the Tanganyi

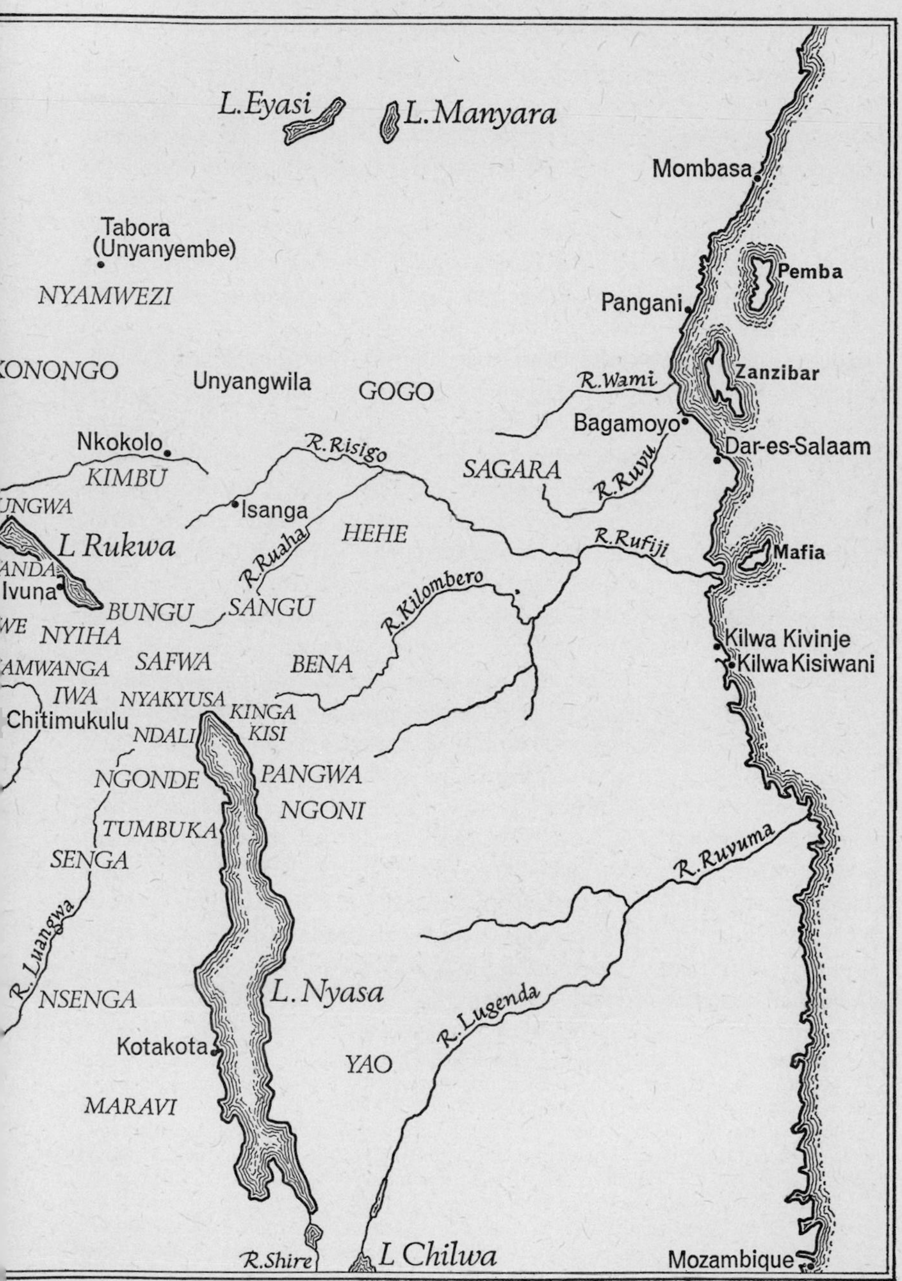

asa Corridor, 1800–1890

the constant activity in Lungu villages, whose inhabitants were engaged in mat-making and spinning and weaving. Lungu living on the Lake Tanganyika shore exchanged dried fish for millet with Lungu on the plateau as well as with people from the Mambwe chiefdom of Fuambo forty miles to the east.[1]

The Mambwe country, more than Ulungu, was known for its cattle and sheep and goats. These herds may have attracted the attacks of the Ngoni. At any rate, after 1870 when the Bemba dislodged a group of remaining Ngoni, some of the Mambwe were obliged to send cattle in 'tribute' to the Bemba, and cattle may have been traded earlier as well. The Mambwe also had iron, from which they made hoes, axes, spears, and arrow-heads.[2]

North of the Mambwe and Lungu, the Fipa live on the plateau between Lakes Rukwa and Tanganyika. Their iron industry was the strongest of the corridor region, as suggested by the fact that it lasted into the colonial period while the others died out. Iron ore was found abundantly in swamps, and Fipa smelters—unlike craftsmen elsewhere in the region—apparently used limestone as a flux in the smelting process. They produced unusually long arrow-heads with spiral ribs to hold poison, spears, several kinds of hoe, large and small axes, scythes, and wood files. The Fipa were also known for their cotton-weaving. Burton heard of it through the Arabs of Tabora in 1857; and Livingstone and Cameron visiting Ufipa in the 1870s both commented on the number of people wearing native cloth. At the end of the century Wallace reported that 'almost every man' engaged in the craft, and their black-and-white-striped cloth was stronger than imported calico. Another product, smoked fish from Lake Rukwa, is today exported as far as Mwanza and Ndola, and may have been traditional as well. Finally, Ufipa's 'luxuriant gardens', so described by E. C. Hore, often yielded an exportable surplus.[3]

[1] A. Roberts, 'A Political History of the Bemba', Wisconsin Ph.D. thesis, 1966, 230 (I am grateful to Professor Anthony Low for allowing me to use his personal copy of this work); Livingstone (1874), II, 259; I, 219; E. C. Hore, 'Voyage to the south end of Lake Tanganyika in 1880', and A. Carson, 'Journey from Quillimane to Niamkolo, 1886', both in the Archives of the London Missionary Society, Central Africa Mission Journals, Box 3; W. V. Brelsford, *The Tribes of Northern Rhodesia,* Lusaka, 1956, 67.

[2] Roberts (Ph.D. thesis, 1966), 193; Brelsford (1956), 68.

[3] R. G. Willis, *The Fipa and Related Peoples of Southwestern Tanzania and Northeastern Zambia,* London, 1966, 25; R. F. Burton, 'Lake Regions of Central Africa', *Journal of the Royal Geographical Society*, 1859, 381; Livingstone (1874), II, 239; V. L. Cameron, 'Southern Half of Lake Tanganyika', *JRGS*, 1875, 212; L. A. Wallace, 'The Tanganyika-Nyasa Plateau', *Geographical Journal,* XIII, 1899, 601 ff.; Hore, L.M.S.A., loc. cit.

With such a range of resources Ufipa might appear to have had few needs which people buying her goods could supply. One such need, however, was salt. The Wanda, who live on the Rukwa shore adjacent to the Ivuna salt-pan, had no smiths and received their iron tools and weapons from the Fipa. They probably brought salt to the plateau in exchange. The Nyiha, further south, brought the bulbs of a particular plant gathered in the Rukwa valley to the east for arrow-poison, in exchange for Fipa arrow-heads. Other peoples trading with the Fipa simply duplicated Fipa products. For example, the Rungwa chiefs from the northern end of Lake Rukwa were said to seek investiture from the Fipa chiefs, bringing gifts of hoes, native cloth, and a slave.[1]

South-east along the corridor from the Fipa, Mambwe, and Wanda lie the Namwanga (and related Wiwa) and the Nyiha. The Namwanga paramount chieftaincy was traditionally founded by a man from Bisa country named Musyani—which is said to mean 'blacksmith' in the Namwanga and Nyiha languages. Musyani brought from the Bisa hoes and seeds, and is said to have taught the Namwanga how to forge and to cultivate. In the early colonial period the Namwanga were reported to have paid tribute to the Bemba of grain, livestock, and hoes. It can be assumed that these goods were also taken in trade, for the same account, describing the functions of Bemba border chiefs, gave the example that a Namwanga trader would be asked to pay toll of a slave or a cow at the border.[2]

Tobacco and cotton were grown by both the Namwanga and Nyiha, and Kerr-Cross observed in 1890 that every Nyiha village 'boasts of two or three looms' and all the people were 'decently clothed in the product'. Iron was also abundant in Nyiha country and Nyiha smiths provided it to their Safwa counterparts, who did not smelt. The Nyiha arrow-poison mentioned above was also used by the Safwa. Another specialist craft among the Nyiha was that of the master elephant-hunters, who had to be initiated into the ritual requirements of their work by another master. While ivory export probably belonged to the later period of professional trade, the fact that Nyiha hunters are mentioned in Fipa, Bungu, and Ngonde political traditions, suggests that hunting was also a serious pursuit earlier. Probably in exchange for

[1] W. D. Raymond, 'Tanganyika Arrow Poisons', *Tanganyika Notes and Records*, 23, 1947, 62; Mgr. Lechaptois, *Aux Rives du Tanganyika*, Algiers, 1913, 71. For a discussion of Ivuna, see Ch. 2, above, p. 28.

[2] B. Brock, 'A Preliminary Description of the Nyiha', Leeds M.A. thesis, 1963, 249; C. Gouldsbury and H. Sheane, *The Great Plateau of Northern Rhodesia*, London, 1911, 24.

ironware, salt from Ivuna was brought by the Namwanga and Nyiha, as well as by the Safwa. In addition, Bemba traditions of a salt trade from the Chibwe salt-pans near Mpika north along the line of the present Great North Road suggest that this was a source of salt for the Wiwa and the southern Namwanga.[1]

On the south-eastern end of Lake Rukwa, north of the Nyiha, is the country of the Bungu (or Wungu). The country was settled, according to the traditional history, by immigrants from Usagara. The Wasagara, clad in skins, found people in the Rukwa valley who grew and wove cotton. They traded a particular food—a relish prepared from an insect called Mawungu—for this cloth over the years, before conquering the weaving people. References to trade occur later in their history as well. An eight-year famine is recorded (apparently in the late eighteenth century) during which the Bungu sought food in Usafwa, Unyiha, Umalila, Unamwanga, Uwanda, and Ufipa. Although tradition alleges that the Wabungu 'begged' for food in these countries, it goes on to record that hoes, axes, and cotton were taken to Ufipa to secure the return of the rightful ruler of Ubungu whose banishment by an usurper had contributed to the famine. The gifts taken to Ufipa may have been payment for food, as well as encouragements to the Fipa king (as tradition maintains). When Johnston visited the Bungu in 1890, they were again suffering a prolonged drought and consequently drying game-meat to exchange for grain in the north and south-east.[2]

The probable source of grain for the Bungu in the south-east was the country on the Lake Nyasa end of the corridor, most prominently peopled by the Nyakyusa. From the time of the first European visitors, the Nyakyusa have been described as living in a splendid isolation, made possible by the ruggedness of the mountains which surround them on three sides and by the agricultural fertility of their country. Cattle, bananas, and grain flourished: 'each family produced for its own needs, so that trade was the merest trickle.'[3] But the evidence for that 'trickle' represents as broad a range of articles as that documented for any

[1] D. Kerr-Cross, 'Geographical Notes on the Country between Lakes Nyassa, Rukwa, and Tanganyika', *Scottish Geographical Magazine*, 1890, 289; E. Kootz-Kretschmer, *Die Safwa*, Berlin, 1926, I, 180, cited by W. Cline, *Mining and Metallurgy in Negro Africa*, Menasha, Wis., 1937, 24; Brock (M.A. thesis, 1963), 50 ff.; Lechaptois (1913), 46; Mwene Ilongo II, *Story of Wawungu*, trans. F. G. Finch, *Tanganyika Notes and Records*, 52, 1959, 86; K. R. Robinson, 'Recent Archeology of Ngonde', *J. Afr. Hist.*, VII, 2, 1966, 170; Roberts (Ph.D. thesis, 1966), 161 ff.

[2] Mwene Ilonga II (1959), 84; H. H. Johnston, 'Journey to the North of Lake Nyassa', *Proceedings of the Royal Geographic Society*, 1890, 225.

[3] M. Wilson, *Good Company*, Oxford, 1961, 11.

group. The ancestors of Nyakyusa chiefs traditionally came from the Kinga, in the Livingstone Mountains on the north-east shore of Lake Nyasa, bringing the knowledge of ironwork with them. Nyakyusa smiths could make spears, tools, and cow-bells but continued to depend on the Ukinga as a source of iron. Kinga religious leaders joined Nyakyusa in rituals at Lubaga in honour of a common hero-ancestor and these occasions facilitated the exchange of ironware for cattle.[1]

The Kinga also brought salt from Bena country—probably from the source at Saja mentioned at p. 29, n. 1. On the thin strip of mountain-side between the Kinga and the lake, the Kisi exploited a clay of particularly good quality and made pots, the trade of which made up for their poor agriculture. Thomson found their market at Pupanganda famous among the neighbouring Nyakyusa in 1879, and excavations at Mbande suggest that Kisi pots were traded with the Kinga for ironware, and with the Pangwa across the mountains for agricultural goods.[2]

From the Sangu in the north, through the Mahasi, the Nyakyusa imported a red root for a dye and cosmetic. From the Ndali in the west bark-cloth was brought. To the Nyakyusa, the greater the distance from which it was carried, the more preferable the medicine. War medicine was procured from the Kinga and Sangu, *muavi* poison from the Ngonde or Nyasa, and other medicines from Ndali and further afield.[3] It seems likely that Nyiha iron and perhaps Ivuna or Chibwe salt also reached the Nyakyusa.

This commercial survey of the corridor, though necessarily incomplete and uneven due to the varied nature of the sources, evokes the image of a vast tract of country humming with activity from one end to the other and supporting exchanges of a wide variety of products. It may be asked whether it is accurate to describe the area surveyed as an economic region, or a 'network' of trade. To describe the sum of the exchanges mentioned as a network suggests first that the individual patterns of exchange were going on simultaneously and, secondly, that the patterns were all related to one another. Although the evidence of the various exchange patterns is culled from reports spanning the last hundred years, it all refers to a *type* of trade which Brian Fagan has

[1] M. Wright, 'German Evangelical Missions in Tanganyika 1891–1939', London Ph.D. thesis, 1966, 68; M. Wilson, *Communal Rituals of the Nyakyusa*, Oxford, 1959, 97.

[2] J. Thomson, *To the Central African Lakes and Back*, 2 vols., London, 1881, I, 263; Robinson (1966), 172 ff.; O. F. Raum, 'Changes in African Life under German Administration', in (ed.) V. Harlow *et al.*, *History of East Africa*, II, Oxford, 1965, 195; Tanganyika Territory, Annual Reports of the Provincial Commissioners, 1931, 18.

[3] Wilson (1961), 61, and id. (1959), 151.

shown was carried out *many* centuries ago. The patterns of supply of such basic items as salt and iron are determined largely by physical factors, and would have had to have been in operation for the populations to live. It is therefore not unreasonable to suppose that most if not all of these patterns were established by the beginning of the nineteenth century.

To say that the patterns are related to one another does not mean that the Tabwa knew anything about the Nyakyusa, or even necessarily that any Tabwa product reached the Nyakyusa (although, as will be discussed below, at least one product may have travelled through the whole system). But throughout this area, from Tabwa to Nyakyusa and Kazembe to Ubungu, there is no frontier over which, if drastic economic change took place on one side, it would not be felt on the other side of the barrier. Thus if the Tabwa obtained a new product, they could buy Lungu ironware with it as well as with salt, and the Lungu might pass it on to the Fipa for grain, and so on. Obviously the boundaries of such a network are largely arbitrary: I have ignored on the south the Chisinga knife-makers, the Bisa fishermen, the Senga weavers, and on the north the Urua and Marungu goatherds, the Kimbu ironsmiths, and so on, whose produce also entered the margins of the corridor network.

While the sources available suggest the existence of this network of local trade they yield little information about its organization. To portray adequately the economic state of the corridor and its readiness to spawn professional, market-oriented trade, it would be important to describe not only the directions of trade and the goods exchanged, but the frequency of trade, its mechanics, and its relative role in the economic life of individuals and communities. With the exception of the Kisi pot-market observed by Thomson, there appear to have been no regular markets such as those Livingstone found busy every four days in Manyema country. Among many of the peoples of the corridor —such as the Fipa, Nyiha, and Namwanga—it has been recorded that the chief received tribute in goods and services. There are some indications that, as among the Bemba and Lunda, corridor chiefs distributed gifts as well as received them and thus provided some focus to trade. But this may have become important, along with the common provision that the chief receives one ivory tusk of every pair taken in his district, in later days when coastal demand had reached the area.

In the absence of concrete evidence for the corridor itself, Marvin

Miracle's findings among the Lamba and Senga, neighbouring the corridor peoples in the west and south, may illustrate a situation common to the corridor network. Local trade among the Senga was casual and irregular but not uncommon. A few men would take their wares to a village where they had done business before. Either side could initiate trade; but the Lamba recalled a tendency to avoid journeying away from home as long as caravans or small groups visited them, unless a bad harvest forced them to trade for food abroad.[1]

There are differing indications of the degree of dependency on trade. For all communities imports provided a few basic necessities, and exports an insurance against famine, but the main business seems to have remained subsistence agriculture. Chisholm alleged that the Namwanga 'had no differentiation of labour. Every man makes what he requires for himself. . . .' But he added that those more skilled at making hoes sold them to their fellows. Beverly Brock described the skilled hunters, weavers, and master ironworkers of the Nyiha as 'part-time specialists'. Moore went further with respect to the Kabwile and Tabwa saltworkers: 'Although these are agricultural people the soil is not fertile and they depend to a large extent on the proceeds from sale of their salt for sustenance.'[2]

On balance it would seem that though these individual producers were professional in the sense of relying on their industrial expertise for part of their livelihood, they were not 'professional traders'. Their production and trade remained tied to agriculture. Though they, or their chiefs, might have served as middlemen in the course of their normal functions, they did not specifically devote their full energies to the role. These producers were the sort of economic élite who in the case of the Yao ironsmiths developed into professional traders, but further factors were necessary to touch off a similar development in the corridor.

The corridor local trade network has so far been considered in isolation from its surroundings. One of the prerequisites for professional trade would seem to have been the communication of the coastal demands for such goods as ivory and slaves, and of the new luxuries available, which made professional trade worthwhile. By the early nineteenth century the Nyamwezi professional traders were operating

[1] Miracle (1962), and id., in Bohannan and Dalton (1962), passim.

[2] J. A. Chisholm, 'Notes on the Manners . . . of the Winamwanga and Wiwa', *Journal of the African Society*, IX, 1910; Brock, 'The Nyiha of Mbozi', *Tanganyika Notes and Records*, 65, 1965, 5; Moore (1937), 131.

to the north-east of the corridor region as the Bisa were to the south-west. The effects of their activities probably radiated toward the corridor, followed by the professional traders themselves. But because of the Lunda's geographical position and early involvement in market-oriented trade, it would seem reasonable to suppose that the first intimations of professional trade should have come from the Kazembe.

It has been clearly documented that the Lunda of Kazembe were involved in market-oriented trade in the latter part of the eighteenth century. Traditions suggest that the very founding of the Kazembe kingdom was related to commercial interests. Portuguese descriptions indicate the commercial significance which the sophisticated Lunda political organization may have assumed, especially with regard to tribute. Pereira described how Bisa chiefs, 'conquered by the Kazembe, pay tribute to him in stuffs, for which he always returns ivory. . . .' The reciprocal nature of 'tribute' is also mentioned by the *pombeiros,* who found on the way from Mwata Yamvo to Kazembe a chief Muginga Mucenda, installed by Kazembe 'to supply all travellers coming from the Muropue [MwataYamvo] to Kazembe, taking tribute, . . . as also for those who come from Kazembe to Muropue, taking the tribute. . . .' Thus tribute was a state-organized system of exchange rather than simply a burdensome tax.[1]

It is not clear how much the Kazembe actually organized caravans. It seems that Bisa were the actual carriers of most trade to the east. Lunda carriers, however, fetched salt and carried goods west; missions sent to the Portuguese in 1798, 1814, and 1830 were headed by Lunda aristocrats; and Kazembe spoke of himself to the Lacerda expedition as 'he who, opening the roads . . . [closed by a Bisa chief], had sent his vassals to buy cloth, and to bring whites with much treasure to his kingdom'.[2]

There is some evidence that Kazembe did not ignore the abundant local trade of the corridor to the east. According to Lunda traditional history,[3] the third Kazembe, Lukwesa (thought to have acceded to power in about 1760 and to have died in 1805) left his people on the Luapula and marched east and north saying, 'I am going to capture Kela [a Mambwe chief], Chincinta, Ntenda, Tangu, and Chungu we

[1] R. F. Burton, *Lands of Cazembe,* London, 1873, 37, 176.

[2] Burton (1873), 122.

[3] Mwata Kazembe XIV, *Historical Traditions of the Eastern Lunda,* trans. I. G. Cunnison, Rhodes-Livingstone Institute, Livingstone, 1961, 49, 63 ff.; see also I. G. Cunnison, *The Luapula Peoples of Northern Rhodesia*, Manchester, 1957, 154.

Timbwe for I have heard they all have many cattle.' His party moved to Tabwa and Lungu, stopped before the Bemba sub-chief Mwamba, out of respect for the tradition that the Lunda and Bemba are related, but pushed beyond as far as Ngonde and returned by Mambwe and Inamwanga. Following this foray Kazembe received tribute—honey from Lusenga, fish from Mpweto, salt from Puta (the latter two in Bwile on the north-east shore of Mweru), and 'men, mpande shells and many other things' from Mambwe, Tabwa, and Lungu. During Gamitto's visit to Kazembe in 1830, a *chilolo* or Lunda noble who had been sent to the Lungu chief (identified by Roberts as Makupa Kaoma) to fetch tribute returned with some thin cattle, a few slaves, and some iron wire bracelets. The nature of tribute has been discussed above; in these cases it is certainly unlikely to represent political control by the Kazembe over the Lungu or the Mambwe, or to have gone unreciprocated. Shortly after Gamitto's visit, according to Lunda tradition, or earlier according to the Bemba, Chileshye, the famous Bemba paramount, visited Kazembe and received gifts which included, in varying versions, war magic, an instrument of divination, seeds, cloth and beads, or court singers and craftsmen. Finally, Livingstone passed what he was told was a 'Lunda' smelting site near Chibwe, on the borders of the Bemba and the Lungu; there is no way of telling whether Lunda craftsmen habitually operated so far from their home, but the incident does suggest a Lungu–Lunda iron trade.[1]

All of this suggests that Kazembe was a part of the corridor's local trade network. But it does not suggest that Kazembe played a dominant role in it, or that he drew it into a professional trading system. The Lunda's relations with their eastern neighbours seem to have had the same character as the relations between other peoples in the corridor. Whatever 'tribute' came to Kazembe from the corridor peoples consisted largely of local products such as cattle and iron, rather than the stock of professional trade such as ivory or the European cloth Kazembe obtained from the Bisa. The Lunda's professional trade continued to be directed toward the Bisa and the Mwata Yamvo; neither the idea nor the techniques nor the goods of professional middlemen seem to have been passed on to the corridor peoples. But if the corridor was not initiated into a new style of commerce by Kazembe, it did not long remain isolated from all contact with professional trading systems. The first reverberations of coastal trade

[1] A. C. P. Gamitto, *King Kazembe*, trans. I. G. Cunnison, Lisbon, 1960, II, 35; Roberts (Ph.D. thesis, 1966), 172, 115 ff.; Kazembe XIV (1961), 70; Livingstone (1874), I, 201.

seem to have come into the corridor from the east, particularly through the Sangu and the Bungu.

The Sangu appear to have developed institutions of a centralized chieftaincy by the 1830s and to have made themselves felt by their neighbours by raiding for cattle and later for slaves. Under their paramount, Merere I, they suffered a temporary setback from the Ngoni in the early 1840s, but regained their strength and continued to expand their field of activity. Before this, Isanga and Isenga, to the north-east of Usangu, were the western termini of the Arab traders from the coast, and as the coastal trade was extended north-east into Unyamwezi, the route continued to pass through Isanga/Isenga. In 1837, Burton was told twenty years later, the Kimbu living beside Isanga/Isenga were forced by Sangu attacks to move north. As the route suffered increasingly from Sangu depredations, the bulk of the coastal-Nyamwezi trade shifted north to a route through Ugogo.[1]

But the Sangu did not lose contact with the coastal trade. In 1857 Burton found that a route went south from Tabora through Isanga/Isenga to Usangu and Ubena beyond. While it was then unusual for caravans to come up to Tabora via Usangu, one had recently done so, and more often caravans passed through Usangu when returning to the coast. The Sangu seized slaves in attacks on the Bena, Kimbu, Hehe, and Konongo, and drove them to the coast or to slave traders in Usagara. In addition traders found cattle, ivory, and iron in Usangu.[2]

It is difficult to say whether the Sangu owed their rise to power to their proximity to the early coastal route; or whether, on the contrary, the trade-route found its way to Isanga/Isenga because of an already manifest commercial potential in Usangu, with the attractions of cattle and iron as well as slaves and ivory. It is possible that the Sangu drew upon the wealth of the corridor to the south-west to achieve their strength.[3] Such coastal goods as beads and such intangibles as the appreciation of ivory as a valuable commodity may have radiated from Usangu. But the countries of the corridor are not mentioned by Burton as being subject to the raids of the Sangu, and there is little

[1] Burton (1859), 145, 300; A. Smith, 'Historical Introduction' to *Maisha ya Hamed bin Muhamad* (Tippu Tip), trans. W. W. Whiteley, supplement to the *Journal of the East African Swahili Committee,* 1958/9, 10; M. Wright (Ph.D. thesis, 1966), 60; A. Shorter, 'Ukimbu', Oxford D.Phil. thesis, 1968, 435–42.

[2] Burton (1859), 299–302.

[3] As Marcia Wright has observed, 'Burton notes that the heavy iron spear of the Sangu was a key to their success. Early trade with the Kinga iron-producers of the Livingstone mountains may be indicated': 'Chief Merere and the Germans', *Tanganyika Notes and Records,* 1969, 4.

evidence that the Sangu initiated regular, professional trade links with them.

As mentioned above, the Bungu traditionally immigrated from Usagara. The founders of the Nyitumba chiefdoms of Ukimbu, with whom the Bungu are associated in the migration, have been credited with having 'opened up a route linking the interior to the coast' and with bringing such coastal goods as conus-shell emblems of chieftainship as would eventually attract the interior people into coastal commerce.[1] It is doubtful that the Bungu maintained commercial contact with the coast from the time of their migration before the mid-eighteenth century. But they were certainly in a position to profit when in the nineteenth century coastal trade began to reach the Sangu, Kimbu, and Nyamwezi to their north.

A route to Ubungu south from Tabora was established before 1857 and the Bungu were described to Burton as a 'warlike people, rich in cattle and ivory'. On Burton's map was drawn a route to a spot east of Lake Rukwa labelled 'Ivory Mart'. Chief Ilonga, who ruled Ubungu from the 1830s to 1856, invited the Ngoni to aid him against the Sangu, and had some difficulty with the Ngoni overstaying their welcome, but they eventually moved north. Ubungu was left sufficiently prosperous for Ilonga reportedly to have sent men to Unyanyembe to buy cattle, who set themselves up in such 'a style of grandeur' that chief Fundikira had them killed.[2] Ilonga's successor Kilanga threatened a war of vengeance, but he probably did not allow the crisis to interfere with more profitable activities. He gained a reputation as a warrior, attacking Unyiha, Unamwanga, Uwanda, Ukimbu, Rungwe, Ukonongo, and Usafwa, according to the Bungu tradition, taking slaves in tribute. Fipa tradition records an incursion of the Bungu in the mid-nineteenth century which made off with some women of the royal family; and tradition among the Wabende mentions Ubungu as the source of guns sought by a disappointed aspirant to the throne.[3]

One indication that the effects of the coastal contacts of the Sangu and the Bungu might have been passed fairly rapidly on to the corridor is a Kimbu traditional song telling of the great famine in Ukimbu in the late 1830s: 'We are wiped out . . . [they sang]. Let us flee to those who

[1] Shorter (D.Phil. thesis, 1968), 415. For further discussion, however, of this statement and the Kimbu role in trade, see the Note on p. 228, below, by Father Shorter.

[2] Burton (1859), 304 (I am grateful to Andrew Roberts for bringing this reference to my attention). For Burton's map, see R. F. Burton, *Lake Regions of Central Africa*, London, 1860; for the dating of the Bungu tradition, see Shorter (D.Phil. thesis, 1968), 324.

[3] Ilonga (1959), 88; Lechaptois (1913), 35, 58.

have food. . . . Let us go to Ubungu. . . . Let us go to Ubemba. . . . Let us go to Ugogo. . . . Let us go to Ugalaganza. . . .'[1] The mention of Ubemba may be anachronistic, or it may well indicate that an avenue of trade was already open directly from Unyamwezi, Ukimbu, and Ubungu—all engaged in trade with the coast—right through the corridor to the Bemba. Unfortunately, in any case, the way in which the impact of long-distance trade on the margin of the corridor region was conducted through the regional trade network cannot be determined. There was too little time for the corridor peoples to register a reaction to the advance effects before they were more directly confronted with the coastal presence. Almost simultaneously with the developments among the Sangu and the Bungu outlined above, Arabs, Swahili coastmen, and Nyamwezi were pushing through the corridor and beyond. Thus in the Fipa and Bende traditions mentioned, Arabs appear in the same era as the Bungu.

It is difficult to date precisely the first instance of this penetration by foreign[2] traders. In a confused passage, the *pombeiros* reported that in 1806 a people named 'Tungalagaza' were bringing slaves, brass bracelets, cowries, and palm-oil to Kazembe. This has been interpreted as referring to Nyamwezi—from Ugalagansa, the name of a district in western Unyamwezi (which later came to be applied to the Nyamwezi in Katanga). The context seems to indicate that these people were coming from the west, which could perhaps mean that they had come across Lake Tanganyika and to Katanga through Uruwa before returning via Kazembe. That they were carrying indigenous, not coastal goods, would support this hypothetical route, and would perhaps also match what might be expected of Nyamwezi at this period. But the ambiguities remain such that this cannot be regarded as conclusive evidence of Nyamwezi activity; and even if it can be definitely shown from further study of the archaeology and traditions of the area that Nyamwezi had reached Kazembe and Katanga by this date, it does not appear that they had come through the corridor.[3]

It is worth noting before leaving the *pombeiros*' account that copper ('brass' being a common Portuguese misnomer) is mentioned as one of

[1] Shorter (D.Phil. thesis, 1968), 448.

[2] For the purpose of considering the economic region of Kazembe and the corridor, Nyamwezi as well as coastal Arabs and Swahili will be labelled 'foreigners'.

[3] Burton (1873), 88; A. Verbeken and M. Walraet, *La Première Traversée du Katanga*, Brussels, 1953, 75; for the interpretation of Tungalagaza as Nyamwezi, see J. Vansina, *Kingdoms of the Savanna*, Madison, 1966, 227, and A. Smith, 'The Southern Interior 1840–1884', in R. Oliver and G. Mathew (eds.), *History of East Africa*, I, Oxford, 1963, 265.

the first objects of professional trade. As shown above Katanga copper was already being traded west through the Lunda and south-east through the Bisa. Burton found copper traded to Ujiji and the northern shores of Lake Tanganyika, and the traditions of the interlacustrine kingdoms date the arrival of presumably Katanga copper much earlier. It may be that copper was traded in a professional way long before ivory attained a commercial significance.

The first indisputable evidence of coastal traders at Kazembe[1] is Gamitto's record of meeting there in 1830 'two dark coloured negroes with *kofio*' (Muslim prayer caps worn by Swahili), 'Moors' from the '*pwani*' or coast. But it cannot be asserted that these 'Moors', any more than the mysterious Tungalagaza, definitely travelled through the corridor; the fact that they were familiar with Mozambique and conversed with Gamitto in the Makua language suggests that they may have come by way of the Yao–Bisa route south of Lake Nyasa.[2]

Evidence from Bemba traditions, however, suggests that by the beginning of the second quarter of the nineteenth century the corridor was pierced. Some time after 1827 Chileshye became the Chitimukulu, or paramount chief of the Bemba, by driving out Susulu. The latter fled to Mambwe, where he died; Chileshye had to send gifts to the Mambwe to retrieve Susulu's body. Tradition records that the gift was cloth (and perhaps guns) obtained from Arabs. Another Bemba tradition asserts that Arabs entered the country to buy slaves after the war Chileshye waged against the Bisa (of which Gamitto saw the effects in 1830). Another intriguing piece of evidence of the passage of traders through the corridor is that in 1872 Livingstone met a sixty-year-old Nyamwezi chief in Tabora who claimed to have travelled as a boy to Katanga with his father, a 'great trader', by 'the same Fipa route' Livingstone himself was to take.[3]

Whenever the first foreign traders entered, it is generally agreed that it was in the 1840s that Arabs and Swahili reached the Kazembe area in numbers. Mohammed bin Saleh, whom Livingstone found settled at Kazembe, said that his father had 'opened' the country to Arab trade. Mohamed himself claimed to have been at Kazembe when

[1] Livingstone heard a story that traders from Ujiji had been at Kazembe at the time of the Lacerda expedition, but it seems hardly likely that such trading rivals would have been ignored in the expedition's diary: Livingstone (1874), I, 246.

[2] Gamitto (1960), II, 119.

[3] Roberts (Ph.D. thesis, 1966), 132 ff.; Ann Tweedie, 'History of the Bemba from Oral Sources', in E. Stokes and R. Brown (eds.), *The Zambesian Past,* Manchester, 1966, 210; Livingstone (1874), II, 180.

Gamitto visited, but, as Livingstone observed, 'Mohamed . . . never tells the whole truth.' He claimed at various times to have been imprisoned by Kazembe for ten, twenty, and twenty-five years; actually it seems that poverty forced him to stay at Kazembe after he had unsuccessfully attacked Nsama of Itabwa in 1841–2. Other examples of traders present from this period were those met by Livingstone near Lake Nyasa, who had been 14 years in Katanga; and Said bin Habib, who after leaving Zanzibar in 1844 crossed from Ujiji to the western side of Lake Tanganyika and down to 'Mpulungu', whence to Kazembe and later Katanga.[1]

It was in the 1840s that the father of Msiri—the Nyamwezi who later set up the Yeke state—is said to have come to Katanga around the southern end of Lake Tanganyika and to have made blood-brotherships with several Katanga chiefs. Msiri himself returned in about 1856 and obtained permission from Kazembe to cross the Luapula and establish himself in Kazembe's western dominions. Msiri soon made himself master of Kazembe's former vassals, chief Katanga of the Lamba and chief Ponde of the Sanga. When Kazembe's nephews went to attack Msiri in about 1865 they were killed, provoking a reaction in Kazembe's kingdom against all foreign traders, in which the veteran Mohamed bin Saleh was imprisoned, his gradually accumulated wealth stolen, and one of his sons and several followers killed.[2]

By 1857 Burton found several routes established to the corridor. One lay from Ujiji through Ufipa to Ulungu (although Fipa traditions maintain that Arabs entered the country for the first time two or three reigns after the Ngoni invasion of about 1842). Another route went from Unyanyembe south-east of Unyangwila and then south-west through Kiwele and Nkokolo in Ukimbu. From Nkokolo the route passed south past Lake Rukwa to Ufipa and from there through 'Iwemba' to Kazembe. By 1860, at the time of Chileshye's death in Bemba country, this route may have been sufficiently valuable for Mwamba, offered the position of Chitimukulu, to have begged out of the job because it would have meant moving eastward to a place less advantageous for trade. The route which Burton records to Ubungu may be assumed to have also led onwards to the corridor. Moreover there were various points at

[1] Livingstone (1874), I, 247, 276, 287, 297; Burton (1859), 256; Livingstone, *The Zambesi and its Tributaries*, London, 1865, 259, cited by I. G. Cunnison, 'Kazembe and the Arabs', in (eds.) Stokes and Brown (1966), 228; Sir John Gray, 'Trading Expeditions from the Coast', *Tanganyika Notes and Records*, XLIX, 1957, 232.

[2] A. Verbeken, *Msiri, Roi du Garenganze*, Brussels, 1956, 40 ff., 63 ff.

which traders crossed Lake Tanganyika for Ulungu and Kazembe as well as Uruwa and Katanga.[1]

In 1863 Tippu Tip took another route—from the coast by the 'old' road to Usangu (where he found the trade bad) and on to Fipa, Namwanga, 'Ruemba', and Lungu. With his brother he made a second journey through Usangu to the Bemba chiefs Mwamba and Chitimukulu. It was on this occasion that he (with other Arabs) defeated Nsama of Itabwa, and met Livingstone. On a third journey in 1870 he went from Tabora and Ukonongo through Ufipa, along Lake Tanganyika to Ulungu and Itabwa again, and then back to the Bemba chiefs, before pushing on beyond Lake Mweru to Uruwa.[2] Magaru Mafupi, whom Livingstone met at Chitapankwa in 1867, had also come through Usangu, and from there perhaps to Chikanamuliro—the Namwanga chief. Livingstone was told that it was the first time they had 'come so far' by that way, but the wealth of description which he was given of Merere and the Sangu by Arabs in Bemba and Lungu country suggests that the corridor extension of the Sangu route was well known.[3]

By the time of Livingstone's travels between 1867 and 1873 the entire country between Lakes Mweru and Bangweulu and Tanganyika was saturated with Arabs, coastmen, and Nyamwezi; some passing through on their way to Katanga or back to Tabora or the coast, and others established for a few seasons or semi-permanently. But despite all this traffic, a main artery of trade, such as the Kazembe–Bisa–Yao–Kilwa or the Ujiji–Tabora–Bagamoyo routes, never developed through the corridor. This was partly because the way to Katanga through the corridor was rivalled by both the other two routes. In both 1861 and 1866 Livingstone met Bisa who continued to trade on the southern route despite the interruptions of the Bemba and the Ngoni. If the Bisa seemed to fail in about 1870, coastmen had stepped in to take their place. Mention has been made of some of these that Livingstone met in 1861. In around 1840 a Swahili had established himself as 'Jumbe' at Kotakota—where a ferry took slaves across Lake Nyasa to Losewa—and he undoubtedly sent expeditions north-west along what had been the Bisa route. On the nothern route, Burton had found in 1857 that the

[1] Burton (1859), 234, 259, 305; Roberts (Ph.D. thesis, 1966), 153.

[2] Tippu Tip (1958/9), 43, 45, 49 ff., 75.

[3] Livingstone (1874), I, 187, 212, 214, 218, 225; for the tentative identification of the southern stages of Magaru's route, including Chikanamuliro, see Roberts (Ph.D. thesis, 1966), 239.

'western terminus of the Zanzibar trade' lay in Uruwa south-west across Lake Tanganyika from Ujiji. From there traders were already going south to Kazembe and Katanga. When Msiri became established, this route became monopolized by Nyamwezi, but Arabs continued to work across Lake Tanganyika further north in Manyema.[1]

If the trade-route through the corridor never achieved the status of the Nyamwezi or Bisa routes, it was partly because there were no indigenous peoples who had had sufficient opportunity to develop the entrepreneurial talent of the Nyamwezi or Bisa. Neither Kazembe nor the peoples of the corridor appear to have taken the initiative in the establishment of long-distance trade. In the case of Kazembe this can be explained by the fact that he did not need another outlet to the coast; he was too involved in keeping the southern route clear to look to the north. The incursions of the Bemba and Ngoni apparently did not stop the Bisa traders coming to Kazembe until perhaps in 1870, by which time there were so many Nyamwezi and Arab traders about that Kazembe did not need to exert himself to open a road. Far from lacking an outlet for his trade-goods, Kazembe was overcome by demands he could not meet. Thus Livingstone could describe the Kazembe, whose predecessors had been so imperious towards Portuguese visitors, as a 'poor' man, forced to confess his inability to supply any ivory, while his subordinate Mwenimpanda was in heavy debt to the Arab traders. Livingstone blames the Kazembe's cruelty for having driven away his common subjects, and his stinginess over rewards for having driven away his elephant-hunters.[2] But it is more likely that, faced with fierce coastal competition, Kazembe was simply unable to compete with the many new opportunities for the hunters' skills, and unable to enforce the monopoly of trade which would have provided the largesse with which to maintain adherents.

In the case of the other peoples, it appears that there was insufficient time, between their first opportunity for professional trade and the march of foreign traders past their doorsteps, for them to have seized the initiative and established themselves in a major way. Having been denied the opportunity to develop entrepreneurial initiatives on their own, however, some of the corridor peoples were drawn into professional trading patterns by the great influx of foreign traders.

Naturally, the foreign traders formed local alliances. The Fipa, Burton was told in 1857, 'welcomed' merchants seeking slaves and

[1] Roberts (Ph.D. thesis, 1966), 134, 237; Burton (1859), 255; Thomson (1881), II, 46.

[2] Livingstone (1874), I, 254, 265, 295, 305.

ivory, and Livingstone's men passed two Arab caravans heading for Ufipa in 1873. One Ngombe Sase was settled at Kapufi's capital, whom Thomson described as the Fipa chief's 'prime minister' and as wielding 'considerable influence'. Further south Ulungu was found by Tippu Tip and another Arab acquaintance of Livingstone to be a great source of ivory. Burton described 'Marungu' and Thomson more particularly Iendwe as 'the most important place . . . on Lake Tanganyika' (besides Ujiji), because it served as headquarters to Arabs and Nyamwezi. Ulungu struck the traveller coming across the corridor from Lake Nyasa as obviously on a trade-route—as evidenced by both the quantity of imported cloth and ornaments and the manners of the people.[1]

In some cases people from the corridor may have become independent professional traders in their own right. The examples of the Sangu and Bungu have already been discussed. Elton found the Sangu in 1877, though momentarily under duress from the Hehe, well-armed with firearms, accustomed to receiving Arab traders, and acting as hosts to the trader Suleiman and a Baluchi who served as Merere's military adviser. When the Sangu were finally forced by the Hehe to abandon their homeland and move west into Usafwa, they underwent considerable hardship, but began to raid their new neighbours with renewed vigour and continued exporting slaves.[2]

The Bungu chief Kilanga was described in tradition as not only having conquered surrounding countries but as also having traded ivory, slaves, hippo teeth, and rhinoceros horn to visiting Arabs. He and his children were even said to have become Muslims. He too had a foreign military adviser, a Baluchi named Amran Masudi, who, it is said, urged Kilanga to attack the Sangu, with the disastrous consequences that both Kilanga and Amran were killed in 1872–3. Eight years later Nyungu of the Kimbu helped the Bungu prince Zunda to seize the throne from his brother Wangu, but business continued as usual. A scene recorded by Johnston in 1890 epitomizes the wholehearted engagement of the Bungu in long-distance trade: the chief was found playing bao using bullets as counters! Many Bungu spoke Swahili fluently, and slaves and ivory were still exported to Unyamwezi.[3]

[1] Burton (1859), 259–65; Livingstone (1874), II, 334, 336 ff., 180; Thomson (1881), II, 217; II, 16; I, 304; Tippu Tip (1958/9), 43.

[2] M. Wright (Ph.D. thesis, 1966), 62; J. F. Elton, *Travels and Researches among the Lakes and Mountains of Central Africa,* (ed.) H. B. Cotterill, London, 1879, 345 ff.

[3] Ilonga (1959), 89; Shorter (D.Phil. thesis, 1968), 492 ff., 524; Johnston (1890), 226.

There are a few indications that others as well as the Bungu and Sangu were not simply servants to the foreign professionals but traded in a new style on their own account. E. C. Hore met in Ujiji in 1879 a 'little party of Fipa natives come on a trading expedition'. After travelling along the Fipa coast he referred to the Fipa as 'inveterate slave-traders'; his colleague Swann met in Ulungu large Fipa canoes loaded with grain, whose crew were willing to take only slaves in payment. Farther away, in Itabwa, some Fipa elephant-hunters settled, one in the service of a Swahili, but others perhaps on their own. Among the Tabwa themselves, there is no evidence that chief Nsama organized caravans, but the fortune in copper and ivory which he had amassed by 1867 (and which on his defeat in that year fell into Tippu Tip's hands) suggests that he may have been involved in professional trade in some capacity.[1]

None of these hints from the available sources give conclusive evidence of professional trading in imitation of the foreigners, but they suggest that the corridor was not perhaps entirely passive. Marcia Wright has suggested that a study of the Namwanga in particular might yield valuable information on corridor reactions to professional trade. The long genealogy of the Namwanga paramountcy—indicating early centralization and stabilization; the fact that Tippu Tip, his fellow-trader Saud bin Said, and Magaru Mafupi all visited Unamwanga; and the observations by Kerr-Cross that the Namwanga chief had recently dealt much with the Arabs, obtained guns, and raided his neighbours; as well as the observations by Fuchs that Namwanga had adopted many Nyamwezi phrases: all suggest a fruitful field of enquiry.[2]

Despite the few examples of indigenous professional traders which may be uncovered, the style of most of the corridor peoples' engagement in trade remained essentially different from that of the Nyamwezi. This is illustrated by Tippu Tip's description of his return journey to the coast in 1867–8. The Urungu were friendly and transported his goods as far as Mambwe. When he fetched another contingent from Bemba country, Bemba porters also carried the ivory as far as Mambwe. But the people were

[1] E. C. Hore, *Tanganyika: Eleven Years in Central Africa*, London, 1892, 91; id., L.M.S.A., loc. cit.; A. J. Swann, *Fighting the Slave Hunters in Central Africa*, London, 1910, 98; Brelsford (1956), 74; Tippu Tip (1958/9), 47.

[2] Personal communication from Marcia Wright; Tippu Tip (1958/9), 43, 57; Kerr-Cross (1890), 287; P. Fuchs, *Die Wirtschaftliche Erkundunge des Ostafrikanischen Sudbahn*, Berlin, 1906. I am grateful to Andrew Roberts for bringing the last reference to my attention.

fearful of one another. So the people of Mambwe transported the ivory to Unamwanga and they, in turn, transported it to Nyiha and the people of Nyiha took it as far as Usafa and they continued as far as Urori [Usanga]. . . . On our arrival at Urori, porters were not available for the trip to the coast so I decided to go to Tabora and fetch Nyamwezi porters. . . .[1]

Tippu Tip ascribed his troubles to the unrest following Nsama's defeat, but the Nyamwezi traders were not deterred by the interminable political wrangles in Unyamwezi, Ugogo, and elsewhere. The corridor peoples largely remained local, subsistence-oriented traders.

The coming of professional trade to the corridor, though it did not become the immediate business of most people, had considerable effect on the continuing network of local trade. New goods were passed along the old channels and new demands placed on the old production skills. In addition to the European imports of beads and cloth which the foreigners injected into the local trade network was the African commodity of copper.

As indicated above, copper figured in the earliest professional trade. Some copper may have found its way to the corridor from Kazembe in the pre-professional period, but its circulation was certainly boosted by foreign traders. When he was unsuccessful at obtaining ivory, the Arab trader Mohamed Bogharib bought copper south of Kazembe to take north to Uvira to exchange for ivory. Livingstone found Nyamwezi apparently smelting copper on their own 'for the Manyema market'. And it passed east as well. Near Chitapankwa's Bemba capital, a copper bar one foot by three inches was offered in sale to Livingstone. Chitapankwa himself wore numerous copper leglets. At the city of Chitapankwa's subordinate, Mwamba, wire-drawers (whom Roberts identifies as probably of Yeke origin) were settled, producing the anklets which adorned Mwamba's wives. In the following decades, visitors found leg and arm adornments of copper wire in Itabwa, Ulungu, Mambwe, and Nyiha. But the most significant evidence of the trade of copper through an expanded local trade network comes from the Nyakyusa, whose country was not crossed by the foreign traders. In 1877 Cotterill remarked upon the 'delicate tracery of brass and copper wire' inlaid on the shafts of Nyakyusa spears. (The 'brass' is probably a mistake by Cotterill.) The copper wire may have been scarce, as the first reference to copper body-belts, 'amayeta', was by Kerr-Cross in

[1] Tippu Tip (1958/9), 55–7.

1893, when British imported brass and copper wire was reaching the area. Fotheringham's claim that brass wire in Ngonde, south of the Nyakyusa, was imported from Britain before 1889 would not account for the observations of Elton and Cotterill, the first Europeans to reach Nyakyusa. Evidence that the Nyakyusa were linked in trade with the corridor peoples north-west of them has already been presented above. That copper was coming to them from the west is further suggested by Thomson's observation that, among their neighbours the Nyiha, copper ornaments as well as beads became more and more numerous as he moved west.[1]

The most obvious case in which foreign traders increased demand for local products was in foodstuffs, but other goods were involved as well. Thus Arabs are reported to have bought iron ingots, as well as slaves and ivory, from the Mambwe. Fungafunga, a Nyamwezi trader Livingstone met south-east of Kazembe, was trading for hoes as well as copper and slaves. Indeed many of the professional traders entered into thoroughly 'local' patterns of trade to facilitate their passage. Nyamwezi waiting for the rains to stop in Itabwa in 1868 supported themselves by hunting and selling buffalo meat to the local people for grain and cassava. Livingstone passed two Nyamwezi in Ulungu who were carrying salt from Kabwile to the Bemba chief Mwamba. Trivier met a party in 1889 similarly taking salt from Mweru wa Ntipa to buy slaves in Ulungu and Mambwe; while Giraud in 1883 found Nyamwezi at the Bemba chief Nkula's selling ironware, bark-cloth, and bark-boxes for salt. Livingstone himself engaged in such local trade. Near Kazembe he bought five hoes for two or three yards of calico each, with the intention of buying a goat in Kabwile. At Kabwabwata he found he could get a large pot of ground-nut oil for a hoe; while his servant Susi bought a hoe with gunpowder which he sold then for a large quantity of 'dura' grain. On Lake Bangweulu Livingstone hired a canoe with hoe and beads. A large quantity of fish he received from Kazembe he used to buy flour at Chikumbi, where he also found salt better than beads for buying provisions.[2]

As the goods which the foreigners brought moved further than the professional traders themselves, so their effect on local production

[1] Livingstone (1874), I, 298, 321, 184; Roberts (Ph.D. thesis, 1966), 242; Fotheringham and Kerr-Cross, cited by M. Wilson (1961), 61 n.; Elton (1879), 322 n.; Thomson (1881), I, 292.

[2] Brelsford (1956), 66; Livingstone (1874), I, 278, 268, 272, 314, 316; Trivier and Giraud, cited by Roberts (Ph.D. thesis, 1966), 230–31.

extended beyond their immediate dealings. Andrew Roberts has suggested that the arms, which Lungu smiths provided for the Bemba, grew in quality and quantity over the nineteenth century, as they were paid for in imported trade-goods. As Roberts commented, 'The presence of alien traders and craftsmen, and the introduction of new commodities, helped to stimulate exchange across the plateau, and consequently the exploitation of local resources.'[1]

Yet if the immediate effect of the influx of professional traders on the local trade of the corridor was beneficial, in the longer term it was crippling. The foreigners, by their own needs, by the incentive of their new goods, and by their expansion of the distribution of local products, stimulated the production of the subsistence traders. But they also monopolized the enlarged entrepreneurial role which attended this heightened production. The positions of middlemen in an expanded local trade should have been the first logical steps towards an indigenous professional trade. By their first appearance in considerable numbers the foreign traders had denied the opportunity for corridor peoples to develop into long-distance professional traders. By their subsequent involvement in the local trade network they seem to have denied the subsistence traders the opportunity to professionalize in the more immediate context in response to the new commerce.

The political consequences of the presence of large numbers of foreign traders restricted the activities of local traders even further. One of the first casualties of long-distance trade was the Tabwa chiefdom of Nsama, who was humbled by a group of Arabs including Tippu Tip in 1867. At the same time Kazembe was under pressure from all sides. Msiri, who established himself in Katanga with Kazembe's at least formal acquiescence, had risen to control a far larger territory and trade, and was in a position that blocked Kazembe's access to the Mwata Yamvo. When one of the last of his vassals went over to Msiri, and his nephews were killed, Kazembe could only exercise his impotent anger on such foreigners as Mohamed bin Saleh who happened to be within his grasp. In 1868 the Nyamwezi settled south of Kazembe, although they had defended the country against Ngoni raids, had so aroused the jealousy of the inhabitants that they were forced to withdraw northwards. Kazembe apparently joined in his neighbours' quarrel, and suffered the worst of the counter-attacks. In 1872 the Kazembe was driven from his capital and later killed; his successor met

[1] Roberts (Ph.D. thesis, 1966), 245.

the same fate soon after, when a trader helped install a Lunda pretender to the throne.[1]

The erosion of the independence of other peoples took place more gradually, but equally inexorably. The eastern end of the corridor, as Marcia Wright has pointed out, was by the 1890s divided into 'spheres of interest' of the (Songea) Ngoni, Hehe, and Sangu. The Sangu, from their new base in Usafwa, extracted tribute from the Kukwe (a sub-group of the Nyakyusa) to the south and the Wainji to the east. The Hehe had annexed the old lands of Usangu, and ruled those Bena who had not fled to the Ulanga valley in the east. Other Bena fell under the Ngoni, who also raided the Pangwa, Kinga, Kisi, and Nyakyusa.[2]

To the west of these spheres lay that of the Bemba. All the travellers of the late nineteenth century who passed from the north end of Lake Nyasa up into the corridor and towards Lake Tanganyika were struck by the difference between the open settlements of the Nyakyusa and the tightly stockaded villages of the Nyiha and other peoples of the plateau. The stockades were apparently a very necessary protection against the Bemba. Chitimukulu Chitapankwa mounted an expedition against the Lungu chief Zombe, which was repulsed with the aid of other Lungu chiefs shortly before Livingstone reached there in 1872, but the Bemba apparently returned between 1880, when Hore found Zombe flourishing, and 1883 when the Ulungu coast lay in desolation. In the following decade the London Missionary Society pioneers at Niamkolo tried to grant some shelter to refugees from continuing Bemba raids. The Mambwe came under attack from 1870 onwards, when the Bemba expelled a last Ngoni contingent and set out to punish Mambwe collaborators. In 1886 Carson found the Mambwe chiefs Tangasi and Wanbankura allied with the Bemba and thus at war with their fellow Mambwe chiefs Kela and Fuambo, who maintained their independence.[3]

To the north the Namwanga and Bungu maintained their own circles of power, though the Bungu fell under the shadow of the Kimbu lord Nyungu ya Mawe. In the Fipa country bordering on Lake Rukwa, an adventurer named Kimalaunga established himself some time in the

[1] Livingstone (1874), I, 335; II, 194; Cunnison in (eds.) Stokes and Brown (1966), 233; A. Roberts, 'Tippu Tip, Livingstone, and the Chronology of Lunda', *Azania*, II, 1967, 128–9.

[2] Wright (Ph. D. thesis, 1966), 65.

[3] Roberts (Ph.D. thesis, 1966), 189–90; Hore, L.M.S.A., loc. cit.; id. (1892), 183; Carson, L.M.S.A., loc. cit.

1860s. A member of the Sangu royal family who fled the dynastic struggles after the death of Merere I, he was granted permission to settle in Ufipa by chief Zumba Piloa, who hoped for assistance against Kapufi, head of the rival Fipa chiefdom. But Kimalaunga quickly achieved such strength as to drive the two Fipa chiefs into an alliance to try to withstand his raids.[1]

A common factor among the masters of all these spheres is that they were known as raiders, not traders. Contemporary European descriptions of events in the corridor, emphasizing the European role as protectors and saviours of the innocent from the evil warlords, must be regarded with caution, but there is considerable evidence that the activities of these powers did serious damage to the earlier patterns of local trade.

Already in 1867 Livingstone found in Ulungu that 'much cloth was made in these parts before the Mazitu [Ngoni] raids began', with the implication that the raids cut this production. Namwanga tradition records that the last Namwanga hoe-maker died or was killed in a war with Kimalaunga. The Moravian missionary Backman found most iron-furnaces in Unyiha in disuse. Johnston claimed after a visit in 1889 that the plateau people would be cattle-breeders, were it not for the ever-present raiders. He found no direct road from Zowa in Unyiha to Lake Tanganyika; each village seemed to be at war with the next.[2] Thus it seems that the common people scarcely had the time or space in which to grow adequate food, let alone produce such things as iron-ware and cotton cloth.

The corridor peoples, unable to benefit from the new opportunities for middlemen, were, in the besieged state of the region in the late nineteenth century, increasingly unable to pursue their old forms of trade. But, if the arrival of the Arabs had stifled local entrepreneurship, the entry of the Europeans dealt the death-blow to local production. The missions brought stores with which to build their stations and hire labourers, and in a very short time the country was flooded with imported metalware, cloth, and even salt, in such quantities that the local industries could not compete. By 1902 the London Missionary Society was importing over 15 tons of trade-goods annually. Already by 1911 it could be written of the Bemba that they 'seem to have no special inclination for trading since they buy all they want at the local

[1] Shorter (D.Phil. thesis, 1968), 470; Lechaptois (1913), 60.

[2] Livingstone (1874), I, 207; Mbeya District Book; Wright (Ph.D. thesis, 1966), 172; Johnston (1890), 734.

European store'.[1] There are striking examples of the skills acquired in the old trading patterns being put to use in new circumstances, such as the blacksmiths who turned from smelting to beating out scrap and casting new parts for firearms and other gadgets; but whatever residue of the traditional was maintained in these activities they were performed in an economic context so different that they must be considered as something totally new.

The examination of the local trade network of the Tanganyika-Nyasa corridor assails once again the old stereotype of eastern Africans living in completely self-sufficient family units with no needs to import and no products to export, and demonstrates in detail the extensive and varied nature of the local trade which supplemented subsistence agriculture. But this trade, complex as it was, remained on a subsistence plane, and did not lead to the development of professional long-distance traders as elsewhere. The failure of the corridor peoples to take the initiative shown by such other interior peoples as the Nyamwezi and the Yao in establishing trade with the coast may in the main be due simply to lack of time. The possibilities of long-distance commerce were transmitted to the corridor only a few years before foreign professional traders entered the region. New entrepreneurial roles were filled by these outsiders before indigenous traders had a chance to appreciate them.

A Note by Dr. Aylward Shorter

On page 215, there is a quotation from my Kimbu thesis (p. 415) concerning the founders of the Nyitumba chiefdoms of Ukimbu that they 'opened up a route linking the interior to the coast'.

Taken by themselves these words could be misleading, and, indeed, they could have been better chosen. On page 360 of my Kimbu thesis I also call the Nyitumba 'intermediaries who acted as a stimulus for early Nyamwezi traders'. I think, however, that it is sufficiently clear from the contexts of my chapters 7 and 8 that I do not wish to suggest that the Nyitumba Kimbu were in direct contact with the coast at any time before the early nineteenth century. Nor do I wish to suggest that they acted as 'middlemen' in a trade with the Nyamwezi.

All that I am maintaining is:

(a) The Nyitumba (and Igulwibi) Kimbu pioneered a long route

[1] R. I. Rotberg, 'Rural Rhodesia Markets', in (eds.) Bohannan and Dalton (1962), 583; Gouldsbury and Sheane (1911), 284.

linking the highlands of eastern Tanzania with the Nyamwezi area and the Iramba area. This route later became one of the principal trade-routes in the early nineteenth century when Nyamwezi started travelling to the coast.

(b) There is evidence that the Kimbu had the conus-shell disc-emblem before the Nyamwezi and that the Nyitumba (and Igulwibi) Kimbu brought it, and popularized the idea. The conus-shell, of course, originates on the coast. Nyamwezi (particularly Sumbwa) traditions all maintain that the first object in going to the coast was to obtain these shells. It is therefore, I think, justifiable to say that the Nyitumba Kimbu were a stimulus for the Nyamwezi traders.

The Nyitumba route was not simply used for one never-to-be-repeated trek. The Nyitumba, the Igulwibi, and the Bungu founders all passed along it. Kimbu traditions show that people passed back and forth along the route, and there is evidence that it was used by people going to fetch seeds of new crops.

Nyitumba traditions mention 'ivory' and 'cloth' in the myth of origin. These I take to be anachronisms. The southern Kimbu state explicitly that they were not aware of the commercial value of ivory until the Arabs came. Bungu traditions (Chief Ilonga's history) maintain that the founders from Sagara were wearing skins, and only learned the use of cloth made from kapok from the people of the Rukwa valley. Two versions of the Nyitumba myth of origin state that they went on to Ubemba for ivory and slaves. Most versions say they returned to Usagara before the final conquest of south-eastern Ukimbu. I think, therefore, that this is not reliable evidence for a link with Ubemba.

Were the Kimbu entirely passive when the early Nyamwezi trader-heroes began their journeys? The earliest traditions concern Nyamwezi travellers. However, it is clear from the first written sources that the Nyamwezi included also the northern (Igulwibi) Kimbu. Both Macqueen and Cooley say that Unyangwila (Ukimbu) is Unyamwezi ('eastern limit' of Unyamwezi or 'first town'). The Igulwibi Kimbu appear to have been the first of the Kimbu to become aware of the value of ivory, since most of the myth-charters of their chiefdoms (of the turn of the eighteenth century) speak of elephant-hunting.

Burton calls the people of the Kimbu chiefdom of Ngulu 'Wakon-ongo'. This is another very relative term. Nyamwezi travellers were called Konongo by the Hehe and other tribes on the road to the coast. Burton says (1860, I, 307) that the Gogo called the Nyamwezi 'Wakonongo'. Burton himself (1859, 169) calls Unyangwila one of the 'principal provinces of Unyamwezi'.

I think it probable that the Igulwibi people in Iramba and northern Ukimbu, being astride the two main routes from Unyamwezi to the coast, were active in the early trade to the coast. Unyanyembe, it must be remembered, which had built up such wealth by the time of Burton's visit, was a Nyamwezi (Sagali) chiefdom with an Igulwibi (Kimbu) dynasty.

The first reference to a Kimbu chief making a journey to the coast is, as far as I know, the reference to Madereka, son of Kasanda, seventh chief of Ngulu, in the Swahili history of Ngulu (NAT, Regional and District Files, 47, 29/4). This states that 'Madereka went on a journey with chief Lyowa of Ugala. They went to Ugogo and when they arrived in Ugogo, they were killed by the Wagogo.' *(Mtemi Madereka akasafiri na Mtemi Lyowa wa Ugala. Wakaenda Ugogo. Walipofika Ugogo, wakauawa na Wagogo.)*

This event can be dated to the early 1840s. In about 1839 Chief Mkumbamkikile was driven by a Ngoni attack to Ukonongo. One of his slaves usurped the chiefdom but Mkumbamkikile's son, Masanja, returned and ousted the usurper. Before he could call his father back, the latter had died. Mkumbamkikile was succeeded by a brother who died young from an illness. The latter was succeeded by a sister's son who was ousted and killed by one of his own brothers. This was Madereka. These events must have followed in fairly quick succession. Madereka was the great-grandfather of Malingo, son of Kanyanka, the chief of Ngulu driven out of his country by Mnwa Sele in 1860–65. The earlier we place Madereka, therefore, the easier it is to fit in the requisite generations.

It will be remembered that Kafuku of Usumbwa, the traveller hero of the Sumbwa Nyamwezi, was killed by the Gogo in about 1825, perhaps later. At any rate, Madereka's journey and Kafuku's are not so far removed in time.

11

Zambian Trade with Zumbo in the Eighteenth Century

NICOLA SUTHERLAND-HARRIS

Many of the peoples in the great arc of Zambia to the north-west of Zumbo—the Tonga, Lenje, Lamba, Ambo, Kunda, and Nsenga—traded with Zumbo in the eighteenth century. This arc lies between the comparatively well-known trading areas of the Lozi on the one hand and Kazembe's Lunda on the other. On the area between these two, little has been published by historians, but the remarkable extent of its trade with the Portuguese and Goans on the Zambezi emerges even from a cursory reading of just a few of the letters written in the eighteenth century from Zumbo, the Portuguese post furthest up the Zambezi.[1] Zumbo itself was set up at the beginning of the eighteenth century, when Changamire destroyed the fairs in Monomotapa's lands. Before this time, Portuguese contacts with Zambia were sporadic at most. Zumbo's main *raison d'être* was to tap the Butua gold which had formerly come through Monomotapa's kingdom, but it also had an active trading frontier to the north in the eighteenth century, just as it did in the later nineteenth.[2] The main item of trade, then as later, was ivory. Some provisions and cattle were also involved, but the items which prove the most useful clues in the identification of the trading areas are copper, worked iron, and, occasionally, gold. To the Africans were sent in exchange cloth, beads, and presumably other luxury goods, and possibly firearms.

At Zumbo, the limit of the foreigners' trading frontier, just as in the better-known cases of the Kamba and Nyamwezi, the vital trading initiative seems to have come from the Africans. This can be clearly

[1] The sources used are entirely Portuguese rather than African and are confined to 1750–1800, haphazardly spread even over that short period.

[2] See, e.g., A. Roberts, 'The nineteenth century in Zambia', in (ed.) T. O. Ranger, *Aspects of Central African History*, London, 1968, 81.

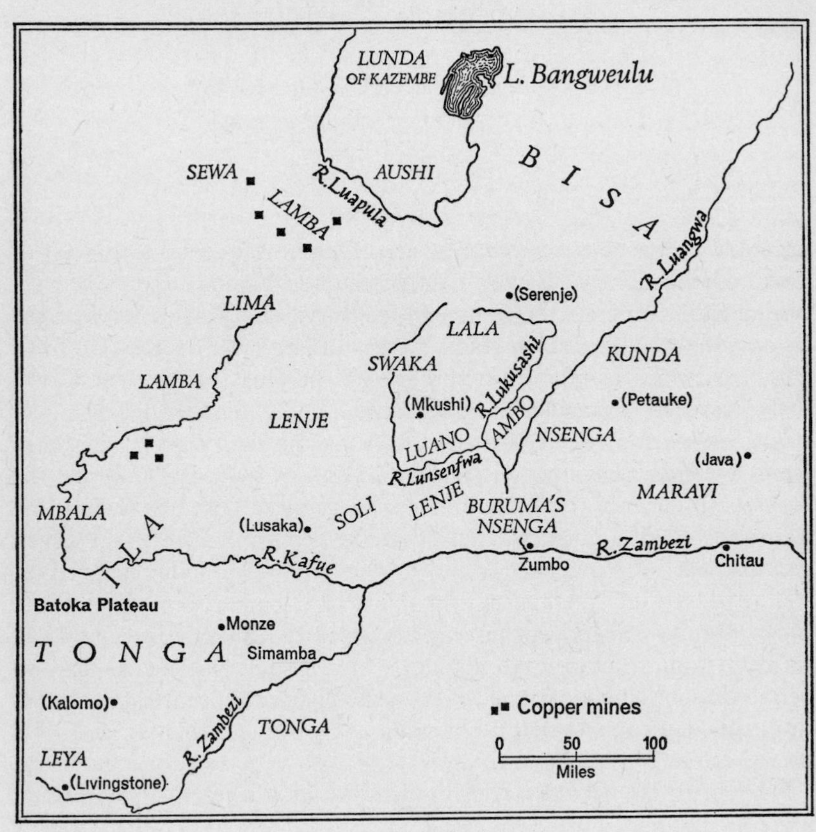

Map 13. Zambia and Zumbo in the Eighteenth Century

seen in two cases—the arrival at Zumbo of the people of the region of Urenje described in an account of 1762 and of the 'manamucates' (envoys or agents) of Chief Mamba in 1781—and it seems probable that this reflects a general trend. It was only later that 'mussambazes' (African agents) were sent out to these places by the merchants of Zumbo, following routes already open.[1] After the early stages, the arrival of African traders at Zumbo is not mentioned, but it is likely that they still came, especially in periods when trade between Butua and Zumbo flourished and diverted attention away from the north.

We hear little else about the trade of this great arc and only adverse comments on its effect on the Africans of the interior. The flood of trade-goods was said merely to stimulate internecine wars between ambitious rival chiefs.[2] There is no indication of the building up of great states on the basis of foreign trade, and the whole area probably remained divided into very small chiefdoms. As will be seen below, there is some indication, although slight, of the growth of the Lenje and the Nsenga as an entrepreneurial people, parallel to the well-known examples of the Bisa and Yao elsewhere.

Of the northern areas with which Zumbo traded, Urenje (in Portuguese Orenge, sometimes Orange) was the best-known to all in the Lower Zambezi area, and almost certainly the most important. According to the 1762 'Memórias' already referred to, the people of Urenje

> come every year to Zumbo to trade in ivory and in copper, which they bring ready smelted in great bars and of which there is great abundance and for its quality it is preferred to European in India. The greater part of the ivory which comes to Senna is from this region . . . but the merchants never trade extensively in these two commodities, except when the gold supply fails or to use up spare trade-goods.[3]

Because of this central importance of Urenje, its identification is of particular interest and as yet no solution is agreed. The word denoted a

[1] 1762—'Memórias da Costa d'Africa Oriental', in A. A. Andrade, *Relações de Moçambique Settecentista,* Lisbon, 1955, 204. No 'mussambazes' went there because there was no gold. 1781—Account of Adjunto of Zumbo on 6/11/1781 in Arquivo Histórico Ultramarino, Moçambique, caixa 17 (seen on microfilm). In a letter of António Caetano da Souza of 25/4/1783 from Zumbo (ibid.), caravans were being sent to Urenje, and in the 1766–8 period, when Butua was unproductive, Zumbo merchants were particularly eager to send their servants elsewhere (see, e.g., letter of Coelho de Campos of 23/1/1768, in 'Inventário do fundo do século XVIII do Arquivo Histórico de Moçambique', in *Moçambique—documentário trimestral*, 89 (1957), 163).

[2] Letter of Manoel José de Sta. Anna from Zumbo, 24/9/1767, in A.H.U. Moç., caixa 12.

[3] Andrade (1955), 204. (Own trans.)

'great region', which had within it many chiefs. It is variously described as fifteen days' walk up 'the river' (Luangwa or Zambezi), forty days to the north-east, and bordering on Caronga's (that is the Maravi). It was often said to be necessary to pass through Buruma's to reach it.[1] Pacheco almost certainly referred to the same place when, in 1862, he spoke of Zumbo's former trade with 'Arenje', and he was quite clear who the 'Varenjes' were: they lived west-north-west and west of Zumbo and Buruma's subjects were related to them.[2]

The Lenje of the present day are found in one small pocket fairly close to Zumbo on the north-west—no doubt those referred to by Pacheco. Their main country lies further north-west, between the Kafue and the Lunsenfwa; the name of Bene-Mukuni used to distinguish these people from the smaller group of Lenje.[3] The two names are now synonymous and the peoples must always have been closely related. The Lenje of Chipepo (Tembo clan) are said to have helped the Ambo on their first arrival in their present area and some Lenje, were also expelled early by the Nsenga.[4] Lane-Poole's tradition also connects the Bene-Mukuni with these Nsenga of Petauke district, for in it Undi, the Maravi paramount, went to Mukuni's and on his return journey established the Nsenga there. The story itself may have been discredited, but the connection may still exist.[5] In the other direction the Leya chief Mukuni claims descent from the Lenje chief Mukuni.[6] It is, then, possible that the Lenje covered a considerable area—Alenje, which may be identical with Urenje—either living in it or trading over it. It may even be that the community nearer to Zumbo was a colony of disappointed Lenje traders who originally settled down to await the next trading season. The 'Memórias' of 1762 describe how the payment in

[1] Varella, 'Descripção de Moçambique 1788', in L. F. Carvalho Dias, *Fontes para a história e geografia de Moçambique*, XVIII, Lisbon, 1954, 307; Andrade (1955), 204; Fr. Manoel de Sto. Thomas, for Academia Real da História Portuguesa, in *Cronista de Tissuary*, 4 vols., Goa, 1866–9, IV, 61; meeting of Adjunto of Zumbo on 28/11/1782, A.H.U. Moç., caixa 18.

[2] A. M. Pacheco, 'Viagem de Tete a Zumbo 1861–2', trans. in P. Guyot, *Voyage au Zambèze*, Paris, 1895, 301, 313, 320.

[3] J. Torrend, *Specimens of Bantu Folk-Lore from Northern Rhodesia*, London/New York, 1921, 1 (map); R. Apthorpe, *Central Bantu Historical Texts*, I, Rhodes-Livingstone Communications 22, Lusaka, 1961, vii, quoting Panabantu Milimo.

[4] B. Stefaniszyn, *The Social and Religious Life of the Ambo of Northern Rhodesia*, London, 1964, xx; E. H. Lane-Poole, *Native Tribes of the Eastern Province of Northern Rhodesia*, Lusaka, 3rd ed. 1949, 42. Probably both happened in the eighteenth century.

[5] Lane-Poole (1949), 39; R. Apthorpe, 'Problems of African History; the Nsenga of Northern Rhodesia', *Rhodes-Livingstone Journal*, 1960.

[6] B. M. Fagan, *Southern Africa during the Iron Age*, London, 1965, 175, quoting a MS. by the chief.

cloth for the ivory and copper they brought every year could only be made when the merchants had enough cloth left over from the Butua trade.[1]

Other possible identifications of Urenje lie further away, in the present-day Congo. Thus, both Burton and Cameron quoted Livingstone as having discovered, or been told of, Lake Ulenge or Kamalondo, which seems to have been a confusion of the Lake Kisale group of lakes and one near Bambarré Mountain much further north. Livingstone also met an Arab in Tabora who was travelling west to a land west of Katanga called Uranjé. The various Uranjes even further down the Congo, found by Stanley, may be discounted entirely.[2] Thus, linguistic evidence alone is clearly not conclusive. Some, on logical grounds alone, identify Urenje with Kazembe's Lunda kingdom, since it controlled the best-known copper supplies of the region. Nonetheless, Pacheco's evidence cited above lends strong support to the theory that Urenje was indeed the land of the Lenje, in roughly their present area. Undoubtedly, even if this was the origin of the word, it came to be a 'blanket term', covering a larger area than could properly be said to be inhabited by Lenje.

In the 1766–7 boom period a mass of ivory, provisions, cattle, and butter were the products of Urenje, but, both before and after this, copper was also mentioned. In 1762 they brought an abundance of copper in great 'barras'. In 1788 Varella claimed that ivory, machilas (cotton cloths), copper, and worked iron were to be found in Urenje.[3] Although there was supposed to be no gold there, there may have been the one mine found by two merchants in Frei Pedro's time (before 1751), although it did not last long.[4]

In return, the people of Urenje received cloth, small beads, and bigger vermilion ones from Balagate in India. When the 'mussambazes' started going into these lands themselves, they claim to have paid vast amounts in tolls to each chief en route, as well as frequently being barred altogether by Buruma and by wars in Urenje.[5]

There is no indication that the Lenje people worked iron particularly

[1] Andrade (1955), 204; Fr. Manoel José (1767).

[2] R. Burton, *The Lands of Cazembe*, London, 1873, 36; V. L. Cameron, *Across Africa, 1873–5*, 2 vols., London, 1876, I, 351; D. Livingstone, *Last Journals*, 2 vols., London, 1874, II, 176; H. M. Stanley, *Through the Dark Continent*, 2 vols., London, 1878, II, 175, 287.

[3] Andrade (1955), 204; Carvalho Dias (1954), 307.

[4] Fr. Manoel José (1767); Carvalho Dias (1954), 307.

[5] Fr. Manoel José (1767); António Manuel de Mello e Castro to José de Vasconcellos de Almeida, Sena, 17/7/1780, A.H.U. Moç., caixa 16.

well, although they had good iron ore which, later at least, they sold to the Plateau Tonga. However, the Soli (only called a tribe since the European administration) who lived in the same area had outstandingly good ironwork.[1] In the Lusaka district (as in Soli country) there have been sporadic gold-mines and traces of copper-mines, although the main copper-mines of the district are further west in the Hook of Kafue, where the Kaonde have now come to live.[2] It is not probable that any of these produced great quantities of copper, and perhaps the Lenje bought it in their turn from the Lamba and Sewa further north on the modern Copper Belt. As to provisions, the Lenje did have good land and own large numbers of cattle. Pacheco gives a picture of them as apathetic and without skills, but he might also be implying that they were traders, since they bought everything 'abroad'.[3]

Chief Mamba or Momba is sometimes referred to as a chief within the Urenje district, but more frequently as a separate trade partner.[4] I have found no indication of Mamba's whereabouts, although clearly it was in the same direction as Urenje. Perhaps the most likely candidate is Mambwe, the Kunda chief, who came to the district east of the Luangwa probably from Aushiland.[5] However, the name and others resembling it are common and there are many other possibilities.[6]

[1] M. P. Miracle, 'Plateau Tonga entrepreneurs in historical inter-regional trade', *Rhodes-Livingstone J.*, 1960, 40; Guyot (1895), 319—they had foreign artisans to work it for them; B. M. Fagan, 'Pre-European Iron Working in Central Africa', *J. Afr. Hist.*, 1961, 208—results of the examination of two nineteenth-century Soli chiefs' graves near Lusaka are described.

[2] *Report of the Land Commission of Northern Rhodesia*, Lusaka, 1946, 44; E. W. Smith and A. M. Dale, *The Ila-Speaking People*, 2 vols., London, 1920, I, 17; J. M. Mowbray, *In South Central Africa*, London, 1912, 72; J. D. Clark, *Prehistory of Southern Africa*, London, 1959, 305 (map). The Hook mines were largely sulphide and difficult to work. There was silver too at one.

[3] Guyot (1895), 319; *Land Commission* (1946), 36. Torrend (1921), 24, concerns a trading expedition.

[4] Letter of 26/11/1781 from Zumbo, A.H.U. Moç., caixa 18—this might mean that there were outposts of Lenje in Mamba's lands; letter of 28/11/1782 (ibid.) describes him as Regulo Mamba de Orenje; on the other hand, the two are separate in a letter of Caetano Manuel Correia 24/11/1785 (ibid., caixa 22) and of J. Pereira 10/1/1800 from Tete in 'Fundo do séc. XVIII' (cit.) in *Moçambique*, 82, 79.

[5] The Kunda were of Luba origin, but not directly connected with the Lala group (see below). Many Nsenga probably came with them. See Apthorpe (1960), 53; id. (1961), I, xvii; Lane-Poole (1949), 49–50. Lane-Poole's genealogies (77) put Mambwe *c.*1840, but all his dates have to be put drastically back because of the telescoping caused by the identification of alternate generations by Central African peoples, and indeed Gamitto appears to mention the Kunda in 1831–2: A. C. P. Gamitto, *King Kazembe*, trans. I. G. Cunnison, 2 vols., Lisbon, 1960, II, 157–8.

[6] Thus, two alternatives put his chiefdom in much the same area: Mambwe Chisaka was a half-brother of Lungu, the Ambo chief who pushed south in the eighteenth century:

The only product of Mamba's land mentioned was ivory, but in this commodity it was an important area for Zumbo and must have gained a significant amount of trade-goods in return in good years.

Again connected with the region of Urenje, but probably not precisely in it, was Chief Comcomba. He may merely have been a small chief of a Lenje people more widely spread than they are at present, but the name is irresistibly suggestive of Kankomba, the praise-name of the Nyendwa clan—the 'royal' clan of the Lala and their offshoots the Ambo, Swaka, Luano, and Kunda—because it was the name of their first leader out of Lambaland and is the honorific title of the chief.[1] The Nyendwa clan were in Lambaland perhaps in about 1625, moved to Aushiland, and thence Kankomba set up an important people in the Serenje district, spreading gradually southwards, Bwashi going into Swakaland in one direction and Lungu with the Ambo into 'Nsengaland' in the other. So, Kankomba's land in the eighteenth century could mean the Serenje district or perhaps lands already 'colonized' to the south.[2] The sources give no details of trade-goods or organization in this area except the usual complaints of robbery and loss. The Lala, however, used to work iron and own cattle. In the middle of Mkushi district there is some copper, not now mined and possibly not mined in pre-European times either. The Nyendwa royal clan also claimed all ivory, although this could have been a nineteenth-century innovation.[3]

It is possible that the Nyendwa clan's people were known as the Ambo, rather than Lala, on these journeyings, although now the Lala form the largest unit. This could explain the Bisa reference

---

Stefaniszyn (1964), xx; Mumba Chundu was the chief in 'Nsengaland' at the Lunsenfwa/Lukusashi confluence conquered by Lungu: J. T. Munday, 'Kankomba' (1944), cited in Apthorpe (1961), I, 19; but also, Chief Momba lives near Kalomo, with Nkoya and Tonka people under him: W. V. Brelsford, *Tribes of Northern Rhodesia*, Lusaka, 1956, 52; Simamba is a chief of the Valley Tonga E. Colson, *The Social Organisation of the Gwembe Tonga*, Manchester, 1960, map; the Mumba clan supplied two chiefs of the Luano (a Lala offshoot) in Mkushi district: Apthorpe (1961), I, xv, etc. It is not likely to be just 'mambo', a generic name for a chief, as the Portuguese were perfectly familiar with this usage.

[1] See J. T. Munday, 'Some traditions of the Nyendwa clan of Northern Rhodesia', in *Bantu Studies*, 1940, 435; id. (1944), in Apthorpe (1961), I.

[2] ibid.; W. Whiteley, *The Bemba and Related Peoples of Northern Rhodesia*, Ethn. Surv., London, 1950, 34. The 1625 date is based on generations. All that is certain is that they left Lambaland before *c.* 1775 (C. M. Doke, *The Lamba of Northern Rhodesia*, London, 1931, 36, 40), but a considerable time before is likely. Bwashi was apparently a nineteenth-century chief, but Lungu probably preceded him in the mid-eighteenth century. (See genealogies in Stefaniszyn (1964), xx–xxi.) References to Comcomba are to be found in 'Fundo do séc. XVIII', *Moçambique*, 84, 84 (1769 letter); letter of 9/9/1781, in A.H.U. Moç., caixa 18 and of 26/11/1781 (ibid.).

[3] Whiteley (1950), 34, 4; *Land Commission* (1946), 22; Munday (1940), 448.

in 1798 to the peoples to the south of them as the Aramba and the Ambo, omitting the Lala who lie between them and the present Ambo. These Ambo and Aramba (clearly the Lamba—in their present area) were on peaceful terms with Kazembe and traded with the Africans in the neighbourhood of Zumbo.[1] This may refer to the African 'mussambazes' of the merchants or to the Nsenga peoples around Zumbo. Doke states casually that it is well known that the Lamba went on trading expeditions to the Nsenga.[2] Elephant-hunting was a respected and important activity. Probably in the eighteenth century the Lamba mined copper, as did the Sewa, their offshoot in the present-day Congo. They were probably also trading in the other direction, with Kazembe, at the time.[3] So, copper and ivory may both have filtered down to Zumbo from here.

Most intriguing of all these trading regions is Ambara. Caetano Xavier in 1758 said that the copper seen in the Zumbo and Tete area was from Ambara and the trade in ivory from there was hindered only by the mountains. Worked iron and hoes also came from them but were costly. 'Mussambazes' were sent there for copper and ivory and what ivory they did not buy was used for stockades.[4] There are two indications of the whereabouts of Ambara. In 1768 the lands of Senga and Ambar were near the gold-mine of Mixonga, which from other sources we know was in Maravi country between Zumbo and Tete. Pinto de Miranda described the gold-mine of Pemba, discovered by Frei Pedro, as in the 'jurisdiction of Ambara', where there was iron and copper, close to Zumbo.[5] These sources indicate some location up the Luangwa, and Lane-Poole's information that an area near Petauke is called Mbala and the people of it (although part of the Nsenga) are sometimes called Ambala seems to provide the clue. These Nsenga of the Petauke area may be a combination of people from the west and from the Maravi and were perhaps distinct from the Nsenga further

[1] Lacerda's Journey to Cazembe (1798), in Burton (1873).

[2] Doke (1931), 30 n. One of his fables is set on such a journey: id., *Lamba Folk-Lore*, New York, 1927, 262.

[3] Whiteley (1950), 59, 57; B. M. Fagan, 'The Iron Age of Zambia', in *Current Anthropology*, 1966, 460; W. Cline, *Mining and Metallurgy in Negro Africa*, Menasha, 1937, 56.

[4] I. Caetano Xavier, 'Relações do Estado . . . de Africa Oriental', in Carvalho Dias (1954), 197; Varella (ibid., 308) said that the same 'mussambazes' that went to Changamire went to Ambararà for ivory and copper.

[5] 'Fundo do séc. XVIII' in *Moçambique*, 88, 133 (letter of 1768): see Guyot (1895), 301; Pinto de Miranda, 'Memória da Africa Oriental (*c.* 1766)' in Andrade (1955), 281 (but Carvalho Dias (1954), 88, reads it as Ambava). The Banda-Pemba mines were described as 6 leagues from Zumbo: see Guyot, loc. cit.

south at that stage. There is also apparently an old working for gold in this area.[1] Livingstone's reference to Chief Monze's on the Batoka Plateau as the farthest point west that the Ambala came up the Zambezi for ivory provides an instance both of the Nsenga being called Ambala and of their trading activities. Possibly his other reference to an old headman of Namilanga (north of Livingstone) whose father twice went to Bambala, where white traders lived, when he himself was a young boy (about 1790 or 1800) signifies the Petauke Ambara too.[2] It is possible, however, that the last quotation refers rather to the Mbala people north of the Ila, or indeed that Bambala meant the people of the north, as it did to the Ila. These Mbala did trade iron goods to others, for instance the Plateau Tonga, and were close to the copper-mines of the Hook of Kafue. Although they may have been the Bambala spoken of by Tonga, it is not likely that their land was the Ambara known to the merchants of Zumbo.[3]

Ambara, then, was probably the present Nsenga country near Petauke. This may also have been identical with the country of the Anvuas or Amuvas, mentioned, it seems, only in the seventeenth century. Barreto said that the Amuvas lived along the Zambezi (conceived as flowing from the north) above the Maravi and had a great deal of ivory (of which they made fences), for which transport was very difficult. Caetano Xavier's remarks about Ambara may be an echo of this. Frei António da Conceição in 1696 described the Anvuas as bordering on the Zambezi, as being situated on the way to the silver-mines, and as possessing ivory and apparently also copper, and says that through their districts Africans come from Angola.[4] Probably these two refer to a country stretching further south and east than it did in the eighteenth century but none the less the same. Retreating still further in time, perhaps this was also the Mõbara of António Fernandes, where copper was sold to Monomotapa's people across a great river.[5]

If the Petauke district is a correct identification, it is unlikely that copper came precisely from there, although ivory probably did.

[1] Lane-Poole (1949), 41; Clark (1959), 305 (map).

[2] D. Livingstone, *African Journals 1853–6*, ed. I. Schapera, 2 vols., London, 1963, II, 350–51, 336.

[3] M. A. Jaspan, *The Ila-Tonga Peoples*, Ethn. Surv., London, 1953, 12; Miracle (1960), 39.

[4] M. Barreto, 'Informação do Estado e Conquista dos Rios de Cuama 1667' in *Records of South-Eastern Africa*, ed. G. M. Theal, 9 vols., Cape Town, 1898–1903, III, 481; Fr. António da Conceição, 'Tratado dos Rios 1696' in *Cronista de Tissuary*, II, 65.

[5] Veloso's report in H. Tracey, *António Fernandes Descobridor do Monomotapa 1514–15*, Lourenço Marques, 1940, 24. Tracey prefers a Lomagundi area identification.

Possibly the Nsenga-Lenje connection lubricated a route for copper from the Lenje themselves or the Lamba further north.

It is clear that the Portuguese had trading connections with the Tonga peoples spread either side of the Zambezi valley and over the Plateau as far as the Kafue.[1] Perhaps Livingstone's Tonga man who journeyed to Bambala was taking part in this trade. Of the Portuguese accounts, the clearest is Frei António da Conceição's of 1696, before Zumbo itself was established. The furthest point he mentions is Muzimo, which Axelson identifies near the Kafue confluence with the Zambezi. There the Africans wore ill-made beads and copper bangles. They sold copper and gold but mostly ivory to the merchants coming up from Tete. Again Africans were said to cross to Angola from there.[2] There were apparently copper and gold mines on the Tonga Plateau, and copper crosses have been found over the area.[3]

Finally, an evident omission from the account so far is a discussion of trade with the Bisa. It would be extraordinary if these great traders, who reached Lake Malawi and Tete carrying Kazembe's goods, had not found Zumbo. Indeed Pacheco does mention them and the Bemba as trade partners of the merchants there. However, I have as yet found no recognizable reference to their presence at Zumbo or of trade with their area in the eighteenth century and indeed it seems that they did not come even as far south as the mine of Java until about 1793.[4] Their statement to Lacerda that the Lamba and Ambo declare that they trade with those near Zumbo suggests a lack of first-hand knowledge, at any rate at that stage. If the Bemba traded with Zumbo, it was clearly at a later date, after they had made their thrust southward.

The volume of trade with all these areas varied immensely, so that the few figures available cannot be used to imply trends. None the less, they give some indication of the importance of the trade. For ivory from these areas, Barreto (1667) said that one merchant alone bought 50 bars from the Amuvas (but was robbed of half); Frei António da Conceição in 1696 puts Muzimo's production at 200 bars a year; in 1762, the

[1] See, e.g., letter of Costa of 1769 in 'Fundo do séc. XVIII', *Moçambique*, 84, 84. I am dealing in this essay only with the longer trade-routes. Obviously there was trade too with Buruma and other chiefs near Zumbo.

[2] Fr. António da Conceição, in *Cronista de Tissuary*, II, 65; E. Axelson, *The Portuguese in South-East Africa*, Johannesburg, 1960, 190–91. Muzimo is mentioned again in 1781: accounts enclosed in a letter of 29/3/1781, A.H.U. Moç., caixa 17.

[3] Fagan (1965), 167, 170.

[4] Guyot (1895), 301; Manuel Caetano Pereira (1798), in Burton (1873), 35, said the Bisa had heard of his father at Java 'years before'—but it had only been mined since 1790.

greater part of the ivory which came to Sena came from the region of Urenje, and from the whole of the Rios 40 bars were exported, worth 60,000 xerafins; in 1800 Jeronimo Pereira said that, a few years before, Mamba had been producing 70–80 bars of ivory a year.[1] For copper the only indication I have found is the 1762 account, which gives as the product of the Rios 200 arrobas (about 2–3 tons), worth 20,000 xerafins. This came largely from Zumbo, but, as we have seen, in some years no copper came there at all.[2]

The reciprocal importance of trade for Zumbo and this great arc of Zambia was underestimated in the more general Portuguese accounts of the Rios. For them, Butua was the vital trade partner of Zumbo, because it produced gold. None the less, on the spot, the merchants clearly appreciated the northern trade as much, and especially that with Urenje. In 1783 it was even said that Urenje was the only area of trade left to Zumbo, and it was always prized there. In 1767 it produced a mass of ivory and in 1762 a great abundance of copper.[3]

The effect of the trade on the African peoples is not yet known, but one might speculate that the production and transportation of two or three tons of copper in one year required the development of a considerable organization, however indirect the routes used. These routes may have provided channels for commercial information and perhaps even cultural change. Although the name Urenje may simply be a blanket term used by the Portuguese, it is possible that it indicates that the Lenje enjoyed a wider sphere of influence than they now do, and that this influence was commercially based. The Nsenga too have emerged prominently in this account as traders with the Portuguese, and although the evidence as yet is inconclusive, either or both of these peoples may have provided a middleman service for the area. Certainly, with the early preoccupation of the Zumbo merchants with Butua, it was necessary for the initiative in this northern trade to come from Africans, and it duly came, from the people of a wide area of modern Zambia. Thus there developed an active eighteenth-century trade,

[1] Barreto in (ed.) Theal (1898–1903), III, 481; Fr. António da Conceição, quoted by Axelson (1960), 191; Andrade (1955), 204, 219; J. Pereira letter of 1800 in 'Fundo do séc. XVIII', *Moçambique*, 82, 79. In one instance, 7 tusks = ½ bar (1781) and this may be a fair rough estimate. Officially *c.* 1333 xerafins = 1000 cruzados, but in 1750, 1000 cruzados' worth of ivory would only fetch *c.* 600 xerafins in India: F. Mello e Castro, *Descripção dos Rios de Sena, 1750*, Goa, 1861, I, 19.

[2] Andrade (1955), 219; A. Lobato, *Evolução Administrativa e Económica de Moçambique 1752–63*, Lisbon, 1957, 243.

[3] Letter of 28/5/1783 in A.H.U. Moç., caixa 19; see also above, p. 235.

mainly in ivory, which, although not conducted on the grand scale of Kazembe's for example, was of importance to both partners and long preceded the better known nineteenth-century traffic in the same region.

12

Trade and the Rozwi Mambo

NICOLA SUTHERLAND-HARRIS

The Rozwi area of Butua, in modern Rhodesia, for centuries produced relatively large quantities of gold, which was sent to the Indians, Arabs, and Portuguese on the coast. In the seventeenth and eighteenth centuries, as well as at an earlier period, considerable amounts of pottery, metal goods, ivory, and foodstuffs were also exchanged within the area. A flourishing economy might, then, be expected here, based on profitable foreign and internal trade. In fact, although it is true that the volume of both external and internal trade was great, trading operations were strictly controlled and confined by the Mambo or Changamire, who had a monopoly of gold, the main export, and whose tribute-network formed the major lines along which exchange took place within the country. This was 'state control' designed for the benefit not of the whole community, but of a small, oligarchical group.

Two other sources of the Mambo's power, the religious and the military, were, however, more obvious to his subjects. The Mambo was held in mystic awe and, perhaps, seclusion. As the representative of the land, he may not have been allowed foreign foodstuffs or even, perhaps, other goods. There is evidence that the Mambo himself was a religious figure in that he prayed for rain for the people, and the Rozwi as a whole had a reputation for being closer to Mwari than others.[1] However, the main religious functions were served by the priests of Mwari to whom the Mambo sent messengers with 'tribute' for rain, as the Mukurudzi is now sent by Rozwi chiefdoms in the south. It may be that the secular and spiritual worlds were at one time more united, but by the nineteenth century stories of dispute between them are frequent in

[1] *Acrescimento* to 'Memória sobre a doação do território Bandire', in Arquivo Histórico Ultramarino, Moçambique maço 21, doc. of 1/6/1831; K. R. Robinson, *Khami Ruins*, Cambridge, 1959, 13, 162.

tradition. The widespread Mwari cult was, however, clearly an important unifying feature in the 'empire' or 'confederacy'.[1]

Portuguese accounts are full of praise for Changamire's military strength. Although Rozwi buildings were designed for effect rather than defence, their weapons were exceptional—axes, daggers, clubs, and leather shields—and their battle-axes impressed even the Ndebele.[2] Rozwi war-medicines too were respected. It seems that Tumbare, one of whose functions may have been to act as regent during an interregnum, had the task of administering these to the armies. They probably used forts, with palisades of elephants' tusks, as well as their 'stone houses'. It *may* be that there was some form of age-regiment, but this could have been a late development imported from the south. In 1758 Caetano Xavier mentioned a division of the army into two squadrons, one to fight and one to chase the fugitives.[3] Sebina remarks on the 'unflinching obedience' of the people of Mambo. One method of fighting was to send 'nhabazes' with men of war, giving them a hoe as a token that they were entitled to clear the land of the enemy and cultivate it.[4]

None the less, the Rozwi state was not a unified, despotic organization, but a very loosely connected confederacy. Political communications were maintained by annual tribute and possibly by the bringing of new fire by messengers to each chiefdom every year. This is suggested by the Hera myth of fire being introduced by a Mrozwi and was the case in the sixteenth-century Monomotapa's chiefdom.[5] Certainly at the death of a local chief the contact was stressed by a system of confirmation of the new chief by the Rozwi. Botelho described the operation of

[1] M. Gelfand, *An African's Religion,* Cape Town, 1966, 41, for Mukurudzi; see D. Abraham, 'The roles of Chaminuka and the mhondoro cults in Šhona political history', in E. Stokes and R. Brown, *The Zambesian Past,* Manchester, 1966.

[2] Robinson (1959), 15–16; P. Schebesta, 'Die Zimbabwe-Kultur in Afrika', *Anthropos,* 1926, 248–9; I. Caetano Xavier, 'Notìcias dos dominios Portugueses na Costa d'Africa Oriental' (1758), in L. F. de Carvalho Dias, *Fontes para a história e geografia de Moçambique,* XVIII, Anais IX, Lisbon, 1954, 177–8; A. J. B. Hughes and Van Velsen, *The Ndebele,* Ethn. Surv., London, 1954, 61.

[3] Caetano Xavier (1758), in Carvalho Dias (1954), 178; G. Fortune, 'A Rozi text with translation and notes', *Native Affairs Department Annual (N.A.D.A.),* 1956, 81; A.H.U. Moç., 1/6/1831; E. Smith, 'Sebituane and the Makololo', *African Studies,* 1956, 61.

[4] P. M. Sebina, 'The Makalaka', *African Studies,* 1947, 86; letter of Costa 13/3/1769 (referring to the wars against the Mahias), in 'Arquivo Histórico de Moçambique, Inventário do Fundo do século XVIII', in *Moçambique-documentário trimestral,* 72–89, Lourenço Marques, 1952–7, 84, 92.

[5] F. W. T. Posselt, *Fact and Fiction,* Salisbury, 1935, 21; *The Book of Duarte Barbosa,* Hakluyt Soc., London, 1918, 13.

this system in Sanga (Quissanga) in the mid-eighteenth century. The aspirant went to Changamire and, if Mwari duly sent his rain in blessing, was treated with medicines and sent back with Changamire's men to proclaim him. In modern times the Rozwi officiating may catechize the new chief on his duties. The paramount never had more than this veto over appointment and the actual choice lay with the family and people and perhaps ancestors of the chiefdom.[1]

The area covered by the Rozwi state fluctuated. The Mambo probably had no permanent seat but travelled to different centres—Khami, Dhlo Dhlo, N'natali, Ntaba zi ka Mambo, and others—in which he had indunas installed. These were generally members of his own family such as his wives, his mother, and his sons.[2] The area of polychrome 'band and panel' pottery and decorated stone ruins generally identified with the Rozwi is restricted to the south-west of modern Rhodesia,[3] although traditions of Rozwi hegemony remain from Manicaland to the Shankwe.[4]

Although the religious and military bases of the Mambo's power, and the slenderness of that power politically, must be borne in mind, the Mambo's intervention in trade was also vital to his position and influence. This intervention may be seen in three spheres. Within the Rozwi area of influence, tribute was paid in gold, copper, iron goods, ivory, and foodstuffs to the Mambo, and probably through the same network foreign trade-goods—cloth and beads—filtered. The part played by independent traders was of minor importance. The second sphere was external inter-African trade, that is with peoples of the Transvaal, Botswana, Zambia, and possibly even Congo, mainly in metal goods. This trade seems to have developed little, perhaps

[1] S. X. Botelho, *Memória Estatistica,* Lisbon, 1835, 167 (reporting a hundred years before); J. N. Jenkinson, 'Marauke's installation', *N.A.D.A.* 1959, 46–7; A.H.U. Moç., 1/6/1831; M. Gelfand, 'The great Muzukuru; his role in the Shona clan', *N.A.D.A.*, 1966, and *An African's Religion* (1966), 17; J. F. Holleman, *Shona Customary Law*, London, 1952.

[2] S. Nenguwo, 'Oral work among the Rozwi: a few notes', Central African History Conference of the Rhodes-Livingstone Institute, Lusaka, 1963, 1; K. R. Robinson, 'History of Bikita District', *N.A.D.A.*, 1957, 77; id. (1959), 163.

[3] Probably even Great Zimbabwe was not an important centre at this time and was, rather, ancestral to the Mambo's civilization under discussion. See K. R. Robinson, 'The archaeology of the Rozwi', in Stokes and Brown (1966); P. S. Garlake, 'The value of imported ceramics in the dating and interpretation of the Rhodesian Iron Age', *J. Afr. Hist.*, IX, 1, 1968, 28.

[4] Relevant traditions are generally late eighteenth-century and early nineteenth-century, and many may concern only a 'Southern Rozwi' influx from the Transvaal about this time. See H. von Sicard, 'Ruins and their traditions on the Lower Mzingwane and in the Beitbridge area', *N.A.D.A.*, 1961.

because of strict control. The third sphere was trade with non-Africans, where, whoever the agents involved (and they were usually African), the ultimate trade partner was European or Indian. This part of Rozwi trade was largely confined to gold but included some ivory. The main routes into the Rozwi area were from Zumbo on the Zambezi and from Manicaland. Again, here, the Mambo tried to keep a monopoly over gold production and to control trading activities, to his own advantage.

The organization of internal trade was largely dependent on the Mambo himself, with other traders playing only a minor role, and the wide 'tribute' network was the basis of most exchange. Tribute collection was centrally, not hierarchically organized. According to one tradition, there were four groups of officers who went out to collect tribute each year; in another, Mambo Nechadzike punished the Bakwa of Wankie district for killing the tribute collectors.[1] One of the items of this tribute, at least at Khami, may have been grain, since large grain-stores but few grindstones have been found there. This may have been used for the supply of officials at the capital of the day, which had little good agricultural land around it, or there may have been some kind of redistributive system in times of scarcity. It is possible that grain tribute was organized as it had been by Kiteve (Quiteve) in the sixteenth century, where each village worked one of its fields for the king.[2] Some forms of 'tribute' were paid in person at the court; the Lilima and Humbe women, for instance, came up to make pots for the Mambo and then returned. These are probably the makers of the 'band and panel' pottery characteristic of Rozwi decorated ware.[3] On the other hand, the Mambo himself is said to have travelled to Maguswini (Dett, near Wankie) to obtain a substance for strengthening spears. This may have been carbon for steel, as there were once said to be 'steel mines' in the rivers, but it is more likely that it was some form of medicine.[4] It is probable that the Mambo gave as much as he received for some of these goods, as the loose structure of the confederacy would have allowed of nothing else. Certainly Monomotapa paid for *his* tribute, at a fixed price even, as when he sent two cows for

[1] Robinson (1957), 77; Posselt (1935), 145.

[2] Robinson (1959), 161; J. Dos Santos, 'Ethiopia Oriental' (1609), in G. M. Theal, *Records of South-Eastern Africa,* 9 vols., Cape Town, 1898–1903, VII, 222.

[3] Robinson (1959), 61. Undecorated pottery differs markedly at different sites, e.g. Dhlo Dhlo and Khami.

[4] ibid., 164; D. Mello e Castro, 'Notícias do Império Marave e dos Rios 1763', in Carvalho Dias (1954), 126.

500 reis of gold.[1] Beads reached all corners of the area, perhaps largely in this way. Therefore there is sufficient justification for calling 'tribute' an exchange of goods and including it in a discussion of trade. There is no evidence that the Mambo took any part in the up-keep of communications, but it seems that the Rozwi did develop the use of oxen to ride and to carry their loads.[2]

In the independent sector of the economy, inter-village trade probably flourished uncontrolled. There is no evidence of market-places or organized markets. Usually, it seems, the customer went to the ironsmith, for example, and made a specific order, and in modern examples even brought his own iron and helped in the work in addition to paying for it.[3] None the less, there are also examples of itinerant traders who travelled into foreign districts within the general Rozwi sphere, although how far these were controlled by the political authority is unknown. Thus, the Zezuru became known as 'bashabi'—pedlars—whose trade of iron hoes, axes, and knives to the Budja may be ancient and who may also be identified as the inhabitants of Usesuro, whence the people of 'Changoé' (Shankwe presumably) obtained their iron weapons. The Lemba too were known as 'vashavhi' and have strong traditions of wandering selling luxury goods south of the Zambezi.[4]

The goods and routes involved in trade, whether organized by the Mambo or independently, are indicated diagrammatically in Map 14. The main goods travelling were probably iron, copper, gold, ivory, building stones, salt, medicines, and cattle, and presumably there was a good deal of local trade in different kinds of tobacco and in skins.[5] Iron was a particularly frequent commodity. Weapons were brought from all directions as 'tax' to Khami. Nenguwo collected traditions in the Bikita reserve to the effect that hoes were brought from the Kateve people to the court at Bulawayo and spears from the Zambezi. The Hera and Njanja certainly paid tribute to the Rozwi in iron implements. They lived around Mt. Wedza, where there are extensive ancient workings for iron. Equally, in the Vuxwa Hills, Mulungwani Hills

[1] J. de Barros, 'Da Asia' (1552–1613), in Theal (1898–1903), I, 271–2.

[2] A.H.U. Moç., 1/6/1831; Marodzi, 'The Borozwi', *N.A.D.A.*, 1924, 90.

[3] H. von Sicard, 'The Ancient Sabi-Zimbabwe Route', *N.A.D.A.*, 1963, 60; J. S. Hatton, 'Notes on MaKalanga Iron-Smelting', *N.A.D.A.*, 1967, 42.

[4] Budja tradition, in H. Kuper, *The Shona*, London, 1954, 27; A. Pacheco, 'Voyage de Tete à Zumbo 1861–2', in P. Guyot, *Voyage au Zambèze*, Paris, 1895, 287—probably reporting tales of earlier days; Lemba, in H. Stayt, *The Ba Venda*, London, 1931, 27; N. J. Van Warmelo, *The Copper Miners of Musina and the Early History of the Zoutspansberg*, Pretoria, 1940, 62.

[5] See Posselt (1935), 156.

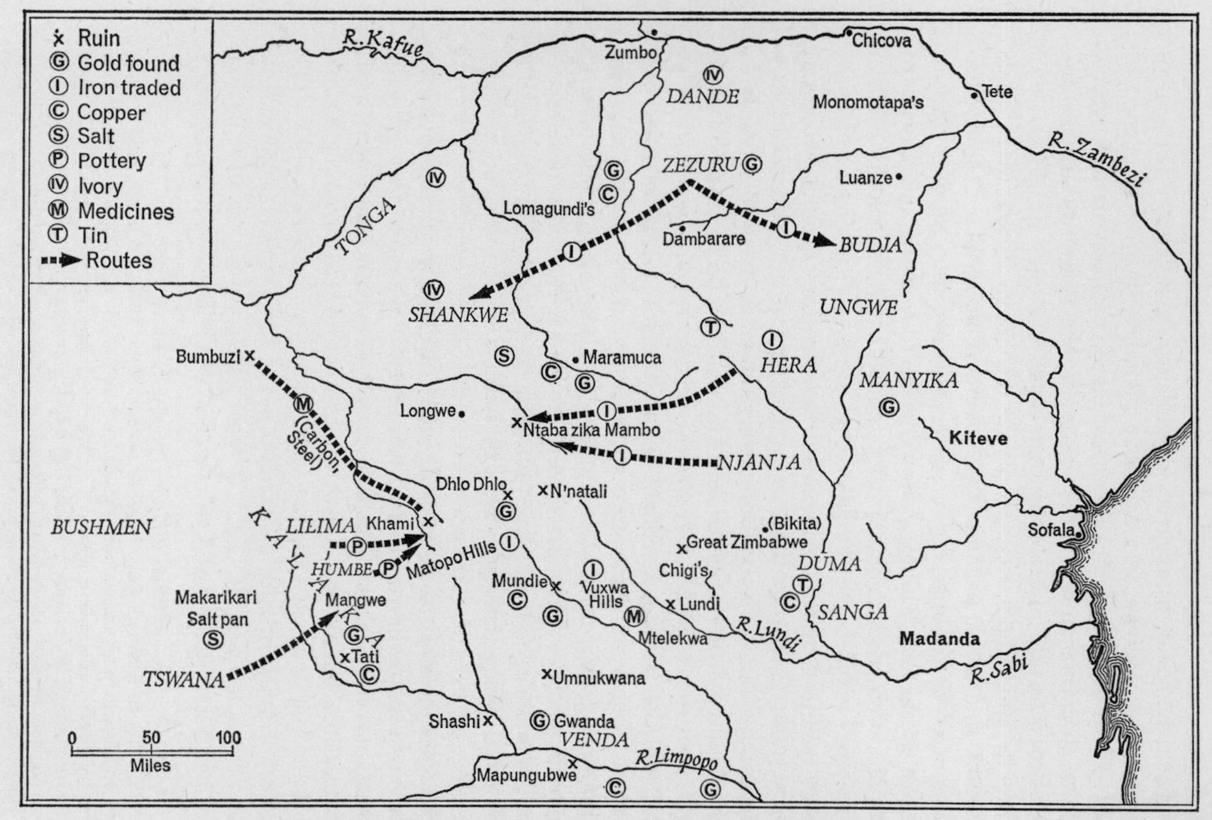

Map 14. Rozwi Internal Trade-Routes and Goods

(Bulawayo), and Manesi Hills (Charter), iron ore and slag were found in quantities suggesting the supply of a large region.[1] Apparently there are no traditional accounts of copper being traded or brought as tribute, although it presumably was. There are considerable deposits at Selkirk, near Tati, and in the Lomagundi area as well as smaller ones elsewhere.[2] Gold too must have travelled considerable distances to satisfy the demands of the Mambo and the aristocracy and of export. All trade in gold seems to have been inspired by the Mambo, and more will be said of his monopoly later. The main ancient workings are marked on the map, following Summers.[3] There are many traditions of stones being brought to build the Mambo's houses as tribute and it is probable that the tribute included the laying of them too. Perhaps the traditions of attempts to move mountains recall this. However, in practice stone was never far away. It was said that the Christian prisoners taken by Changamire at the fairs in the seventeenth century had the task of repairing the palace.[4] The desire for salt and ivory is given as a reason for the Rozwi invasion of the Shankwe[5] inspired by the Mambo, who presumably received these goods afterwards as tribute. Finally, the exchange of medicines by 'ngangas' (diviners) over long distances was doubtless common, the exotic remedy always being the more effective. One hint of such a trade might be seen in the statement that one of the medicines for making divining dice effective was only obtainable in the Vuxwa Hills.[6] There was, no doubt, an ever-changing pattern of trade in such commodities. Probably the most valued objects to exchange for any other goods were cattle, ornaments, and foreign trade-goods. Thus the Mambo, in his turn, paid tribute to Mwari in beads, cloth, hoes, and gold, and black oxen—the black symbolizing rain-clouds—were brought and killed at religious feasts.[7]

[1] Robinson (1959), 164; Nenguwo (1963), 6—Bikita Reserve traditions; Posselt (1935), 24, on Hera; on Vuxwa Hills, H. von Sicard, 'Places of Ancient Occupation in Chief Negove's Country', *N.A.D.A.*, 1956, 32; F. P. Mennell and R. Summers, 'The "Ancient Workings" of Southern Rhodesia', Occ. Papers of the National Museums of South Rhodesia, 20, 1955, 768.

[2] W. Cline, *Mining and Metallurgy in Negro Africa*, Menasha, 1937, 58.

[3] R. Summers, 'Environment and Culture in Southern Rhodesia: a study in the "personality" of a land-locked country', *Proc. American Philosophical Society*, 1960, 281 (map).

[4] See traditions in Robinson (1959), 159; Fortune (1956), 82–3; 'Descripção Corográfica do Reino da Manica Seus Costumes e leis' (? 1787), in A. Lobato, *Evolução Administrativa e Economica de Moçambique 1752–63*, Lisbon, 1957, 63.

[5] D. M. Coley, 'The Fate of the last BaShankwe Chief', *N.A.D.A.*, 1927, 65.

[6] H. von Sicard, 'Vuxwa Hills and their Inhabitants', *N.A.D.A.*, 1958, 75.

[7] R. S. Summers, 'Carl Mauch on the Zimbabwe Ruins', *N.A.D.A.*, 1952, 12–13; Fortune (1956), 82.

The demand for goods, predominantly by the Mambo and court, led to a certain degree of specialization and exploitation of the country's resources. Specialization in the craft of pottery has already been mentioned. The Lilima and the Humbe were both said to have made pottery as tribute. Although normally similarity in pottery over an area, as here in the south-west, indicates cultural unity, it may be that some credit is due here to trade or tribute in it.[1] Bent in the 1890s was told that there were whole villages which specialized in pottery-making[2] and these may well have existed earlier. The Lilima also seem to be mentioned by tradition as 'professional' builders, in that they built Bambuzi for the Nanzwa and were paid for it.[3]

Again in the 1890s Bent saw Chibi's village which specialized entirely in iron, selling it to obtain basic foods, and was told there were others like it. The blacksmith's art is inherited through possession by a 'mashavi' (special skill) spirit, which usually falls on a relative of the preceding medium, so that a kin-based village could easily become a specialist community. There is some justification for reading this situation back into the past, since Mambo's people (at Ntaba zi ka Mambo), for example, were said to be ironworkers who paid for work done for them in iron hoes.[4] Working of iron could be done anywhere that the skill had been developed, but for smelting good charcoal was required, so that this also was often divorced from the mining operation. There is evidence of considerable iron-smelting industries at Shashi, Vukwe (near Tati), Ntaba zi ka Mambo, and Dhlo Dhlo.[5]

The Rhodesian ruins, however, are famous for finds of the more precious metals. Caetano Xavier's dictum that Africans looked upon gold and ivory only as items for the export trade[6] clearly does not apply to the Rozwi. Hall and Neal found 700 oz. of gold at Dhlo Dhlo, much of it in the form of ornaments, often in burials, of which the most sumptuous contained 72 oz. In all Matabeleland 2,000 oz. were said to

[1] Robinson (1959), 118.

[2] J. T. Bent, *Ruined Cities of Mashonaland,* London, 3rd ed. 1902, 45.

[3] Robinson (1959), 161.

[4] Robinson (1959), 164; Bent (1902), 45, 272; H. Tracey, 'The Mashavi', *N.A.D.A.*, 1934.

[5] H. A. Wieschoff, *The Zimbabwe-Monomotapa Culture,* Madison, 1941, 67–8; at Ntaba zi ka Mambo (K. R. Robinson, 'The Leopard's Kopje Culture', *South African Archaeological Bulletin (S.A.A.B.),* 1966, 16) there are different periods of Leopard's Kopje industry topped by a small layer of 'band and panel' pottery; G. Caton-Thompson, *The Zimbabwe Culture: Ruins and Reactions*, Oxford, 1931, 169.

[6] Caetano Xavier (1758), in Carvalho Dias (1954), 179.

have been found.[1] These ornaments were made during the Rozwi period, although perhaps decreasingly, as is suggested by the stratification of Khami and by a tradition that Mambo's wives only picked up in the ruins the gold they wore. The ornaments were manufactured within the ruins themselves; for instance, gold wire was drawn at Dhlo Dhlo.[2] The smelting of gold, both for home and export consumption, is not so much in evidence at the ruins themselves, except at Mundie, where Hall and Neal claim to have found five furnaces near the surface, and perhaps at N'natali and M'telekwa.[3] The methods of gold-mining were similar to those described in other parts of Rhodesia,[4] although it is interesting that old workings at Tati appear to have had underground tunnels, whereas elsewhere mines were open stopes or shafts with bell-shaped chambers at the bottom. Tati may, however, have been used later than other mines. The workings at Gwanda of 160 and 120 feet depth are some of the biggest anywhere in Rhodesia.[5]

Copper was also worked extensively into ornaments and bars—the latter perhaps being for transportation or for use as currency. Bronze too was alloyed in the country, some of the tin used being mined in Africa, as tin slag was found at Dhlo Dhlo; but some was perhaps imported through Zumbo, where it was used as a trade-good.[6] Hall and Neal describe a copper-and-gold alloy at Khami, and copper and lead may have been combined, as they were by the Venda to the south, although lead has only been found on its own.[7] As to silver, although mines are not now found in Rhodesia, there was a little in the Hartley Hills which might have been the source of the raw silver, bangles, and beads at Dhlo Dhlo. However, most of the silver hoard at Dhlo Dhlo was clearly imported.[8]

Other crafts too were highly developed, particularly at the court.

[1] R. N. Hall and W. G. Neal, *The Ancient Ruins of Rhodesia*, London, 1902, 144–7, 94, 91.

[2] At Zimbabwe it seems that most of the gold came from Period IV (Robinson (1966), 23), which may be ancestral to or contemporary with the Western ruins; Posselt (1935), 153; see Hall and Neal (1902), 93.

[3] Hall and Neal (1902), 85, 290–91, 149.

[4] See B. M. Fagan, *Southern Africa during the Iron Age*, London, 1965, 87–8.

[5] On Tati, see H. Stabb, *To the Victoria Falls via Matabeleland, 1875*, ed. E. C. Tabler, Cape Town, 1967, 58; F. C. Selous, *Travel and Adventure in South-East Africa*, London, 1893, 338; in general, see Mennell and Summers (1955).

[6] D. R. McIver, *Medieval Rhodesia*, London, 1906, 43; for Zumbo, see Accounts of March 1781 in A.H.U. Moç., caixa 17.

[7] See Hall and Neal (1902), 151–2, 144–7; Stayt (1931), 65.

[8] Hall and Neal (1902), 144–7; Caton-Thompson (1931), 164–75; T. Baines, *The Gold Regions of South-East Africa*, London, 1877, 30.

Ornaments were made of shell and ivory as well as metal. The ostrich-egg shell was used for many beads, and divining dice, little lions, and beads were carved of ivory at Khami Ruins and probably elsewhere.[1] Ivory was strongly associated with chieftainship. The Mambo received the ground-tusk of any elephant killed, as did many African chiefs, and he was said to sit on an ivory throne. Ivory bracelets may also have been confined to chiefs and their wives as among the Venda.[2] There is evidence of cotton spinning in the pottery whorls found frequently at Khami, and certainly elsewhere in south-east Africa cloths (machilas) were made locally.[3] Bark-cloth and skins none the less provided the ordinary people's regular clothing, and at court imported cloth was prized.

Although these 'industries' were considerably more developed than those of many other African peoples of the same era, they were still peripheral in a predominantly subsistence economy. Rice and '*mixoiera*' (a kind of millet) were said to be the main staples of Changamire's lands in 1831,[4] but the former probably grew only in the Sabi valley. It may be that maize had been introduced, although by the late nineteenth century sorghum was apparently the staple crop of Matabeleland and maize of the land nearer the Zambezi.[5] Butua, however, was famous for its cattle and Changamire's own connection with cattle is indicated in the tradition told to the Portuguese that he had been Monomotapa's cowherd before his rebellion.[6] Perhaps this could refer to some post in the Monomotapa's kingdom, whose incumbent had a duty to supply cattle to the Monomotapa as tribute, as the same story was told of Matuzianhe (a rebel against the Monomotapa) early in the seventeenth century. Interestingly, too, the name Chirisamuru—one of the Rozwi Mambos—means 'little calfherd'.[7] Finally, the Rozwi seem to have hunted a great deal, and there used to be many elephants and

[1] Robinson (1959), 146; id., 'Excavations at Khami', in *Proceedings of 3rd Pan-African Conference on Prehistory, 1955*, Oxford, 1957, 359, 363; McIver (1906), 45.

[2] C. R. Bullock, *The Mashona*, Cape Town, revised ed. 1927, 37; Stayt (1931), 25.

[3] Robinson (1959), 142; Monclaro, 'Viagem . . . com Francisco Barretto 1569', in Theal (1898–1903), III, 229.

[4] A.H.U. Moç., 1/6/1831.

[5] J. Walton, *The African Village*, Pretoria, 1956, 62, however, implies that maize was grown all over Rhodesia by 1560; as to the nineteenth century, see Hughes and van Velsen (1954), 57 (quoting a 1910 source), and Selous (1893), 48.

[6] A. Gomes, 'Viagem que fez . . . ao Império de Manamotapa' (1648), ed. E. Axelson, *Studia*, 1959, 197; Lobato (1957), 64; Robinson (1959), 5; Frei António da Conceição, 'Tratado dos Rios de Cuama 1696', *Cronista de Tissuary*, 4 vols., Goa, 1867, II, 105.

[7] A. Bocarro, 'Décadas', in Theal (1898–1903), III, 364–5.

buffalo around the ruins area. Fortune's Rozwi text mentions meat which was brought as tribute to Mambo Lembeu at the flat rock at the court of Bulawayo (probably Dhlo Dhlo or N'natali).[1]

Upon this basis of subsistence, then, were grafted the metalwork, carving, and pottery industries described. They served local demand, for example, for iron tools, but owed their development and momentum to the demands of the Mambo and his court. These demands were largely supplied by the Mambo's own organization of an exchange network where tribute goods were brought to him, probably in return for foreign trade-goods or ornaments as well as for his protection. In this way the trading sphere left to 'private enterprise' was small and the Mambo's economic power considerably enhanced his political standing. He had the means to reward those who served him, who formed an oligarchical class, living in the stone enclosures, dominating the rest of the population.

Trade with other African peoples outside the Rozwi area was probably not of great importance. Contacts with the east are largely entangled with non-African trade and will be dealt with in that context. Thus, there was probably considerable contact with the Monomotapa throughout, both economic and political. The political contact was frequently unfriendly,[2] which may have had a major disruptive influence on trade. Manicaland was at some periods subject to Rozwi hegemony but may be regarded as external in that it was much more a part of the coastal, Portuguese trading network. Some Rozwi gold went to Manicaland and, it seems, birds' eggs,[3] presumably ostrich-egg-shells for making beads. Cattle may also have been sent there as this is where the reputation of Butua cattle seems to have been so great.

To the west, again, political relations and domination fluctuated greatly,[4] but some trade is mentioned, such as that in dogs (presumably for hunting) from the Tswana to Mangwe district. The exchange of metal for cattle between the Kalaka and the Ngwato is described in Smith's diary of 1835, but many Kalaka were outside Rozwi influence by that time. Later on, the Matabele had considerable traffic with the Amasili/Masarwa of the edge of the Kalahari, exchanging iron, dagga, spears, hoes, and knives for ostrich-egg-shell beads, ivory, feathers,

[1] Fortune (1956); see also Robinson (1959), 5.

[2] See Lobato (1957), 55.

[3] ibid., 64.

[4] Mambo Dombo fought against the MaNgwato (Tswana): Posselt (1935), 145. The Ngwato frequently invaded the Kalanga in the far south-west, and in 1826 their king, Kgari, was killed there: E. Smith (1956), 61, quoting Mackenzie.

horns, and skins. It is possible that the Rozwi had a similar relationship.[1]

To the north some Rozwi probably did go to Barotseland to live, fleeing from invaders or their fellow-Rozwi, but there is no evidence that they maintained trading links along the Zambezi.[2] The routes *immediately* to the north of the Rozwi may have run along the Zambezi, rather than north and south. For example, the Batonga (of the Gwembe Valley) sold ivory for slaves to their neighbours, who presumably sold it to the merchants at Zumbo.[3]

The only indications of trade with lands north of the Zambezi come from archaeology. Ivory figures reminiscent of Congo ones can probably be dismissed, as both merely show Portuguese influence.[4] At Khami, however, were found a copper-inlaid axe-head and a bronze spear-head perhaps cast by the 'lost wax' method, both suggestive of Congo origins. The socketed iron spear at Khami has no parallel further south than Ufipa. All these were found in the final phase at Khami.[5] Iron gongs or bells may belong to an earlier period.[6] These are generally associated with the Congo region but others have been found scattered widely (e.g. in Buganda). Dos Santos mentions that in the sixteenth century Kiteve had drums, irons (*ferros*), bells, and pianos, and he may be referring to these bell-shaped iron gongs. As early as about the fourteenth century they were present at Ingombe Ilede on the Zambezi.[7] Finally, the copper crosses too have caused speculation on trading contacts with Katanga, and must be considered, although they were not found in the undoubtedly Rozwi ruins. Portuguese references to these crosses seem confined to the sixteenth and seventeenth centuries.[8] However, as the eighteenth century was a

[1] Robinson (1959), 164 (tradition at third hand); H. von Sicard, 'Rhodesian Sidelights on Bechuana History', *N.A.D.A.*, 1954, 89–90 (quoting A. Smith); E. C. Tabler, *The Far Interior (1847–1879)*, Cape Town, 1955, 94–5.

[2] See, e.g., Sister Mary Aquina, 'Tribes of the Victoria and Chilimanzi Reserves', *N.A.D.A.*, 1965, 41, and M. Mainga, 'The origin of the Lozi: some oral traditions', in Stokes and Brown (1966), 241–2.

[3] Posselt (1935), 131.

[4] But see Robinson (1959), 119.

[5] ibid.; see B. M. Fagan, 'Pre-European iron-working in Central Africa', *J. Afr. Hist.*, II, 2, 1961, 209.

[6] Finds: 3 at Zimbabwe, Period IV (R. S. Summers, K. R. Robinson, and A. Whitty, *Zimbabwe Excavations 1958*, Occ. Papers of the Nat. Mus. of S. Rhod., III, 23A, 1961, 328); 1 at Dhlo Dhlo (Hall and Neal (1902), 144–7); some at Umnukwana (J. Walton, 'Some features of the Monomotapa culture', *Pan-African Conf. on Prehistory* (1957), 350).

[7] Fagan (1965), 97; see Wieschoff (1941), 85; Dos Santos (1609), in Theal (1898–1903), VII, 202; see also above, p. 27; D. W. Phillipson and B. M. Fagan, 'The Date of the Ingombe Ilede Burials', *J. Afr. Hist.*, X, 2, 1969, 199–204.

[8] Crosses were found at Zimbabwe in Period IV (Summers, Robinson, and Whitty

period when considerable amounts of copper (if not in cross form) came down from the north to Zumbo, possibly from the Copper Belt, it may be that those south of the Zambezi still benefited as well as the Portuguese. The objection to the inference that this evidence indicates trade is that the connections may well be cultural, since the Karanga may have come from the Upper Congo originally and may well have brought these ideas and techniques with them. The cross-shaped ingot mould found in the Great Enclosure at Zimbabwe[1] supports this view. Altogether the evidence of a long-distance northern trade-route amounts only to tantalizing hints.

Trade with the area south of the Limpopo may not have been very great in the seventeenth and eighteenth centuries. Probably some copper was obtained from the Messina mines. It seems unlikely that tin or ready-made bronze came to the Mambo from Rooiberg since there are ancient workings for tin in Rhodesia, and Rooiberg tin contains arsenic, while most tin analysed in Rhodesia does not.[2] The Paraotte story of coming to 'Monomotapa' with gold may suggest a north-south connection in the early eighteenth century.[3] Some components of the Venda people now living south of the Limpopo split off from the Rozwi, however, perhaps early in the eighteenth century,[4] and since then have kept up considerable contacts with the shrine of Mwari, and one might assume that at some periods this was conducive to trade. The Lemba too are scattered from the Zambezi to Pietersburg.[5]

In contrast to internal and external inter-African trade, trade with non-Africans was dominated by one commodity—gold. During the first millennium A.D. beads reached the far corners of Rhodesia, probably

---

(1961); and at Ingombe Ilede. António Fernandes, according to Almada, saw '*aspas*' of copper in 1514 in Ambar (H. Tracey, *António Fernandes, Descobridor do Monomotapa*, Lourenço Marques, 1940, 34), which Tracey identifies as the Lomagundi area but was perhaps north of the Zambezi (cf. eighteenth-century references to Ambara). Fernandes apparently 'knew' that they were made in the Copper Rivers of Manicongo (ibid.). Almada himself had seen them at Sofala in 1516: E. Axelson, *South East Africa 1488–1530*, London, 1940, 260. Gomes (1648), in Axelson (1959), 203, saw them north of the Zambezi (? in Caronga's). M. Barreto describes the 'massonta' (a currency of the Rivers) as two copper St. Andrew's crosses joined by a bar: Theal, 1898–1903, III, 505.

[1] See Caton-Thompson (1931), 228.

[2] Caton-Thompson (1931), 220; but see R. Summers, 'The Iron Age in S. Rhodesia', *Current Anthropology*, 1966, 466.

[3] A Dutch diary of 29/12/1725, in Theal (1898–1903), I, 420; but see discussion below, p. 261, and in Ch. 13, pp. 275-6, as to their whereabouts.

[4] Stayt (1931), 12. Others have suggested the late eighteenth century: H. von Sicard, *Ngoma Lungundu*, Uppsala, 1952, 176.

[5] Stayt (1931), 18.

by indirect routes and in return for gold. By the Portuguese period 'Butua' was famous for its pure gold. However, the identity of Butua is by no means clear, nor necessarily single, since it is merely an 'outsider' word.[1] Abraham distinguishes, for the sixteenth and part of the seventeenth century, Changa's kingdom from Togwa's, Changamire during the seventeenth century conquering the Togwa's kingdom (perhaps reducing that line to spiritual office only).[2] Many of the seventeenth-century references to Butua have been traced to lands further east than the ruins generally identified as Rozwi.[3] None the less, there is some archaeological evidence of Portuguese trade to the western ruins, at any rate by the seventeenth century, which were probably under Changamire's domination.

One route from the Portuguese to the south-west passed from Tete through the Monomotapa's lands in which there were fairs, such as Luanze, Dambarare, and Ungwe (Ongoe), and probably the nearest to the Rozwi area that the Portuguese came to live was Maramuca in the present Hartley district.[4] Garlake provides evidence of the trade of Khami and Dhlo Dhlo with the Portuguese, particularly those of what may be Luanze in that the beads at the Luanze site are identical with those of Khami group II, and the blue and white Chinese porcelain at Khami is similar to what was found at Luanze and at another Portuguese site in the Maramuca region. The Khami porcelain belongs to the first half of the seventeenth century and, taking this evidence in combination with that of the beads, Garlake thinks that these finds suggest trading contacts around this time rather than forcible seizure in 1693 in the attack on the fairs.[5] At Dhlo Dhlo the Chinese porcelain seems to be later in date, mostly after 1644,[6] and some of it may belong

[1] M. D. W. Jeffreys, 'The Batwa—who are they?', *Africa*, 1953.

[2] D. Abraham, in Stokes and Brown (1966). In traditions Togwa is only mentioned by informants of the eastern part of Rhodesia; see D. Abraham, 'Ethno-history of the Empire of Mutapa', in (eds.) J. Vansina, R. Mauny, and L. V. Thomas, *Historians in Tropical Africa*, London, 1964, 18; E. Lloyd, 'Mbava', *N.A.D.A.*, 1925.

[3] Thus Bayão, who in 1644 went to Butua to counter Mohammedan intrigue and restore the king, probably went to a Hera chief (see H. von Sicard, 'A proposito de Sisnando Dias Bayão', *Studia*, 1965); two documents (of *c.* 1650 and of 1652) refer to missionaries being sent, one to Butua, but the other certainly to Togwa (see D. Abraham, 'Porcelain from the Hill Ruin, Khami', *S.A.A.B.*, 1962, 33).

[4] Abraham has located this convincingly in the Hartley area: D. Abraham, 'Maramuca: an exercise in the combined use of Portuguese records and oral tradition', in *J. Afr. Hist.*, II, 2, 1961.

[5] See Garlake (1968), 30; id., 'Seventeenth-century Portuguese Earthworks in Rhodesia', *S.A.A.B.*, 1967.

[6] Garlake (1968), 30.

rather to the Zumbo route used in the eighteenth century. Porcelain was probably not a regular item of trade so much as a gift to the Mambo. The main trade-goods were no doubt beads and cloth, and the porcelain is merely useful for dating, although its use even for this purpose has been doubted since such objects were kept for long periods.[1] The so-called 'Jesuit's Treasure' and articles such as a bell, key, oil lamps, and silver embossed plate found at Dhlo Dhlo[2] may have served the functions of gifts too (not necessarily in the eighteenth century) rather than indicating the presence of a priest (otherwise unattested), or they may indeed be booty from the invasion of the fairs.

The Zumbo route took over when that through Monomotapa's ceased after Changamire's destruction of the fairs in the late seventeenth and early eighteenth centuries. The fairs in Monomotapa's lands never recovered despite attempts, such as that in 1769, to resurrect Dambarare.[3] Changamire's connections with Zumbo seem to have started early in its life, since the *capitão-mor* was always known to Changamire as 'pereira', the name of the first founder.[4] It is as yet impossible to discern the fluctuations of trade along this route, although some details are reasonably clear. For example, in about 1766 there were succession wars in Changamire's chiefdom and the Mahias (unidentified) caused much disruption to Zumbo's trade with the Rozwi area.[5] The frequent complaints by merchants at Zumbo of robberies in Butua have to be treated with caution as they were always used to excuse default on debts, but none the less a certain amount of goods must have been lost this way, and in what the 'mussambazes'—African agents of the merchants—regarded as unjustifiable tolls and lawsuits.

Changamire did not always fully control the long trade-route to Zumbo. For example, in 1784 mussambazes had, he complained, stopped going by the old-established routes and started passing through Chereya's land, from which Chereya was becoming rich and over-mighty. Chereya was probably Chireya, still a chief of the Shankwe district. Changamire said that he had suspended punishment of this chief because he valued the trade with Zumbo so highly, and asked the mussambazes to keep to the old route in future.[6]

[1] Garlake (1968), 30; Robinson (1959), 143. [2] Hall and Neal (1902), 144–7.

[3] Letters of 'Fundo do séc. XVIII', *Moçambique*, 84.

[4] ibid., 94; A. A. Andrade, *Relações de Moçambique Setecentista*, Lisbon, 1955, 543.

[5] Costa, letter of 13/3/1769, 'Fundo do séc. XVIII', *Moçambique*, 84, 92.

[6] Report of reception of an embassy of 'Borozy of Changamire', 2/4/1784, in A.H.U. Moç., caixa 19; R. R. Tapson, 'Some notes on the Mrozwi occupation of the Sebungwe district', *N.A.D.A.*, 1944, 32.

In general, Changamire's control of this foreign trade within his lands was formidable. It was said that he allowed no non-Africans into his lands,[1] so that the merchants of Zumbo had to depend on the mussambazes who travelled out in October and, if all went well, returned in March/April, being paid half in advance and half on their return. These mussambazes, although living in danger of robbery and fire, seem to have owned cattle, and perhaps land near the mines. They may, indeed, have been responsible for the foreign architectural influence on Ruswingo wa Kasekete, if that is an eighteenth-century site.[2] Sometimes it was not worth their while to return to Zumbo, as when they knew there would not be enough cloth to pay them.[3] Changamire's control over them no doubt fluctuated, but it seems clear from all the accounts that he had a monopoly over the production of the gold. Thus Mello e Castro said that an African in Changamire's country could not own gold on pain of death, except that of the poorest quality which he might exchange for trivia. Similarly, in 1769, Changamire was reported to have sent 'munhais' (soldiers/messengers) to punish some subjects for not disclosing the discovery of new mines.[4] This monopoly must presumably have been exercised by confining trade with foreigners strictly to organized markets, whether near the mines or at his capital. There seems to be no evidence of Rozwi subjects taking gold to Zumbo themselves or of the Mambo sending caravans, although he did send ambassadors. Probably he feared the loss of his control if his agents dealt directly with the merchants at Zumbo.

Although gold was the predominant export to Zumbo, ivory played some part. There is some reference, too, to a medicinal root which came from Butua.[5] Ivory is mentioned by Da Costa as a product of Butua for which it would be easier to trade from Dambarare. However, this probably came mostly from the Dande area nearest to

[1] J. J. Nogueira de Andrade, 'Descripção do Estado . . . da Capitania de Mossambique de 1789', in *Arquivo das Colônias*, Lisbon, 1917, I, 117; Caetano Xavier (1758), in Carvalho Dias (1954), 198; but see Souza, letter of 7/11/1783, in A.H.U. Moç., caixa 20, and p. 259 below.

[2] Morais Pereira, 'Notícias dos Domínios Portugueses na Costa Oriental da Africa' (mid-eighteenth century), in Lobato (1957), 247; 'Memórias da Costa da Africa Oriental 1762', in Carvalho Dias (1954), 230; Costa (1769), in *Moçambique*, 84, 92; K. R. Robinson, 'A note on iron-age sites in the Zambezi Valley and on the escarpment in the Sipolilo district', *Arnoldia* (Rhod.), I, 27 (1965), 3.

[3] Coelho de Campos, letter of 10/1/1768, *Moçambique*, 88, 122.

[4] F. de Mello e Castro, *Descripção dos Rios de Sena 1750*, Goa, 1861, 33; Costa (1769), in *Moçambique*, 84, 92.

[5] Caetano Xavier (1758), in Carvalho Dias (1954), 199; J. B. de Montaury, 'Moçambique, Ilhas Querimbas, etc.', *c.* 1778, in Andrade (1917), 360.

Zumbo, which was sometimes under Changamire, sometimes independent.[1] Caetano Xavier refers to the use of the ivory which was not bought by mussambazes for stockades in Ambara and Changamire's land, and again no attempt by Rozwi to take ivory to Zumbo is mentioned.[2] Morais Pereira rather weakly attributed the lack of ivory from this region to the expense of its transportation, but more often the problem was lack of cloth to pay for more than the first-priority commodity—gold.[3]

The most common goods imported along this route were beads, cloth, and strong liquor.[4] In addition, many weapons and military trophies have been found. The latter[5] may have been obtained in a raid, but arms certainly were traded to Changamire. In 1769 the ambassadors sent by Changamire to Zumbo were given a musket and some lead bullets, although they would have preferred, it seems, a fort to protect Changamire against the Mahias.[6] Flintlocks and lead bullets were found by Hall and Neal. Apparently in 1831 Changamire had four pieces of artillery, and according to tradition two old cannon bought from the Portuguese were used by the Rozwi against the Nguni.[7]

Although the volume of these imports is unknown, some idea may be formed of the amount of gold involved in trade along this route. Frequently and consistently in the eighteenth century the mines of Butua were said to be the most important in the Rivers, even with the development of those worked by slaves of the Portuguese around Tete and Zumbo.[8] Mello e Castro in 1750 said that Butua alone used to produce 500–600 *pastas* in a good year; Azevedo Coutinho de Montaury in 1762 put the figure at 300–400 *pastas,* apparently including the closer mines around Zumbo; and in the robbery of 1756–7 1000 *pastas* were said to have been stolen.[9] For the rest of the eighteenth and early

[1] Letter of 2/3/1769, *Moçambique*, 84, 82–4.

[2] But see p. 254, on ivory from the Batonga; Caetano Xavier (1758), in Carvalho Dias (1954), 197.

[3] Morais Pereira, in Lobato (1957), 249.

[4] See, e.g., Carvalho Dias (1954), 230.

[5] Principally a brass bugle, metal epaulette, leg-iron, and handcuffs from near Dhlo Dhlo (see F. Marconnes, 'The Rozwis or destroyers', *N.A.D.A.*, 1933, 81).

[6] Costa (1769), in *Moçambique*, 84, 94–6.

[7] Hall and Neal (1902), 144–7; Caton-Thompson (1931), 194; A.H.U. Moç., 1/6/1831; S. S. Dornan, 'Rhodesian Ruins and Native Tradition', *South African Journal of Science*, 1915, 508.

[8] e.g. Mello e Castro (1861), 31; Galvão da Silva, 'Viagem . . . a Manica 1788', in Guyot (1895), 218, referring to the Manica outlet as well.

[9] Mello e Castro (1861), 32; M. A. Azevedo Coutinho de Montaury, letter of 15/7/1762, in Andrade (1917), 593; Caetano Xavier (1758), in Carvalho Dias (1954), 198; Galvão da Silva, ibid., 316. 500 *pastas* were worth 400,000 cruzados, equal in 1947 to £20,000: see H. V. Livermore, *History of Portugal*, Cambridge, 1947, 478–9.

nineteenth centuries figures are not available for Butua production alone.

Although the outlet through Zumbo for Rozwi gold was certainly the most important in the eighteenth century, an alternative lay through Manicaland and from thence either to Sofala or Sena. Dos Santos in 1609 mentions Butua Africans who came to Manica. Gomes may refer to the western part of Rhodesia when he describes Butua as 'beyond the kingdoms beyond Manica' and mentions three or four fairs there. These were Mohammedan fairs, and Butua themselves had not been to Manicaland for fear of tales told them by the Mohammedans of the Portuguese.[1] On the surer ground of the eighteenth century, a few years before 1762, at the fair in Manicaland, Africans had come from distant lands bringing ivory, gold, wax, seed-pearls, rock-crystal, honey, raw cotton, skins, and cattle.[2] Some of these may have been Rozwi. By 1788 that fair was flourishing again, Changamire having given the Portuguese permission to hold it in return for tribute paid in cloth and one of his wives had even been established in Manicaland.[3] Gold, ivory, and iron were the main exports to the coast from here. Copper also came to Manicaland (presumably largely for local consumption) from the Duma, six days away. They were in the Sabi valley probably until about 1850 when they moved near Zimbabwe.[4] Although in the 1820s on the coast there seemed to be no one going from Sofala to Changamire, Africans who had been there said in 1831 that there were no impediments or robberies on the roads from Kiteve (which took one month) or Sanga (fifteen days) to Changamire's court.[5] It seems that pigs and rifles may have been brought along this route from Manica to Changamire, as they were said to come from the people of Sena.[6] None the less this Manica route was of minor importance in terms of the volume of trade along it from the Rozwi to the outside world.

The other routes to the coast were even less used. There has been much speculation about the importance of the Sabi-Lundi river as a

[1] Gomes (1648), in *Studia*, 1959, 195; but see von Sicard (1965); Dos Santos (1609), in Theal (1898–1903), VII, 274.

[2] Carvalho Dias (1954), 222.

[3] Galvão da Silva (1788), in Guyot (1895), 219.

[4] Galvão da Silva, ibid.; see generation evidence in Aquina (1965), 9, but see also Robinson, in Stokes and Brown (1966), 7.

[5] A.H.U. Moç., 1/6/1831; Ferão, 'Account of Portuguese possessions' (?1820s), in Theal (1898–1903), VII, 377.

[6] A.H.U. Moç., 1/6/1831; tradition of Budja in F. W. T. Posselt, *Survey of Native Tribes in Southern Rhodesia*, Salisbury, 1927, 30.

route inland, particularly to Zimbabwe. This mostly concerns the Arab and early Portuguese periods.[1] In 1744 a Dominican seemed to regard the Sabi as the outlet for the 'palace of Sheba' (in the land they called Mambone) with the 'inscription in strange characters'. Father Manoel de S. Thomas regarded this 'lettering in the kingdom of Mahongo' as eighty leagues direct from the Sabi, bordering on Manica and Kiteve. The similarity of the names Sabi and Sheba, however, seems to have been the main basis for such comments.[2] It is possible then that the Sabi-Lundi river was followed. Certainly the lower Sabi was navigated to collect ivory throughout MaDanda until the Landins invaded.[3] Gold dust was found in Lundi ruin and gold was washed in these rivers.[4] If my location of the Paraotte is correct (see below) the 'Moetonge' may have come from Sofala trading for the Portuguese to the Gwanda area, and the Sabi is a possible route.

For evidence of contact between the Rozwi and the coast further south, one has mainly Portuguese fears of Dutch penetration. A viceroy of India reported in 1730 that the Dutch had penetrated two hundred leagues inland from Inhambane and found gold-mines.[5] These might have been on the south side of the Limpopo—the nearest source marked on Hall and Neal's map—rather than in the Rozwi area. However, Gwanda, a large mine towards the south of Rhodesia, did contain a brass tray, dated to the eighteenth century at the earliest,[6] which indicates that there may have been at least indirect links between this mine and the coast in this period, and the outlet was probably Inhambane or Delagoa Bay. The Dutch gin-bottle at Dhlo Dhlo might also have come there by this trade-route. It is tempting to place the Paraotte in the Gwanda district (sometimes subject to Mambo's influence), in which case they were taking gold to the Dutch at Delagoa Bay in 1725 as well as to the 'Monomotapa' (? Mambo) in the north.[7] Whatever the route, it seems unlikely that a great amount of trade came to the Rozwi from this direction. At Delagoa Bay, what gold there was

[1] See, e.g., von Sicard (1963), and R. Mauny, 'Notes sur le problème Zimbabwe-Sofala', *Studia*, 1958, for discussions of the physical practicability.

[2] C. R. Boxer, 'A Dominican Account of Zambezia in 1744', in *Boletim da Sociedade de Estudos de Moçambique*, 1960, 10; Frei Manoel, in *Cronista de Tissuary*, IV (1869), 43.

[3] Botelho (1835), 173–4.

[4] von Sicard (1963), 12.

[5] Letter of 2/1/1730, in *Arquivo Portugues Oriental* (Nova ed., Bragança Pereira), Tomo IV, vol. II, pt. II, p. 242.

[6] Mennell and Summers (1955), 773; Hall and Neal (1902), map.

[7] See Theal (1898–1903), I, 420, and Ch. 13, below, pp. 275–6. Gwanda is quite close to the Venda, if Inthowelle is indeed to be identified with them.

came mainly from the south, down the Nkomati and Maputo (Usutu/Pongola) rivers.[1] However, in 1758 Caetano Xavier said that the purest gold was to be found at Delagoa Bay and the Dutch were not only spoiling the market but wanting to go up the river to Changamire, 'which they well could from there'.[2] How much this observation was built on geographical assumptions or on experience one cannot tell. Finally, a Portuguese document of the late eighteenth century says that although most of the gold came from the mountains of Matolla (up the Nkomati), great numbers of Africans brought gold from Kiteve to Delagoa Bay.[3] This is an interesting route since Kiteve was so close to Sofala anyway, but it gives no hint of connection with the Rozwi. Unfortunately all the meagre evidence we have so far is from the European end, so that there is no way of saying what the activities of the Africans might have been.

The claim that the Rozwi possessed a route to Angola is based on the shakiest evidence and is not intrinsically plausible. A blanket was said in the sixteenth century to have come from Angola to Manica via Butua, but it might equally have come from Mohammedans on the Zambezi and still have seemed miraculous to the Portuguese in Manicaland. Gold in the Congo was once assumed to be from Butua, but there were in fact gold-mines much nearer. In the seventeenth century the presence in Butua of 'buzeos, which is the cowry of Angola,' was also adduced as evidence, but these may have been East Coast cowries.[4] *Perhaps* the name Angora, used of a trading place far up the Zambezi in 1696, may give a clue to Butua contacts with 'Angola' if these were based on reports by Africans.[5] The one really suggestive piece of evidence for a West-Coast route is the reference to a route from Muzimo (where a

[1] Bolts, for example, in 1776 was planning to go up the R. Maputo for gold: G. M. Theal, *History and Ethnography of South Africa*, London, 1907–10, I, 3.

[2] Caetano Xavier (1758), in Carvalho Dias (1954), 189.

[3] Quoted by H. A. Junod, *The Life of a South African Tribe*, 2 vols., London, revised ed., 1927, II, 142.

[4] Blanket—Dos Santos (1609), in Theal (1898–1903), VII, 274; gold in Congo—D. de Couto, 'Da Asia' (early seventeenth century), in Theal (1898–1903), VI, 392, and (ed.) W. Bal, *Description du Royaume de Congo et des contrées environnantes par Filippo Pigafetta et Duarte Lopez (1591)*, Louvain, 1963, 110; shells—Gomes (1648), in *Studia* (1959), 197; for *buzios*, see M. D. W. Jeffreys, 'Cowry: ndoro', *N.A.D.A.*, 1953.

[5] Frei António da Conceição (1696), in *Cronista de Tissuary* (1867), 2, 65; E. Axelson, *The Portuguese in South-East Africa, 1600–1700*, Johannesburg, 1960, 190–91, identifies it as near the Nyakasanga River. This might then tell us more about Butuan links with the area north of the Zambezi than with the West Coast. The whole suggestion is, however, too tentative to build upon.

Portuguese trader had brought copper and gold) to Angola.[1] This evidence is not first-hand, but all that can be said is that, if the Rozwi did travel west, it might have been by such a route.

Within the Rozwi area itself, one has the impression of a vigorous economy where goods were traded over considerable distances. There was specialization by whole villages in crafts such as pottery and iron, which indicates the beginnings of a true market economy. There were 'professional' traders such as those of the Zezuru and Lemba, but still most trading was done *ad hoc* without markets even. It is not certain how far even these 'professionals' used the proceeds of their trade as their main means of livelihood. It may be that internally it was the Mambo's peace which kept the way open for travel and trade. Certainly it seems to be the case that much of the trade was stimulated by the demands of the court, and that direction of trade came from the top.

Indeed it does seem to be true, as so many have pointed out,[2] that the cleft between the top 'Rozwi aristocracy' and the masses, who were exploited by them in the mines, is not as Eurocentric a view as it sounds. The 'aristocracy', or, better, oligarchy, were rulers and priests, although it *may* be that some of them also owed their position to technical skill in iron work. The richness of the country, particularly in minerals, provided the Mambo with one of the sources of his political power. With his near-monopoly of the gold trade with the outside world he had the bulk of the resources for rewarding service. Internal consumption of gold, too, was limited, it seems, to the aristocracy in the high-walled embellished cities; gold was not worn in the villages where it was actually mined. None the less, one does not have the impression that this was a despotic state, far from it. At times the Mambo's military strength may have inclined it that way, but his main strength, for his subjects, was religious, his closeness to the ancestors and his power to bring rain. The Mambo was normally limited by custom and conscience, supernatural sanctions, his family and counsellors.[3] The usual view indeed is more of a loose confederacy than of a unified empire.

As to the beneficial or detrimental effects of trade with non-Africans for the Mambo's political power, it is possible that the expansion of

[1] Frei António (1867); Axelson identifies it near the confluence of the Kafue with the Zambezi.

[2] See Fagan (1965), 124.

[3] See the retribution and recrimination for breach of custom by Tumbari in Sebina (1947), 86.

Changamire's influence during the seventeenth and eighteenth centuries is connected with an increase in trade with foreigners. Probably there was an increase in the building of decorated stone walls in this period because of prosperity, going hand in hand with political power for one class. To this extent the state may have been built on long-distance trade. Perhaps the exclusion by Changamire of non-Africans, deliberate or fortuitous, helped him to retain control and not to go the way of Monomotapa who let the Portuguese move in. The Mambo managed to have the best of both worlds. His people, on the other hand, remained isolated, their economy having no momentum of its own, themselves bound to Mambo's wishes in trading affairs, rather than seeking the profits for themselves.

13

Delagoa Bay and the Trade of South-Eastern Africa

ALAN SMITH

Between the mid-sixteenth century and the early nineteenth century the Delagoa Bay area was transformed from an isolated region, far removed from the mainstream of East and Central African commerce, into one of the most important commercial centres on the East African coast. This was the result not only of additional opportunities created by the increasing commercial activities of Europeans, but also of the development, on an extensive scale, of the entrepreneurial skills of African traders. The evolution and development of the trade of Delagoa Bay, and the interaction of European and African traders, were accompanied, however, by intense competition and continuous conflict among the participants. In fact, much of the political history of the bay area was determined by these conflicts, and by the different responses of the various peoples to the opportunities and problems arising from the growth of trade.

The Portuguese were the first Europeans to establish a regular trade with Delagoa Bay. Although the bay had been visited several times during the early years of the sixteenth century, it was not until the 1540s that the Portuguese attempted to incorporate it into their East African trading system. By this time ivory had apparently come to play a larger role in their mercantile thinking and it was decided to investigate the lands to the south of Sofala. To this end, Lourenço Marques and António Caldeira were commissioned to investigate the trading possibilities at 'two rivers' in the south, and in 1544 the two explorers submitted an extremely favourable account of what they had seen. At the mouth of the Limpopo, they reported, copper was abundant, and the people promised to sell it at very reasonable prices. Further south, in Delagoa Bay, they saw great herds of elephants and

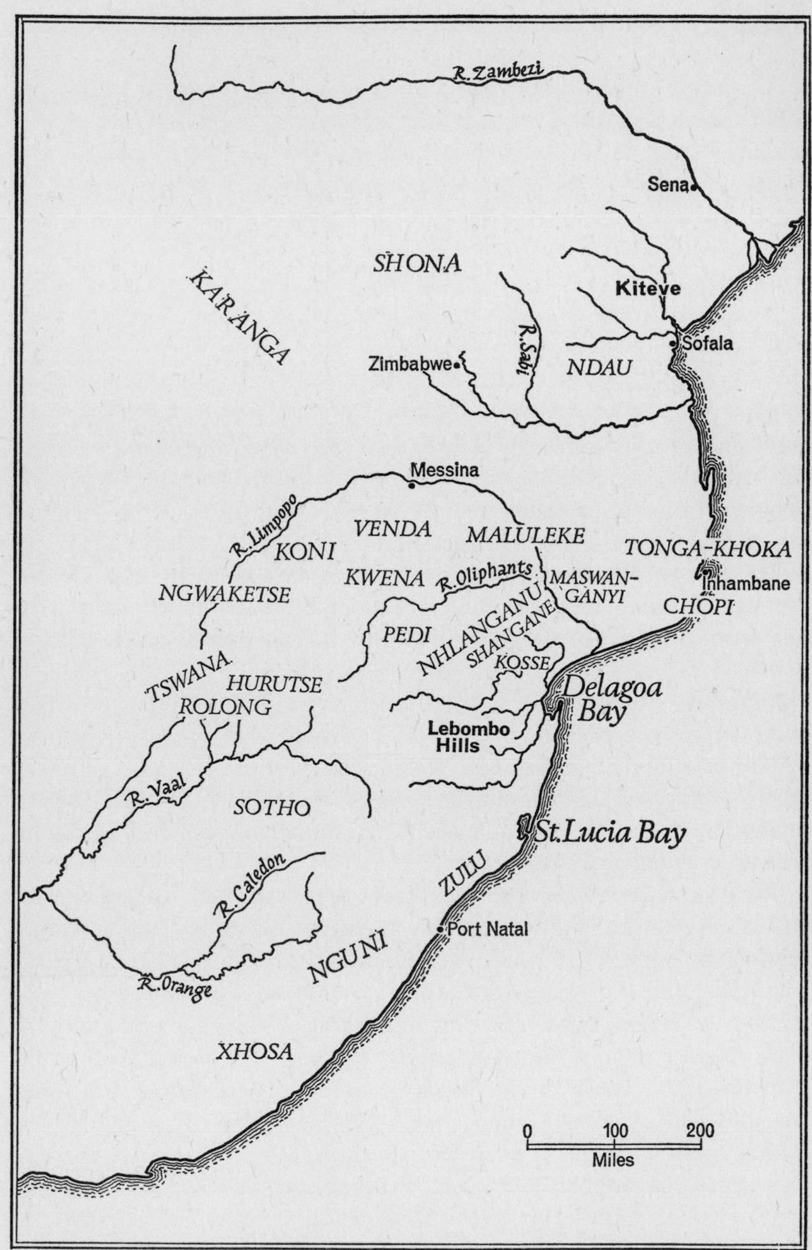

Map 15. South-Eastern Africa

again received promises that great quantities of ivory could be obtained very cheaply.[1]

As a result of this report, the Portuguese began a regular trade with what became known as the 'bahia de Lourenço Marques'. Each year a trading vessel, commissioned by the governor in Mozambique and trading on behalf of the crown, was despatched to Delagoa Bay with the tail-end of the southward monsoon. This 'pangayo' remained in the bay approximately from December to June and then returned northward before the monsoon winds began to blow toward the south again. During their years of trade at Delagoa, the Portuguese switched the base of their operations from the Espirito Santo river to the Nkomati and Maputo rivers, before finally deciding that a temporary factory, constructed on an off-shore island, provided them with the most security and offered the best means of conducting their trade. From this off-shore island, men were despatched to trading sites on each of the five rivers, and every ten days the goods would be brought down and stored on the island.[2]

The establishment of a regular trade at Delagoa Bay brought the Portuguese into contact with the Ronga people of the bay area, who form the southernmost group of the Thonga-speaking peoples of southern Mozambique. The Thonga live in the area from the south of Delagoa Bay to the Sabi river in the north, and extend inland from the east coast to the mountain ranges in the west, near the borders of the Transvaal and Rhodesia. The terms 'Ronga' and 'Thonga' are linguistic and cultural classifications, which were not used by the people themselves, but which are used here for the sake of clarity.[3] It should also be noted that the Thonga of southern Mozambique are distinct from the Tonga-Khoka of the Inhambane area, the various Tonga groups of the Zambezi Valley and Zambia, and the 'Lakeside Tonga' of Malawi.[4]

[1] Caetano Montez, *Descobrimento e Fundação de Lourenço Marques,* Lourenço Marques, 1948, 13–22; Colin Coetzee, 'Die Kompanjie se Besetting Op Delagoa-baai', *Archives Yearbook for South African History*, II (1948), 176.

[2] Montez (1948), 32; Jan van de Capellen, 'Rapport van Jan van de Cappelle . . . aan den . . . Goveneur van de Kaap Colonie', in (ed.) George M. Theal, *Records of South-Eastern Africa* [*RSEA*], 9 vols., Cape Town, 1898–1903, 6, 409; Bento Teyxeyra Feyo, 'Account of the Wreck of the Ships Sacramento and Nossa Senhora da Atalaya . . . 1647', *RSEA*, 8, 355.

[3] See Henri A. Junod, *The Life of a South African Tribe,* 2 vols., New York, 1962.

[4] For ethnographic surveys of southern Mozambique, see Henri-Philippe Junod, 'Notes on the Ethnological Situation in Portuguese East Africa on the South of the Zambezi', *Bantu Studies*, 10, 3 (Sept., 1936), 293–312; António Rita-Fereira, *Agrupamento e Caracterização Etnica dos Indígenas de Moçambique*, Lisbon, 1958.

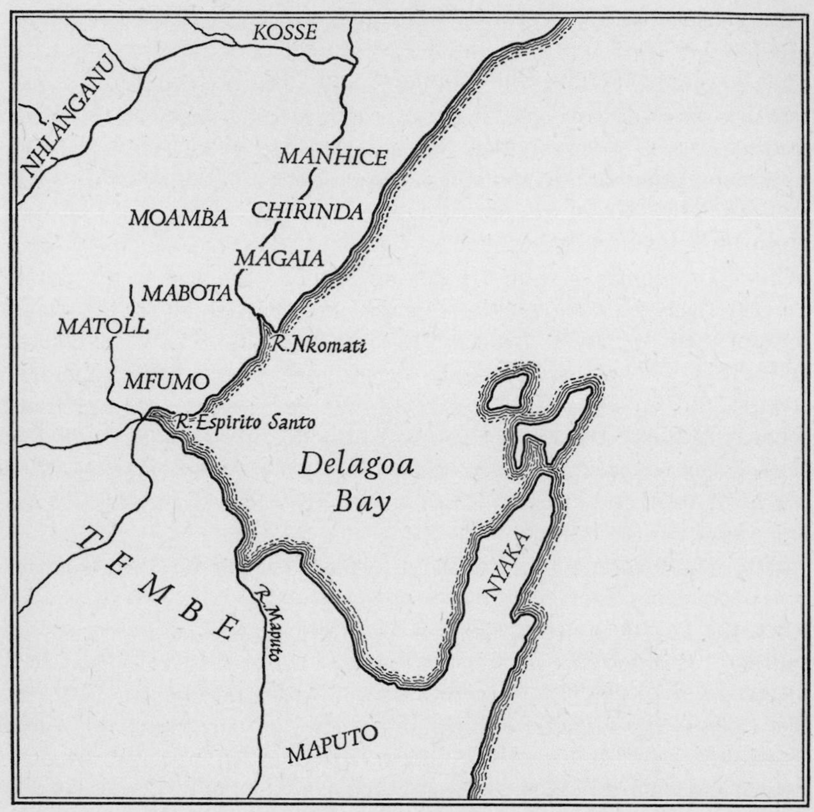

Map 16. Delagoa Bay

From the descriptions provided by the Portuguese, it is possible to suggest certain characteristics of the Ronga political units of the sixteenth and seventeenth centuries, which were to have important bearings on the power relations among the chiefdoms of the bay, and consequently on the role that they were to play in the trade of the area. In the middle of the sixteenth century, the Portuguese learned of five chiefdoms which bordered on the littoral of the bay. These chiefdoms, Nyaka, Tembe, Mfumo, Nondwana, and Manhice,[1] continued to exist as recognizable units until the nineteenth century. From the

[1] Report of Manuel Perestrello, 1575, in Levy Maria Paiva Manso, *Memória Sobre Lourenço Marques*, Lisbon, 1870, 68; Henri A. Junod, 'The Condition of the Natives of South-Eastern Africa in the Sixteenth Century . . .', *South African Journal of Science*, 10 (1914).

reports of the early Portuguese, it is apparent that the Ronga chiefdoms showed a marked tendency toward fission. In some cases, such as the split between 'Tembe, the Younger' and 'Tembe, the Elder',[1] the segmentation resulted in only partial and temporary divisions. In other cases, however, complete fission could not be avoided and independent chiefdoms resulted. By the end of the eighteenth century, the chiefdoms of Machavane, Matoll, Maputo, and Mabota, had been derived from and added to the five observed by the Portuguese in the sixteenth century.

The reports of the Portuguese suggest several other important characteristics of the Ronga. For example, they made a clear distinction between the Ronga, whose political units they called 'kingdoms', and the people of Natal, whose political units they called 'inkosis',[2] thus suggesting that in the sixteenth century the political process of consolidation was already fairly well developed among the Ronga. Judging from the facts that Nyaka's armies raided as far south as the St. Lucia river, were alleged to have 'stolen' other peoples' lands, and at the same time feared aggressions from Tembe,[3] it might be suggested that relations among the chiefdoms were often hostile, and that the conflicts, which were greatly to alter the balance of power in later centuries, were already a characteristic feature in the sixteenth century. Finally, the eagerness with which the Ronga received the Portuguese, and the willingness of one chiefdom to denounce its neighbours and thus attempt to improve its own trading relationship with the Europeans,[4] are early indicators of the role that trade would come to play and of the competition it would generate among the Ronga.

Since the Portuguese had no permanent factory or fort in Delagoa Bay, they took little part in local politics. Unlike their establishments at Sofala and ports further to the north, where permanent occupation at times afforded them some control of the immediate area, and where reprisals could be taken, the traders who sailed to Delagoa Bay were almost always on the defensive in their dealings with the Ronga. As a result of grievances arising from alleged misdealings in matters of trade, the relations between the Portuguese and one or another of the chief-

[1] Feyo, in *RSEA*, 8, 355.

[2] Diogo do Couto, 'Narrative of the Shipwreck of the Great Ship São Thomé . . .', in (ed.) Charles R. Boxer, *The Tragic History of the Sea*, Cambridge, 1959.

[3] H. A. Junod (1914), 153; João Lavanha, 'Shipwreck of the Great Ship Santo Alberto . . . 1593', in Boxer (1959), 157; 'Narrative of the Great Galleon Saint John . . . 1552" *RSEA*, 1, 139.

[4] *RSEA*, 1, 139; do Couto, in Boxer (1959), 82.

doms of the bay often became hostile. Soon after they began trading in the bay, the Portuguese, forced to move from their original trading site in the mouth of the Espirito Santo river because of the constant conflict between the traders and the people of Tembe,[1] began to concentrate their efforts on the chiefdoms of Manhice and Nyaka. Complaints against their trading practices, however, were also to involve them in difficulties in these new areas. In 1594, the people of Manhice 'plundered' the ship of that year in revenge for crimes which they felt the captain had committed.[2] In the early seventeenth century, the chief of Nyaka, also angered by the behaviour of certain Portuguese, took a similar action. In response, the Portuguese temporarily discontinued the voyage to Delagoa Bay.[3] When difficulties arose, it can be seen that the Portuguese were forced to retreat.

Despite the difficulties between the Portuguese and the Ronga, however, the trading voyages from Mozambique to Delagoa were maintained with some degree of regularity from the middle of the sixteenth century until the beginning of the eighteenth. Owing to the absence of adequate documentary material, it is difficult to determine with precision the frequency of these voyages. From royal regimentos and shipwreck records it seems safe to assume that for the first forty years the voyage was made annually. After 1590, there was a change in policy and the ship was now supposed to be despatched only during alternate years.[4] Although the documentary record indicates that there were gaps of more than two years between voyages, it is likely that these periods were exceptions to the general rule.[5] For in addition to the various chroniclers of Mozambique, who, during the seventeenth century, universally maintained that the voyage was biennial, there were Portuguese traders mentioned in some of the few surviving first-hand accounts of Delagoa Bay.[6] Thus it seems likely that the biennial voyage was maintained in practice almost as well as in theory.

[1] Manuel Perestrello, 'Narrative of the Wreck of the Ship St. Benedict', *RSEA*, 1, 282.

[2] João dos Santos, 'Ethiopia Oriental', *RSEA*, 7, 366.

[3] Francisco Vaz d'Almeida, 'Account of the Misfortune that Befell the Ship Sao João Baptista', *RSEA*, 8, 116.

[4] Montez (1948), 40.

[5] One of the periods was when there was a four-year interval between voyages due to Nyaka's murder of a Portuguese priest. Rather than official policy, this absence may have been due to difficulty in finding people to make the voyage. See n. 3 above.

[6] dos Santos, in *RSEA*, 7, 322; Manuel Barreto, report of 1666, *RSEA*, 3, 466–7; also *RSEA*, 4, 228, 366; Mean Mocquet, 'Voyages en Afrique . . .', in (ed.) Edward Strangman, *Early French Callers at the Cape*, Cape Town, 1936, 38; *Voyage of Linschoten to Indies*, Cambridge, 1935; 'Correspondence Respecting the Claims of Her Majesty's Government

During the seventeenth century, the trade of Delagoa Bay was not a monopoly, however, and by the 1680s English traders were more active and more successful than the Portuguese. English contact with the bay apparently began as early as 1597, when three ships sought permission to open a factory and brought 'fine blue cloth and blue coral'.[1] When the survivors of the 1622 shipwreck passed through the bay, they saw many articles of English manufacture, among which English brass had become a highly esteemed commodity.[2] Although there are no eye-witness accounts until the latter stages of the seventeenth century, it is possible that the intervening years witnessed increasing penetration by English traders.[3] In the 1680s as many as five English ships were sighted in the bay in one year and English traders had established themselves on an off-shore island and were manufacturing copper bracelets.[4] Reports from various sources indicate that English trading activity continued into the early years of the eighteenth century.[5]

The increasing pressure of English traders placed a great strain on the Portuguese, who found that the Ronga preferred to trade with the English, because they brought better trading goods. On one occasion the pangayo returned to Mozambique virtually empty, because 'from the quantity of ivory bartered by the English there [was] virtually none left in the country'.[6] When the governor of Mozambique suggested that the voyages be discontinued, he was overruled by the viceroy, who felt that the royal fazenda had to continue to bear the loss until some decision could be reached.[7] Although the Portuguese did attempt to continue the trading connection, the loss of a ship and its entire cargo to a French pirate apparently determined the end of the trade with Delagoa.[8] Faced with mounting difficulties all along their coastal

. . .', *Accounts and Papers*, LXXXIII (1875), 209; Feyo, in *RSEA*, 8, 355; 'Voyage . . . van de Noord', in (ed.) E. C. Godee Molsbergen, *Reizen in Zuid-Afrika in de Hollandse Tijd*, 3, The Hague, 1922; Alexandre Lobato, *Quatro Estudos e Uma Evocação Para a História de Lourenço Marques*, Lisbon, 1961, 39.

[1] 'Lista da Navegação de Moçambique . . .', in Montez (1948), 159.

[2] d'Almeida, in Boxer (1959), 248.

[3] Alexandre Lobato, *História da Fundação de Lourenço Marques*, Lisbon, 1948, 4.

[4] Molsbergen (1922), 130.

[5] Thomas Boteler, *Narrative of a Voyage . . . to Africa . . .*, 2 vols., London, 1835, I, 22–3; Jacob Bucquoy, 'Zestinjarige Reize . . .', in (ed.) Charles Walckenaer, *Histoire des Voyages*, Paris, 1821, 21, 415; (ed.) John Bird, *The Annals of Natal*, 2 vols., Cape Town, 1965, 1, 56.

[6] D. Miguel de Almeida to viceroy, 6 August, 1686, and Manuel de Fonseca, enclosure I, *RSEA*, 4, 296.

[7] D. Rodrigo da Costa, 24 January, 1687, *RSEA*, 5, 295.

[8] van de Cappellen, in *RSEA*, 1, 408–9.

settlements, the Portuguese could no longer compete effectively in the south, and in 1703 all voyages to Delagoa Bay were discontinued.

During the years of the Portuguese trade, the products exported from the bay consisted mainly of rhinoceros horns, amber, 'azeite', and ivory. Of these, ivory was both the most consistent and most important article of export. A fair percentage of this ivory was probably obtained locally, while additional supplies were acquired from inland areas. Evidence from the Portuguese shipwrecks indicates that ivory originating several hundred miles within Natal was brought to Delagoa Bay.[1] The absence, on the other hand, of any mention of gold, tin, or copper suggests that a similar development of trade-routes between Delagoa and the metal-producing areas of the South African high veld and Rhodesia did not take place. Thus in the sixteenth and seventeenth centuries, there seems to have been no connection between the trading network of Delagoa Bay and the networks of the South African high veld and Rhodesia.

In 1721, Delagoa Bay was occupied by the Dutch East India Company. From the time of van Riebeeck, the east coast of Africa had been of interest to the governors of the Cape, who were primarily concerned with penetration to the gold-producing areas of the 'Monomotapa'. After 1680, the favourable reports on the commerce of eastern Africa, which the Cape governors received from English ships, further stimulated their interest and caused them to press the council of seventeen for more action. The council, however, remained unconvinced and the negative report of the captain of the *Noord*, which visited Delagoa in 1688, did nothing to change their minds. No final decision regarding Delagoa Bay and the east coast had been reached, however, when the advent of war in Europe caused the question to be shelved. After the conclusion of the war, the council became increasingly wary of English and French designs in the Indian Ocean and began to look more favourably on a settlement in Delagoa Bay. The final impetus seems to have come from the publication of Jean Pierre Purry's *Mémoire sur les Pays des Caffres . . .*, which described the land of Natal as the richest part of southern Africa. Spurred on by this favourable report, the company decided in 1719 to occupy the bay.[2]

Soon after they had established a residence in Delagoa Bay, the Dutch found themselves beset with a multitude of problems. Contrary to what they had expected, actual residence in the bay did not improve

[1] Lavanha, in Boxer (1959), 133.

[2] Coetzee (1948), 188–225.

their trading position. Whenever the opportunity presented itself, the Ronga chose to sell their ivory and amber to the English, whose brass goods they preferred to the heavy copper brought by the Dutch.[1] A more serious cause of alarm, however, was the high sickness and mortality rate, which rapidly depleted the size and efficiency of the garrison. A report to the Cape summed up the situation: 'sickness very bad.... Hardly any food for the garrison and nothing to buy from the natives. Affairs . . . in a deplorable state.'[2] The station was then attacked by pirates, who sacked it, took what they liked, and after a two months' stay, departed with one of the company's ships, as well as a number of employees who had had enough of the company's service.[3]

After 1724, conditions at the bay suddenly, markedly, and inexplicably improved. The high death rate, which had been a constant cause of concern, suddenly disappeared and the health of the station was regarded as satisfactory.[4] Trade with the Ronga also improved and the only complaint emanating from the bay concerned the insufficient supply of trading beads.[5] Another positive factor was that by 1724 the Dutch had begun to acquire slaves for use at the Cape, thus eliminating their voyages to Madagascar.[6] The appearance of gold and tin, brought by people from far in the interior, however, proved to be the most satisfying news of all.[7] Hopes of contacting the 'Monomotapa' and the legendary wealth of the interior soared. As the settlement became more prosperous and stable, the decision to occupy the bay began to appear to have been a wise one.

The good fortune of the station, however, was short-lived. Penetration of the interior had been one of the primary goals envisioned by the company, and several expeditions had been sent inland along the Nkomati, Espirito Santo, and Matoll rivers. None of these, however, succeeded in reaching the gold-producing areas and only one voyage along the Nkomati was able to penetrate any distance inland, before a large force of armed Africans forced it to turn back.[8] From this

[1] van de Cappellen, in *RSEA*, 1, 416.

[2] *Précis of the Archives of the Cape of Good Hope,* Cape Town, entry of April, 1722, 288.

[3] *Cape Archives,* entry of 12 July, 1723, 294–5; Coetzee (1948), 255.

[4] ibid., entry of 19 September, 1724, 298.

[5] ibid., entry of 8 February, 1725, 299.

[6] M. L. van Deventer, 'La Hollande et La Baie-Delagoa', *Tijdschrift van het Aardrijkskunig Genootschap Gevestigd te Amsterdam,* 11 (1883), 12; Henri Deherain, *Le Cap de Bonne-Espérance au XVIII Siècle,* Paris, 1909, 200.

[7] *Cape Archives,* entries of 13 March, 1724, 296–7, and 15 January, 1726, 302.

[8] '. . . Rapport en Journaal, . . . Examineerde de Noord Revier . . . ofte die van St. Espirit', *RSEA,* 1,437.

experience and other evidence that they were unwelcome in the hinterland, the Dutch realized that the interior would probably remain beyond their grasp. Concurrently with this realization, the garrison once again began to suffer from the effects of the lowland climate. As the death rate began to climb again, the constant need to replenish the diminished garrison placed additional demands on the company's resources.[1]

These, however, were not the only difficulties experienced at Delagoa Bay. Trade, which had flowed briskly for several years, began to dry up, as a series of wars closed down the trade-routes. The good relations which the Dutch had been able to maintain with the Ronga began to break down, especially after one of the Dutch officers, assuming that his cattle post was about to be robbed, ordered his men to fire on a group of Africans.[2] Finally, the general dissatisfaction of the garrison, which previously had been expressed by desertion, resulted in an attempted mutiny and the punishment of sixty-two men.[3] Faced with this multitude of problems, the council decided in 1730 that the establishment should be disbanded, 'the sooner, the better'.[4]

During the years of the Dutch residence in Delagoa Bay, there was constant fighting among the chiefdoms of the bay. One of the most serious conflicts involved Tembe and Machavane, in which Tembe won several victories,[5] which seem to have led to the incorporation of Machavane into the chiefdom of Tembe. Another series of wars involved the smaller chiefdoms on the northern side of the bay. There were wars between Mateky and Nondwana, Nondwana and Mfumo, and finally a coalition of Mambe, Matoll, Mateky, and Nondwana, against the Mfumo.[6] The last of these wars resulted in a decisive defeat for the Mfumo, who, as the senior branch of a group of related chiefdoms, apparently had attempted to exercise too much control over the others. The repercussions of the realignments of the power relations among the bayside chiefdoms arising from this series of wars will be seen when the later period is considered.

These, however, were not the only conflicts during this period. Realizing the precariousness of their position as middlemen, the bayside Ronga strove to maintain their monopoly. In order to effect this end, they attempted to prevent the 'Machicossers' and the 'Sanganers',

[1] *Cape Archives*, entries of 10 April, 1727, 307; 1 November, 1727, 308; 7 November, 1728, 313; 26 April, 1729, 316.

[2] Coetzee (1948), 266–7.

[3] *Cape Archives*, entry of 15 February, 1729, 314.

[4] ibid., entry of 12 June, 1730, 318.

[5] Coetzee (1948), 264.

[6] ibid., 264–6.

people from the interior, from trading directly with the Dutch.[1] During the years 1726 and 1727, the trade-routes remained closed, while the Ronga and the 'inlanders' fought several skirmishes.[2] The Ronga apparently were successful, because when the 'inlanders' returned, their trade was either handled by the Ronga or the Ronga accompanied them to the Europeans and evidently received a percentage of the profits.[3] Ultimately, the 'inlanders' ceased to come to Delagoa because they were continually exposed to 'irregularities' and robbery by the Ronga.[4]

From the information supplied by the 'inlanders', it seems possible to identify their homeland. Some of these people identified themselves as being from 'Paraotte' and 'Machicosse'. The accounts they gave of the interior, or perhaps the Dutch transcriptions of these accounts, are somewhat contradictory. From the several versions, the only consistent fact which helps in determining the location of their homeland, is that 'Machicosse', 'Inthowelle', and 'Paraotte' all lived in the same area.[5] Regarding ethnic affiliation, it has been suggested that the name 'Machicosse' in fact corresponded with Mashakatsi, chief of the Maluleke Thonga, who lived on either side of the Transvaal-Mozambique border, between the Oliphants and the Limpopo, and that 'Inthowelle' corresponded with the first of two Venda chiefs, named Vele.[6] Since these assumptions seem to correspond with the genealogies of the Maluleke Thonga and the Venda, agree with Venda traditions of migration and state formation, and also correspond with the ethnological map of the area,[7] it is to be supposed that they are substantially correct. In addition to the information about where they lived, the 'inlanders' mentioned that 'Inthowelle' ruled over all the people of the area.[8] It seems likely, therefore, that the area to which the

[1] van de Cappellen, in *RSEA*, 1, 414. The 'Sanganers' have been equated with the Nhlanganu Thonga, who lived to the north of the bay. See F. R. Paver, 'Trade and Mining in the Pre-European Transvaal', *South African Journal of Science*, 30 (1934), 605.

[2] Coetzee (1948), 264.

[3] See 'Journaal van . . . de . . . Snuffelaar', in Molsbergen (1922), especially 248.

[4] Jacob Francken, '. . . Reize van het . . . Schip de Naarstigheid . . .', *RSEA*, 6, 494.

[5] 'Extract Uit het Journaal Gehouden te Fort Lagoa . . .', *RSEA*, 1, 420; *Cape Archives*, entry of 15 January, 1726, 302.

[6] Paver (1934), 605–8.

[7] See Paver (1934), Henri A. Junod, *Grammaire Ronga*, Lausanne, 1896, Introduction; H. A. Junod (1962), 26; also Hugh Stayt, *The BaVenda*, London, 1931; (ed.) N. J. van Warmelo, *The Copper Workers of Musina*, Union of South Africa Ethnological Publications, Pretoria, 1940, 8, 81–2.

[8] *RSEA*, 6, 420.

trading links of Delagoa Bay extended at this time, was located in the north-eastern Transvaal, where Venda and Thonga peoples had mixed, and which was controlled by a Venda chief, named Vele.

The significance of the appearance of the men of 'Machicosse' and 'Paraotte' stems not only from the fact that they brought the first gold and tin to be exported from Delagoa Bay, but also that they were connected with trading networks whose outlets were normally directed toward the north. The Dutch learned that their land was visited by 'black men with black hair' from Chifalle (Sofala), who came to trade for gold. They called these men 'Moetonge', which probably corresponds with the Tonga-Khoka of the Inhambane area,[1] some of whom evidently functioned as itinerant traders between the inland areas and the port of Sofala. In addition it is quite possible that the people of 'Paraotte' and 'Machicosse' had regular trading contacts with the Rozwi or other Rhodesian peoples. For one of them claims to have been to the 'Monomotapa' and he mentioned that in the land of the 'Monomotapa' 'there was a great deal of gold, which out of his land [Paraotte] and other lands was brought' to be sold.[2] Although 'Monomotapa' at this time might have meant any number of people, the Changamire Mambo would appear to be the most likely candidate, since gold originating from any other 'Monomotapa' would have travelled by an extremely circuitous route to have been exported southward through 'Paraotte'.

Whatever the complexities of the inland trading patterns, the fact that these people, who usually used other outlets for their goods, came to Delagoa Bay during the period of permanent occupation by the Dutch, seems more than coincidental. Whether this resulted from the fact that Delagoa Bay may have been of easier access than other ports in Mozambique, a desire to escape from trading with the Portuguese, to benefit from the new opportunities offered by the Dutch, or some factors of interior politics, the salient point is that permanent occupation of Delagoa Bay stimulated a short-lived change in the pre-existing trading patterns. As in the case of early sixteenth-century coastal Muslim traders, who found new routes to the interior when the Portuguese took control of the old ones, and in that of the Yao, who in the eighteenth century switched their trade from Kilwa to Mozambique, the speed with which the inland traders seized the opportunity

[1] *Cape Archives*, entry of 15 January, 1726, 302; van de Capellen was told that the Thonga called the people near Inhambane 'Moetonge': van de Capellen, in *RSEA*, 1, 415.

[2] *RSEA*, 1, 420.

of trading to Delagoa Bay demonstrated an astute commercial awareness in the interior.

By the second half of the eighteenth century, Delagoa Bay seems to have become a more consistent supplier of export goods. Much of the information concerning this period was supplied by the Portuguese, who, as part of what was intended to be a general revival of their establishments in Mozambique, attempted to re-enter the trade at Delagoa Bay. The attempt began poorly when the first ship sent to the bay was wrecked on the return voyage,[1] and after this disaster the governor remained reluctant to send another, despite the fact that a private trader from Mozambique returned from a voyage in 1756 with a profit of more than one thousand per cent for his effort.[2] Not until 1762 did another ship venture southward, and this one, as well as those which followed during this decade, found the trade to be brisk, but for one reason or another the Portuguese were unable to take advantage of the opportunity.[3] When the Portuguese governor raised the duty on ships going from Mozambique to Delagoa to forty per cent, whatever slim chances Portuguese traders had of successfully competing with other Europeans were removed and the trade was once again abandoned.[4]

Despite the second withdrawal of the Portuguese, the Ronga were not without a ready outlet for their goods. By mid-century some French vessels had apparently begun to pay occasional visits to Delagoa, and the Dutch also continued to send trading vessels.[5] The lion's share of the trade, however, remained concentrated in the hands of India-based English traders. Armed with ample supplies of inexpensive trading beads and cloth from Surat, the English established a semi-permanent trading factory and stationed boats in each of the rivers. The trade of the bay had become 'big business' and the merchants of Bombay and Surat were becoming wealthy from it.[6]

[1] António de Andrade, *Relações de Moçambique Setecentista,* Lisbon, 1955, 514–15.

[2] Inacio Caetano Xavier, 'Notícias dos Dominios Portugueses . . . 1758', in Andrade (1955), 157–8.

[3] Montez (1948), 99–100; António José de Mello to governor of Moçambique, July, 1763, *A & P*, 380–81.

[4] Montez (1948), 100.

[5] King to viceroy, 1748, *RSEA*, 5, 194; João Baptista Montaury, 'Moçambique . . .', in Andrade (1955), 372; Francken, in *RSEA*, 6, 477; Bird (1965), 1, 272.

[6] Manuel Pereira do Lago, 'Instrucção . . . a Quem lhe Suceder Neste Governo', in Andrade (1955), 318; Montaury, ibid., 372; Bombay Report on External Commerce for 1802/3, Paragraph 40, India Office Library.

The increased trade in Delagoa Bay was probably due to its connections with Natal. The fact that during this period there were only small quantities of metals offered for sale indicates only a limited contact with the metal-producing regions across the Lebombo hills.[1] Instead, the commerce of Delagoa Bay remained confined almost exclusively to what might be considered its traditional exports, that is, ivory, amber, and rhinoceros horns.[2] Moreover, a further link with Natal is suggested by the fact that the best trading posts were in the rivers on the southern side of the bay,[3] while the fact that the Portuguese felt that the trade from the area north of Delagoa Bay travelled not to the bay, but to the Portuguese establishment at Inhambane,[4] is a further indication that Natal must have been the principal supplier of the Delagoa exports.

The evolution of Inhambane as an export site in many ways had differed considerably from that of Delagoa Bay. Located more than one hundred miles to the north of Delagoa, Inhambane had also been visited by an annual voyage from Mozambique. After the discontinuance of the voyage to Delagoa Bay, the Portuguese had continued to make regular visits to Inhambane and had fairly successfully prevented 'foreign intrusion'.[5] After 1731 the Portuguese permanently occupied Inhambane with a force which, although pitiably weak at times, afforded them some degree of control. During the eighteenth century, the export trade, which consisted mainly of the same products as at Delagoa Bay with the important addition of a considerable slave trade, increased significantly. By the second half of the century, Inhambane had surpassed the rapidly declining Sofala in importance and among the Portuguese trading sites ranked second only to Sena as an exporter of ivory, while its slaves were considered the best of the entire Mozambique coast.[6]

A Portuguese described the area from which these exports were derived as '*vastissimo*'.[7] By the second half of the eighteenth century, a good part of the trade which had previously been exported from Sofala, had been diverted southward to Inhambane.[8] Since the entire hinterland from Inhambane to Delagoa Bay depended on Inhambane, the

[1] Francken, in *RSEA*, 6, 493; Xavier, in Andrade (1955), 158.
[2] de Mello to governor, July, 1763, *A & P*,. 281.
[3] Francken, in *RSEA*, 6, 492.
[4] 'Memórias da Costa da Africa Oriental . . .', in Andrade (1955), 212.
[5] '. . . Rapport en Journaal . . . Inhambano . . . Junij 1728', *RSEA*, 1, 463–4.
[6] Montaury, in Andrade (1955), 372; Andrade (1955), 212.
[7] Montaury, in Andrade (1955), 371.
[8] João Julio da Silva, 'A Brief Description of the Town and Port of Sofala', P.R.O., Adm 1/2271, 'Cap. O', 35.

overland trading connections between Inhambane and Delagoa Bay, which had functioned from the sixteenth century, or before, probably continued.[1] During the Dutch period, for instance, it was observed that the people from the Ronga chiefdom of Manhice went to Inhambane in the months of the dry season and returned with hoes, axes, and assegais, which in turn were traded with the other peoples of the bay.[2] Portuguese traders, 'both black and white', were also allowed to pass along the coastal trade-routes[3] and thus direct the flow of goods towards a point of embarkation of their choice. If, as the Portuguese contended, these trading patterns remained consistent after about 1750, it is likely that the struggle between Delagoa Bay and Inhambane for their mutual hinterland was being won by Inhambane.

The appearance of yet another European factor into the trade of south-east Africa was once again to change the patterns of trade. Under the direction of William Bolts, the Austrian Asiatic Company of Trieste occupied Delagoa Bay in 1777. Bolts had formerly been employed by the British East India Company and he had learned of the value of the Delagoa Bay trade during his residence in India. After his dismissal from the company service, Bolts went to Europe to seek capital for his proposed settlement at Delagoa Bay. Upon receiving the necessary financial backing at the Austrian court, he gathered together a makeshift crew of Germans, English, Portuguese, Arabs, French, and Italians, and proceeded to Delagoa to begin his establishment. Soon after the arrival of the company, treaties were signed with Matoll and Tembe, forts and factories were constructed, and trading with the Ronga was commenced. Aided by excellent trading goods and the willingness to pay high prices for their merchandise the 'Austrians' soon began a brisk trade. An employee of the factory remarked that commerce was excellent, and one historian, who has used the company records, has remarked that the commerce was 'extremely voluminous'.[4]

The Austrian venture, however, was to be short-lived, for Bolts had unwittingly provided the Portuguese with an opportunity to seize control of the bay. Although it had never occupied Delagoa Bay, Portugal had nevertheless consistently maintained that it was her property. During the Dutch occupation the Portuguese king had sent a protest to the Dutch East India Company, threatening expulsion if

[1] Charles Fuller, 'An Ethnohistorical Study of Continuity and Change in Gwambe Culture', Northwestern Ph.D. dissertation, 1955, 49.

[2] van de Capellen, in *RSEA*, 1, 411.

[3] Boteler (1835), 323–4; *RSEA*, 1, 431.

[4] Lobato (1948), 15–27.

the bay were not evacuated.[1] When it was feared that an English occupation was imminent, a similar protest had been despatched.[2] By the mid-century, occupation of Delagoa had become an important consideration in the intended overhaul of the Portuguese administration of Mozambique. However, a combination of lack of adequate transport, hostility to the idea from the Ronga chiefs, and fear of the diplomatic repercussions of a conflict with either the Dutch or the English soon dissuaded the Portuguese from the plan of occupation. As expressed by the king, it would be better to 'conserve what we have in peace, without extending commerce or territory, when we do not have the means to sustain them', than to come into conflict with either the English or the Dutch.[3] While the Portuguese had been in no position to contest either the English or the Dutch, a private company offered an opportunity to take control without a direct confrontation with a powerful nation. As soon as Bolts began operation, the Portuguese crown acted swiftly and decisively. Two warning despatches were sent, and when no satisfaction was received, an expedition was sent to destroy the Austrian factories. The company garrison, which had been depleted by illness, surrendered without a struggle.[4]

Between 1782 and 1796, the Portuguese failed in their attempt to maintain exclusive control of the export trade from the bay. At first, control of trade was given over to two companies, which by attempting to exchange goods at unreasonably low prices invited foreign competition,[5] which a garrison depleted by illness could not prevent. African chiefs, who had been warned not to trade with 'foreigners' soon expressed their independence and protested 'that the land was theirs and that they could trade with whomever they pleased'.[6] Unable to prevent foreign competition or to control the African population, the governor was instructed to tread warily and avoid causing too much of a disturbance.[7] By the 1790s, this administrative laxity had become open corruption, as sailors who were in the port illegally were entertained in the governor's home, and foreign traders occasionally even purchased their merchandise within the walls of the fort.[8] Not to be lost sight of,

[1] Letter of king, 1723, *RSEA*, 5, 130.

[2] King to East India Company, April, 1721, ibid., 5, 116.

[3] King to João de Mello, 20 March, 1759, in Andrade (1955), 53.

[4] Vicente Godinho, 14 March, 1782, in Paiva Manso (1870), 91.

[5] Captain general of Mozambique to secretary of state, 12 August, 1783, in Alexandre Lobato, *História do Presídio de Lourenço Marques*, 2 vols., Lisbon, 1949/1960, 1, 190; secretary of state to governor general of Mozambique, 5 April, 1785, ibid., 1, 198.

[6] ibid., 2, 118. [7] ibid., 2, 30. [8] ibid., 2, 116.

however, is the fact that in addition to the increasing number of Portuguese voyages to the bay,[1] these years witnessed renewed contact with the English and Dutch, as well as the appearance of Indian and French traders.[2] From the sheer number of participants, it seems safe to conclude that the 'big business' begun in the 1750s continued throughout most of the 1780s and 1790s. In 1796, however, this period was brought to an abrupt end by the destruction of the fort by French men-of-war and the resultant Portuguese abandonment of the bay.

After an absence of almost seven years, the Portuguese reoccupied Delagoa Bay. This time, however, they were able to make their monopoly more effective. One factor with which the Portuguese no longer had to contend was the competition of Dutch traders, who after the loss of the Cape apparently ceased to visit the coast of East Africa. During the Portuguese absence, only one English ship had sailed to Delagoa. This ship made handsome profits and had been well received by the Ronga, who for a time had been without customers. The Portuguese soon returned, however, and closed the port to foreigners.[3] Between 1803 and 1815 no English ship ventured into the bay, and when Captain Ramsden attempted to test the Portuguese monopoly in 1815, he found that the trade was still closed to foreigners.[4] Thus in the early years of the nineteenth century the trade had come completely into the hands of the Portuguese and the monopoly, which they had sought so long, had become a fact.

Before considering the question of the evolution of the trading patterns of the late eighteenth and early nineteenth centuries, a word should be said about the development of 'Ronga' politics and how local politics affected control of trade. Until the turn of the eighteenth century, the trend which began during the Dutch period was continued. Tembe, which in a series of wars against the chiefdom of Machavane had gradually absorbed parts of that chiefdom, continued its expansion against the remaining sector of Nyaka, reducing it to negligible size and importance. Until the civil war of the 1790s, which resulted in the creation of the new chiefdom of Maputo, Tembe remained the most powerful chiefdom of the bay.[5] In the struggle between Matoll and Mfumo, dominance remained with Matoll. In

[1] Lobato (1949/60), 2, 408.

[2] Secretary of state to captain general of Mozambique, 25 April, 1784, ibid., 1, 192.

[3] Bombay, Report on External Commerce for 1802/3, paras. 41–4, India Office Library.

[4] Mabel Jackson, *European Powers and South-East Africa*, London, 1942, 126.

[5] See Francken, in *RSEA*, 6, and Santa Thereza, 'Plano e Relação da Bahia Denominada por Lourenço Marques', in Montez (1948), 164–7.

1781, Matoll attacked, decisively defeated, and virtually ended Mfumo's independence.[1] In addition to, and probably as a result of, their political supremacy, during the later years of the eighteenth century Tembe and Matoll were the leading trading chiefdoms of the bay.[2]

Although the evidence is limited, it seems likely that the two diminished chiefdoms sought aid and protection in a European alliance as a response to their subservient status. From the published materials, the precise nature of the relationship between the Nyaka and the Austrians cannot be determined. Yet the facts that the Austrians had established a factory in Nyaka, that Nyaka was the only chiefdom to protest against their expulsion by the Portuguese, and finally that Nyaka enjoyed a temporary trading renaissance during this period, strongly suggest that Nyaka may have received aid from the Austrians.[3] The relationship between the Mfumo and the Portuguese is much more easily determined. When the Portuguese seized control of the bay in 1781, Mfumo had recently suffered a severe defeat at the hands of Matoll. Thereafter, the Portuguese apparently supported the Mfumo in their wars and helped it to regain its lost stature. When the Portuguese were forced to evacuate the bay, Mfumo quickly came under Matoll's dominance again.[4] In the nineteenth century, when the Portuguese returned again, Mfumo was the only chiefdom to remain consistently allied with them.[5] By supporting the Mfumo, the Portuguese probably hoped to secure a foothold at the bay and also to reap the advantages of the trading skills of the Mfumo. For the Mfumo, the alliance not only guaranteed their survival, but since the Portuguese became the sole merchants in the export trade, it probably also promised advantages in matters of trade.

The increase in trade during this period was due partly to alterations in the directions of the flow of goods, but also to the further development of existing lines of communication. Despite the fact that the exports from Delagoa Bay were being drawn from an ever widening area, Natal remained the single most important source of supply. It was observed that a great deal of ivory came down the Maputo river from Nguni-speaking peoples.[6] Further confirmation of the connections of the bay and Natal is derived from the fact that the Tembe, which among the bayside chiefdoms handled the largest amount of trade,

[1] Lobato (1949/60), I, 10–11 n. [2] Santa Thereza, in Montez (1948).
[3] Paiva Manso (1870), 108; Santa Thereza, in Montez (1948), 162–4.
[4] William White, *Journal of A Voyage* . . ., London, 1800, 41.
[5] Jackson (1942), 126. [6] Santa Thereza, in Montez (1948), 164.

received their ivory from the lands to the south.[1] An early nineteenth-century source, written at the other end of the trade-route, indicates that at least by that time the trading connections of Delagoa Bay extended all the way to the eastern Cape frontier.[2]

The trading connections of Delagoa Bay also penetrated into the interior of Mozambique, at least as far northward as the kingdom of Kiteve. At one time the Kiteve kingdom had been a principal supplier of the export trade of Sofala. However, by the early years of the eighteenth century, Kiteve had been considerably weakened by internal difficulties and the continuous encroachment of the Portuguese.[3] Parts of the kingdom subsequently were conquered by 'Landeens' from Inhambane, who then directed the trade to that port.[4] After the 'Austrians' occupied Delagoa, a part of the Kiteve trade was channelled further toward the south. For it was observed that 'a large number of Negroes from the kingdom of Quiteve come down from the mountain and come . . . there to make exchanges, they bring a large quantity of gold. These Negroes all are Landins.'[5] It would appear that one of the incentives to seek out the Austrians at Delagoa must have been the low price ceiling which the Portuguese had established at their ports. While they were only offering forty pannos for an arroba of ivory, the Austrians were paying eighty.[6]

The emergence of the Kosse chiefdom of the middle Nkomati as a powerful and important intermediary was another significant development of the trade with the northern interior. By a combination of blocking the river route to the bay and establishing good commercial relations with the Europeans, the Kosse had established themselves as the inland market to which African traders brought their goods. Even after the expulsion of the Austrians from Delagoa Bay, the people from Kiteve, as well as peoples along the coast to the north of the Limpopo, seemingly continued to bring their wares to the Kosse.[7] From here

[1] Anonymous letter, 1785, *A & P*, 247.

[2] Report of Colonel Collins, 1809, in (ed.) Donald Moodie, *The Record*, Amsterdam, 1960, 43. For further discussion of the link between Natal and Delagoa Bay and its political significance, see Alan Smith, 'The Trade of Delagoa Bay as a Factor in Nguni Politics, 1750–1835', presented at the UCLA Conference on Southern African History, held at Lusaka, Zambia, July 1–5, 1968. (The papers and proceedings of this conference will be published by the African Studies Centre, UCLA.)

[3] Senhor Ferão, 'Account of the Portuguese Possessions within the Captaincy of the Rios de Sena', *RSEA*, 7, 376–82.

[4] J. J. da Silva, in P.R.O., Adm 1/2271, 'Cap. O', 35.

[5] Anonymous, *A & P*, 247.

[6] Lobato (1948), 21.

[7] Anonymous, *A & P*, 247–8.

porters either paid tolls to be allowed to continue southward to the bay, or sold their goods to the Kosse, who during the season of high water in the river were visited by boats coming up from the coast.[1] Although the ascendent position of the Kosse, and indeed the restructuring of a significant portion of the trade of southern Mozambique away from Inhambane toward Delagoa Bay, may have only been a temporary phenomenon,[2] this once again indicated that these routes were sufficiently flexible to be altered when it served the purposes of the African traders.

During this period the trade between Delagoa Bay and the South African high veld probably became more intensive. As we have seen, people from the high veld were bringing gold, copper, and tin in limited quantities during the 1750s. Unfortunately, for the later period there is no document which specifically identifies trade or traders as being from the Transvaal area, although it is quite possible that the phrase 'many people come from the mountain' with gold, copper, and ivory,[3] refers to goods brought from the high veld. In any case, evidence from traditional sources and from early European travellers in the interior of South Africa confirms that there was a substantial trading connection between the two. From one traditional account it is learned that there was trade between Delagoa Bay and the Koni of the Transvaal and additionally that this trade existed 'in the very old days'.[4] The trade of Delagoa Bay also extended to the copper workings of Musina in the very north of the Transvaal and to the country of the Venda in general, with whom ivory, copper, and hoes were exchanged for beads and a certain type of black cloth which was prized by the miners of Musina.[5] That the trading links penetrated further to the west can be inferred from the information provided by John Campbell, one of the first Europeans to visit the Tswana, who found that the Kwena and the other peoples obtained articles of clothing and beads of European manufacture, which he thought came from the east coast.[6] While travelling through Tswana country in the early 1820s, Thompson

[1] Santa Thereza, in Montez (1948), 168; anonymous, *A & P*, 247.

[2] It is impossible to determine if this pattern continued, because there is no significant primary information after the two Portuguese documents of the 1780s. With the end of the period of 'open trading' in Delagoa, it appears that a primary motive for taking goods southward would have disappeared.

[3] Santa Thereza, in Montez (1948), 166.

[4] (ed.) N. J. van Warmelo, *The Bakoni of Mametsa*, Union of South Africa Ethnological Publications, Pretoria, 1944, 15, 48.

[5] van Warmelo (1940), 82–3.

[6] John Campbell, *Travels in South Africa*, London, 1815, 255.

learned that prior to the appearance of the Mantatis, a trade-route existed from Lattakoo, passing through the 'nokeunig', the Rolong, 'Marotzies', 'Manemasons', the 'Maquins', and lastly to Delagoa Bay.[1] Finally, from the journal of Arbousset, it is learned that the Pedi received European goods by way of Delagoa Bay in exchange for ivory, horns, and cattle,[2] and although this information in itself suggests an extensive trading system, it is to be supposed that the trade was not limited to those areas for which information is available.

The extension of trade to the high veld brought Delagoa Bay into contact with an area where a highly developed commerce had already emerged. Cattle, tobacco, sheep, animal skins, and other products were circulated in a complicated trading network, which undoubtedly percolated through almost all of southern Africa. The most essential goods exchanged among these high veld peoples, however, appear to have been iron and copper. In South Africa, there were several sources of copper, and it seems to have been widely circulated, either as in the case of Musina, where 'all the people', the Venda, Shona, and Sotho, were alleged to have come to trade,[3] or by a system of having it passed from neighbour to neighbour. It appears that iron was usually circulated in the same way. Especially in the cases of copper and iron, there was a good deal of economic specialization. The copper-workers of Musina, for example, shunned the growing of crops, and concentrated almost exclusively on their speciality.[4] In the matter of iron-working, the Rolong had established a reputation for skilled ironwork, and from the raw materials brought to them they fashioned assegais, hoes, knives, and axes.[5] Thus in the eighteenth century there appears to have been a considerable amount of economic specialization among the peoples of the high veld.[6]

Another indication of the developed nature of trade on the high veld was that many of these transactions were financed with beads.[7]

[1] '. . . From Capetown . . . to Cape Correntes', in Walckenaer (1821), 21, 13.

[2] T. Arbousset, *Relation d'un Voyage d'Exploration au Nord-Est du Cap de Bonne-Espérance,* Paris, 1842, 357.

[3] van Warmelo (1940), 81.

[4] ibid., 81–2.

[5] George Stow, *The Native Races of South Africa,* London, 1906, 489.

[6] For a summary of the opinions expressed by Europeans, all of whom were impressed by what they saw on the high veld, see W. Desborough Cooley, 'A Memoir on the Civilization of the Tribes Inhabiting the Highlands near Delagoa Bay', *Journal of the Royal Geographical Society,* 3 (1833), 310–24.

[7] See, for example, William Burchell, *Travels in the Interior of Southern Africa,* 2 vols., London, 1822/1824, 2, 375.

In fact, beads became somewhat of a circulating currency.[1] The role of beads in the exchange of goods is illustrated by the case of Dutch traders at Delagoa Bay in 1731. Although some 'inlanders' apparently came a long way to trade with the Dutch, they refused to sell their ivory, because the Dutch could not produce a bead which could be exchanged in the interior.[2] This case not only indicates that beads were used to finance exchanges in the eighteenth century, but it also throws light on another consideration. Although beads were used as currency, the exchange value of any particular type seems to have lasted for only a short period of time.[3] Since these beads could easily be obtained through the exchange of ivory, by supplying a continuous flow and furnishing different varieties of beads the long-distance trade may have been an important stimulus to the internal trade of the high veld.

We have seen that the trading connections of Delagoa Bay extended several hundred miles across the high veld, northward into the interior of Mozambique, and southward to the eastern Cape frontier. Each area on the periphery of the routes from Delagoa, it should be noted, was connected with another source of European goods. The Tswana, for example, received beads and sheep from Khoi traders, who came from south of the Orange.[4] By the late eighteenth century, the high veld may also have had trading contacts with the west coast.[5] On the eastern frontier, the Xhosa had been receiving copper, brass, and beads, also transmitted by Khoi intermediaries, since the seventeenth century. Although European farmers gradually replaced the Khoi and assumed the role of intermediaries, the trading connections between the Cape and the Xhosa continued.[6] By supplying different varieties of beads and cloth, the overlapping of trade-routes further stimulated the exchange of goods in the interior, and the alternate lines of supply may have maintained an interest in trade if the routes from one direction were blocked. Thus by the late eighteenth century southern Africa

[1] Martin Legassick, 'Notes on Sotho-Tswana Trade' (unpublished paper).

[2] Molsbergen (1922), 241–7.

[3] In a little more than one hundred years the colour of the beads desired at Delagoa changed several times. The survivors of the *Santo Alberto* found that red beads were wanted; the *Noord* found that white beads were desired; the *Snuffelaar* was unable to buy much because they had neither blue nor yellow beads. The same phenomenon seems to have been true in the interior, and in some places beads had completely lost their purchasing power by the 1830s.

[4] Burchell (1822/4), 2, 380.

[5] Legassick (unpublished paper).

[6] See Gerrit Harinck, 'Interaction between Khoi and Xhosa . . . 1620–1750', presented at UCLA Conference on Southern African History, 1968 (cf. p. 283, n. 2, above).

had developed an intricate trading system, in which the trade from Delagoa Bay played a very significant role.

The extension of the routes from Delagoa Bay largely depended on the entrepreneurial skill of the Thonga. Ronga traditions remember that commercial voyages were undertaken to lands as far away as the Nyai country in Mozambique.[1] The development of the trade with Kiteve also seems to have been due to the Thonga, since it is quite evident that the 'Landeens' in reality were Thonga people. The first indication of this fact is that the homeland of the 'Landeens' was in the Inhambane area,[2] which would rule out the possibility that they were Karanga-speakers. Secondly, there is evidence in Portuguese sources which distinguishes 'Landeen' from the Tonga-Khoka of the Inhambane area, which further substantiates the hypothesis that 'Landeen' and Thonga were one and the same.[3] Thus it can only be concluded that when the documents speak of 'Landeens' from the kingdom of Kiteve, they are speaking of migrant Thonga, who went north to capture the trade which was exported to Sofala.

The Thonga were also instrumental in the development of the trade of the high veld and apparently continued to be the principal intermediaries in the trade between the interior and the coast. Among the various Ronga groups, it was the Mfumo who first began trading expeditions to the high veld area. High-veld traditions remember that the beads and cloth brought from the east coast were first brought by people from Mfumo.[4] In addition to the Mfumo, who it must be remembered were closely allied with the Portuguese, other groups, who cannot at this stage be properly identified, but who were obviously Thonga, penetrated into the interior to sell their wares. These people were called 'Mathlekas' and 'Malaquini', and from physical descriptions, which emphasize incisions in the nose and other characteristics of the Thonga, it is quite apparent that these people were from the Thonga cluster.[5] Further confirmation of the fact that the Thonga maintained their position as carriers of the inland commerce is provided by the facts that the Pedi, who were relatively close to Delagoa Bay, insisted that 'other people' brought the European goods to them,

[1] H. A. Junod (1962), 2, 143. [2] Ferão, in *RSEA*, 7, 382.

[3] In 1758 Xavier called the Bila, a Thonga group, by the name 'Landeen': Xavier, in Andrade (1955), 145. Santa Thereza called the Tembe Landeen, in order to distinguish them from the Nguni: in Montez (1948), 164.

[4] van Warmelo (1940), 82–3; id. (1944), 48.

[5] Arbousset (1842), 357; Andrew Smith, *The Diary of Andrew Smith 1834–1836*, 2 vols., Cape Town, 1939, 2, 193.

that the Venda also maintained that they rarely undertook long trading excursions, their European goods being obtained from people who came to them from the coast, and that the 'Magwambwa', who accompanied Louis Trigardt from the high veld, could still make themselves understood in broken English, which they could only have learned at Delagoa Bay.[1]

During the eighteenth century, the role of the various peoples who took part in the Delagoa trade changed significantly. In the early years of the century, most of the trading initiative seems to have come from peoples in the interior, who sought out the Delagoa market. Although the people of the Ronga chiefdom of Manhice did conduct seasonal trips to Inhambane, the role of the Thonga seems at this stage to have remained essentially that of stationary middlemen. By the end of the eighteenth century, however, the commercial voyages undertaken by the Thonga indicate that their function had been altered. Rather than remaining content with a relatively passive role, they had become the initiators of the trade between the east coast and the interior. The example of a group from Delagoa Bay which traversed the whole of Natal and travelled all the way to the kraal of the Xhosa chief, Gaika, illustrates that the Thonga were not content with known sources of goods, but were prepared to seek out new possibilities.[2] Since the Thonga were able to procure European goods fairly easily, they were well received in the interior and soon were recognized as the only people capable of supplying these goods.[3] Judging from the initiative, skill, and preoccupation of the Thonga with matters of trade, and their acceptance by the people in the interior, it would seem that during the eighteenth century they emerged as what can be called 'professional traders'.

Another indication that their role had changed to that of 'professional traders' is the fact that there is a distinct possibility that an incipient migration of Thonga peoples, similar to that of the Yao of northern Mozambique, was taking place in the late eighteenth and early nineteenth centuries. Since many Thonga later fled into the Transvaal as a result of the Shangane wars, this earlier dispersal of Thonga has passed virtually unnoticed. As we have seen, however, Thonga peoples

[1] Arbousset (1842), 357; Stayt (1931), 76; Claude Fuller, *Louis Trigardt's Trek across the Drakensberg*, Cape Town, 1932, 8. For an explanation of 'Magwambwa', see opposite.

[2] Louis Alberti, *Description Physique et Historique des Cafres, sur la Côte Méridionale de l'Afrique*, Amsterdam, 1811, 4–13.

[3] See Henry Francis Fynn, *The Diary of Henry Francis Fynn*, Pietermaritzburg, 1950, 48.

conquered parts of the kingdom of Kiteve and apparently settled there. In the Transvaal, people of the Maswanganyi, whose home was near the confluence of the Limpopo and Oliphants rivers in southern Mozambique,[1] settled among the Venda and used this settlement as a 'rendezvous for all the Thonga traders'.[2] Numbers of the Mfumo also settled in the Transvaal and, in exchange for payment of a share of their profits 'to the owners of the country', were allowed to take up permanent residence.[3] The very name 'Magwambwa' by which all the Transvaal Thonga came to be known, derived from certain immigrants into the Transvaal, who went there to trade, and who later settled down and took wives from among the indigenous people.[4]

Unlike the situation in northern Mozambique, where the Yao dispersal continued throughout much of the nineteenth century, this incipient migration of Thonga peoples, as well as the entire trading patterns, including much of the market-oriented trade, which had evolved during the eighteenth and early nineteenth centuries, were irreparably disturbed by subsequent events. The Difeqane, the relocation of various Nguni and Sotho groups, and the Great Trek created a new set of conditions in south-eastern Africa. The role of the Thonga was gradually pre-empted by the Portuguese, and firearms and slaves, rather than beads and ivory, came to play the leading role in the trade. Thus, in trade, as in so many other ways, the nineteenth-century revolutions in southern Africa initiated a new era.

[1] H. A. Junod (1962), I, 17. [2] van Warmelo (1940), 68. [3] ibid.
[4] H. A. Junod (1896), 21.

Index